November, 2010

Dear Jon,

Pray for us.

Yours friend,

Abbot Melvin

Miracle on High Street

Miracle on High Street

The Rise, Fall, and Resurrection of St. Benedict's Prep in Newark, N.J.

Thomas A. McCabe

Fordham University Press | New York 2011

Library of Congress Cataloging-in-Publication Data

McCabe, Thomas Allan.
  Miracle on High Street : the rise, fall, and resurrection of St. Benedict's Prep in Newark, N.J. / Thomas A. McCabe.
    p. cm.
  Includes bibliographical references and index.
  ISBN 978-0-8232-3310-6 (cloth : alk. paper)—ISBN 978-0-8232-3312-0 (ebook)
  1. St. Benedict's Preparatory School (Newark, N.J.)—History. 2. Preparatory schools—New Jersey—Newark—History. 3. Minorities—Education (Secondary)—New Jersey—Newark—History. I. Title.
  LD7501.N6M336   2011
  373.749'32—dc22   2010032685

Printed in the United States of America
13 12 11   5 4 3 2 1
First edition

To Susie, Tommy, and Maggie
and
for the monks of Newark and St. Mary's abbeys

Contents

Acknowledgments ix

**Introduction: Downtown Monks
and the Miracle on High Street**   1

1. **Newark's Forgotten Riot**   7

2. **"Necessary, Useful, and Beautiful": Founding Fathers
   and a Catholic Day College, 1868–1900**   18

3. **The Making of a Modern Catholic Prep School,
   1900–1926**   36

4. **St. Benedict's Prep from Depression to War, 1926–1945**   61

5. **The Duke, Divine Comedy, and Discipline
   at St. Benedict's Prep**   82

6. **Benedict's Hates a Quitter: Athletics
   at a Catholic Prep School**   108

7. **"He Was Afraid of the City": Abbot Patrick, the
   Monastic Family, and Postwar Newark, 1945–1967**   134

8. **"Camelot Is Dead": The Newark Riots and the
   Closing of St. Benedict's Prep, 1967–1972**   156

9. **"A Possible School": The Resurrection of St. Benedict's Prep, 1972–1977**   190

10. **The Headmaster and the Street, 1977–1986**   224

     Conclusion   254

Notes 259
Index 303

Acknowledgments

When Father Jerome Flanagan looked to find a fitting mascot for the athletic teams at St. Benedict's Prep in 1924, he settled on a bee because "a bee, with all its concentrated activity, just about symbolized the St. Benedict's spirit." Writing the history of St. Benedict's has demanded such concentrated activity, but it has also required support and guidance from other "worker bees," especially colleagues, friends, and family.

Many thanks to the monks of Newark and St. Mary's abbeys for telling me their stories in countless interviews, hallway conversations, and telephone calls, and of course, to all the "Benedict's men" who shared their insight that has illuminated the history of their extraordinary school. Likewise, a debt of gratitude to the faculty and staff, past and present, who make things happen on High Street, especially Candace Bradsher, Dorothy Brooks, Tony Carnahan, Glenn Cassidy, Keith Corpus, Jim Duffy, Bernard Greene, Ron Jandoli, Didier Jean Baptiste, Doris "Juju" Lamourt, Ivan Lamourt, James "Big Jim" McKerry, Mike Scanlan, Paul Thornton, and Elizabeth Yarbrough.

Many thanks to Ginny Yans, who has been there from the beginning. She has always provided me with the courage to tell a story and the freedom to do so. I am forever grateful to mentors who read this manuscript and made wise and wonderful suggestions for its improvement, especially Jack Dougherty, Margaret McGuinness, Peter Wosh, and Jim Reed. Likewise, Fredric Nachbaur, Eric Newman, and Nicholas Taylor at Fordham University Press helped improve the manuscript, as they each made thoughtful and needed suggestions. Fordham University's Jim Fisher, who has recently written a magisterial book on the

Irish waterfront in New Jersey and New York, has been a constant supporter and adviser of this story about a school on High Street. As always, I thank him for his guidance, good humor, and great New York City lunch dates. I met Clement Alexander Price through his scholarship on the African American community in Newark as an undergraduate student many years ago, which in no small way influenced my decision to take a job at St. Benedict's in 1991. Four years later, Clem Price became a mentor as I began my graduate studies, and upon my finishing graduate school he asked me to teach his "History of Newark" course at Rutgers University–Newark. That course—a cheap imitation of the real thing—has helped me contextualize the story of a school in a city, and this journey would never have been started, or finished, without Clem. He is the epitome of a gentleman-scholar, and one of Newark's true gems.

The monks of Newark Abbey have not only been my employers for almost all my professional life, but they have also been the inspiration behind this success story. To witness their commitment to the city and the young men in it has been an inspiration. Many thanks to Father Augustine Curley for his unconditional help with the Newark Abbey Archives, and to Father Albert Holtz for many conversations about the school's history. Father Albert also generously shared his personal journal, and its insights clearly made the tale a better one. Father Boniface Treanor always took my calls, especially to answer questions about "the Duke" and his discipline methods. Abbot Giles Hayes of St. Mary's Abbey–Delbarton has always been one of my heroes, and his advice, guidance, and knowledge of monastic history in New Jersey have been indispensable. Abbot Melvin Valvano always encouraged me to tell the *real* story of Benedict's, and his photograph graces the front jacket for good reason: he has been the spiritual leader behind Newark Abbey's remarkable sojourn in faith for almost forty years. The inimitable Father Edwin Leahy fielded every question that I had with his usual passion, honesty, and humor.

I thank my fellow "Newark dorks" for sharing their love of this great city's past, especially Tim Crist, Warren Grover, Mark Krasovic, and all the members of the Newark History Society. The historian

Simon Schama once declared, "History needs to declare itself unapologetically for what it is: the study of the past in all its splendid messiness." Newark's history has indeed been messy at times, as has the history of the abbey and school just out of its downtown; but its telling has been made easier by the men and women who marshal its primary sources in the city's various archives and depositories. First and foremost, thanks to all the good folks in the New Jersey Division of the Newark Public Library. Charles Cummings, George Hawley, James Osbourn, James Lewis, and Deirdre Schmidel have all made the long research hours most enjoyable in one of my favorite places in the city. Likewise, both Natalie Borisovets and her excellent "Newark Experience Page" at Rutgers-Newark's Dana Library are treasure troves of source material. Also, I thank Linda Epps, a Benedict's mother, and the rest of the good folks at the New Jersey Historical Society.

I first met Pat Napoli when we both joined the faculty at St. Benedict's in the months after college graduation. Ever since, he has been a great friend and motivator. He is a major reason why this long-delayed history is now finished. I owe you, Pat, and the next round of the "tour" is on me. Countless other friends endured this decade-long project, and they too are thrilled to see it completed, but special thanks to Chris Condron, Lyman Dally, Jasper Malcolmson, and Paulo Nunes for their friendship along the way.

It is also fitting that St. Benedict's Prep has always been a family school, because this project is very much rooted in family. My grandfathers, Allan E. Murtaugh and Thomas E. McCabe, kindled my love of stories, and their families have always supported this one. My father, Don McCabe, is my hero and the man I most want to be like. As only a mother can and will do, D. J. McCabe lovingly read each and every word of this manuscript—twice! Her suggestions helped improve each successive draft, and it was a joy to share the work with her. My dear sisters, Melissa and Beth, encouraged me every step of the way and fended off our nagging father on more than one occasion. My wife, Susie, is not only my best friend, but she has been the patron of this project. Her love and patience helped me see it through. Our children, Tommy and Maggie, endured this project as well, and they can be assured that Daddy now has more time to play! I love you all.

Miracle on High Street

Introduction: Downtown Monks and the Miracle on High Street

Just outside of downtown Newark, New Jersey, sits an abbey and a school. For more than 150 years Benedictine monks have lived, worked, and prayed on High Street, a once-grand thoroughfare of Victorian mansions, churches, synagogues, and hospitals. For much of the twentieth century, High Street belonged to the strivers of the city's bygone industrial era. Germans—whether Protestant, Catholic, or Jew—followed by Irish Catholics, Greeks, and later African Americans, all settled and built institutions along the two-mile stretch of "Striver's Row." Most left in the years after World War II when the city suffered from a trinity of woes: massive deindustrialization, high-speed suburbanization, and racial violence. Newark's Striver's Row became its Skid Row. As the city and its struggling neighborhoods deteriorated around the monks, they too wrestled with whether to remain in Newark.

Over the last 1,500 years, Benedictines have lived in self-governing communities according to *The Rule of St. Benedict*, whose spirit is best summed up by the motto *ora et labora* ("pray and work"). Many monasteries have founded schools, thus establishing the Order's reputation as a "teaching order." The most distinctive feature of Benedictine monasticism, though, has been a vow of stability of place, an ancient pledge that roots a monastery in a particular location, and binds an individual monk to it for the rest of his life. Boniface Wimmer, the father of the Benedictine Order in the United States, also recognized the importance of a second attribute—adaptability—that allowed monks to respond to conditions particular to their locale.[1] As men of both stability and adaptability, the Benedictines were well suited for the trials and tribulations of running a school in an old American city.

While the story of St. Benedict's Preparatory School is about an institution's rise and fall, its resurrection and renaissance, it also reveals the variety of Catholic responses to the "urban crisis" in the second half of the twentieth century.[2] Monks, students, parents, alumni, and friends often saw the tumultuous events of the 1960s and early 1970s in different ways. The infamous Newark riots of July 1967 ultimately led to the closing of the school in 1972. St. Benedict's reopened a year later in part because of the Benedictine virtues of stability and adaptability. One local historian has even claimed that the downtown monks helped save the city by resurrecting its prep school; some have even called it the miracle on High Street.[3]

Founded in 1868 to teach the sons of German Catholic immigrants, St. Benedict's also taught the children of successive waves of immigrants, including Irish, Italian, and Polish newcomers. The school had its roots in bloodshed as Know-Nothings, an anti-immigrant group, attacked and ransacked St. Mary's in 1854, the parish started by German priests in the 1840s. Two Catholic men died in the violence, and others were injured. In response, the Benedictines rebuilt the torched wooden church, this time with brick and mortar, and eventually started a "day college" for young men, firmly setting down roots in an ever-expanding industrial metropolis.[4]

St. Benedict's remained relatively small throughout the nineteenth century, but it did grow with the city and advertised itself as a "home or day college," not a boarding college like Seton Hall in nearby suburban South Orange. At St. Benedict's, three programs of study existed, in the classical, commercial, and preparatory departments; and males ranging from ten to twenty years old studied under the watchful eye of mostly German-educated monks. Almost all the students were German and Irish Catholic residents of Newark's numerous ethnic neighborhoods. "The peculiar advantage offered by St. Benedict's College is in its combination of thorough classical or commercial instruction with what we may term Home Education," boasted the 1874 catalog. "The parents, having their children (save in the hours at school) at home, under their own eyes, are naturally led to take greater interest in both their studies, their morals and manners."[5] Together, parents and monks hoped to make "Catholic gentlemen," ones who also looked to ascend the socioeconomic ladder into the city's burgeoning new middle class. As one of the country's leading industrial, banking, and insurance centers, Newark offered ample opportunity for upward mobility.

The school population exploded after the institution was classified as a college preparatory school in 1915, growing from more than two hundred students to more than seven hundred in 1925. Though a "prep school," St. Benedict's never oozed elitism; its historically modest tuition led one reporter to call it "the poor man's prep school."[6] There was always a healthy mix as the sons of white-collar professionals went to school alongside the sons of the blue-shirted working classes. By mid-century, the school had established itself in New Jersey and elsewhere as an academic and athletic powerhouse. Graduates went on to some of the best colleges and universities in the country, including Notre Dame, Georgetown, and Holy Cross, before making their mark in professions like law, government, business, and the clergy. St. Benedict's Prep was a thriving, self-confident institution at the peak of its influence in the years after World War II. Looking back on the 1950s, Father Benedict Tyler, a longtime faculty member and administrator, recalled, "There were no concerns at all, everybody thought St. Benedict's would be the same for years and years to come. It felt secure in itself; it had its own niche and was set to go on that way forever."[7]

In 1960, the year John F. Kennedy was elected the first Roman Catholic president in the history of the United States, St. Benedict's enrolled more than eight hundred students for the first time. But unlike the very first students in the 1870s, most of those in the 1960s did not walk from their homes to the school's front doors. As one alumnus put it, it was "a largely expatriate student body" by then, as young Catholic men traveled from suburbia to the city each day for their educations.[8] Prior to 1970, only a handful of talented African Americans had enrolled at St. Benedict's, but Newark was in the process of changing its complexion. Between 1940 and 1960 the African American population skyrocketed from 45,760 to 207,458 while the city's white population plummeted from 383,534 to 168,382. By 1970, more than 50 percent of the city's residents were black.[9] The neighborhood surrounding the school had become virtually all black, and many residents lived in substandard housing, attended failing schools, held low-paying jobs, and routinely suffered the indignities of racism and discrimination.

A violent and bloody riot broke out in Newark for a week in July 1967. Twenty-six people died, more than one thousand were injured, and more than ten million dollars' worth of property was damaged. Cities were in crisis as most Americans saw them as violent, unhealthy, and unlivable; one news magazine called Newark the "worst American city."[10] White flight to the suburbs picked up speed, and fewer and fewer families were sending their children into places like Newark for their schooling. As a result, urban Catholic grammar schools and high schools began closing. But at the school's centennial celebration in 1968, Abbot Martin Burne, a monk attuned to the stirrings of the civil rights movement and the sweeping changes of the Vatican II–era Catholic Church, asked a large gathering of alumni and friends to accept "the challenge of a lifetime": "I challenge a society that talks a great deal about helping the underprivileged to let St. Benedict's do just that."[11]

As more and more African American students attended the school in the late 1960s and early 1970s, total enrollment declined from more than 800 to 460 in the seven years after the riots. In 1972, the school graduated 144 seniors, but only 50 freshmen had registered for the upcoming year. For decades the monks never had trouble attracting students, but now they were losing money and some blamed changes in the city and the church for the reversal of fortune. Within the monastic community, a bitter "ideological schism" over the future of the school and monastery pitted one group of monks against another. In short, some monks did not see a future in the city beginning in the 1960s, while others saw the city as fertile but extremely challenging ground on which to live out their vocations as monks.[12] Unable to achieve a resolution, St. Benedict's Prep closed on Ash Wednesday, 1972. Sixteen Newark monks, about one-third of Newark Abbey's monastic family, left the city for another monastery.

The monks who remained found work outside the monastery; some even continued to teach. "In the summer of 1972," remembered Father Albert, "many of us felt like foreigners in our predominantly black neighborhood in the crumbling center of the city, and suspected that our lifestyle was so bizarre as to make us more of a curiosity than a witness."[13] After some serious soul-searching, though, the monks decided to reopen St. Benedict's after a one-year hiatus. Teaching was their life's work, and it was one of the things the city needed most from them. Under the leadership of Abbot Melvin Valvano and the longtime headmaster Father Edwin Leahy, the revival of St. Benedict's has been spectacular.

The school reopened in 1973 with ninety-six students, almost all of them African American, and more than thirty years later it has nearly six hundred. Newark Abbey and St. Benedict's Prep now occupy twelve buildings on fifteen acres; its facilities match those of many colleges and universities, including those in the University Heights section of the city. The monks and their staff provide a solid college prep curriculum for a consciously integrated student body, which is now 63 percent African heritage, 22 percent Latin heritage, 10 percent Caucasian, and 5 percent other. By design, more than 60 percent of the student body hails from the nearby urban neighborhoods of Newark, East Orange, and Irvington. Ninety-five percent of graduates go on to study at a wide range of colleges and universities, proving that the educational achievement gap that exists between white and black Americans as well as rich and poor ones can be bridged. St. Benedict's "merits special attention," wrote Robert J. Braun in the *Newark Star-Ledger*, "because it is an institution dedicated solely to the dignity of children often deemed less than worthy by other institutions, because the struggle to survive was so difficult and because the effort emerged, not from mandated government policy, but from personal values and hard work."[14]

Perhaps the school's greatest achievement, though, has been its ability to bring young men of all sorts of backgrounds together over time to create a school community in a fractured and still fragile city. In the last quarter of the nineteenth century, students of German and Irish heritage went to school together, and at the beginning of the twentieth century Italian and Polish students arrived. The first waves of African American and Latino students came in the 1960s, and after the school reopened it became a veritable United Nations, with students from a variety of national, racial, ethnic, economic, and religious backgrounds. Only 40 percent of the current student body is Roman Catholic, but most of the students are Christian; Muslim and Jewish young men attend the school too.

The bells of St. Mary's have rung for as long as there has been a St. Benedict's in Newark. Over nearly the last century and a half, the sun has passed over the monastery and school, bringing with it a shadow from the cross high above St. Mary's Church. The shadow traverses High Street and the school's buildings by midday and ends up traveling toward Newark's downtown by late afternoon. The first students at St. Benedict's studied and played, laughed and learned, under that shadow, as have successive generations of "Benedict's men."[15] All the while men of both stability and adaptability, the downtown monks have remained rooted to their mission: the education of young minds, bodies, and souls, regardless of where they have come from or what they look like. On High Street, perhaps the miracle has been the long and enduring impact of one venerable institution that has shone in the shadow of the cross.

1

Newark's Forgotten Riot

The miracle on High Street actually began on William Street.

On September 5, 1854, three thousand men, most of them wearing Prince Albert coats, round felt hats, and red sashes slung over their shoulders, paraded through the streets of Newark. Thirteen different lodges of the American Protestant Association, all marching behind their own banners and bands, wanted to make a show of force on behalf of the Know-Nothing Party before the November elections. Since 1850 the nativist political party had garnered swift support for its anti-Catholic and anti-foreigner platform. Nationwide the party now had over one million members and had put thousands in office, ranging from the grassroots level to the halls of Congress. That day, almost all the men carried swords and pistols. Marching four abreast, the "long and imposing" procession sang anti-Catholic ditties and shouted the party's motto, "Americans must rule America." They eventually stopped for lunch at Military Hall on Market Street, where they ate and drank for the next two hours.[1]

Just a few blocks away on William Street, Father Nicholas Balleis, a Benedictine missionary from Austria, dined with three other priests at his living quarters adjacent to St. Mary's, a small wooden church built in 1842 to minister to the growing number of German Catholic immigrants in the neighborhood. Father Nicholas had read about the parade in the morning's paper—the *Newark Daily Advertiser* noted, "Know-Nothingism is said to be spreading, not only in this city but in all the surrounding towns and villages"—but he did not make much of it until he heard music playing outside. Scheduled to march through a nearby native Protestant neighborhood, the parade's course was changed after lunch, partly because of the unseasonably hot day, and as a result it staggered up William Street at three o'clock in the afternoon. As the various lodges ascended the hill, they shouted and sang and fired their pistols into the air. By the time the Henry Clay Lodge reached the tiny church, a sizeable crowd of men, women, and children gathered to witness the spectacle. In particular, men working in the Halsey and Taylor leather works, and other nearby factories, rushed out to see the parade. Across the street, students watched the scene unfold through the school windows. One student recalled, "The Orangemen discharged their firearms and hurled stones and other missiles at the white Cross on the apex of the Church, but they could not get it down." In the tense moments that followed, men hurled insults and threats, and some threw more stones. The riot was on![2]

Nativist marchers, fueled by their hatred of Catholics and also by hours of drinking, quickly broke ranks and brawled with the onrushing Catholic workingmen. Some rioters sidestepped the melee, fought their way into the church, and ransacked St. Mary's, leaving the altar overturned, a statue of the Virgin Mary decapitated, and the organ pipes twisted and destroyed. A frightened Father Nicholas hid under his bed. His assistant, Father Charles Geyerstanger, displayed more courage and forced his way through the raiding party to retrieve the Blessed Sacrament. He took it to a neighboring home and quickly returned to sound the alarm. Sensing imminent danger, Fathers Nicholas and Charles shed their cassocks, fled the rectory, and disappeared into a parishioner's home. Moments later several men broke into the rectory looking for the departed clergymen but found only an old German housekeeper. Pointing revolvers at her head, they demanded to know where the priests went. She replied, "Shoot! I am only a poor woman!" She then took her broom and brandished it in defiance.[3]

Outside there were repeated calls to torch the church, but the combination of crowd resistance, the arrival of police, the work of marshals to reform the procession, and the warnings of Father Charles, who had returned to the scene, prevented it. As word spread of the riot, thousands came to watch the unfolding violence; others hid, including a nun and her charges at a nearby Catholic orphanage, fearing the wrath of the marauding mob. At St. Mary's, Father Nicholas gave last rites to

Rev. Nicholas Balleis

Father Nicholas Balleis was the first Benedictine in Newark, and while he ministered to the German Catholic community at St. Mary's Church in the 1840s, he left the city in the wake of the 1854 Know-Nothing riot.

Thomas McCarthy, an Irish Catholic tanner who had been gunned down by one of the marchers. Another man, Michael McDermott, a watchman at a trunk factory, would die several days later after being repeatedly stabbed in the back. Others, struck by stones, lay severely wounded. The police made only two arrests, and armed parishioners guarded the sacked church through the night. It was a "typical Know-Nothing riot," argued one historian, as armed Protestants marched through a heavily Catholic area, incited local residents, reacted to the violence with force, and then claimed self-defense. The day after the riot, the *Newark Daily Mercury*, a mouthpiece for the Know-Nothing Party, blamed the victims, saying that eyewitnesses "impute the blame entirely to the Irish Catholics."[4]

Talk of the riot dominated conversation in the city for days, and some newspapers eventually retracted their accusations in reaction to pressure from Newark's bishop, James Roosevelt Bayley. While Bayley excoriated the press for placing the blame on Catholics, priests sought to quell their seething coreligionists. Although some wanted revenge, Fathers Bernard McQuaid, the future president of Seton Hall College, and Patrick Moran, the pastor at nearby St. Patrick's, preached calm in the days and weeks after the attack. The historian Joseph Flynn commented on the riot's aftermath, writing, "The tempest passed, and, while its trail was long visible, still it bore fruit." Newark's forgotten riot on William Street led to at least one fortunate event: the unlikely but ultimately fruitful arrival of the Benedictines to the city, which they announced by overseeing the completion of a new church. Made of brick and mortar and almost three times the size of the tiny wooden edifice it replaced, the new St. Mary's now faced High Street.[5]

City upon a Hill

In 1857, as the Benedictines settled just outside Newark's downtown, they set out to build a new "city upon a hill." Newark's first European settlers had pledged to do the same nearly two hundred years earlier, in May 1666, when Puritans from the New Haven founded the last theocracy in the American colonies on the banks of the Passaic River. Lauded as a "Terrestrial Canaan . . . where the Land floweth with milk and honey," the small, isolated town revolved around farming and "godly government" for the better part of a century, and its inhabitants were described as "remarkably plain, simple, sober, praying, orderly, and religious people." But Newark could not remain an exclusive religious outpost forever, and after a period of road and bridge building in the 1790s and canal and railroad construction in the 1830s, the once quiet and tranquil community transformed itself into a hub of industry, invention, and immigration.[6]

While many native Newarkers welcomed industrialization, they did not always welcome immigrants. The Irish began arriving in the 1820s—men dug the Morris Canal, laid railroads, or worked in a variety of small factories, while women most often labored as domestics—but immigration reached epic proportions in the wake of the Irish Potato Famine beginning in 1845. Pushed out of Ireland by starvation and disease, the Irish crowded into a handful of distinct neighborhoods throughout the city. The largest concentration was in "Down Neck," a swampy, malaria-infested section that provided cheap rents and "a comfortable distance from unfriendly Protestant areas of town." The sons and daughters of Erin had a difficult time adjusting to life in Newark; rural, poor, and Catholic, they struggled to make their way in an urban, industrial, and Protestant society. Depicted as stupid, lazy, drunk, and aggressive, the Irish in Newark were often the object of ridicule and derision. Protestant ruffians hurled insults during the city's inaugural St. Patrick's Day parade in 1834, routinely hanged "St. Paddy" in effigy during the 1840s, and disturbed the procession of James Roosevelt Bayley's installation as bishop in 1853.[7]

In the late 1840s, German immigrants, many of them refugees of the failed revolutions of 1848, joined the Irish in Newark, settling in the "Hill District" around St. Mary's Church. There they recreated important elements of the fatherland, including beer gardens, song festivals, and Turner societies, and often worked in neighborhood industries as shoemakers, trunk makers, brewers, and jewelry manufacturers. While Germans were generally more literate and skilled than the Irish, they too faced prejudice, in particular for playing sports, drinking beer, and singing songs on Sunday afternoons. The Irish and German immigrant influx into the city caused Newark's total population to skyrocket from seven thousand in 1820 to more than one hundred thousand in 1870, more than a tenfold increase. By 1860, one-third of Newark's population was foreign-born. White Anglo-Saxon Protestants often felt that Newark was a city under siege.[8]

Despite industrial progress and the promise of even more to come, urban life in the antebellum United States was in turmoil. People questioned traditional notions of authority, violence was commonplace, social tensions multiplied, and the economy fluctuated between the extremes of boom and bust. Many native-born Americans often blamed a growing list of social, economic, and political problems on recently arrived immigrants. By 1850, Newark was the "nation's unhealthiest city" as it suffered from a variety of public health crises, including epidemics, poor sanitation, inadequate water supply, and massive pollution. Higher than normal rates of poverty, alcoholism, and criminality among the Irish increased hostility toward them further still. One in three German immigrants were Catholic, and they were not without enemies either, since they insisted on preserving their language and culture in a strange land. Whether in Newark, Boston, Philadelphia, or New York, native-born Protestants viewed Catholics as foreign, mysterious, and increasingly dangerous to their way of life, and as a result, hostile mobs often threatened to burn churches, rectories, and convents, and to physically harm priests, nuns, and other defenders of the faith.[9]

In Newark, tension between natives and immigrants came to a boil over the schools. Catholic clergy questioned the validity of the public school system by asking if Protestant prayers and devotional practices were acceptable in a publicly financed institution. They argued that mandatory use of the King James Bible or certain textbooks that incorporated a detectable anti-Catholic bias seemed to sanction a state religion, and flew in the face of religious tolerance. Bishop Bayley worried about the influence of the public schools, arguing, "The Protestants make the greatest efforts to pervert our youth, mainly in establishing free schools, supported by the state." Catholic clergy demanded that local government support parochial schools as well, but determined Protestant opposition precluded any financial help, especially since the fledgling public school system needed all the resources it could get. But lack of public support for parochial schools did not deter Bayley from issuing a statewide rallying cry for a parallel system shortly after he was installed as the first bishop of Newark. In 1853 he wanted to see "every Catholic child in the State in a Catholic school." When the bishop called on the Benedictines in the weeks after the Know-Nothing attack on St. Mary's Church, he knew all too well that they were also world-class educators.[10]

Stability and Adaptability

A week after the riot Father Boniface Wimmer, the founder of the Order of St. Benedict (OSB) in the United States, traveled from Latrobe, Pennsylvania, to Newark in order to console and advise a visibly shaken Father Nicholas Balleis. Wimmer was well aware of the threat of nativists in his own state, observing, "Our newest political sect, the Know Nothings, would like to eat us, skin and hair, but it does not go so easily. The pressure on them is as it was on the Egyptians; they see us grow but they cannot stop us." An emboldened Wimmer thought that more property should be acquired so a bigger church could be built. Traumatized by the riot and embroiled in a string of controversies with his parishioners, though, Father Nicholas quickly transferred church property to Bishop Bayley and left for another assignment. In turn, the bishop redoubled his efforts to bring Benedictines to Newark and offered the parish to Wimmer, telling him, "I am most anxious to have your Order established here." It was part of his strategy to fortify a Catholic community under attack.[11]

Nicknamed the "Project Maker," Father Boniface led the active, aggressive lifestyle of a missionary. Upon his arrival in southwestern Pennsylvania in 1846, for example, he wielded an axe as he and his fellow Benedictines quickly got to work felling trees, clearing fields, and constructing the new monastery's first buildings. Quick-tempered but tolerant, he had a grand vision of what his Order could accomplish in the United States. A year before founding the first American Benedictine monastery, he wrote, "Benedictines are men of *stability*; they are not wandering monks; they acquire lands and bring them under cultivation and become thoroughly affiliated to the country and people to which they belong." Moreover, based on more than a millennium of experience, the Benedictine Order could "very readily *adapt* itself to all times and circumstances." Benedictines took three vows: conversion of life, obedience, and stability of place. The vow of stability, unique among religious orders, anchored them in a specific location. As a result it was inevitable that a particular monastery would become "thoroughly affiliated to the country and people to which they belong." The interplay of these two essential elements—stability and adaptability—

proved to be among the greatest assets of Benedictine monastic life in the United States.[12]

Father Boniface preferred mission work in farm country to that in teeming cities, yet only a year or so after settling in rural Pennsylvania he started receiving letters from Newark. Father Nicholas first wrote in 1847, asking him to send priests to minister to the city's growing German Catholic population. One monk arrived the following year, but stayed for only six months, and it would be another four years before Father Charles, who heroically saved the Holy Eucharist during the attack on St. Mary's, came to the city. During the 1850s, when Father Boniface looked to start other monasteries, he looked only westward, preferring to follow the flood of German immigrants across the Midwest. Even before the riot, he had a lukewarm attitude toward St. Mary's in Newark, confessing to his superior in Germany, "It is true, the parish has a fine location, the city can easily be reached, but I am afraid of cities." After the riot, he wrote Bayley, "Why should we rush into cities to draw upon us the wrath and hatred of others?"[13]

Bayley ignored Wimmer's rebuff and asked again. This time, the German monk elaborated on his reluctance to come to the city, saying, "In the country, far from the noise of the cities, we lead a happy life, and if we are not doing first rate we are doing at least well. . . . How would we do in a city, I do not know." Wimmer feared that monastic observance might suffer in an urban setting, as he pondered whether "we might lose the simplicity of manner, the poverty in our diet, the spirit of self-denial and the pure intention of our efforts." His own experience raised "great doubts as to whether it would be good or evil for the Order to settle in cities." Over the course of their three-year correspondence, Father Boniface indicated his preference for founding new monasteries in the West, which continued to flummox the eastern bishop. Bayley wrote Wimmer in 1857, "I cannot understand what East or West has to do with the matter when the question is the salvation of souls." An exasperated Bayley did not yield, and pressed the matter further, writing, "Newark is so near to New York, as to be a suburb of that city. The German Catholic Population here is already large, and is increasing. It would give you a great center of influence,"

The founding father of American Benedictinism, Boniface
Wimmer, OSB, of St. Vincent Archabbey in Latrobe,
Pennsylvania. Although wary of establishing the Order of
St. Benedict in the city, Abbot Wimmer committed men to
Newark in 1857, and the monastery's growth since has been
unique in the annals of the Order's history—a full-fledged
abbey grew out of a simple city parish.

and "I am certain that those who come to take charge of this Mission,
will find plenty to do."[14]

A final answer came in the spring. St. Vincent had recently been
elevated from a priory to an abbey, with Wimmer becoming the first
abbot, and Pope Pius IX told the missionary monk to continue to grow
and expand the Benedictine Order in the United States. Possibly it was

this directive that pushed him from ambivalence to acceptance of the city. In May 1857, Abbot Boniface traveled to Newark to witness Bishop Bayley sign over the legal title to the St. Mary's property to the Benedictines. Towns and cities had grown up alongside Benedictine monasteries as they became religious and cultural centers in Europe, but for missionary monks to settle in an already sprawling American city was an unprecedented move, and it was ultimately faithful to Wimmer's enduring mantra, "Forward, always forward, everywhere forward. We must not be held back by debts, bad years or by difficulties of the times. Man's adversity is God's opportunity." The new foundation was called "St. Mary's Benedictine Priory," and Abbot Boniface assigned three monks to the new urban monastery. Setting down roots, he also purchased three houses facing High Street for a total of eight thousand dollars.[15]

The Benedictines did have "plenty to do" in Newark. As more and more Germans immigrated to the city, St. Mary's parish grew, and the school founded as the first German Catholic parochial school in the state flourished. Benedictine sisters came from St. Mary's, Pennsylvania, to staff it and over four hundred children were soon under their

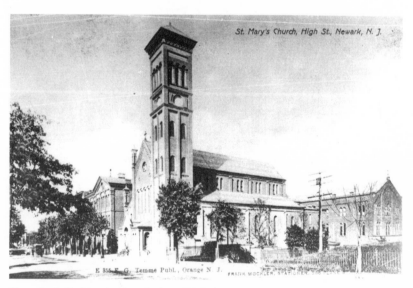

The rebuilt St. Mary's Church along High Street, 1915.

care. Bishop Bayley dreamed of founding a boarding college for men, and Seton Hall College was founded in 1856. But Bayley also dreamed of a second college in the city, and in the mid-1860s he would petition the Benedictines to start one. Such plans were a far cry from the days of the tiny wooden church on William Street, the very one that suffered the wrath of the American Protestant Association on September 5, 1854. Benedictine folklore has it that the man who decapitated the statue of the Virgin Mary suffered an industrial accident in the months following the riot. His right hand was so badly cut that he eventually died of "blood-poison, a raving maniac." Mary's head went missing for many years, but it was found eventually at St. Vincent Abbey in Latrobe. The monks at St. Mary's reassembled the statue and displayed it in the church as a reminder of the many obstacles Catholics faced in the city. It also came to symbolize the monks' stability, adaptability, and willingness to commit to a future in the city.[16]

2

"Necessary, Useful, and Beautiful": Founding Fathers and a Catholic Day College, 1868–1900

It was a family school from the start. John and William McGurk, teenage sons of poor Irish Catholic immigrants, walked to school each morning from their home in a predominantly Irish working-class neighborhood of Newark. Within a few blocks of their apartment they climbed one of city's grand avenues, the aptly named High Street—home to many of Newark's well-to-do citizens, who could literally look down on the McGurks from their perch. High Street was in the Hill District, a section of the city that overlooked downtown Newark and Manhattan in the distance. First settled in the 1840s, the "Hill" was full of Germans, ones who had made it in the rapidly industrializing city and others who were still on the rise, as well as their churches, shops, breweries, and factories. As the brothers strode by Newark Academy—the oldest prep school in the city, where wealthy Protestants sent their sons—and crossed William Street, they stood in the shadow of the steeple of the rebuilt St. Mary's Church, now one of the tallest structures in the city. Two doors down, John and William entered a humble two-story frame house, where they encountered a handful of bearded, black-robed Bavarian monks teaching the sons of Catholic immigrants.[1]

The McGurk brothers were among the twenty or so pioneering scholars to enter St. Benedict's after the Order of St. Benedict was incorporated in the state of New Jersey in 1868. Originally called a high school, a literal translation of the German *Hochschul*, a new name—Collegium Sancti Benedicti, or Saint Benedict's College—was used by 1870. In the late nineteenth century St. Benedict's did confer college degrees, including a two-year "Master of Accounts" degree, but it was a preparatory school for the most part, and in the early part of the twentieth century the monks abandoned the college program for good. John and William McGurk never received a degree because their father struggled to pay the modest tuition of fifteen dollars per quarter. The brothers remained at St. Benedict's for only two years, and ten years later they still lived in the same house, at that point with their widowed mother and four other siblings. William was employed as a hatter and John was a foreman in a local factory. But it was altogether fitting that they were the first recorded students at St. Benedict's, as it foreshadowed the unique mix of students that the school would commit to serve for years to come.[2]

On December 22, 1870, the city was in the midst of a cold snap, but four priests huddled in the pastoral residence of St. Mary's Church to adopt bylaws for the "Order of St. Benedict of New Jersey." Abbot Boniface Wimmer traveled from St. Vincent Abbey to meet with Father Roman Hell, who, despite his demonic surname, was the spiritual leader of the Newark monastery, and two pastors of local German Catholic parishes, one of whom was Father Peter Henry Lemke, a missionary priest who had helped persuade Wimmer to come to the United States twenty-five years earlier. Abbot Boniface and his monks now operated a successful seminary, college, and preparatory school in Latrobe, Pennsylvania, based on a straightforward educational philosophy. "Only God can create something out of nothing," reasoned Wimmer, which led him to believe students should be taught "first what is *necessary*, then what is *useful*, and finally what is *beautiful* and will contribute to their refinement."[3] In 1866 Wimmer assigned Hell to Newark, where he helped found one of the first Catholic secondary schools and colleges in New Jersey. When Wimmer and Hell met with the two other priests, they unanimously agreed on the following: "The objects of this corporation are divided between the spiritual guidance of souls and the educational training of youth."[4]

The founding of St. Benedict's was sandwiched between two great events in Newark's history: the two hundredth anniversary of its founding and the Newark Industrial Exposition of 1872. The first event paid tribute to a city's founding fathers and their Puritan ideals, while the second saluted Newark's industrial diversity and manufacturing might. A second set of founding fathers, a band of religious brothers from the Order of St. Benedict, now set their sights on building their own "city upon a hill," this one amid a budding metropolis during a century of sustained immigration. As we have seen, Roman Catholic immigrants were not always welcome in time-honored Puritan towns like Newark, but the old order was in the process of changing. Immigrant Catholics, and their offspring, built institutions to help them remain true to their faith but also become productive citizens in a new and often strange land. The founding of St. Benedict's was part of this very American strategy, and between 1868 and 1900 the Benedictines in Newark relied on the Order's two main virtues—stability and adaptability—to successfully establish "a day college for young men." Based on those early efforts to overcome all obstacles and hardships, future generations of St. Benedict's students were able to walk to school each morning too, and some would even retrace the steps of the two immigrant sons, John and William McGurk.

"A Day College for Young Men"

Bishop Bayley's position on education was well-known, and he was an early and fervent advocate for the construction of Catholic schools. Writing one pastor in 1855, he said, "Nothing is nearer to my heart than the establishment of good parochial schools." The bishop's heartfelt attachment to Catholic schools was due in large part to his perception of the pubic schools as a Protestant-dominated free system that made "the greatest efforts to pervert our youth." Bayley's position had hardly changed by 1872, when he wrote, "The public schools in this State are virtually Protestant schools, as much so as if Protestantism was the established religion of the State."[5] A Catholic newspaper attacked the public school system as "godless" and "pagan," and even spearheaded a campaign to force Catholic parents to send their children to parochial schools. In 1875, the Vatican went so far as to ask American priests to prevent Catholic children from attending public schools.[6] Bayley also believed in secondary and postsecondary Catholic education, and he approached the Benedictines to open up the second college in the diocese as early as 1867. Seton Hall College had been founded in 1856 and moved to its present location in South Orange, only four miles outside Newark, in 1860, but the bishop coveted another institution of higher learning. The Benedictines almost always ran schools, and one monk-educator commented, "There can be no question of a monastery without a school." Another added, "If we cannot win Catholic youth with Catholic schools, our mission will ultimately fail."[7]

Differing considerably from today's colleges, early men's Catholic colleges housed several different educational activities under one roof. At St. Benedict's, three programs of study existed: those in the classical, commercial, and preparatory departments. The classical course was modeled after the Bavarian gymnasium, a six-year course of study that saw males ranging in age from ten to twenty engaged in a traditional liberal arts curriculum. This included classical and modern languages (Latin, Greek, English, and German), history, mathematics, science, music, and religion. Some of these students planned to move on to the seminary and study for the priesthood, but most left to study further or enter the workforce. The second option at St. Benedict's was a commercial course that blended a traditional liberal arts program with more practical technical training for those headed toward a career in business. Students in the commercial course took many of the same classes as those in the classical track, but spent time mastering bookkeeping and penmanship too. In addition, the youngest students entered a preparatory department designed to aid those students not yet prepared to start in either the classical or commercial tracks.[8]

Close to home, inexpensive, and easy to get into, what really set St. Benedict's apart from its competition was the fact that it was a day college for young men. "The peculiar advantage offered by St. Benedict's College is in its combination of thorough classical or commercial instruction with what we may term Home Education," boasted an early school catalog. "The parents, having their children (save in the hours at school) at home, under their own eyes, are naturally led to take greater interest in both their studies, their morals and manners." Another advantage was the considerably lower cost when compared to a boarding college; it was the administration's "earnest wish that no great expense debar anyone, even of small means, from the acquisition of a thorough education." Modest admissions standards proved little obstacle too, as the only students not admitted were those "unable to read or write with tolerable facility, to perform operations in the four fundamental rules of arithmetic, and who has not at least some idea of grammar."[9]

The school day began at 8:30 A.M. and ended at 3:00 P.M., with an hour recess beginning at noon, a schedule that allowed monks to keep monastic observance as they prayed communally in the morning, at midday, and in the late afternoon. The academic year consisted of four quarters, starting on the first Tuesday of September and concluding in the last week of June. Father William Walter, the college's first president, let students know their academic standing by reading progress reports aloud each month in the presence of all professors and students before sending the grades home. A local reporter praised mid-year examinations in the early 1870s, saying, "In these days of deceptive show, when all that glitters is not gold, but very poorly plated glass, it is quite a treat to witness an *honest* college examination." Father William's faculty included a combination of monks, local priests, and lay professors. Monks taught Latin, Greek, English, algebra, and Christian doctrine, while Father Charles A. Reilly, pastor at nearby St. Columba's, instructed students in elocution and oratory. John Schulte, "the great poly-linguist from Westphalia," taught "Modern Languages," John Mindnich conducted music lessons, and John Johnson provided a "thorough, practical English mercantile education, qualifying the student for the office, the warehouse or the bank." Lay teachers figured prominently in the school until 1877, after which only monks served on the faculty.[10]

St. Benedict's was not interested solely in matters of the mind, as the monk-teachers wanted to look after the souls of their earthly charges too. The monks persuaded parents to enroll their sons because the school could best attend to their intellectual *and* moral development. "Secular education, whether classical or commercial, may help a young man to get on in the world, but it cannot fit him to discharge properly his duty either to his Maker or to society, nor can it really profit himself," stated the school catalog. "For what doth it profit a man, if he gain the whole world and lose his own soul?" A comprehensive education had to include "other lessons than merely those which relate to the day book or ledger, to Demosthenes or Cicero." Parents could now have "the best of both worlds . . . by sending [their sons] to St. Benedict's, where, in connection with secular instruction, they are also taught those lessons which will make them worthy candidates of heaven." In describing the atmosphere, a reporter observed, "The whole edifice is crowned by the firm and vigilant supervision . . . thereby insuring the presence of those great wants in American schools, as well as in American families, order, obedience and rule."[11]

The school quickly outgrew its old frame building, and plans "to erect a more suitable and commodious edifice on the site of the old building" were underway by July 1871. Workmen removed the original building, which was sold at auction for three hundred dollars, and broke ground on a new one. Classes were held in a nearby house until the three-story brick and tin-roofed structure was completed six months later. The new academic building accommodated up to two hundred "day scholars," which was a clear sign of ambition since only

Faculty and students of St. Benedict's College, 1891.

twenty-five students were on the books in 1872. Two years later, though, more than eighty students attended St. Benedict's, and the monks had faith that they could fill all those empty seats. In 1870, both William and High streets were macadamized, the first streets in the nation to be paved over with asphalt. The monks probably thought that the road to a new "day college" was paved with their good intentions, and that in the era of horse and buggy it would also be the smoothest of rides.[12]

In the summer after the construction of the new college building, the city hosted the Newark Industrial Exhibition to celebrate its status as a "monster workshop." Over the course of fifty-two days, an estimated 130,000 guests, many of them Newarkers, viewed the exhibition, which showcased a plethora of the city's industries and products. "The trunk you travel with is, in 9 cases out of 10, of Newark manufacture; the hat you wear was made there, the buttons on your coat, the shirt on your back, your brush, the tinware you use in your kitchen, the oil-cloth you walk on, the harness and bit you drive with, all owe Newark their origin," noted the *New York Times*. "And as to your wife's chain, bracelets, earrings and pedants, they have been fashioned by some cunning Newark goldsmith."[13] Any monk who walked through Newark's old skating rink, the site of the exposition, would not have been surprised by the multitude of manufactures, as many of the fathers of the first students were trunk makers, hatters, tailors, harness makers, and jewelers. As industries prospered, immigrants continued to flock to the city, a trend started by the Irish and Germans in the 1840s, but one that would accelerate toward the end of the century. Between 1840 and 1870, Newark's population increased sixfold, from 17,290 to 105,159; by 1880, 136,508 residents lived within the city's boundaries, and by 1900, nearly a quarter of a million people, many of them Catholic, called Newark home.[14]

A typical student entered as a thirteen-year-old, second-generation Irish or German immigrant from one of the city's immigrant neighborhoods. He lived within a mile of St. Benedict's and his family, which was usually five to seven strong and neither wealthy nor destitute. His father was most likely either a member of the new middle class or was employed by a local factory as an artisan. His mother stayed at home raising children and "keeping house." The family belonged to one of nearly a dozen German or Irish Catholic national parishes within the city limits. He could have either walked or taken a trolley or streetcar to get to school, and as a student in the commercial course he most likely studied for two years before qualifying for work in "the office, the warehouse or the bank." After leaving St. Benedict's, he might have worked as a clerk in one of the local businesses or followed in his father's footsteps and entered a trade, thus continuing his family's advancement in the United States, which often meant leaving his central city neighborhood for a better situation in an outlying district. Still, by 1900 more than 70 percent of the student body at St. Benedict's hailed from Newark.[15]

No matter where a young man lived, it was easy to get to St. Benedict's, as the school's front door was within one hundred paces of the intersection of High Street and Springfield Avenue, a routine stop on the city's expanding public transport network. Indeed, early school advertisements emphasized the school's convenient location. Located in "a most desirable part of the city," the school catalog boasted that the location was within "easy access from any part of the city or depot of the city . . . almost entirely secluded from the bustle and noise of business thoroughfares." It was all a bit of an exaggeration, though, as the city's busiest intersection was less than a half mile away and the church, monastery, and school were surrounded on the north and east by the city's oldest patent leather factory, Newark Academy to the south, and an open field and a brewery to the west. In October 1876, just a month after St. Benedict's began its ninth year, a reporter from *Harper's Monthly* toured the neighborhood and described it as "a snug, compact, well-paved city within a city." She called it "Germantown" since a "wondrous tide of Germans [had] flooded Newark, dropping into all the vacant lots about the factories . . . until it numbers about one-third of the voting population."[16]

Some even considered Newark to be a German city, a claim that both Newark's Anglo-Protestants and its surging Irish community surely contested, but at least in the two-square-mile Hill District "German habits and German customs" did prevail. German love of lager beer explained the nearly ten breweries and countless beer gardens in the area, and just up William Street stood the Newark Turnverein, the German community's athletic center. Churches and synagogues provided services in the immigrants' native tongue. A German newspaper, *New Jersey Freie Zeitung*, regularly published local news, including newsworthy bits on St. Benedict's. At the time, the German community was mostly middle class, but there were glimpses of both poverty and extreme wealth. Perhaps no other figure represented the industry of the local German immigrant population more than Gottfried Krueger, one of Newark's most fantastic rags-to-riches stories. Wearing wooden shoes, he came to Newark in 1854 as a teenage boy to work in his uncle's brewery, and through hard work and saving he bought the brewery just over a decade later. He went on to have a career in local politics and was a well-known philanthropist. Both Krueger and Christian Feigenspan, another apprentice turned beer baron, eventually built magnificent mansions along High Street, just a few blocks south of St. Benedict's.[17]

St. Mary's Church and St. Benedict's were both founded with the local German Catholic population in mind, but even though the parish and school were nestled in the middle of Germantown it quickly became apparent that both institutions would not be exclusively German. The McGurks were among the first group of Irish Catholics at the school, and while students had to study the German language, every other class was in English, a clear departure from some of the German-English schools in the city at the time. Baptismal records at St. Mary's indicate that the Irish attended the English-speaking service that was held at nine o'clock in the morning, before the German Mass a few hours later. Likewise, one chronicler of the school's early history argued that it "was anything but a German national school," despite the fact that it was situated in the middle of a predominantly German neighborhood. "It did much to help the younger generation of immigrant Catholics to join in a common effort, rather than form national units of the ghetto types which their elders were prone to do."[18]

One of the most striking features about the early years at St. Benedict's, then, was the presence of the Irish. Originally, Benedictine missionaries intended to minister only to German Catholics, but they came

to learn that German and Irish immigrants usually lived in close proximity to one another. Boniface Wimmer admitted Irish students to St.
Vincent College after it opened in 1846, and in doing so he believed
he was contributing to the "amalgamation of the two Catholic elements
in the church in America, which, so far, are opposing one another to
the detriment of both."[19] The same was true for St. Benedict's. Even
though it was designed on a German model and was staffed by monks
born in Germany, the sons of Kerry and Cork outstripped those of
Baden and Bavaria. In the early years, when St. Benedict's was small
and the German presence should have been felt most strongly, more
than 30 percent of the first students were of German heritage, more
than 60 percent had Irish roots, and a sprinkling of students with
French and Swiss heritage contributed flavor to the school's multi-
ethnic, multi-class stew.

An advertisement for the college in the *Irish Citizen* claimed that
"this useful and creditable institution is open to students of all classes
and creeds," and while there might have been only a handful of non-
Catholics at St. Benedict's in its early years, there was certainly a mixture from Newark's lower, middling, and upper classes.[20] A close examination of the economic background of the first students dispels the
long-cherished myth that they were mainly poor and disadvantaged.
While Newark's Catholic community comprised many immigrant families concentrated at the bottom of the occupational ladder, over half
the students at St. Benedict's came from middle-class families whose
fathers were employed as dry goods grocers, manufacturers, and
clerks. A still-thriving artisan class of tailors, shoemakers, and masons
made up a third of the families, while only 14 percent of the student
body came from unskilled laboring families.[21] St. Benedict's appealed
to immigrant Catholic parents who had secured more than a foothold
in the United States.

Irish families accounted for nearly seven out of every ten middle-
class families at St. Benedict's, while the Germans dominated the artisan class. Grocers (26 percent), manufacturers (18 percent), clerks (13
percent), and salesmen (13 percent) made up the majority of this new
middle class, with grocers and manufacturers the most prosperous
among them. Some grocers began as peddlers in the 1850s, hawking

their wares door-to-door through Newark's streets, but ten years later they owned their own stores and earned steady incomes. The most prominent was Martin Burne, a wholesale and retail grocer who had accumulated holdings of more than $150,000. Burne lived up the street from the school in a mansion with a large extended family, including his stepsons, whom he sent to St. Benedict's. In many families, children had to work. Matthew Hogan's father was a shoe manufacturer and he and his two sisters all worked in his factory. Before Bernard Naughton entered St. Benedict's in 1872, a census report for 1870 listed him as dressmaker.[22]

Some of the shoe, leather, hat, and brick manufacturers acquired property and amassed modest wealth too. Economic success made home ownership, another index of social standing within the Catholic community, possible for nearly a third of all families at St. Benedict's. Sixty-three percent of all property owners came from the new middle class, with 30 percent from the artisan class and only 7 percent from the unskilled laboring class. Seventeen percent owned more than ten thousand dollars' worth of property, 23 percent owned between five and ten thousand dollars' worth, and another 57 percent owned between one and five thousand dollars' worth. Only 3 percent of home owners had a home valued at less than one thousand dollars. In addition, almost half the families at St. Benedict's employed live-in domestic servants, almost all of them young women from Ireland.[23]

A small fraction of laborers, tanners, hatters, and railroad workers sent their sons to St. Benedict's in the early years, but the ones who did were often quite successful despite being classified as unskilled. If Newark was like any other northeastern city, more than half of all Irishmen worked as unskilled laborers, earning no more than four hundred dollars a year. But among the "unskilled" families at St. Benedict's, four out of every ten owned homes. Michael Cadden's father worked as a laborer but was still able to own more than one thousand dollars' worth of property in 1870. Another father did the hard and dirty work of a tanner, but his holdings topped four thousand dollars. Still another was employed as a switch tender in a local railroad yard and accumulated more than six thousand dollars.

It would be unfair to say that St. Benedict's ignored the poor and struggling Catholics in Newark, but it is clear that they targeted families successfully making their way in the city. Benedictines had a tradition of accepting the poor in their monasteries and schools, and at St. Vincent College some students paid a fraction of tuition, room, and board, while "several orphans [were] kept entirely free."[24] The poor and orphaned came to the doors of St. Benedict's College too; one orphan was the ward of a local Catholic priest who paid his entire tuition. Francis Farrell, only ten years old when his father died in an industrial accident at a nearby factory, had two years' worth of tuition paid in full by an unknown benefactor. Several other boys and young men lived in female-headed households, because of the death or desertion of their fathers, but the monks usually found a way to alleviate the burden by reducing fees on a case-by-case basis.[25]

For many, paying tuition proved to be a willing sacrifice even though it put a strain on household finances. James McKeever's father could not afford tuition, but perhaps the monks overlooked this in order to foster a vocation to the priesthood. James became a priest and served as pastor of St. Rose of Lima in the city for decades. Alexander Haffert, a saloon keeper born in Germany, was both steady and sober in his approach to paying the bill, appearing at the beginning of each month to pay six dollars in cash. In hard economic times, families had tough decisions to make. William Carrolton, a hat manufacturer and father of six, usually paid the bill in full at the beginning of each academic year, but when the Panic of 1873 hit, he went an entire year without making a payment. The following year his son, James, did not return to St. Benedict's. The majority of families paid tuition quarterly, and less than 10 percent ever let accounts go delinquent, the only exception being the two academic years after the panic, when the number of accounts with an overdue balance doubled. But the monks showed leniency and tried to keep students enrolled.[26]

Throughout the school's first decade of existence, two factors conspired to hinder the growth of St. Benedict's, so much so that the monks had "to persevere in the face of what seemed to be insurmountable difficulties." First, the Panic of 1873 had wreaked havoc on the country, and national unemployment reached a staggering 14 percent by 1876 as countless businesses failed and factories shut down. Newark would not recover until 1879. Second, an upsurge of anti-immigrant and anti-Catholic feeling coincided with the tough economic times. The historian Dermot Quinn called nativism mid-century New Jersey's "besetting sin," and Catholic schools were often the target of slander and propaganda. In Newark, talk about the "parochial school disease," and how Catholic schools repeatedly "demonstrated their utter inferiority to the public schools, their inability to prepare Roman Catholic youth for the duties of life and of American citizenship," undermined the ability to attract more students. "Continual defamatory insults, heaped by bigoted fanatics upon the educational establishments of the Church," noted a proponent of a Catholic day college, continued to negatively affect enrollment.[27]

An additional factor curtailing growth was the fact that few boys and young men planned to study in secondary school or beyond. As the immigrant church in Newark expanded, so did the network of Catholic schools, and by 1870 nearly 70 percent of all parishes had grammar schools. Both St. Patrick's and St. James's Catholic schools, for example, had enrollments of more than one thousand boys and girls; St. Mary's Grammar School enrolled nearly four hundred. In one sense, there was no shortage of prospective students, but attracting boys to St. Benedict's remained a difficult task for the simple reason that most boys in the city stopped their formal education before the end of elementary school. With jobs readily available at a young age, there was no premium put on furthering one's education. The college's commercial department attracted some as they looked to move up the occupational ladder, but throughout the 1870s the college's attendance averaged only fifty-three, with a high of eighty-one in 1873–74 and a low of twenty-five in 1871–72. Perhaps the school's greatest accomplishment during those early, lean years was preparing a dozen young men to study for the priesthood, a handful of whom would come back to join the monastery and lead the school in the future.[28]

Even though the student population remained small, St. Benedict's was "steadily rising in popular favor," as word-of-mouth traveled through Catholic educational circles and the local press printed a number of complimentary articles. The *Newark Evening Courier* observed that St. Benedict's, "conducted by the hard working and zealous Fathers of the Order of St. Benedict," was "now a credit to the city," and the *Newark Daily Journal* commented that "it may now be classed among the foremost Roman Catholic institutions of learning in the land" because "the Benedictines thoroughly understand their business."[29] Yet the lofty goal of two hundred "day scholars" was not to be realized for another four decades.

An Urban Abbey

"God have pity on me," he wrote to a friend. "I was chosen on the second ballot." Such was the reaction of a thirty-five-year-old monk upon learning that he would be the first ever abbot of St. Mary's Abbey. James Zilliox had grown up right around the corner from the monastery he would now lead. Born in Newark and baptized at St. Mary's Church, young James had attended St. Mary's Grammar School and spent one year at St. Benedict's before his talents and vocation pointed him to Latrobe, Pennsylvania, where he studied to be a priest at St. Vincent College. The bookish monk's father still lived on William Street, and his grandmother was the housekeeper who fought off the Know-Nothing men when they raided the church in 1854. His Newark roots ran deep, but he wished that another monk had been elected. At his installation, on July 22, 1885, he could barely look up, not to mention look around the ornately decorated church, festooned with flowers and plants for the special occasion. Two bishops, three other abbots—including Zilliox's mentor, Boniface Wimmer—and a college president were among the hundreds there to celebrate, but Abbot James was far too shy, serious, and embarrassed to enjoy all the pomp and circumstance.[30]

The year 1885 proved to be momentous for the monks and students on High Street. The monastery was elevated to abbatial status and a native Newarker was its first spiritual leader. For the first time, more than one hundred students attended St. Benedict's, even though forty-five studied in the short-lived night school, and Mayor Joseph Haynes

A lithograph of St. Benedict's College on High Street.

attended graduation exercises, a clear sign of the school's growing reputation in the city. A local pastor delivered the commencement address, and he praised the monks for the care they gave their students, saying, "They have taken great pains to incline these twigs—and some of them are very tender saplings—in the right direction in the way of morality and virtue as well as profane knowledge." The following year, Mayor Haynes brought Governor Leon Abbett with him to the closing ceremonies. A new monastery building had been completed and a fourth floor was added to the school building in order to accommodate new physics and chemistry laboratories. Moreover, the New Jersey State Legislature had passed bill 345 on March 21, 1881, which legally raised the status of St. Benedict's to the level of a college, granting it "the right and power of conferring the usual academic and other degrees granted by any other college in this state." St. Benedict's College emphasized its new status in all its literature, and the student population doubled between 1881 and 1885.[31]

Ironically, the very foundation that Abbot Boniface Wimmer was afraid of most turned out to be one of the least troublesome; the Newark monastery was more or less self-sufficient, ran a successful parish and two schools, and produced its share of vocations to the priesthood. It had earned its independence. Abbot James, the second of eleven children, began his tenure in charge of twelve other monks, and he immediately started to shape his vision for an urban abbey. In the very first chapter meeting (a regular conclave to discuss and vote on issues affecting the monastery and school), the monks voted to discontinue the night school at Benedict's, sell its farm in Morris County, and start a scholasticate, a college-level program to prepare young men for entry into the Order. In a subsequent meeting, the monks considered acquiring more land along High Street to eventually expand the school. Perhaps more tellingly, the new abbot returned several parishes to the bishop, thus curtailing the monks' weekend assignments outside the monastery. The inward-looking Zilliox believed that the monks should divide their time between only two things: proper monastic observance and their educational apostolate. His approach to monasticism clashed with his mentor's style. Wimmer advocated a more "muscular, action-oriented, and purposeful" strategy, believing that the Catholic faith had to be preserved in the era of the immigrant church. Likewise, he believed that churches, schools, and monasteries had to be built and cultivated.[32]

Abbot James's abbacy lasted only sixteen months, as health issues related to tuberculosis caused him to resign. At first, the new abbot, Hilary Phraengle, shared some of Zilliox's concerns about overextending the monks, but within a few years he took on new parishes, including one in New Hampshire. Knowing that the Newark monks were educators, the local bishop soon requested that they start a Catholic college in New Hampshire. Abbot Hilary wrote Boniface Wimmer seeking advice in 1887, and the aging monk responded, "Newark— your day school there must be your main care, since your Abbey depends chiefly on its good standing." The Newark community was too young, too small, and too saddled with debt from its recent building campaign to start another monastery and college, but two years later, in 1889, St. Anselm College was founded as the third-oldest Catholic college in New England. The decision proved to be a considerable drain on the Newark community, as both monks and money left the city for the new foundation in New Hampshire. Over the next twenty-five years, the monks voted to spend more than four hundred thousand dollars for the expansion of St. Anselm; they spent half that on the Newark operation. Moreover, during the 1890s, Abbot Hilary left Newark to live in Manchester for five years to ensure that the fledgling monastic community and college survived, no small feat considering that a deep and far-reaching depression was the decade's decisive event.[33]

Despite the New England venture and the Panic of 1893, St. Benedict's made solid progress, and perhaps the arrival of steam heat in the monastery, church, and school (a luxury in 1886) was a clear sign of middle-class status. By 1903, the "steam heat" monks mirrored the upward mobility of the "steam heat" Irish, and purchased part of the Halsey estate next to their current High Street property. The monks still educated three basic groups: younger boys in the preparatory department, those aspiring to work in local businesses in the commercial department, and those who sought our professional schools and the priesthood in the classical department. They performed their duties well, and according to one local newspaperman, "St. Benedict's College has turned out some very clever young men, who have made their way to leading positions in the different professions, who always refer with great pride to their early training." "The story of rejection, then acceptance," and finally of achievement in Newark and beyond, noted the historian Dermot Quinn, can be "best told in names."[34]

Of course, the story could begin with a young James Zilliox, one of the first students at St. Benedict's, who then became the abbey's first spiritual leader. Zilliox turned out to be the first of a kind, since Joseph Helmstetter (from the Down Neck section of the city) entered St. Benedict's in 1872 and spent a few years at the school before expressing an interest in a vocation. He too was sent to St. Vincent's to study for the priesthood before returning to his beloved Newark in 1885, and then spent the next twenty years on the faculty, even serving as headmaster on two separate occasions. Martin Burne, the wealthy grocer who sent his two stepsons to Benedict's in 1870, also started a long family tradition. Nearly one hundred years later another Martin Burne became abbot, and his vision for St. Benedict's proved crucial to the school's more recent history.[35]

There was more than a monastic legacy, however, as some of Newark's most prominent businessmen studied at the school. Andrew and Edward Radel, sons of a German immigrant coal dealer, both graduated in the 1870s before going on to become executives of a local railroad company. Bernard M. Shanley, owner of the state's largest contracting business, built the Pennsylvania Railroad between New York, Newark, and Philadelphia. He did not attend the school, but he sent his son, Bernard Jr., who went on to become a wealthy jeweler and one of the most prominent Catholic laymen in the city. Peter Hauck Jr. studied at both Newark Academy and St. Benedict's, a rare combination, before taking over the family brewery in nearby Harrison. A member of the prestigious Essex Club and a director of Federal Trust Company of Newark, Hauck married Elizabeth C. Smith, the daughter of a local political boss and U.S. senator, James "Big Jim" Smith Jr.[36]

Big Jim, a product of the Catholic school system himself, made his way in business through the J. H. Halsey and Smith Company, the patent leather factory adjacent to the monastery's property. He became good friends with the monks, and even delivered the commencement address in 1891. Smith gave the graduates advice on the importance of self-confidence and persistence, and warned them to be wary of diffidence, "the rock that wrecked many a well-equipped ship." Finally, he talked about work ethic and how "the race is not always to the swift but to the persistent. The slow, plodding, persevering fellows frequently reach the goal first." It was a fitting message, not only for the graduates, but also for the monks who had built up the monastery and school. Father Ernest Helmstetter, who taught mathematics, chemistry, and physics at St. Benedict's in 1891, was among the dozen monk-teachers in the crammed St. Mary's Hall to hear Smith's speech. In just over a year, Father Ernest would become the new director of St. Benedict's, and over the next few decades the Newark native would also serve as abbot. Under his leadership the school that was founded in the era of the immigrant church to be "necessary, useful, and beautiful" would be transformed into a modern Catholic prep school.[37]

3 The Making of a Modern Catholic
Prep School, 1900–1926

Some students called it the "pickle factory," but the new four-story facility was one of the best school buildings in the state when it was completed in September 1910. Boasting three floors of classrooms, modern science laboratories, an assembly hall, and a recreation facility, the red brick exterior may have looked like one of the local factories, but it was most certainly part of the "City Beautiful" movement in Newark. It was not as grand as the recently constructed Essex County Courthouse, Newark Public Library, or Newark City Hall, but it did have some interesting features, including ornate tin ceilings, chestnut millwork in every classroom, and eventually a Tiffany & Co. stained-glass canopy over the front stoop. Ten years later, a "larger and more pretentious structure" was added, and together the two new buildings closely resembled the downtown department store L. S. Plaut & Co. The store's ceaseless activity and network of honeycomb windows had earned it the nickname the "Beehive"; in 1924, St. Benedict's would acquire its own nickname, the "Gray Bees," and the school building was dubbed the "Beehive" too, or simply the "Hive." This era of "brick and mortar Benedictinism" symbolized the ascendancy of St. Benedict's as it evolved from a small, traditional day college to a large, modern Catholic prep school.[1]

Between 1900 and 1926, the modernization of St. Benedict's occurred within the context of a rapidly changing society, church, city, and educational system, and two central figures, Ernest Helmstetter and Cornelius Selhuber, helped shepherd the school through the transformation. The German-born Selhuber came to study at St. Benedict's after immigrating to Newark with his parents, and he provided the vision and leadership that made St. Benedict's one of the great Catholic high schools in the region. A leading light among fellow monk-educators, Father Cornelius served as chairman of the High School Department for the Benedictine Educational Association, and his ideas and methods influenced other Benedictine secondary schools. His approach to curriculum reform, character education, and teacher training was that of a "conservative progressive," one who believed in "healthy conservatism" rather than "destructive liberalism."[2] Notably, he looked to other schools for insight into programs and standards, in particular other prep schools and big-city public school systems. All along he was encouraged and enabled by the third abbot of St. Mary's Abbey, Ernest Helmstetter, a native Newarker and former headmaster himself.

St. Benedict's Prep flourished in the first quarter of the twentieth century, as the school grew from 75 students in 1900 to over 735 in 1925, almost a tenfold increase. Newark grew exponentially too, from 246,070 in 1900 to over 400,000 in 1930, a direct result of the arrival of "new" immigrants to an "old" immigrant city. In particular, southern and eastern Europeans, as well as African American migrants from the American South, inundated an already-crowded city in search of work in what the Newark Board of Trade called the "City of Industry." Many flooded into the neighborhoods around St. Benedict's, resulting in overcrowding and unhealthy living conditions. The neighborhood would be renamed the Third Ward in 1917, and for the first time it began to show signs of decline. Yet St. Benedict's Prep came of age in a thriving, somewhat progressive, and increasingly diverse city, and issues of educational reform, boosterism, ethnicity, and race came to affect the school's development. While St. Benedict's still possessed traditional objectives that emphasized character formation, discipline, spirituality, and academic achievement, the school also became a more confident, modern, urban, and American institution.

"Teaching Is Our Life's Work"

Intrigue surrounded the decision to expand in the city, though, as Abbot Hilary Phraengle told his fellow monks at a chapter meeting in

August 1909, "here in the city we would always be pressed for space and could not develop as we ought." He proposed buying a farm "not too far from the city," and some suggested that he might move the monastery one day. Two months after breaking ground on the new school building, Abbot Hilary died suddenly, and his body was found in a second-floor bathroom after he failed to appear for dinner. The new abbot, Ernest Helmstetter, had grown up in the city and attended St. Benedict's, and the potential for a move from his hometown was laid to rest, at least for the time being.[3]

Abbot Ernest would build again in 1920, when the school had grown enough to warrant the erection of another classroom building and state-of-the-art gymnasium. The construction campaign coincided with a name change too. St. Benedict's College was changed to St. Benedict's Preparatory School in 1910, which simply confirmed what the school had been for decades already: a high school. Ironically, after 1881, when an act of the New Jersey State Legislature raised St. Benedict's to the rank of a college, it turned out far more high school graduates than college ones. In fact, there were never more than eight college graduates in a given year between 1881 and 1910, and usually there were only two or three. College graduates accounted for less than 10 percent of all students, so the focus for some time had been on the younger students in the classical and commercial departments. The monks stopped advertising St. Benedict's as a day college by 1900, and a 1907 advertisement emphasized that St. Benedict's was the "Catholic High School of Newark." When the Board of Trustees met in 1910, they finalized the decision to abandon the college program but retained "college" in its name for the prestige. In 1914 the school was called "St. Benedict's College and Preparatory School," and it was not until World War I that the monks officially discarded the "college" name. By 1922, one advertisement confidently boasted, "Your Boy Is Assured of the Best Educational Advantages at St. Benedict's Preparatory School."[4]

The push to modernize St. Benedict's as a high school began just before the turn of the century during Father George Bien's seven years as headmaster. From 1898 to 1905, he refined the curriculum, made certain that the school had the latest and "most modern apparatus" for the science program, and championed the burgeoning athletics program. Father George was also a meticulous numismatist, and his coin collection became part of the "Cabinet of Natural History," a hodge-podge of "rare coins, minerals and curiosities of various kinds." The coin collection consisted of some three thousand "specimens," including Roman coins dating back to A.D. 350, papal coins from the 1500s, and old American pennies dating to 1792. The cabinet, which included donations by Andrew Carnegie, the Gilded Age's most generous industrialist, also displayed some eight thousand stamps. The coin collection was neglected and even "lost" after Father George's death, but it was discovered again decades later and served the school extremely well in a time of financial need (see Chapter 10).[5]

Ernest Helmstetter enjoyed his second stint as headmaster following Father George's passing, and his affinity for city, school, and abbey were unparalleled. Forever interested in the school's progress, Helmstetter introduced weekly Saturday faculty meetings, and on one such occasion a dozen monks gathered to listen to a lecture on "Method of Teaching." Father Anselm Kienle, the Latin and Greek teacher, was renowned for his deft handling of Virgil's *Aeneid*, but he also kept abreast of the latest educational trends. His long discourse began with a defense of the priest's role in Catholic education:

Thorne in his *Globe Review* one time said that a priest can not be a good professor except in theology, maintaining that he will either neglect his duties as priest or as professor. I do not agree with this opinion. The history of our Order and also of other teaching Orders disabuses us of this. A secular teacher is prompted by various motives: instruction of youth, a natural inclination to his vocation, display of learning, and last but not least a fair salary. A conscientious religious will perform his duties prompted by higher, supernatural motives. *Teaching is our life's work.*

"The school is what the teacher makes it," Father Anselm continued. "It is largely a reflection of himself. If he is listless, aimless and indifferent, his pupils will be listless, aimless and indifferent also, but if he is earnest, devoted and determined, they will be so also." Teachers' knowledge, dedication, and patience enabled "good results [to] be confidently expected." But that would only get a teacher so far, because he also had to understand "boy nature." Father Anselm explained: "The teacher must have sympathy with his pupils. He must be able to look on things with their eyes and feelings. He must have power to enter into their thoughts and to share in their sorrows and joys."[6]

The recent changes in structure, philosophy, curriculum, and student body all seemed to coalesce when Abbot Ernest asked Father Cornelius to become the new headmaster in 1910. St. Benedict's not only had a new building, it now had a straightforward school leader who also possessed the vision, energy, and stubbornness to push through his ideas. He listened to his colleagues and kept his fingers on the pulse of educational trends, but he was self-assured enough to remain steadfast to his vision, a variation of Archabbot Boniface Wimmer's mantra, "Forward, everywhere forward!" In the end, it was "under [Selhuber's] aegis" that St. Benedict's Prep grew "both in numbers and prestige." Significantly, Father Cornelius's "manly and kind way," coupled with "a thorough understanding of [students'] capabilities," contributed to his standing among his charges. "We all knew that all the students looked to him as their primary guide and counselor, and that all loved him," praised students in the 1920 yearbook. "During our four years in his happy company, we had many opportunities to see that his interest, enthusiasm and generalship is the *secret motive power* of St. Benedict's."[7]

Catholic high schools grew and matured alongside an expanding public school system, often mirroring changes they saw in their secular counterparts. Historians of education locate the emergence of the public high school in the Progressive Era, but prep schools, most of them along the eastern seaboard, emerged during this period too. The same holds true for Catholic high schools, as they made the transition from colleges/academies to four-year secondary schools. Ample evidence exists that St. Benedict's routinely looked to private and public high schools for ways to improve its curriculum and programs. Benedict's required only two years of science, but that changed to four after Father Cornelius lamented, "We are not on even terms with the High Schools." English courses were revised to model those at a large public

Headmaster Father Cornelius Selhuber, OSB, was "the
secret motive force" behind the phenomenal growth at
St. Benedict's Preparatory School from 1910 to 1926.

high school in nearby Jersey City. St. Benedict's also looked to other
elite prep schools for ideas and innovations, in particular Newark
Academy, which stood across William Street until it moved to another
part of the city in 1929.[8]

Nonetheless, the monks fretted over their decision to identify as a
high school. During of the summer of 1912, Father Cornelius toured
the city in a new automobile to interview parents; he wanted to know
if they would still send their sons to St. Benedict's if it dropped its
college status. In 1914, the Catholic schools superintendent designated

St. Benedict's one of six high school centers—along with Seton Hall and St. Peter's, and three girls' schools, including the nearby St. Vincent's—as part of a plan to coordinate secondary education in the Newark diocese. Under the plan, some parishes even paid for students to attend these schools, which proved to be a godsend to St. Benedict's. The student rolls jumped to over two hundred for the first time in school history; as the school built its reputation as a high school, it had a ready pool of potential students. Roman Catholics now outnumbered any other religious sect in the city, with an estimated population of 105,000.[9]

As St. Benedict's successfully transitioned from a college to a high school, Father Cornelius continued to promote high academic standards, but he did not want them to be too cumbersome. The school had insisted on three hours of "home study" each day in order to "reasonably expect satisfactory results." But that changed to two hours a night in 1912, when Father Cornelius informed parents that homework would be "given consistently" but in "moderate doses." He also convened the faculty to discuss common testing standards, asking that they "would be neither too easy, nor too hard." In assigning grades, he opted for giving the boy "the benefit of the doubt whenever possible." The curriculum still proved challenging, as some students remained "conditioned" from the previous year. Having not met the passing mark of 70 percent from the previous year, promotion came with the stipulation that they become proficient by the first quarter of the following year. Poor-achieving students were required to attend after-school tutoring sessions too, and if additional help was required, a student could receive a private lesson for the sum of fifty cents.[10]

In June 1914, an assassin's bullet killed Archduke Franz Ferdinand of Serbia, precipitating a chain of events that led to World War I. But the prospect of American involvement in the war remained distant, and an isolationist stance enabled Newark to continue enjoying its "golden era." Proof of progressivism and civic accomplishment was everywhere. Newark boasted the first county park in the country, a new city hall and courthouse, and its first skyscraper. In 1911, former President Theodore Roosevelt dedicated a sculpture of Abraham Lincoln at the foot of the courthouse steps, just down the street from St. Benedict's. Throughout the week, but especially on weekends, people flocked to shop at Bamberger's, Hahne's, and Plaut's, often before eating dinner in one of the city's many restaurants and then going to the theater or the movies. Newark was a destination. In September 1914, nearly 250 students attended St. Benedict's, the largest enrollment in its nearly fifty-year history. The promising start to the year so pleased Father Cornelius that at Christmas he presented each member of the faculty with a box of fifty cigars. In 1916, Newark celebrated its 250th anniversary, and the following year a reform measure saw the mayor-council form of government replaced by a commission government. But the soaring optimism of progress and progressivism eventually ran aground as one city resident's invention helped drag the country into war.[11]

By the time the Holland family moved to Newark from nearby Paterson in 1900, John P. Holland had been designing and testing submarines for over twenty years. Holland immigrated to the United States from Ireland in 1873, and five years later the schoolteacher turned inventor tested an early submarine in the Passaic River. Aware of his creation's destructive potential, Holland wrote, "The submarine is indeed a 'she devil' against which no means we possess at present can prevail." In the years after his son, John Jr., graduated from St. Benedict's, Holland's "she-devil" terrorized the seas, leading to the sinking of the famed *Lusitania* in 1915, as well as three American ships two years later. Unlimited submarine warfare against American vessels pushed President Woodrow Wilson to ask for a declaration of war on Germany, which Congress provided. At St. Benedict's, a large portion of the faculty were German-born monks, and they had decided as early as 1914 to "refrain from discussing the war either in or out of the class." Now it was impossible not to do so, and the monks and their school completely supported the city and country's war efforts.[12]

Four days after the declaration of war on Germany, Joseph McDonough, the president of the class of 1920, tried to enlist. He was too young, but he later lied about his age and eventually saw action in France. Others enlisted, and still others tried in vain, but the majority of the student body remained at St. Benedict's and joined the war effort by selling Liberty Bonds, volunteering at Knights of Columbus and Red Cross drives, and participating in conservation programs. Individual classes competed against one another to see who was more patriotic, monitoring and measuring their contributions to the war. One student sold more than three thousand dollars' worth of war bonds. Military training was introduced at the school too. While the Western Front's bloody trench warfare ended in a stalemate thousands of miles away, an influenza epidemic in the city proved especially deadly. It reached the doorstep of St. Benedict's and delayed the opening of the 1918–19 school year. The sophomore James Reid was among the 26,235 city residents who contracted the virus, and unfortunately he was one of the 1,133 who died before the epidemic faded in late November.[13]

News of Germany's surrender rippled through Newark prematurely, and despite the recent tragedy of a classmate's death, some students were in a festive mood. Bernard DuPlessis recollected the following in the class of 1921 history:

Several newspapers anticipated Armistice Day, and on the morning of Friday, November 7, 1918, the fake glad tidings were announced. Did we Sophomores ask whether the news was authentic or not? We did not. About fifteen of us crowded into and on Arthur Connolly's seven-passenger car and set out. It didn't take us long to find out we were playing "hookey," but little did we care that morning. We were out for a good time and we meant to have it. The real fun came, however, when we had to explain to out parents the "why" of the absentee notices.

When the real Armistice Day was announced four days later, the monks gave students the day off as they declared November 11 "Victory Day." Bernard and his pals once again set out in Art's car, "but the first day's fun seemed to take the edge off the second." By 8:00 A.M. the intersection of Broad and Market streets, popularly known as the "Four Corners," had been packed with revelers for hours. Strangers embraced, citizens sang, and bands played. The Newark Evening News headline read, "Newark Explodes in a Tumult of Celebration."[14]

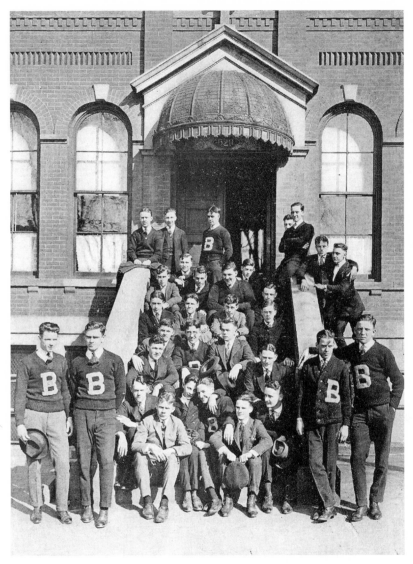

A group of students posing on "The Stoop," the iconic set of steps leading up to the front entrance of the school, 1921.

Roman Catholics had to prove their patriotism once again during World War I, and in Newark there was considerable anti-German sentiment. Federal officials raided the offices of a German-language newspaper. Public school teachers had to take loyalty oaths, and German language classes were suspended. In the Ironbound section of the city, patriotic citizens insisted that some street names be changed; Hamburg became Wilson Place, and Bismarck became Pershing Avenue. War conditions prompted St. Benedict's "to abandon" the semicentennial celebration of the school's founding, but they did not force a change in the curriculum. It was decided that "the German course (in spite of the war with Germany) [would] be continued." In the immediate aftermath of the war, an editor for the St. Benedict's yearbook wrote an essay on patriotism. "We must not let the world ignore the fact that in every war America ever had, Catholics composed nearly half of every army," he argued. "This is true of Washington's day, as he, himself publicly proclaimed, true even when American warred on the weak Catholic Nation of Spain."[15] Someone, perhaps one of the monks, also composed the St. Benedict's Prep alma mater. Sung to the tune of the German Christmas carol "O Tannenbaum," it first appeared in the 1922 yearbook:

> Thy praises now we fondly sing,
>   Ever dear St. Benedict's;
> Our loyal hearts to thee we bring,
>   Ever dear St. Benedict's;
> For God, for Country and for thee.
>   Be this our watchword, trinity;
> Thy sons forevermore are we,
>   Ever dear St. Benedict's.[16]

Parish Boundaries: Ethnicity and Race in a City and School

Victory parades gave way to a tumultuous decade in New Jersey, especially in many urban neighborhoods that seemed to be nothing more than a mixture of tribes. Prosperity returned after an initial postwar recession, but so did discrimination and racism. The 1920s witnessed a revival of anti-Catholic, anti-immigrant, anti-black behavior, so much so that instead of the "Roaring Twenties," the historian John Higham called the decade the "Tribal Twenties." With an estimated membership of sixty thousand in New Jersey, the Ku Klux Klan believed that immigration, industrialization, and urbanization all seriously threatened their native state. Peter F. Daly, a Roman Catholic jurist, spoke at a Benedict's alumni function, and in his talk, titled "The Coming American," he painted "a word picture of a composite individual, formed of the fibers of the various races of the earth, each with its peculiar outstanding characteristic, which will in time be the ideal American and the leader of the universe." John Cotton Dana, the director of the Newark Public Library, agreed with Ryan: "The thoughtful people of Newark welcome foreigners to this city. The more intelligent a man is the better he understands that each new race brings to us some knowledge that we need—some talent, some quality of character, some custom, some knowledge." The Klan disagreed, of course, and in 1923 hooded Klansmen interrupted a Sunday service at a white Methodist church in Newark. One official read a statement from the pulpit defending Klan activities in the state, indicating that the group only wanted to "maintain the solidarity of the white race." Newark's mayor at the time denounced the Klan's presence in the city, declaring, "Newark is a pretty well governed city, and can take care of itself in maintaining law and order without the assistance of the Ku Klux Klan."[17]

The Klan's distrust of all things Catholic was a topic of discussion when some alumni met at Ludwig Achtel-Stetter's restaurant on Broad Street in December 1922. Father Cornelius and Bernard M. Shanley Jr., president of the St. Benedict's Prep Alumni Association and a wealthy jeweler in town, spoke to the assembly of young alumni. Shanley's brief but emotional speech included the bold statement, "I defy anybody to tell me of an Irishman who is not 100 percent American. Benedict's is proud to be called an Irish institution." In his remarks, Father Cornelius commended the young men, saying, "You've got loyalty to your school, which comes from loyalty to your country, and as to our school and country you have loyalty to your religion. That is the spirit we need now." He bluntly concluded, "I'd hate to think of any hooded figures who might come here and challenge our loyalty. I don't think they'd fare very well at our hands." Applause flooded the hall as alumni proudly "raised the roof."[18]

As the Ku Klux Klan spread throughout New Jersey in the 1920s, Catholics responded in a confident and militant manner. The speeches of Father Cornelius and Shanley attest to a new attitude. The staff of *The Kayrix*, the fledgling newspaper at St. Benedict's, approached the revival of nativism with humor and satire when they reprinted an editorial from the *New York Times* in 1924:

Mr. Lowell Mellet tells us in *The Atlantic* that the Klan in Indiana is primarily an Anti-Catholic organization, and that the wildest tales of papal plots are readily believed by apparently sane citizens. . . . There is in Indiana a militant Catholic organization, composed of men specially chosen for strength, courage and resourcefulness. The devoted warriors lead a life of almost asceticism, under stern military discipline. . . . They have shown their prowess on many battlefields. Worst of all, they lately fought, and decisively defeated a detachment of the United States Army. Yet we have not heard of the Indiana Klansmen rising up to exterminate the Notre Dame football team.

A month later, Newark mayor Frederick Breidenbach visited St. Benedict's and addressed the student body on "Good Government and Good Citizenship." "Your good teachers are among our staunchest champions of law and order and respect for duly constituted authority, and you cannot go wrong if you follow their instructions and example," he commented to seven hundred students packed into the school gym. Before leaving, Breidenbach recognized St. Benedict's Prep as "a power for good in this community."[19]

Breidenbach, like most politicians, knew a voting block when he saw one. In 1900, the Catholic population in the Diocese of Newark numbered 290,000; by 1930, when every single member of the 1924 audience would be eligible to vote, it had leapt to 683,297. Catholics represented more than one-fourth of the area's total population during the period, and throughout the 1920s and 1930s they used their parishes "to map out—both physically and culturally—space within [the city]." Within the confines of these parish boundaries Catholics could "carry out almost every activity of life—education, health care, marriage and social life, union membership, retirement and old age—within a distinctly Catholic environment."[20] Entire neighborhoods seemed Catholic, and while the monks lived in a mostly Protestant and Jewish area, they got to know these very Catholic neighborhoods through their weekend parish assignments. Father Cornelius recognized the parishes as a pipeline of potential students, and he advised the monks to recruit for the school during their weekend visits. He called it "a little drumming."[21]

The historian John McGreevy has explained how American Catholics saw "the world as a series of loosely connected enclaves, with various 'racial' groups staking out claims to different sections of the city and different parochial institutions." Perhaps there was no better illustration of that patchwork parochialism, or in other instances tribalism, than a map issued to Newark social agencies in 1912. Titled "A Map of Newark, with Areas Where Different Nationalities Predominate," there were more than thirty distinct districts where one "race" or nationality group dominated. As one walked west from the genesis of Springfield Avenue just out of Newark's downtown, for example, there were three settlements for "Negroes" and a tiny Greek enclave. As one crossed over High Street between the county courthouse and St. Benedict's, a smaller German district lay at the foot of a large Jewish community. On either side of Bergen Street, a huge German neighborhood lingered in the distance. The northern part of the city had two Little Italy's, and discernible Irish, German, Slavic, and Italian sections competed with one another in the mix that was the Ironbound district. There was even a small Chinatown.[22]

Newark's mosaic changed in the interwar years, but a similar map in 1930 or 1940 would still depict a world where nationality, religion, and neighborhood intersected. Ethnic rivalry pervaded the city, and "old" versus "new" immigrant antagonisms were common. "The old Down Neck, when the Irish and Germans were here, was the best place to live in New Jersey—no, I mean the world," recalled one Irish Catholic Newarker. As neighborhood demographics changed, though, he added that some groups were "all right," all "except for the Spaniards and the Portuguese." Irish Catholics often mistrusted and despised

Newark's various ethnic groups formed enclaves throughout the city, many of which had high concentrations of Roman Catholics. These neighborhoods, delineated in this 1911 map, were often anchored by the national parish. (Courtesy of the Newark Public Library.)

newer immigrants, who in turn resented Irish domination of the church, labor unions, and local politics. Parish boundaries not only marked one's religion, but often one's ethnic background. Such distinctions made their way into the yearbook at St. Benedict's; in 1924, for example, *The Telolog* reported that John McLaughlin brought "himself hither every morning from Prospect St. in St. James' parish," and that Daniel Maher traveled to Newark each day from "St. Cecilia's parish, Kearny," otherwise know as "Edinburgh-on-the-Passaic." What happened at St. Benedict's when these sons of St. James's or St. Cecilia's met up with the sons of St. Phillip's and St. Ann's?[23]

St. Benedict's was indeed a gathering place for young men, as different parishes sent students to High Street to continue their Catholic education. Class and ethnicity played a role among students and faculty at Benedict's, but it was not a divisive one in the pan-Catholic setting. Irish and German surnames still accounted for most of the names on the roll in the early 1920s, but Italian and Polish names began to appear and became more numerous in the 1930s. In terms of class, very few Catholics had climbed to the top of society, and the bulk of an expanding Catholic middle class was virtually all German and Irish. Newer arrivals from eastern and southern Europe more often occupied the lower rungs in the class structure.[24]

When asked about ethnic rivalries within the school, St. Benedict's alumni responded, "There was none of that," "I don't recall any rivalries," and "There were no cliques." Interestingly, the students of that era viewed the school as a middle ground where Catholics from various class and national backgrounds met, studied, and played together. Pat McAuley, son of a Scottish immigrant who lived in East Orange, recalled, "My neighborhood at the time was all Irish, but when I got to Benedict's there was more of a mix. You never thought of a guy as Irish or Italian when he was at Benedict's." Like other large urban Catholic schools, St. Benedict's was a pan-Catholic, "translocal" institution." According to the historian Paula Fass, these types of Catholic high schools "vastly expanded inter-ethnic contacts which would eventually facilitate the assimilation forestalled by parish schools with single nationalities."[25]

Yet it is hard to believe that it all went so well among the Irish, German, Italian, and Polish Catholics students at St. Benedict's. Inter-ethnic contacts must have happened on so many different levels as students ventured from their various neighborhoods to the school, bringing with them all sorts of preconceptions and notions about issues of religion, class, ethnicity, and race. In William Farrell's trilogy of novels about working-class life in Irish Catholic neighborhoods in Chicago, one youth tells the main protagonist, Studs Lonigan, that "Polacks and Dagoes, and niggers are the same, only the niggers are the lowest."[26] If such sentiment prevailed in the neighborhoods, did it travel to a place like St. Benedict's?

It probably did, but perhaps in a less blatant fashion. Teenage boys will often look at one another and search for weakness, then exploit it with all alacrity. One's ethnic or economic background could be targeted, as could one's physical appearance, intelligence, athleticism, and ability to attract the opposite sex. These were just some of the traits that were routinely commented on in yearbook entries from the 1920s up through the early 1940s. Students were singled out because they were fat ("Girls, behold pleasingly plump Thomas Meehan. Tom simply hates to be referred to as fat."); hailed from the wrong part of town ("It has been rumored that they now use knives and forks [in the Ironbound] while satiating their appetites."); too hard of a worker ("Ray is one of those chaps who burn copious quantities of midnight oil."); or played sports in a certain manner ("He gyrated and pirouetted about the field as a sylvan nymph.").[27]

What we now call ethnicity was also a ripe target. When Pasquale Baiocchi, Alfred D'Agostini, and Anthony Villanova entered in the fall of 1919, they were some of the first members of the "Italian race" to go to St. Benedict's. Italians, Poles, and Jews were some of Newark's "new" immigrants, and they were considered "inbetween peoples" because they were "not quite white." With dark hair and swarthy complexions, the three new Benedict's students looked so much alike that their classmates dubbed them the "Roman Trio." Hailing from "homes of the consumers of succulent spaghetti," Italians had to "pay their dues" and prove their fitness for citizenship. It was just the way things were done in Newark. "History is forever repeating herself. When the Irish and then the Germans first came to Newark they were looked upon with something akin to distrust by the descendants of the Puritan founders," wrote the historian Frank J. Urquhart. "The Italians were received in much the same way by those already on the ground, and much the same process of amalgamation was begun all over again." "Although Italian by birth," concluded the *Telolog* staff, "Louis Baldacinni is an unhyphenated American in spirit and an ardent supporter of the democratic principles of our government." Benedict's had already helped bring the Irish and Germans together, and their accomplishments led to larger acceptance, however grudgingly it was given; now the cycle began anew.[28]

Irish Catholic stereotypes were perpetuated too. Raymond Donahue was noted for his "amusing stories and Celtic wit." The pugnacious Thomas Duffy "never back[ed] down" and "love[d] a scrap." John "Irish" Duffy came to Benedict's from St. Mary's School in Elizabeth, "where nearly all the fighting Irish are trained in the art of self-defense." Perhaps a lasting image of the daily teasing and tussling among the various ethnicities at St. Benedict's was a scene that took place in the school's main hallway in the 1940s. Father Timothy Dwyer, the bespectacled dean of discipline, watched two strapping football players become entangled in a "test of strength and manliness" on the floor. As he looked down, he calmly puffed on a cigar as the Irish Catholic Sweeney grappled with Cohen, the only Jewish student in school.[29]

A Catholic "racial" view of the world in northern cities came to include African Americans, especially during and after the Great Migration (1910–20), and Catholic immigrant groups quickly distanced themselves from the newcomers. The arrival of a large number of southern black migrants began to alter Newark's image as a predominantly white, working-class city, and resulted in the first well-defined African American ghetto in the city's Third Ward, within walking distance of St. Benedict's Prep. Between 1910 and 1920, Newark's African American population grew from approximately ten thousand to seventeen thousand, an increase of nearly 80 percent. William Ashby, a longtime activist in Newark's black community, said that the races "had an accommodating tolerance of one another" before the migration, but with the continued influx "life in Newark for everyone changed dramatically." The northward migration continued through the 1920s, and at decade's end nearly thirty-nine thousand African Americans lived in the city. "There was little going across the [color] line and mixing with whites except in a condescending or patronizing manner," confessed Ashby. "There were discriminations, prejudices, restrictions, prohibitions. . . . But they never penetrated themselves to the depth of 'race hatred.'"[30]

A condescending comic appeared in the 1922 yearbook, depicting an upperclassman walking to school with a small boy in bedraggled clothes and blackface following behind, who said, "Now, all ah needs is some books, so's ah kin make b'leve ah done go to Saint Benjy Man Dicks!" When the class of 1925 nervously arrived on their first day at Benedict's, they remembered "the upper-classmen were hand-shaking like so many small time politicians at the polls, while we yearlings felt as out of place as a few Negroes at a 'Kluxer' banquet." One student parodied life at St. Benedict's using African American dialect in his newspaper column titled "Uncle Tom's Gabbin'." The school newspaper nonchalantly advertised the "St. Benedict Senior Minstrel" in the spring of 1925: "Folks who are pinin' for ol' Virginny, cravin' for a Mississippi hum, languishin' for the darky songs of Alabam . . . had jes' nachally better not miss the St. Benedict Senior Minstrel." In preparation, two seniors "[took] lessons in Negro dialect from an unbleached Nether Newarker." "Freshman Night" included "a dramatic attempt of 'Amos 'n' Andy.'" In 1930, another blackface minstrel show sponsored by the school took place at a nearby hall, and the performance included song and dance numbers from "end men," soloists, specialty performers, and a large chorus. Patrons included the bishop, the mayor, the deputy police chief, and other city officials. Minstrel shows were an all-too-common entertainment at other parishes and Catholic schools in the area too.[31]

African American students did not attend St. Benedict's until the 1940s. At a meeting of the Clergy Negro Welfare Conference in Newark, Abbot Patrick O'Brien speculated on the impact of integrating the school, saying, "I know that if I for the first time in the history of St. Benedict's Prep School were to admit a Colored student predictions, prophecies and groans would be thrown at me." The monastery had accepted its first "colored brother" in 1903 when Robert Bodee was admitted to simple vows. As one of the first community members to learn to drive, he served as Abbot Ernest's chauffeur and was warmly remembered for selling apples at basketball games in the 1920s. Brother Robert, derisively called "Brother Ink" by students because of his dark complexion, also spoke German and clearly understood a racial slur thrown at him by a beer deliveryman one day. When another monk filed a complaint with brewery officials, the offender lost his job. He returned to the abbey days later with his wife and children to seek mercy. Brother Robert forgave him and helped him get his job back.[32]

A Second Home in the "Master City"

If the "pickle factory" was St. Benedict's contribution to the City Beautiful movement, then the two buildings constructed in 1920 helped usher in the "booster spirit" in Newark. Amid the 250th anniversary celebrations in 1916, Mayor Thomas L. Raymond believed it was time to make Newark "a Master City of which it shall be said, 'Not only does it excel in commerce and industry, but it is dominated by a lofty and aspiring soul which places it by the side of the world's fairest cities.'" Despite a brief postwar recession and the decline of some of Newark's traditional blue-collar industries, signs of a booster spirit were to be found everywhere. One only had to look up to see confirmation of this 1926 newspaper headline: "Newark's Skyline Grows Like a Weed." Banks and insurance companies built glittering new office towers, a new luxury hotel faced Military Park, a world-class museum bordered Washington Park, and Public Service opened a new streetcar terminal. Work began on transforming the old Morris Canal into a city subway system and crews filled in acres of land in the Meadowlands to build the first runway at Newark Airport. Some even foresaw a mighty metropolis on the banks of the Passaic, and the editorial staff of the *Newark Evenings News* stated in 1929, "The giant that is the Newark of the future is awakening."[33]

Benedict's was in the process of awakening too, which was announced by large copper lettering along the top of the new building. The letters soon turned green, but "ST. BENEDICT's" could still be read from downtown. The booster spirit that pervaded 1920s Newark also touched the school, and according to the historian Paul Stellhorn, "boosterism was an attitude, a frame of mind," which "demanded that the city develop in every manner of endeavor: economically, civically, and socially." There was no doubt that St. Benedict's Prep was growing, as more than six hundred students enrolled in 1922, and by then it was the second-largest all-boys Catholic high school in the state and one of the ten largest in the Mid-Atlantic and New England regions. As Benedict's got bigger during the 1920s, it also promised to get better. Abbot Ernest and Father Cornelius sought to improve St. Benedict's in a whole range of areas, especially its curriculum, sports program, disciplinary measures, and college counseling.[34]

On July 8, 1918, Abbot Ernest Helmstetter presided over the first meeting of the Benedictine Educational Association (BEA). Modeled after both the Catholic Educational Association and the National Educational Association, the body convened at St. Vincent Archabbey in

Latrobe, Pennsylvania. Nearly twenty monks gathered on the warm summer day with the purpose of discussing current and future "educational problems" affecting their various Benedictine schools. Representatives from all the Benedictine colleges and secondary schools were there, including Father Cornelius Selhuber, the only other Newark monk present. He played a key role during the three-day conference, as he assumed the chairmanship of the High School Department, a post he would retain until 1926; over the course of the next decade, he helped shape BEA policy, curriculum, and culture.

The monks discussed issues central to Catholic schools, like teaching religion, Latin curriculum, and the role of the priest-teacher. They decided that the catechism was "very burdensome" for high school students, and that religion courses should be "interesting and life-like" and help "train [students] to *live* their Religion." As for Latin, Father Cornelius suggested that a curricular "middle course" should be pursued. "No doubt in time a happy mean will be found combining the best elements of former thoroughness and modern progressivism to form the ideal course for the future," he observed. And when considering the impact of the monk-priest in the classroom, the BEA stated, "What Horace said about poets may be applied to priests: there is no room for mediocrity in priests. The consequences are too serious." It seemed that on a yearly basis the monks also debated what it meant to be a Benedictine school, the most effective disciplinary policies, and the role of athletics in education. Father Cornelius influenced other educators to promote a healthy and wholesome pursuit of sport as well as a mild yet effective disciplinary policy (see Chapters 5 and 6 for more on school discipline and athletics at St. Benedict's). Not only was he the *"secret motive power"* behind the phenomenal growth at St. Benedict's, he was also a moving force for the BEA.[35]

The monastic educational body was also concerned about its status with state boards of education as well as accrediting agencies, a clear indication that the once inward-looking Catholics schools now sought outside approval, not only for validation but for competitive purposes. In the BEA's first meeting Father Cornelius maintained that courses should conform to standard state requirements, and he suggested that the "high school departments should be accredited with State Institutions." BEA members also recommended state certification for teachers, and even proposed starting a Benedictine Teachers College. One monk disagreed with the trend toward accreditation, though, as he "pleaded for independence and moral courage in following our Benedictine educational ideals instead of slavishly trying to conform to the requirements, often arbitrary, of standardizing agencies." "Do not fear," replied Father Cornelius. "A good school will get accredited." St. Benedict's Prep was approved by the New Jersey Department of Education and by the diocesan school system. In the throes of the Great Depression, the school sought and received approval from the Middle States Association of Colleges and Schools, a regional accrediting agency. In seeking outside approval, though, the monks never forgot their constituents: the young men and their families.[36]

In many ways, a strong sense of community created by the monks, and then reinforced by the camaraderie and loyalty of the students, set the school apart from its competition. One student wrote about this family atmosphere in a school publication: "After the home, what is

Students conducting experiments in the new chemistry laboratory, 1922.

more congenial to the schoolboy? It is the school in which he spends much of his time, and where he finds things just as comfortable, as pleasant and as agreeable as at home. The Catholic spirit which pervades the atmosphere ensures this feeling of agreeableness, this feeling of a 'home,' which many boys find St. Benedict's to be." In 1919, another student wrote a paean to "Our Alma Mater": "From our entering day we felt ourselves to be at HOME in her halls, felt our adoption to be real and whole-hearted, and knew ourselves to be her well-loved sons." Ted Langan, a 1923 graduate, agreed, recalling, "That was always our motto. St. Benedict's is a family." It was this understanding of community, how to build and sustain it, that made the monks and students feel that they were creating something special. A sense of confidence in what was being accomplished prompted the inclusion of a new phrase in an advertisement for the school: "We Invite Comparison."[37]

St. Benedict's provided four distinct programs of study—classical, scientific, Latin-scientific, and commercial—all guided by an able and well-trained faculty. Students knew that they had to work hard in order to acquire the school's first-rate education, even though it came at a cut-rate price. To successfully complete the requirements for a diploma, "the vast majority of toilers" had to treat school like a "'healthy' four-year 'job,'" and in a day and age when few moved on to higher education after high school, more and more St. Benedict's graduates went on to college. In 1915, the yearbook noted, "all the members with few exceptions intend to study further." Nearly a decade later, the school newspaper observed the following: "It is interesting to note that the number of college-going graduates increases annually at St. Benedict's, and the records of our boys at institutions of higher learning are such as to justify pride—and stimulate ambition—on the part of present undergraduates here." Alumni started to make their mark in the city and state as politicians, lawyers, doctors, clergymen, educators, and businessmen. On the twenty-fifth anniversary of graduation, nearly 70 percent of the class of 1916 were doctors, accountants engineers, lawyers, or insurance executives. Three members of the class became Benedictine monks.[38]

Perhaps the best-known alumnus was Bernard M. Shanley Jr. Active in the local church, an avid sportsman, and a prominent jeweler in the city, Shanley was the school's first real booster. He loved Benedict's, especially its young athletes, and he visited the school nearly every day. Father Cornelius once said of Shanley, "He knew the boys as well as the teachers did." After the basketball team's successful run to the state championship in 1919, he gave the school twenty-five thousand dollars to build a new gymnasium in his father's memory. Though this generous donation paled in comparison to the seven hundred thousand dollars that Louis Bamberger gave to build the Newark Museum, it was part of the growing booster movement at St. Benedict's. On the heels of the gym and the new building on High Street, Father Cornelius coveted a new athletic facility, and he found and purchased a plot of land in North Newark, across the city subway tracks from the beautiful Branch Brook Park.[39]

Father Cornelius's vision helped make a modern prep school, but his crusade for a new athletic field brought an untimely end to his tenure at St. Benedict's. Other faculty members did not want to assume the financial strain of such a project or solicit large sums of private money to pay for it. But Father Cornelius ignored their concerns and continued his campaign. The slogan "when Benedict men back a movement, it moves" aptly described Father Cornelius's attempts to rally support. In fact, it was the first time in more than fifty years that St. Benedict's had asked for help from alumni and friends. He struggled to get the necessary funds, but "Benedict Field" eventually opened in the spring of 1925. Shanley, who was one of Father Cornelius's best friends and confidants, did not get to see the new complex, however, as he died of a heart attack on October 5, 1924. Newark lost an asset too, as Shanley "believed in it as a residence and business city." Born and raised in Newark, he also always lived in the city, first at the Shanley estate on Washington Street, and later on Broad Street near the new city hall. Shanley had been a true Newark booster, and in order to pay tribute to him the entire student body at St. Benedict's marched down High Street to the cathedral on Washington Street. The bishop presided at his funeral mass.[40]

Father Cornelius mourned his great friend, but he also looked forward to his twenty-fifth jubilee celebration as a monk-priest, and traveled to Europe during the summer as part of the festivities. Yet while he was thousands of miles away, some of his fellow monks conspired against him. They were still angered about his strong-arm approach in building Benedict Field, and they thought it was someone else's turn to lead the school. When Father Cornelius learned of the treachery, he immediately wrote a letter to Abbot Ernest. He had heard rumors that some monks resented his power and executive style but also defended his record. "No one knows what a task it was for you and me to bring St. Benedict's to where it is today," he wrote Abbot Ernest. He thanked the abbot for his encouragement over the years, and offered his resignation, saying, "I shall be very happy to be relieved. I only hope that things will go on as smoothly after I am gone and that you will not be annoyed by the endless squabbles and bickerings among the officials and teachers." But Father Cornelius did feel aggrieved, especially after bringing the school so far, and he left the other "bickering" monks for a Benedictine abbey in North Carolina where he became head of their secondary school.[41]

When alumni and friends gathered again at the Robert Treat Hotel forty-four years later to celebrate the school's hundredth anniversary, Father Cornelius Selhuber was one of the first to be praised. "His was a personality that was both warm and attractive, and his fondness for the School prompted him to canvass actively for the School's growth," lauded Abbot Martin Burne in 1968. "By the time of his retirement from the scene, in 1926, the School had witnessed its greatest development in both personnel and physical facilities, and it remained for his successor, Father Boniface Reger to 'firm up,' so to speak, the many areas that were part of that development." Father Cornelius grew the school during a period of peace and prosperity; Father Boniface had to do so during prolonged periods of depression and war.[42]

4 St. Benedict's Prep from Depression to War, 1926–1945

When Paul Healy and John Kling entered St. Benedict's Prep as freshmen in the fall of 1929, they had already known heartache and hardship. Paul's father died when he was only two years old, and when his mother became ill he was put in an orphanage. After she recovered, Mrs. Healy found work as a dressmaker and was able to bring her son back home. At times, Paul accompanied her to the houses of wealthy Newarkers, and one day a woman in a High Street mansion suggested that he be sent to St. Benedict's Prep. The Healys lived across the city in the Roseville section of Newark, but Paul soon found himself taking the bus across town every day. John Kling, his new classmate, traveled to Newark from nearby West Orange. He too suffered from the absence of a father figure. Mr. Kling had a good job, but he contracted tuberculosis when John was five years old and spent the rest of his life in a sanatorium, unable to work or be an integral part of his family. Mrs. Kling found work, moved her family to her parents' house, and enrolled the children in nearby St. John's in Orange. When it came time to send John to high school, she simply went into Newark and registered him at St. Benedict's, returning to inform her son, "John, you're going to Benedict's."

Perhaps Paul Healy and John Kling were drawn to each other because of their personal histories, but over the course of the next four years their stories were joined by scores of others as the Great Depression wreaked havoc on household after household. As members of the class of 1933, dubbed the "Depression class" because they entered only weeks before the stock market crash, Paul and John managed to stay in school because they secured after-school employment. They helped support their respective families and pay school tuition. Paul answered an advertisement for a messenger boy at a Newark law firm and ended up working for William J. Brennan Jr., the son of a city commissioner and himself a future U.S. Supreme Court Justice. Luckily, John found work at a supermarket, earning fifteen dollars a week, the same amount that grown men supported whole families on. Both went on to study at local colleges. Kling enjoyed a forty-eight-year career with the Great Atlantic and Pacific Tea Company (A&P), while Healy owned and operated the longest-running independent advertising firm in the state. Kling confessed years later, "The Depression marked us." But it was World War II that formed his generation, as nearly 1,600 "Benedict's men," including Kling and Healy, answered their country's call to arms.[1]

Depression and war also marked Father Boniface Reger's headmastership at St. Benedict's Prep. In fact, almost his entire tenure occurred during major international crises, the first dozen years in a global depression and the last three in a world war. Likewise, depression and war dominated President Franklin Delano Roosevelt's three full terms in office, and he concentrated on the search for security amid domestic economic collapse and the international threat of totalitarianism. Roosevelt's New Deal did not produce a full recovery nor did it redistribute wealth, but it did bring economic security to many Americans, including home owners, farmers, laborers, the elderly, and the unemployed. A complete recovery from a decade of depression did not come until war industries, including those in Newark, began to hum at the outbreak of the conflict in Europe. But Roosevelt's New Deal brought back a measure of security as well as confidence and civic pride to all Americans.[2]

Despite economic disaster and later impending war, a sense of security and confidence pervaded St. Benedict's Prep, largely because of the calm, considerate leadership of Father Boniface Reger. He managed the Depression with understanding and sympathy, allowing students to remain at school despite delinquent bills. But Father Boniface also insisted that the school move forward despite trying times, best symbolized by his pursuit of accreditation for the school from the Middle States Association. While the Great Depression and then World War II rightly grabbed the headlines, a fascinating subplot began to unfold within the monastic community that significantly affected the futures of both the abbey and the school. Once again, the monks questioned the suitability of a monastery and its school in the middle of a major city, and even considered moving to the suburbs.

The Great Depression at St. Benedict's Prep

At the end of the 1920s, when many Americans still basked in sunny prosperity and the first clouds of depression had yet to gather, the Republican candidate Herbert Hoover confidently declared in the run-up to the 1928 presidential election, "We in America today are nearer to the final triumph over poverty than ever before in the history of any land."[3] The Democratic nominee that autumn was Alfred E. Smith, the four-term governor of New York State, and John Kling, an eighth grader at St. John's, supported his candidacy enthusiastically. On occasion John caddied at the local golf course, which had a double benefit: no school, and the chance to earn a dollar and maybe a tip. Over the course of eighteen holes, John tried to convince a businessman-golfer that Al Smith should become the first Catholic president of the United States. At the end of the round, the golfer calmly scribbled something on his scorecard before walking away. He did not leave a tip. The caddie master showed John what he had written on the card: "Good caddie. But he's for Al Smith and that makes him no good." Vicious rumors spread about how the pope would move into the White House if a Catholic became president. The KKK burned crosses along Smith's campaign trail, and in the end his religion proved to be an insurmountable obstacle. Newark voted for Al Smith, but he lost to Hoover in a landslide.[4]

Less than eight months into Hoover's first year in office, the stock market crashed, on October 29, 1929. "Black Tuesday" did not immediately throw Newark into a tailspin, but the city would experience the wrath of the global depression soon enough. In the first half of 1930, Newark's industries showed a 25 percent drop in employment, so the

Façade of St. Benedict's Prep, St. Mary's Abbey (now Newark Abbey), and St. Mary's Church, c. 1930s.

city government responded by creating jobs. In December it was decided that the continued excavation of the Morris Canal would proceed by shovel, not steam engine, and more than five thousand men signed up for the backbreaking work. Hundreds of factories continued to close, and desperate Newarkers found work wherever possible, selling fruit, shoveling snow, running errands, or even openly begging in the streets. By 1931, an estimated sixty thousand residents, or 30 percent of the workforce, were unemployed. State aid flowed into the city that year, followed by federal aid after Franklin D. Roosevelt's election in 1932. The city's relief rolls kept growing, however, from approximately 37,500 in 1930 to 94,045 in 1935. Homeless Newarkers built a shantytown, or "Hooverville," under the new bridge spanning the Passaic and Hudson rivers, the Pulaski Skyway.[5]

Between 1935 and 1940 the federal government tried to spend its way out of the Great Depression, as it allocated eight billion dollars on average each year, most of it earmarked for programs like Social Security, the Public Works Administration (PWA), and the Works Progress Administration (WPA). In Newark, the PWA sponsored a spate of school construction and renovation projects. WPA work included the extension of Branch Brook Park into Belleville and the construction of new streets, sewers, and sidewalks, and the Federal Housing Authority built moderate- and low-cost housing projects. These programs brought some security and predictability to many people's chaotic lives. The rest of the city, including city hall, often seemed to be spiraling out of control. Mayor Meyer Ellenstein and his cronies were brought up on charges of defrauding Newark taxpayers out of hundreds of thousands of dollars, and gangsters ran illegal gambling and bootlegging rackets, especially when Newark was "wet and wild" during Prohibition. In 1935, Abner "Longey" Zwillman was believed to have ordered a hit on another Jewish gangster, Dutch Schultz. For the first time in its history Newark was no longer a "destination," and the city lost residents during the 1930s. Newark would not fully recover until 1941, when factories were called on to support the war effort.[6]

American Catholics traditionally had looked to the church in times of stress and need, but during the 1930s they increasingly sought out aid from the city, state, and federal authorities. For one student at St. Benedict's, growing up during the Depression meant that "three things went together: Catholicism, the Irish, and the Democratic Party. The Republicans were those other guys who had to go to school on the feast of the Immaculate Conception because they went to public schools." Not all Irish Catholics affiliated with the Democratic Party, though, and some families, like the Shanleys, remained staunch Republicans. This trinity of religion, ethnicity, and political identification summed up how many white ethnic Catholics became an integral part of the "New Deal coalition." Roosevelt's New Deal measures drew many urban Catholics into the Democratic fold, along with Jews, African Americans, union workers, and white Southerners. This alliance continued well after the war with the G.I. Bill, and one historian has referred even to this as the era when "affirmative action was white."[7]

There was no "new deal" for Newark's African American citizens, even though their population had grown from 38,880 to 45,760 during the Depression. African Americans struggled mightily during the 1930s; their prospects for employment were "pitifully small," and they were denied lodging and relief from some of the city's private agencies. Because one-third of the local African American population sought relief, there was even talk among city and state officials of sending poor southern migrants back to the South. During the interwar years they were corralled into the Third Ward, the old Hill District to the west of St. Benedict's, and it became one of the most densely populated neighborhoods of its size in the entire country: 33 percent of the city's overall population of 442,327 was crowded into just 11 percent of the total land area. Long home to poor Russian Jews, African Americans inherited a section of the Third Ward that had some of the oldest, most dilapidated, and unhealthiest housing in the city. A WPA report on Prince Street exposed its extreme poverty: "The houses there are in the last stages of decay, and some neither have gas nor electricity. Toilets are shared by flats, and there are no bathtubs."[8]

Living conditions worsened as the Great Depression continued, and soon African Americans in the Third Ward became associated with "neighborhood decay, crime, vice and disease." Not surprisingly, a red-light district was allowed to flourish on either side of the ward's eastern boundary, where prostitution, gambling, and illegal drinking were routine. The novelist Curtis Ward summed up the weekend nocturnal activity best when he wrote, "The Third Ward had put God away for another week, and was getting about its business of lewdness and revelry." He also tipped his hat to the "characters on the Hill" because they "are as varied as they come: strong men, weaklings, frustrated wrecks, religious-minded folks, and vicious fellows. Beautiful young girls, and old hags; fortunate, well-kept women, and debased hustlers." The Third Ward also had its downtown monks, as St. Benedict's straddled the neighborhood's boundaries.[9]

St. Benedict's Prep did not empty out during the Depression, but it lost approximately 25 percent of its student body. Many families could not afford the $120 yearly tuition, and Father Boniface's correspondence was filled with letters pleading for clemency and leniency. In 1932, a father wrote, "Permit me, Father, to thank you for the personal attention given this case by you, and to accept my sincere promise that it is my full intention to pay eventually for this manhood training." A mother wrote in 1935 and pleaded for her son to be allowed to move on to college despite not paying tuition, saying, "Thomas has always been a good-living boy and now he has this chance to go to college on a scholarship. He can't accept it unless you will have pity on him and send his marks on as the college has requested. Tommy or I can't help if his father would rather drink than take care of his family." Father Boniface was able to help in both cases, but he could not help everyone. In a letter to a local Catholic grammar school, he confessed, "I wish only that we could have helped all the legion who have sought aid during the recent hard years."[10]

Relief agencies even contacted the school on behalf of struggling families. For example, a caseworker from the New Jersey Emergency Relief Administration wrote to the school about the Collins family. Paul Collins wanted to finish his schooling but could not pay the tuition, despite his part-time job at the local Westinghouse plant. The relief worker "wonder[ed] if it would be possible for you to arrange in some way to take care of his tuition." Father Boniface replied that he "had an understanding with Mrs. Collins that payment may be made when times improve. She is in arrears now for a considerable sum and I have not bothered her about it." Reger sent a similar letter to another relief worker: "His parents have not made a payment on his tuition since April, 1932 but they promised to pay whenever times became more prosperous. With this understanding, I am permitting him to continue his education."[11]

The school routinely granted scholarships for many young men; during the first half of the 1931–32 school year, forty-five students did not pay any tuition and another eighty-three paid only a fraction. Countless others were given "an extension of time for which no interest [was] charged." In addition, parishes often subsidized the education of talented Catholic boys by sending scholarship monies in their names directly to St. Benedict's. Even though this helped, the realties in Newark and the surrounding towns meant that St. Benedict's felt the Depression's repercussions, especially after the 1932–33 school year. For the two academic years beginning with September 1930 and ending with June 1932, the student population hovered just below

Headmaster Father Boniface Reger, OSB, guided the school
through a global depression and world war, and in the
process the school garnered "superior" accreditation ratings
from the Middle States Association of Colleges and Schools.

seven hundred, but during the next two years it dropped to just over
five hundred. By 1937 the school's rolls topped six hundred again, but
they did not reach pre-Depression enrollment until after World War II.
Catholic families could no longer send their sons to St. Benedict's in
the numbers they had previously.[12]

A drop in enrollment at St. Benedict's coincided with a surge at
Newark's public high schools; with a 15 percent increase, the city's
high schools ran at capacity in 1934. Most enrolled because they could

not find work, and many high school graduates could not afford college, including some from St. Benedict's. Father Boniface wrote Harry Hopkins, director of the National Relief Administration, to address the pressing issue:

One of the most regrettable results of the present economic conditions in our country is the lack of employment for our young men, especially graduates of high schools and colleges. At a time when a boy is filled with enthusiasm and eager to undertake things, he finds that he is not wanted and there is nothing for him to do. The effect, as I have observed in many cases, it almost hopeless discouragement and mental stagnation.

May I suggest that a sufficient part of the new and even more generous appropriation which Congress has placed at the disposal of our President be devoted to the further development and extension of educational and recreational programs for our young people. Without question, every provision made for the alleviation of the conditions which today confront our youth will contribute enormously to the welfare and progress of our nation.

One of Hopkins's deputies acknowledged the problem, and within several months the National Youth Administration was created. St. Benedict's received NYA Student Aid funds for the first time in 1938, which allowed students to earn money as hall monitors and cafeteria workers. By 1941, thirty-five of a possible fifty boys were employed under the program.[13]

It was at the height of the Great Depression that Father Boniface first sought accreditation from the Middle States Association, an agency established in 1887 that proved instrumental in defining and clarifying the roles and relationships of schools and colleges. Like his predecessor, Father Boniface was most interested in keeping his school's facilities, curriculum, and methods current. Correspondence with Middle States officials documented an aggressive strategy to seek accreditation for St. Benedict's Prep, and it finally came just before Christmas, 1934. Father Boniface was most pleased, as a thank-you letter to one committee member indicated: "The action of the Commission is most gratifying to us, especially since it gives us the assurance that our school meets the requirements of modern education of which the Middle States Association is the recognized exponent."[14]

Soon other Catholic schools asked for St. Benedict's Prep's advice, and Father Cornelius warned of two factors that often proved to be stumbling blocks for Catholic schools. First, he advised that "the Association insists very much on proper equipment for teaching the sciences, so be sure that your laboratories are up to the standard." Second, he added that "they do not permit overcrowding in the classrooms— not more than 30 as an average. Especially too they insist that the teacher load not be excessive." At St. Benedict's, overcrowding seemed to be under control, in part because of the drop in enrollment owing to the Great Depression. Father Boniface wrote Dr. E. D. Grizzell, chairman of the Commission on Secondary Education, about creating a new course at St. Benedict's in 1936. That fall the "General Course" was added, thus setting the school down the path of accommodating many more students in the near future.[15]

Recognition from Middle States was reaffirmed in 1937 and again in 1939, but in 1941 it came at the expense of Father Boniface's health. His doctor called it "a breakdown of the nervous system, induced by overwork." Although the sick headmaster spent some time resting and recovering in a sanatorium, he soon returned to his post, as it had been "particularly comforting to be told by ten experts that our school deserved to be classified among the good schools. With your helpful suggestions, I am able to continue my work with greater courage and confidence." Middle States rated St. Benedict's Prep as "superior," and before the end of the school year Father Boniface read the following to the students, his pride no doubt conveyed through the crackling of the new intercom system: "A few days ago, the official, printed report reached my office. It was indeed most gratifying . . . curriculum . . . very superior; library . . . very superior; outcomes, i.e., what pupils actually learn . . . superior; staff . . . very superior; administration . . . very superior." No area rated lower than "superior." "This report gives us great confidence and satisfaction," he boasted. "We feel assured that our school is not only as good as the average secondary school, but it is superior, and in some departments, very superior to them."[16]

As part of the application to Middle States, schools officials stated that "Citizenship and Catholicism" went hand in hand at St. Benedict's Prep, because "the student should be trained to be a useful citizen, to be taught the ideals of our country, and be inspired to live up to them." It followed that the Catholic school was the best support for democratic government, as it was there that young people "are taught to respect authority, to obey the laws, and to be loyal to their country, not because it is expedient, but because it is the will of God that they should do so." A young man at Benedict's was often reminded of the following dictum: "A good Catholic and a bad citizen cannot exist in the same person." In the six months before the United States entered another world war, Father Boniface delivered one of his trademark addresses over the intercom about the "twofold allegiance to the cross and the flag."[17]

Victory Drives and Commando Courses

If the 1930s was a decade of social and economic paralysis for the country, then the early 1940s were years of incredible movement and industry. Newark and St. Benedict's Prep bubbled with energy and nationalistic fervor following the Japanese attack at Pearl Harbor on Sunday, December 7, 1941. Jack Dalton, a sophomore at Benedict's, was listening to the New York Football Giants game on the radio when the play-by-play was interrupted to announce the infamous attack on the Hawaiian naval base. The following day, a holy day of obligation, Congress declared war on Japan, and Newark mayor Vincent J. Murphy called for "a united all-out effort in this grave crisis." Police ordered that "all Japanese subjects" be removed from all railroad trains traveling through Newark, and they scouted the Ironbound section to round up any suspicious "Nipponese." Father Maurus McBarron, a physics teacher at St. Benedict's, went to the abbot and sought permission to enlist in the armed services as a military chaplain. Five other monks and five laymen on staff soon joined Father Maurus, leaving their posts at the school to serve in the military. Abbot Patrick O'Brien, elected Abbot Ernest's successor in 1937, attempted to portray a "business-as-usual" attitude at the abbey and school, telling a reporter five months into the war, "The Church and the Order have survived wars and battles for centuries and we will survive this war. To date, the war has not affected our lives or our work."[18]

A "spirit of patriotism and sacrifice" pervaded the school as students and monks joined forces to help on the home front. Students eagerly joined and participated in the Schools at War program, organizing a Junior Red Cross chapter, coordinating multiple war bond drives, and conducting various conservation programs. The focal point of student energy was certainly the war bond drives, as more than 90 percent of the student body purchased bonds directly from the school. Students raised over two hundred thousand dollars during the war and surpassed by wide margins all goals in the "Buy-A-Jeep" and "Buy-A-Plane" campaigns. Even Father Matthew Hoehn, the school librarian, got into the spirit as he conducted a successful Victory Book Drive. Students collected nearly double the goal of one thousand books to be shipped overseas to servicemen. The efforts of students at St. Benedict's did not go unnoticed either, as the school earned the right to fly the navy "E" pennant for their contributions. In addition, two large pictures of the school's wartime activities were featured prominently in windows dedicated to the Schools at War program at Bamberger's on Market Street.[19]

St. Benedict's did all it could to prepare its young men for their potential involvement in the war. Father Hilary Stephan, a history teacher, had warned students about German aggression as early as the late 1930s, and after Pearl Harbor the school rolled out a full-scale preparedness program. One monk taught a course in International Morse Code while others spent long hours tutoring students preparing to take War Department–sponsored placement examinations. The curriculum offered additional math courses and even a new one on aeronautics. Joe Kasberger, the football and baseball coach, and Ernest "Prof" Blood, the famed basketball coach, built a commando course "to prepare the boys for what [was] ahead of them in the armed forces." Consisting of sixteen different obstacles and spread over 250 yards, "it taught endurance, agility, speed, alertness, and balance." Blood taught

Students supporting the war effort through a
variety of efforts at the school.

physical education too, and during the war it became deadly serious as
he put students through a rigid calisthenics routine. As a boy struggled
to execute a chin-up, Blood was heard to ask, "Could you do one in an
emergency? Could you pull yourself out of the water up into a lifeboat?" A St. Benedict's rifle team was formed in December 1944 with
the purpose to train boys in the use and knowledge of firearms.[20]

Many graduates of St. Benedict's answered the call to service, from
alumni of the late 1920s and early 1930s to those allowed to expedite
their course of study and complete high school early. Father Lambert
Dunne chaired a committee to recognize graduates in the armed services, and he kept files on those on active duty. He constructed a "Roll
of Honor" that hung in the school's main hallway highlighting the
nearly 1,600 alumni serving around the world. Through an arrangement with the *Benedict News*, each soldier received "a regular edition
of the School paper wherever this is humanly possible." By 1944, gold
stars accompanied the names of thirty-six "Benedict Men who made
the supreme sacrifice to our Country . . . defending the Stars and
Stripes that freedom might live forever."[21]

During the war, the monastery granted asylum to several European monks, and the school served as an official air raid shelter for citizens in the vicinity. The school was also equipped with "blackout curtains," and four monks became air raid wardens. Of the monks serving in the war, Father Martin Burne, a future abbot, was first stationed with the U.S. Marine Corps in Bougainville, a small island in the South Pacific. Later in Guam, Father Martin was the first priest that locals had seen in over two years, and to their delight he officiated at an annual novena in honor of St. Francis of Assisi. Reflecting on his time with the Marines, the pragmatic and humble priest said, "Taking care of a bunch of Marines is much like running a parish back in the States. About half your parishioners are good, fervent Catholics, another 25 percent are lukewarm and the rest are lax. As far as I could see the war didn't make much difference to the lax ones."[22]

One of the Benedict's men in the service whom the monks prayed for each day sent a letter from the distant sands of the Middle East. Stationed in Iran at the end of World War II, Sergeant David Liddell of the U.S. Army and a member of the class of 1935, penned a letter to "the Priests at the school" just two weeks after celebrating victory over Japan. "My biggest ambition came true today," wrote Liddell. "In this letter I am sending you a Money Order of $33.00 in final payment of the debt I have owed since I graduated St. Benedict's." Like so many others, Father Boniface had allowed him to remain in school despite a past-due account, and Liddell never forgot his generosity. "It was Father Boniface's kindness that allowed me to remain in school," Liddell wrote. "His faith in me was outstanding and today I am a very happy boy for not letting him down."[23]

Dave Liddell's gratitude from a far-off corner of the globe at the end of a world war reflected the sentiments of countless graduates of St. Benedict's. Father Boniface, on a much smaller scale than Roosevelt, provided people with a chance during the Great Depression, literally giving them hope and security amid so much despair and destitution. He also moved the school forward when he and other monks could have called for retrenchment. Neither the headmaster nor the president saw the war out while in office. Father Boniface resigned from his post in 1943 because of poor health and Roosevelt died at Warm

Springs, Georgia, in April 1945, leaving the conduct of the remainder of the war to Harry S. Truman. The new president learned of the atomic bomb in July, and by August the twin bombings of the Japanese cities Hiroshima and Nagasaki brought a swift but sobering end to the conflict. Postwar reconstruction now preoccupied peoples around the globe, and before Father Boniface resigned he suggested that the school faced a similar situation: "The problem confronting St. Benedict's today is whether to build on their property at High Street or to sell this property and erect the new school at their athletic field on Park Avenue in suburban Newark."[24]

The Delbarton Situation

During World War II Father Boniface had suggested that a move to North Newark was a possibility. Earlier, Wilson Farrand, the long-serving headmaster at next-door-neighbor Newark Academy, considered High Street to be "an inconvenient and undesirable location." Farrand relocated to Newark's northern periphery near Branch Brook Park in 1929, before eventually leaving the city altogether in 1964. Across the country, especially after World War II, urban private secondary schools routinely uprooted themselves and followed their clientele out to the suburbs. But for the monks in Newark it was different, because they took a vow of stability dedicating the rest of their lives to a single community in a particular place. Monastery and school were inextricably linked. Although a group of monks could move their community from one locale to another, it was done only after serious reflection. Abbot Boniface Wimmer had reservations in the 1850s about a foundation in a large city, and the debate over the existence of an urban monastery still raged on one hundred years later.[25]

In 1925, the downtown monks paid $155,000 in cash for a four-hundred-acre estate in Morristown, named "Delbarton" after the banking magnate Luther Kountze's three children: DELancey, BARclay, and LivingSTON. Abbot Ernest Helmstetter wanted a place in the country where young clerics could escape the hustle and bustle of the city to prepare for their lives as Benedictines, and to that end he opened a school of theology there in 1927. Yet maintaining the vast property and huge mansion quickly became a burden. The Newark monastery ran a soup kitchen on High Street, feeding hot meals to the poor and unemployed who arrived on a daily basis during the Great Depression, but they also sent relief to Morristown. Beginning in the late 1920s and extending through the early 1940s, one thousand dollars was sent each month to help defray costs there. Some monks talked of selling the Delbarton estate, but Abbot Ernest did not see it as a liability, since he envisioned it as a place for further expansion and as the future site for a large monastery. Regrettably, Abbot Ernest was unable to provide leadership on "the Delbarton situation" because he passed away on July 9, 1937. Over the next two years the monks made preparations to start a "residential high school" in Morristown beginning in 1939.[26]

Father Patrick O'Brien was not present on the occasion of one of his life's most significant moments. Suffering from ill health and convalescing at Glen Falls, New York, on strict orders from his doctor, Father Patrick did not attend the chapter meeting in Newark that elected him abbot on August 10, 1937. The meeting was suspended until Father Patrick's "consent to the election could be sought by telephone," and when he was reached, Archbishop Walsh, his good friend

Old Main, part of the Delbarton estate built by financier Luther Kountze in the 1880s, was purchased by the monks of St. Mary's Abbey in Newark in 1925. The 400-acre estate would be home to a school of theology for young monks (1927), the Delbarton School (1939), and St. Mary's Abbey, Morristown (1956).

and confidant, was at his side. The archbishop encouraged him to accept "this sign of God's will," and when Patrick O'Brien, the son of famine Irish immigrants, returned to the monastery on High Street a few days later, he did so as the fourth abbot of St. Mary's Abbey. Considering that all his predecessors were of German ancestry, one monk commented shortly after the Irish American's election, "An Abbot with the name Patrick O'Brien, that's a first-class miracle." Perhaps even more miraculous than that, though, was the fact that the frail and sickly priest went on to serve as abbot for the next thirty years, providing strong and somewhat controversial leadership.[27]

When Abbot Ernest died, he left a huge void in the monastery, one that members of the abbey were not at all convinced Father Patrick could fill. Monastery lore has it that Patrick O'Brien was elected abbot in large part because of his history of poor health. Abbot Ernest had been a strong and tough leader, and some members of the monastic community wanted somebody weaker than him to become the next abbot. Many monks did not have a true successor in mind when Helmstetter passed away, and they also did not think Patrick O'Brien would live much longer. They figured that by the time he died they would have decided on Abbot Ernest's *real* successor. Ironically, Abbot Patrick's tenure as abbot was three years longer than his predecessor's. Even in death, Abbot Ernest cast a long shadow, one that could have overwhelmed Patrick O'Brien, but the new abbot counted on his experience as a pastor, teacher, and administrator to lead the abbey and school in Newark as well as the priory and school in Morristown.

Throughout the first six years of his administration Abbot Patrick not only worried about the spiritual health of his "semi-cloistered, contemplative" community of religious men, but also about mundane things, including how to spend recreation time, leaving the monastery grounds, receiving gifts, and the use of telephones. In so doing, he was following the dictates of St. Benedict and his *Rule*, described as "a brief, practical, and thoughtful work on how human beings can best live in community." "In drawing up its regulations, we hope to set down nothing harsh, nothing burdensome," the new abbot noted. "The good of all concerned, however, may prompt us to a little strictness in order to amend faults and to safeguard love." In the fall of 1943, Abbot Patrick presented his monastic family with a list of reminders that enabled them to "walk steadily and courageously forward, always aiming toward perfection, though we will never reach it." He assured them that "nothing in it is foreign to the Holy Rule and our Constitution but applies merely to our peculiar conditions in the midst of the turmoil and distractions of a large city."[28]

The most important duty of the Benedictines was prayer. In Newark they prayed communally four times a day, but the day was not consumed by it. The monks taught, of course, and while interaction with teenagers may have kept them young at heart, physical fitness and health were different matters altogether. Abbot Patrick made allowances for two recreational periods each day, and he stressed proper diet and exercise, especially since eight members of the community died between July 1937 and March 1938, most from heart attacks. "Walks may be taken after classes," he instructed, "but this does not include visits to homes or places of amusement, such as movies, plays, etc." Likewise, the abbot mandated that "permission to go out at night should be infrequently given." Going "abroad" was both "dangerous and entirely out of harmony with religious life" because "it engenders a love of the world and worldly things and a disgust for everything that is spiritual." Since monks had been known to sneak in through the back door of the monastery after going out at night, Abbot Patrick instructed them, "When returning at night, the front door only is to be used." City living could be stressful.[29]

Monasteries are otherworldly places in large part because of the fact that they build walls around the perimeter in order to mark off property where something special and different goes on. But as an urban institution, St. Mary's found it difficult to escape its surroundings. A visiting priest from a rural European monastery observed, "The monastery is surrounded by factories which dominate its tiny garden, and its front rises directly from the street, whence comes an incessant din of heavy motor traffic by day and by night. Here, as in all large cities of the U.S.A., there is the almost continuous wail of a siren, and the traffic has to give way to a fire engine, an ambulance, or a police car. Inside the building are 700 day scholars, and the time and energy of the whole community are occupied in this and in its other active works." Yet, observed the monk-traveler, Abbot Patrick, "a frail and delicate man with a holy face which could easily be pictured in a quiet cloister," carried on with his earthly business with his community "in the midst of noisy Newark."[30]

Abbot Patrick also inserted himself into the debate over the Delbarton estate. Insisting that it should not be sold but rather developed, he believed it was time to set a policy for its future development. For him, the future of the abbey lay in Delbarton's convenient location and myriad material advantages, especially since he saw the city as anathema to religious life. In a prepared statement on "the Delbarton situation," he speculated on the day when the monastery and school in Newark had run their course, saying Morristown could be developed "when St. Benedict's Prep, on account of parochial high schools, or a Catholic community school, would no longer have any purpose; when our parishes would be supplied from the secular-clergy; these and many more reasons refute the cry: 'Sell Delbarton!'"[31]

For the present, though, Abbot Patrick also could not see young clerics being trained in the city; he believed this could be accomplished only in the serene and contemplative environs of a country house. He had visions of a large monastery there, saying:

It has everything that could be desired for a present home and for a future monastery. It is conducive to the health of soul and of body. It was bought and developed with the idea of a future expansion of the Community. If we intend to continue our diversified occupations, we must have manpower. And this manpower must be developed in the proper surroundings.

We must have a suitable place for training our clerics. We shall surely agree that the city is no place for such training, for developing sincere members of the Benedictine Order. This has been proved by experience. The distractions in a city hinder not only the progress in study, but also the spirit of recollection, of true asceticism.

Patrick O'Brien was not the first abbot to possess an ambivalent attitude toward the city of Newark; James Zilliox, Hilary Phraengle, and even Ernest Helmstetter all made it clear that they had reservations about a monastery in a city. Abbot Patrick's concerns were not new, but his view of the city's future and the role of the abbey in it may well have been. At the conclusion of his statement, he indicated how he planned to lead the community, declaring, "I personally wish to go on record tonight as being heartily in favor of [Delbarton's] retention and development."[32]

Many monks in Newark thought that St. Benedict's Prep had been neglected as a result of all the money and manpower sent to Morristown. During a discussion of the abbey's annual financial report in 1941, the recording secretary observed a growing consciousness among those in Newark: "Many of the Fathers thought that something should be done for St. Benedict's Prep." Two years later in July 1943, a proposal to allot funds to finish the gymnasium at Delbarton was rejected, as the men in Morristown were effectively told to live within their means and not push the development of the school too quickly. The vote no doubt angered Abbot Patrick, but far more substantial opposition to his Delbarton plans soon followed.[33] It was the first of several rounds in a long family fight.

Amid proposals for funds to further enhance Delbarton, frustrated monks in Newark formulated a petition calling for a definite plan for the further development of the abbey and school in Newark. Signed by almost every member of the community, it was presented to Abbot Patrick in the fall of 1943. He reacted by saying he was "unalterably opposed to the petition and the way in which it was presented." He maintained that some members had been coerced to sign it, and said that it demonstrated "a lack of courage" and was "un-Benedictine." Father Lambert Dunne defended its validity, saying it was "both legitimate and Benedictine," and that the petition was so brief that it was impossible for an intelligent person to be unaware of its intended purpose. Another monk viewed the initiative as an act of courage. After further discussion, the community voted on a proposal to allocate monies to complete the project at Delbarton. It did not pass.[34]

It took almost a year for Abbot Patrick to initiate a planning conference—or as he put it, a "goodwill conference"—to discuss the future plans of St. Mary's Abbey in both Newark and Morristown. Father Richard Studer voiced his opinion that the conference should revolve around St. Benedict's Prep and the recommendations of the Middle States Association; the last report stated the need for a new school auditorium and additional classroom space. Others wanted to focus on the relationship between Newark and Morristown, as the monastery in the country might become a separate abbey one day. Some even suggested that the abbey in Newark become a priory, with the mother-house moving out to Morristown. Abbot Patrick stated that it had been Abbot Ernest's desire to build a large monastery at Delbarton and have the seat of the abbey there. On his deathbed, he reportedly said, "I shall have to leave the erection of the Monastery to my successor."[35]

In the months leading up to the end of the world conflict, Abbot Patrick's "goodwill conference" did yield an olive branch. On March 21, the feast day of the Order's founder, the abbot appointed a handful of monks to a committee for the purpose of "building a new and greater St. Benedict's, to be located in Newark, N.J." St. Mary's Abbey and St. Benedict's Prep had weathered the storms of depression and war, and talk of postwar possibilities now preoccupied the community.

5   The Duke, Divine Comedy, and Discipline at St. Benedict's Prep

Bells ordered the day for Father Dunstan Smith. By the mid-1950s, the bells of St. Mary's Church, rebuilt in the aftermath of the 1854 Know-Nothing riot, had been pealing through her High Street neighborhood for close to a century. They called the monks to prayer three times a day, and Father Dunstan, a stern monk of solid build, welcomed the sound, as it allowed him to escape the hectic world of school discipline. In the confines of the abbey church, he could momentarily forget about the nearly eight hundred young men in his charge; instead of thoughts of discipline and demerits, the bespectacled World War II veteran could sit in a mahogany pew and quietly pray. Prayer was a brief respite, though, as another sort of bell also ordered Father Dunstan's life. The jarring, startling sound of the school bell matched his style: he hit first and asked questions later. A force of nature, in part because "his sense of discipline was a right cross to the chin," he was called "the Duke" by students reared on movies starring John Wayne. A generation of Benedict's men feared the "tough, cop-like" disciplinarian, as any matter, big or small, could find an offender sent to his office. "It was like Rome," admitted one student. "All roads led to Father Dunstan's office."[1]

During the fall of 1956, Father Dunstan grew to loathe the final bell. When it rang at 2:15 every afternoon, a string of seniors darted through the front door, down the steps, across High Street, and into their cars. The Duke, determined to put a stop to the frenzied exodus, calmly walked up and down the sidewalk one afternoon reading from his prayer book. As the final bell tolled, he closed the tiny, leather-bound book, tucked it under his belt, and positioned himself at the bottom of the front stoop. As the first group of seniors cascaded down the steps, Father Dunstan cocked his right arm and delivered a devastating blow into the chest of one unsuspecting student. Like human dominoes, the fleeing students fell back on one another. He then said, in his trademark gravelly voice, "Next time, cross at the corner." He turned, reopened his prayer book, and walked away.[2] Indeed, like the church and school bells, Father Dunstan's complex persona swung back and forth, from the peaceful, prayerful monk to the alarming, student-slugging disciplinarian.

One of the distinctive elements of a Catholic school education has been its emphasis on discipline. At St. Benedict's Prep, discipline has been part of a century-old "endurance formula" that has guided young men toward what the monks began calling "character education" or "manhood training" in the early part of the twentieth century.[3] Regulations and restraints marked the ebb and flow of a typical day at Catholic schools, and punishment often punctuated it. While discipline has always mattered at places like St. Benedict's, the nature of punishment has changed over time, often in surprising ways. As headmasters from 1910 through 1943, Fathers Cornelius Selhuber and Boniface Reger felt a paternal chat was more effective than a right cross, and they appointed disciplinarians who carried out that philosophy. A demerit/detention-based discipline policy advocated dealing with young men in a "mild yet effective manner," an approach that some have called "conservative progressivism." By the late 1930s, though, the student population had become so large and unwieldy that a different approach had to be taken. A string of more authoritarian deans of discipline created an atmosphere of fear, one where physical punishment was always a possibility. Father Dunstan in particular controlled the school through "practicing modified violence, consciously implemented," and while Abbot Patrick O'Brien routinely condemned the practice of physical punishment, it persisted. When Father Dunstan spoke to his fellow monks at a faculty meeting in 1949, he stated that he aimed to be "severe, but fair." By the 1960s, though, Dunstan's rough, ready, and at-times repugnant methods became outdated as students came to question the authority of church and state like never before.[4]

While strict discipline and harsh punishment marked student life at St. Benedict's, the school's atmosphere was also part "divine comedy" because there was occasion for "discipline with room for fun and humor."[5] Who would show up late and have afternoon detention? What about the excuses offered up? Could another student be so dumb as to misspell his mother's name on a forged note? Would chemistry students achieve the annual goal of killing Father Laurence's goldfish? Would the missing grade book reappear? Which student would be in the wrong place at the wrong time and suffer Father Dunstan's wrath? There were so many possibilities. Ultimately, generations of "Benedict's men" endured both the mild and not-so-mild discipline they received at the school, and many have even credited the treatment for helping make them men. In particular, they have come to love the telling, and retelling, of so many of the "cat-and-mouse" antics, because in seeking out the divine, discipline at St. Benedict's was often comic.

"We Incline Toward Healthy Conservatism"

Perhaps there was something funny about why Joseph Quinn was the first student ever expelled from St. Benedict's Prep in 1870, or maybe John Hasel's story of how he and four other students broke a few windows at the school amused his father, a blacksmith by trade. The bill that accompanied the story no doubt shattered John's chance of a reprieve. While these two disciplinary matters can be found in the earliest account ledgers, officials at local rival Seton Hall kept an altogether different book. The size of a small atlas, the college's "Punishment Ledger" offers an insight into the world of discipline and punishment at a late nineteenth-century male Catholic school. In 1867, Seton Hall students committed a variety of offenses, including "unbecoming language," skipping morning prayers, "ignorance of a Greek lesson," "whistling in the dormitory," "smoking and then having the boldness to deny it," and even insulting a priest. As punishment, offenders reported to a detention period, where they sat in utter silence while "writing lines." For an undetermined crime, the disciplinarian once sentenced a student to write one thousand lines of Livy's *History of Rome*.[6]

Character formation and punishment both have deep roots in the Benedictine tradition. At the annual Benedictine Educational Association meeting in 1924, one monk began a talk on "character formation" by reminding his fellow members of the Order's sixth-century founder: "Our Holy Founder Benedict clearly indicated that his Order was to be not only a house of prayer and a school of perfection for matured men, but conjointly a school for boys and young men, to mold them into men of real character and sterling worth." Benedictine schools had a sacred duty to cultivate character, the monk went on to argue, because "character is not given by birth; it must be developed. By nature we are like a field in which both good and bad inclinations grow; proper cultivation roots up or cuts down the bad and lets the better predominate."[7] *Succisa Virescit,* a Benedictine motto, has always guided this process of character formation: "Cut me down, and I'll grow back stronger."

Likewise, American Catholic parents were told to weed out moral defects in their children before they became deep-rooted. "Following the example of the careful gardener, who cuts off the superfluous branches while they are young and tender," wrote Reverend Nicholas O'Rafferty in 1940, "parents should, by prompt correction, cut short any irregularity that may manifest itself among their children."[8] Catechisms, parent guides, and sermons all sought to educate parents in how to properly raise children in the ways of Catholic faith and discipline. Central to all of this, of course, was a clear understanding of obedience and hierarchy within the church, school, and family. The authority exercised by parents over children, and superiors over subordinates, flowed from God.

At times, though, children were disobedient, irreverent, and disrespectful. In those cases, parents often relied on traditional child-rearing practices to justify physical punishment, because to "spare the rod" was to "spoil the child." The historian Philip Greven has established that Protestants "ardently advocated corporal punishment," and "with remarkable consistency and persistence, evangelicals through the centuries insisted that parents must control and break the emerging will of children in the first few years of life." They broke the wills of very young children through systematic spankings, canings, and forced fasts, keeping track of it all in their diaries and correspondence.[9] Roman Catholics approved of such punishment too, and although the historical record is not as cooperative, their catechisms, sermons, parent guides, monastic codes, and oral histories all support the existence of a sustained tradition of corporal punishment in their families and schools.[10]

While a stern look or a severe warning most often worked to chastise children, more serious cases could warrant physical punishment. "No matter how much parents may wish to avoid it, no matter how painful it may be at times to inflict upon a child," concluded the authors of a Catholic parent education book, "there are occasions when the little one's rash behavior must be made to serve him against future offenses."[11] The same reasoning applied to its use in schools, as teachers and administrators sought to make examples out of unruly individuals. In 1909, a professor of mental philosophy at St. Angela's College in New York defended the use of corporal punishment, believing that "suffering of some kind must be inflicted upon refractory boys and girls, otherwise there will be dismay and defeat in the army of teachers, and indolence and insolence and riot and disorder in the ranks of the scholars."[12]

Corporal punishment had its place at Benedictine abbeys and schools too. *The Rule of St. Benedict* sanctioned the practice, as chapter 28 instructed the abbot how to deal with a disobedient monk: "If a brother has been reproved frequently for any fault, or if he has even been excommunicated, yet does not amend, let him receive a sharper punishment: that is let him feel the strokes of the rod." Two chapters later, Benedict addressed the matter of disciplining boys: "Every age and level of understanding should receive appropriate treatment. Therefore, as often as boys and the young are guilty of misdeeds, they should be subjected to severe fasts or checked with sharp strokes so that they may be healed." At St. Benedict's the post of disciplinarian first appeared in 1876, and one of the school's earliest catalogs indicated "good order and submission to the established rules of the College [were] secured by mild, but effectual means." Some evidence suggests that students did suffer the stroke of a paddle, yardstick, or pointer at St. Benedict's. A photograph of some of the first students standing behind a handful of faculty members appeared with the following caption: "The whipped and the whip crackers." One dean of discipline walked the corridors with a yardstick, whacking unsuspecting students from behind. Much more common, though, was a literal "hands-on" approach, as certain monks were notorious for slapping, pushing, and punching students.[13]

Discipline at St. Benedict's took a decidedly different turn in 1905, and once again Father Cornelius Selhuber proved pivotal. Having returned to Newark in 1903 after working at St. Anselm College in New Hampshire, Father Cornelius became active in almost every facet of St. Benedict's as teacher, athletics moderator, and disciplinarian. He spent an inordinate amount of time in the company of boys and young men, coming to know their likes and dislikes, hopes and dreams, successes and failures. Father Cornelius even authored a manifesto on discipline that advocated a different philosophy and disciplinary system, thus shaping how the faculty corrected, chastised, and punished students at St. Benedict's for generations to come.

When he delivered a talk titled "On Punishment" to his fellow faculty members on March 31, 1906, Father Cornelius began by observing, "Nothing seems more out of place than harsh and brutal treatment of the pupils, and there is no virtue for which there is greater demand than patience." Although some monks still relied on corporal punishment to maintain discipline, Father Cornelius argued that it was "surely the best policy to do away with it altogether." By the dawn of the twentieth century, the use of corporal punishment in schools, including Catholic ones, had become a contested issue. New Jersey was the first state to abolish corporal punishment in its schools, doing so in 1869, but a "warm debate" about its re-introduction took place in the New Jersey Assembly on March 20, 1894. During the debate, the bill's sponsor impugned "Newark bad boys," because "little ones not taller than the school desks openly defied their teachers." Other assemblymen argued against the measure, and the bill was soundly defeated by a four-to-one margin. Likewise, in the early part of the twentieth century the monks at St. Benedict's questioned the efficacy of using corporal punishment as a means to "character education."[14]

The pragmatic Father Cornelius argued that harsh and cruel punishment could affect student enrollment, saying, "Methods of severity and harshness, especially those pedantic German methods which most of us have learnt to condemn and abominate most heartily, would empty a College of its students." In 1911, he revised the school's punishment policy by stating that monks would not systematically punish students. The school catalog declared, "Our methods in discipline are mild but effective; we will never resort to corporal punishment to enforce good conduct and regular attendance." School officials continued to forbid its use in each subsequent year. Instead, they argued that strictness tempered with patience and moderation produced the best results, especially since the "dull ones, mischievous ones"—who often turned out to be the "best men"—required that type of approach. The most effective way of correction was "frequent talking to the students in a paternal and serious manner," so Father Cornelius instituted "a weekly talk to remind students of their various duties and shortcomings." In effect, those frequent talks "on ethics and general good conduct" brought the student body "into the confidence of school officials, and by looking upon the boys in the Benedictine family spirit, the best results [were] obtained."[15]

In some ways, Father Cornelius and his fellow Benedictines anticipated the philosophy of character education advocated by Monsignor John Bonner, the superintendent of Philadelphia's Catholic schools from 1926 to 1945. According to the historian Francis Ryan, Bonner chartered a "sane and middle course between excessive rigidity and excessive freedom" in matters of student discipline, which marked him as a "conservative progressive."[16] In a similar vein, when members of the Benedictine Educational Association, which included Father Cornelius as head of the High School Department, discussed discipline and character education, they observed, "We incline rather to healthy conservatism than to destructive liberalism."[17] Under the leadership of Father Cornelius and his most trusted lieutenants, the monks at St. Benedict's Prep sought to rid themselves of old "pedantic German

methods," charting a course toward "healthy conservatism" characterized by a "mild but effective" disciplinary system. The Benedictines
were not alone either. Another local all-male Catholic prep school had
a similar approach to discipline in the 1920s, stating in the school
bulletin, "The system of government combines strict discipline with
kind and gentle treatment."[18]

Over his sixteen-year tenure as headmaster, Father Cornelius
sought out teachers who could manage a classroom, saying, "It is certain that no schoolroom can be well instructed, if it is not well managed." "The teacher's eye is the most effective instrument of
management," he added. "A teacher who knows how, may answer a
question, give a command, grant a request, quell a rising disturbance
by a glance of the eye." When Father Cornelius appointed Father William Koellhoffer to the post of disciplinarian in 1920, Father William
became the very embodiment of the school's new approach, vigilantly
but fairly presiding over matters of discipline for nearly a decade. Born
in Newark to German American parents, Father William was a giant
man with an intimidating stare. "When students would meet for assemblies in the auditorium and make all sorts of a racket, Father William would take off his glasses and put them in his mouth, and a hush
would come over the place," recalled one student. "He didn't have to
say a word." He soon earned a nickname, "the Eagle," because his
"eagle eyes" missed nothing. During an algebra test one day, Father
William warned his class, "I would rather see someone turn in a paper
and get a 50% than turn in a paper and get a 100% when he's cheating." He issued the general warning two or three times before standing
over one student. Looking down, he said, "I wouldn't cheat anymore,
if I were you." Father William pulled the offender out of his chair and,
sure enough, his shirt cuffs revealed the answers.[19]

Aside from his powers of vision, the Eagle used his intuition about
boys and what they wanted to do in order to sniff out potential problems. In March 1922, just before grades had to be recorded, "the big
and general notebook mysteriously disappeared," but Father William
soon found it after "a silent search," with no public threats or recrimi-
nations. He knew how to solve a problem. Years later at the annual
Day of Recollection, a handful of seniors skipped out of the church

service, vaulted the back fence, and headed for a downtown theater. As they rounded the corner and approached the box office, the Eagle awaited them, hands folded across his chest, peering down at them over his glasses. "We never got in because he knew what we wanted to do," remembered Art Guarriello. "In the first place we should've been in vespers and, secondly, it was a burlesque." Not surprisingly, Art and his friends amassed five days of detention for chasing after a cheap thrill.[20]

Father William's instincts and his ability to listen helped him achieve cult status among students; they marveled at his sixth sense to predict what would happen next, but they appreciated his fairness and compassion too. Father William was one of the "best-known and best-loved monks," even though he instituted the demerit system and reinstituted the after-school and Saturday detention periods in the early 1920s. One student described him as "kind, sincere, understanding, sympathetic, forgiving, firm in matters of principle, and altogether human." "He wanted your story. 'Give it to me straight,' he'd say. We trusted him, so we did. Sometimes he made judgments in favor of the student, not in favor of the teacher," recalled another alumnus. In the end, Father William encapsulated much of what the Benedictines thought a disciplinarian should be: "He should strive to be loved rather than feared by his students. He should understand that he is not a 'cop,' or a detective: he is a friend, companion, and advisor of students. He must be just and show no partiality; he must be a gentleman towards his wards at all times; he must be of an even temper under all circumstances."[21]

Along with Father Cornelius, Father William Koellhoffer set the standard for the school's "sane and middle course" on disciplinary matters. Father Valerian Kanetski, born to German immigrants a month after the "Great Blizzard" hit Newark in 1888, took over for Koellhoffer in 1928, and his office to the right of the school's main entrance always experienced a flurry of activity. While he met a great many boys who were not amenable to discipline, "his keen understanding of boy nature" allowed him to direct and guide young men over the next decade. He was crucial to the new headmaster, Father Boniface Reger, as the school continued down its path of character education by way of "healthy conservatism." Father Valerian, a star athlete in college, was a "formidable" and "husky" monk, but as students often remarked, "his bark was always worse than his bite." "Seldom, if ever, did one hear a student complain about unjust handling," recalled one monk. But he was strict. Father Valerian "read the riot act" to some boys after he had received information from the bus driver of one particularly rowdy journey. He got flaming mad when he learned that a handful of other students nearly set rival Seton Hall Prep's school building on fire in the late 1920s after secretly setting a bonfire alight the day before their big football rally (more on this in Chapter 6).[22]

In 1938, when Father Valerian retired as disciplinarian, parents indicated in a survey that they sent their sons to Benedict's in part because of the "friendly cooperation between students and priests." To be sure, there were still cases of monks verbally abusing or physically striking students, but it was a rarity. "At St. John's we had the Christian Brothers, and they would whack you. They'd never hit you at Benedict's. The Benedictines were not hands-on," admitted one student from the early 1930s. "They wanted to help, there was very little criticism, and if you tried, you made it." In many ways, this "friendly cooperation" fulfilled the early vision for monk-student relationships at St. Benedict's Prep. At times, the monks discussed what it meant to be a Benedictine school, and on one occasion they offered three explanations: "We train them to *live* their Religion. . . . The number of students is usually small, allowing a more intimate contact with the teachers, among whom there are few, if any, laymen. Thirdly, the discipline is Benedictine in spirit—the family spirit." Father Cornelius helped cultivate that spirit during his sixteen years as headmaster, and in the process grew the Benedict's family tenfold, from seventy to seven hundred students.[23]

The Duke and the Changing Nature of Discipline at St. Benedict's Prep

The monks had worked hard to cultivate a family spirit at St. Benedict's Prep, and it was certainly a contributing factor to the school's runaway growth in the 1920s and 1930s. Parents wanted to send their sons to High Street like never before in order to help make them into young men. As the student population soared, though, the school's intimate atmosphere had been lost, and disciplining the student body became more challenging. With more than seven hundred hormonal and often mischievous young men, school officials waged a daily battle to shape and control student behavior. As the school grew, students had less and less contact with the headmaster, and discipline largely fell to the dean of discipline and individual teachers. Although corporal punishment was still prohibited, some monks struck students, and a few even paddled them. Parents rarely complained of rough treatment, though, thinking the monks could do no wrong. Well into the 1960s, increased authority and an upsurge in physical punishment, or at least the threat of it, highlighted a not-so-mild but still effective discipline strategy at St. Benedict's Prep.

In particular, the shift toward a more authoritarian and hands-on approach to discipline coincided with the coming of age of a new type of disciplinarian. Up until Patrick O'Brien's election as abbot in 1937, only German and German American monks held the offices of head-master and disciplinarian. When O'Brien became the first abbot of Irish ancestry, he began appointing "a certain type of monk" to the newly dubbed position of dean of discipline, and it was almost always an Irish American who grew up in an urban neighborhood and had relatives in the fire and police departments. For the next three decades, this type of monk became a fearsome, towering figure at the school as he patrolled the grounds like a one-man police precinct. This new approach to discipline and punishment was shaped in part by an Irish Catholic worldview that linked violence and spirituality. Further, it affected other monks in their individual classrooms, as some chose to take matters into their own hands; it was commonly understood that if a monk could not effectively manage his own classroom, he would be sent to work in one of the parishes, ministering to a congregation instead of teaching teenagers. In other words, there was an incentive to not have any discipline problems.[24]

Most monks at St. Benedict's Prep had grown up in city neighbor-hoods and would have been familiar with the hardscrabble world rec-reated by James T. Fisher in his groundbreaking history of the New

York/New Jersey waterfront, *On the Irish Waterfront.* Fisher highlights how local politicians, gangsters, longshoremen, union leaders, and even Roman Catholic priests helped create a particular brand of Irish Catholicism on the docks and in many of the predominantly Irish neighborhoods, one that saw a synergy between spirituality and violence. "Although spirituality and violence are normally understood as mutually exclusive," observes Fisher, "on the Irish waterfront an intimacy with violence *confirmed* spiritual authority like no other gift." While certainly not as brutal and fatalistic as the actors on Fisher's Irish waterfront, the various deans of discipline at St. Benedict's Prep also had an intimacy with both spirituality and violence, enforcing a particular brand of Catholic discipline described as "modified violence, consciously implemented."[25]

"In a large school such as St. Benedict's," noted the school newspaper in 1939, "the maintaining of discipline throughout the school at all times is highly necessary." Father John Doyle, a Boston native, was appointed dean of discipline in 1938, and he signaled the arrival of a new type of disciplinarian, one who became the most active and prominent figure *inside* the school, rather than a dominant, aloof headmaster like Father Cornelius. Students saw him all the time, including when they entered the building each day, in the hallways, or in other common spaces like the cafeteria, gymnasium, or library. In a larger school, the dean became an all-action figure, and one who could effectively strike a select student or two to make all the others fall in line. In his second year in the job, Father John, described by students as a "tough nut, but a fair one," began walking the hallways with a yardstick, "keeping order with an occasional reminder for the offender from behind." His "new method" was to approach "the victim from the rear" and "deliver the decisive 'whack,'" often to a student's backside, "without a word of warning." The sting of his "golden ruler" served as a "friendly warning to behave," otherwise he might have to "subject an individual to an afternoon in [detention] where the desired results are obtained in most cases."[26]

Father John was the busiest monk at the school in 1938, when he coupled his disciplinary duties with those of the athletic director. He spent several nights a week monitoring athletic activities and spent whatever spare time he had telephoning parents to follow up on student behavior both inside and outside school. In 1939 he wrote, "the duties of the Dean of Discipline are many and eternal," but as a general rule he found "the boys rather quick to respond to correction." In a memorandum to students, he told them to be courteous, prompt, attentive, self-reliant, trustworthy, and honorable. For most individuals the demerit system worked well because the boys knew that twenty-five demerits meant suspension and fifty led to expulsion. Likewise, parents were "only too willing to cooperate with the authorities" and "seem[ed] to realize that it is for the personal benefit of their sons that such an interest be taken." To that end, Father John knew that parent cooperation led to the monks achieving their "utmost aim" of "the upbuilding of character and manhood in their boys." St. Benedict's Prep was a "workshop" where students worked not for their teachers, but for themselves. Father John reminded them to "work, do not shirk."[27]

"There was the threat of violence, the possibility of physical punishment, at all times," observed one student from the early 1940s. "It was a continuance of what was going on at home, and the hands-on approach at home was continued at school. It was part of the culture." Father Timothy Dwyer, a native Newarker of solid build, held the post next, and while he did not carry a yardstick, he did "push students around." Many of Dwyer's relatives served as policemen and firemen in Newark, including his father, who had emigrated from Ireland, became naturalized, and went on to be president of Newark's Policemen's Benevolent Association. Like almost all the disciplinarians in the school's history, the big-eared Dwyer possessed "a glare in his eye" that often proved to be enough of a deterrent to head off any mischief or wrongdoing, but he was "sometimes forced to use stern measures to teach [students] that 'crime does not pay.'" Like some of his relatives, Father Timothy walked "the beat" at the school, often puffing on a cigar as he did so. On one occasion, he teased rather than punished a student who forged his mother's signature on a sick note. He made the mistake of misspelling her first name, and when Father Timothy saw him afterward, he yelled out, "Hey, Jim, how do you spell Mabel?"[28]

Demerits and detentions helped both Fathers John and Timothy run St. Benedict's just before and immediately after World War II, and the school's disciplinary code remained basically the same for the next twenty years. Each student had to memorize the code, which included specific provisions on lateness (detention), unexcused absences (fifteen demerits and five days detention), misbehavior in assemblies (five demerits and five days detention), throwing food in the cafeteria (five demerits and detention), violation of the dress code (detention), tampering with the elevator (five demerits and detention), chewing gum, fighting, and gambling (at discretion of dean), stealing (immediate expulsion), defacing or abusing school property (at discretion of dean), smoking on school grounds (immediate expulsion), pushing or becoming loud or boisterous in speech or demeanor in hallways (detention), and poor conduct on public transportation (up to fifteen demerits or suspension). Upon committing an infraction, a student was sent to the dean's office with a "yellow slip," where he had to explain his behavior. Most often he was awarded after-school or on some occasions Saturday detention, nicknamed "JUG," which often resulted in a sullen young man marching back to class. JUG, which stood for "Justice Under God," meant that he would have to explain to his parents why he needed to spend extra time at school, and it often resulted in "worse treatment at home." When a student accumulated twenty-five demerits he was suspended until his parents came in to speak with the dean. When a student amassed fifty, he was expelled and received a blunt letter that read, "We regret having to take this action, but you will understand that it is necessary in the interest of discipline."[29]

The monks were interested in maintaining order not only at St. Benedict's; they also took note of behavior away from the school, at home and in the neighborhoods. Students did not always realize or appreciate that they still represented St. Benedict's even when they were not on campus, but as they often lived in "word-of-mouth neighborhoods," news of misconduct traveled back to school. Father Boniface addressed the issue in a morning broadcast over the school's intercom system in 1941:

Be careful how you behave on the buses, coming to school and going home. Remember that actions which seem funny and amusing to you and the other boys are usually ridiculous, childish and annoying to adults. St. Benedict's boys have a splendid reputation for manliness and refinement. However, a few times every year we have letters and telephone calls, complaining about the behavior of some of our boys. Why should half a dozen foolish youngsters impair the good reputation of the whole school? Bear in mind that whether old or young, we must always be gentlemen. A gentleman is defined as one who never does anything that may displease others.

On rare occasions, un-gentlemanly behavior outside school could result in expulsion. Father Boniface informed one student in 1932 that he had been dropped from the school roster, writing, "Rumors reached me concerning your conduct lately in your town. On inquiries at the Police Headquarters, I find that these rumors were true and that your behavior on that occasion was such as we cannot tolerate in a student of St. Benedict's."[30]

While the various disciplinarians dealt with students on a day-to-day basis, and even watched over their behavior outside school, the headmaster rarely got involved in mundane discipline matters. But he did use the intercom and school newspaper on a routine basis to teach lessons about avoiding sin and building character. Sin, whether of the mortal or venal variety, was a constant threat to manliness, and everyone knew what character meant: people who kept their word and chose "long-term good over short-term gratification, no matter how seductive the pleasures of the moment might be." In his book *Lost City: The Forgotten Virtues of Community in America*, Alan Ehrenhalt argues that much of the educational process at mid-century urban Catholic schools "consisted of implanting guilt in quantities sufficient to provide a bulwark against sin's most attractive opportunities." Father Boniface addressed issues of sin, character, and manliness on a regular basis in his "Headmaster Says" column in the *Benedict News*. In 1940, for example, he wrote, "Be honest, be obedient, be respectful, and, above all, be pure. To accomplish this, you must be careful of the company you keep; you must avoid temptations and dangerous occasion." He took on bullying as well, using the example of Jesus Christ to make students feel guilty about their actions:

Some boys imagine that refinement and kindliness are incompatible with manliness. They believe in "rough and ready." But have you ever tried to vizualize Jesus as a boy of your age? He went to school with other boys. He played with other boys. Do you think He tried to domineer over others? Can you imagine Him kicking and punching smaller boys around? Can you imagine Him using foul language or curse words? Though we associate perfect refinement and good manners with the child Jesus, no one would dare say that Jesus was a "sissy." Make Him your model and you will be a real, manly, and gentlemanly boy.[31]

Not all monks followed the "perfect refinement and good manners" of Jesus' example themselves, and they, like some of the older boys at the school, proved capable of punching, cursing, and domineering over their students. Pat McAuley was ordered to the front of his trigonometry class one day in 1940, and told to bend over by Father Joseph Barkus. Pat was struck on the buttocks by Father Joe, and in the process the monk cut his hand on the spiral notebook in Pat's back pocket. Five years later, the 6'6", 250-pound monk knocked another wisecracker right out of his desk. Father Wilibald Berger, a sour-looking monk, came to St. Benedict's during the war as a refugee priest. According to G. Gordon Liddy, he "didn't bother with demerits," often taking matters into his own hands. When Father Wilibald mispronounced an English word, one rather large student made fun of him. The German monk looked up calmly and said, "You. Stand up." "The boy stood, a smirk on his face, expecting to receive a demerit," recalled a young Liddy, who decades later would be implicated in the infamous Watergate scandal. "The German walked down to him and, with a right-hand lead, knocked him out cold." He then told the boy sitting near the door, "You. *Wasser.*" A few moments later, Father Wilibald threw the cold water on the unconscious boy's face to revive him. After helping the punch-drunk boy up, he turned and walked back to the head of the class and said, "Zo, Unt now ve begin again." With a monk like Berger, observed Liddy, "there was always an atmosphere conducive to learning in their classroom."[32] Unfortunately, physical punishment often helped create that "conducive" atmosphere.

To be sure, Father Ignatius "Iggy" Kohl was a student favorite because he cursed and told off-color jokes that often left his charges in
stitches. On one wintry day, some students opened the windows,
allowing the nippy air to circulate throughout room. When Father Ignatius arrived, he took note of the shivering young men sitting there,
put his books on the desk, and said, "It's cold enough in here to freeze
the balls off a brass monkey." Students charged him with swearing,
but he ably responded, "I didn't swear. I was just being crass and
ignorant like you guys." But Iggy could get physical too. In the fall of
1949, he slapped a student for sneezing, and a year later he detained a
class of seniors until 8:00 each night for an entire week. Compassion-
ately, he offered each student "supper" in the form of a stick of Wrig-
ley's Spearmint chewing gum. "You could never forget his methods,"
remembered Robert J. Aikens, "which included a punch in the ribs if
you didn't shape up!" Another monk used an assortment of fraternity
paddles to punish students. As the art teacher, he bent students over a
drafting table to deliver up to five "whacks" to a student's buttocks.[33]
Such rough treatment was not welcome by students, and it no doubt
traumatized some, but certain monks' violent "methods" were unfor-
gettable and served as future deterrents against misbehavior.

While Father Iggy most often impressed his students with his
sharp wit and off-color responses, Father Paul Huber did so with his
swift fists. Born in Newark to immigrant parents, Huber taught German at St. Benedict's beginning in 1930. An avid and accomplished
boxer who was elected to the New Jersey Boxing Hall of Fame, Father
Paul once became so flustered by a young man's insolence that he
challenged him to a boxing match after class. The student in question
was a postgraduate on the school's powerhouse football team, and as
the nearly forty-year-old priest quietly pulled on his gloves he planned
on giving him a lesson. Several students peered through the gym door
window to witness the spectacle, and one of them observed later,
"Father Paul wasn't there to grandstand, but he did want to teach this
guy a lesson. It was over real quick and it wasn't an issue of him
beating a kid." And Father Paul was not the only monk to don boxing
gloves in order to teach a lesson or two. It was one of the many methods the monks used to make men.[34]

Most students were more or less amused by the monks' various reactions to their antics, and they rarely complained of rough or abusive treatment. Whom would they tell, anyway? Parents sided with the monks in almost all cases, and if a student told his father or mother a monk hit him at school, he could risk even rougher treatment at home. On the rare occasion that Abbot Patrick heard parental criticism of teachers' conduct, in particular those resorting to the use of "ungentlemanly and un-Christian language when correcting the boys," he chastised them. "If one of us is unable to control one's temper, the manly thing to do is ask the abbot to release one from school work," he stated in a chapter meeting. "What has been said of language might also be said as a warning to those who would in a fit of temper, strike a boy," he added. "We profess to be cultured gentlemen conducting a select school. We must make our conduct conform to our ideal."[35] While many of the monks were prayerful monks and cultured gentleman, a handful always utilized physical punishment to control student behavior. Abbot Patrick spoke out against striking students, but teachers who struck students were never relieved of their teaching duties, and in the case of Father Dunstan Smith, violent methods led to his promotion to dean of discipline.

Dunstan Smith was not the ideal of a cultured gentleman, but he did prove to be a legendary disciplinarian. Born in a predominantly Irish neighborhood in Newark four months before the outset of World War I, the young Smith attended a local Catholic grammar school before enrolling at St. Benedict's Prep in 1928. Upon graduating he indicated his desire to study for the priesthood and become a member of St. Mary's Abbey. Ordained in 1940, he spent his initial years as a parish priest, but when the United States entered World War II, Father Dunstan requested permission to volunteer as an army chaplain. Commissioned as a first lieutenant, he first served at Fort Slocum in New York, but he later saw duty in New Guinea and the Philippines. At war's end, he was awarded several medals for his service, including the Philippine Liberation Medal for participating in the landing and eventual liberation of the island nation. When the young monk returned to teach after the war, his experiences helped shape his philosophy of education and discipline. At St. Benedict's, wrote one headmaster, a student "faces

Father Dunstan Smith, OSB, war veteran, religion instructor, and dean of discipline at St. Benedict's Prep.

men, mostly priests, who, having been boys themselves, seem to know all their tricks, their failings and their shortcomings, and waste no sympathy on pretended excuses. He should realize that, though they may be hard taskmasters, they are nevertheless his true and real friends." The hardest of taskmasters, Father Dunstan ran the "dreaded discipline machine" with near military precision for the better part of a decade.[36]

The Duke could put "the fear of God" in an individual with a menacing facial expression or a disapproving frown. His gruff voice sent shivers down people's spines. Even the biggest and toughest students feared him. Although of medium build, he was strong and noted for his stern demeanor and gruff voice. He rarely cut anyone any slack, whether it was the first time a student met him or the last time he crossed him. Upon meeting a freshman with long hair, he asked, "Are you getting a hair cut today, or am I cutting it tomorrow?" He greeted a late-arriving student one morning by knocking his books out of his hands and kicking them down the front steps. When the Duke stormed into an assembly of the freshman class in 1954, he spotted the most imposing student, punched him in the gut, and yelled, "See me in my office after school!" Later, in private, he apologized: "That's my policy. I pick out the biggest guy and hit him. The rest then fall into line."[37] Like John Wayne, Dunstan Smith had presence.

As he patrolled St. Benedict's during the 1950s, Father Dunstan believed that striking a student was "the most effective method of administering punishment." According to the *Benedict News*, a quick punch was "short, sweet, and simple; that was Father Dunstan's way." Many students of the era were simply petrified of him. Gene O'Hara worked in Father Dunstan's office during the early 1950s, and he observed, "His facial expressions froze you. He didn't have to hit people." Yet the Duke did strike students on a fairly regular basis, perhaps not back in his office but most definitely in the hallways and in other common spaces. His "reign of terror" even intimidated the meek and well behaved. "I never did anything wrong in my entire life and he would come down the hall and I'd say, 'I hope I didn't do anything wrong,'" admitted one former student. He often made an example out of one student to get his point across to the rest.[38]

Despite the physical violence at St. Benedict's during the 1950s, school life was part divine comedy because students could not predict what would happen next, especially when it involved Father Dunstan reacting to the various antics of certain students. The Duke could whack you for laughing, especially if it was at someone else's expense. Some students liked to sabotage the Coke machine by poking holes up through the paper cups and then waiting for the next victim to be sprayed with soda. When Father Dunstan inserted his quarter into the machine and pressed the button, soda shot out all over his black cassock. He wheeled around, looking for the perpetrator, but only found a chuckling bystander, who got belted instead. Mathias Hagovsky learned a similar lesson, and remembered "being lifted off the ground by Father Dunstan and experiencing temporary anoxia (he used my tie) because I snickered at someone who was being disciplined." There often seemed to be a crowd around Father Dunstan; indeed, he was a spectacle, a crowd-pleasing star who played his role in the divine comedy—or tragedy if you were the one who got hit—to perfection.[39]

Father Dunstan, the chief enforcer of the disciplinary code, set the tone—one of respect for, and fear of, authority. Like past disciplinarians, he enabled teachers to manage their classes without the need for frequent punishment. The threat of being sent to him was a viable deterrent. The situation was similar to many students' home environments. "The parents of the guys I went to school with would smack them around. It was understood; that was the context," noted one alumnus. "That was what your father was supposed to do." Simply put, the Duke was a father figure at St. Benedict's. He was to be respected, listened to, feared, and even revered. Reminiscing about his Catholic school education, one alumnus observed that the monks substituted punches for the nuns' slaps, and "since no one complained, I surmised that maybe such treatment wasn't so harmful. After all, didn't such shaping mirror my home life? In fact, I came to believe that not only did I deserve physical punishment and humiliation, but also that such trials and tribulations were rites of education, rites of adulthood, and rites of becoming a man."[40] Such an observation clearly contradicted life as comedic at St. Benedict's, but the characterization of the school as a "divine comedy" was agreed on by alumnus after alumnus, in interview after interview. Perhaps many young men became habituated to the violence at both home and school, and look back on it as more comic than tragic.

While Father Dunstan was at the peak of his powers, many Americans became increasingly concerned about an increase in juvenile delinquency and a decrease in respect for authority. The upsurge in physical punishment at St. Benedict's, whether by the Duke or one of the other monks, mirrored a noticeable increase in corporal punishment across the nation. In Newark, an official for the National Association of Women Lawyers advocated for repealing the ban on corporal punishment in the state's public schools, arguing in 1946, "Timely punishment, properly applied, has a therapeutic value for many delinquents." In 1955, the New Jersey Bar Association suggested that teachers be allowed to inflict corporal punishment on unruly pupils. Roman Catholic priests blamed "the wave of juvenile delinquency" on parental

Unidentified student sits dejectedly outside the dean of discipline's office." *The Telolog*, 1958.

neglect, and the National Catholic Educational Association entered the fray too, promising to do all it could to halt "family disintegration in America" and vowing to teach children "to respect, obey, love and serve parents." In attempts to curb juvenile delinquency and protect the family unit after the war, an apparent tolerance for harsher discipline, including physical punishments, surfaced in many communities.[41] Far from simply a peaceful, prosperous era, the 1950s proved to be a key transitional period, setting up what one historian has called a "a traumatic identity crisis for American Catholics by the end of the twentieth century," one that is wrapped up in authority, violence, and abuse.[42]

During the 1960s the United States lost its innocence and its appreciation for how authority helped build community. In 1960, John F. Kennedy was elected the first Roman Catholic president; three years later, the March on Washington marked a highpoint of the civil rights movement; and by the middle of the decade, the ecumenical council called by another John, Pope John XXIII, left the Catholic Church utterly transformed. Yet Kennedy's assassination in 1963, the persistence of an unpopular war in Vietnam, the sexual revolution, urban rioting, and the aftershocks of Vatican II all characterized a society about to unravel. Among other things, authority, tradition, and even community were openly questioned, mocked, and disregarded. A decade that began with the illusion of order, hope, and optimism closed in defiance, confusion, and gloom. A cartoon that appeared in the *Benedict News* in 1965 captured the uncertainty of the times, as two students stood on the blacktop playground behind the school. They peered at the brick walls that surrounded them and one student said to the other, "I wonder if they're protecting us from the world or the world from us."[43]

Despite the turbulent times, the monks at St. Benedict's maintained order and discipline at the school as best they could. The demerit system remained unchanged through the early 1970s and the dean of discipline still lorded over the school. Father Francis O'Connell followed Father Dunstan Smith, and his matter-of-fact style contrasted sharply with the fiery, unpredictable Duke. Father Francis carried a small black book in which he kept track of infractions, walking around the school meting out demerits and detentions. In 1960, when the abbot appointed Father Boniface Treanor as disciplinarian, students still feared the man and the post he represented. A tall, thick monk with massive hands, Father Boniface rarely "roughed" students up, as the threat of violence still prevailed (a legacy of the days of Dunstan Smith perhaps), but when he did strike students he used his open hand. Discipline had transitioned "from a punch to a slap." But behavior outside school concerned him as much as behavior inside. For example, a monk jumped out of the bushes to catch several students trying to crack open a few beer cans outside a dance at a girls' Catholic school. "We never got to drink a beer, but we did get suspended," recalled one culprit.[44]

Pranks still figured prominently in the daily life of the school too. Prior to the annual football contest with rival Seton Hall Prep, some students at Benedict's marched through the halls chanting, "Sink the Pirates." Others took them literally as they clogged the toilets and sinks with paper, allowing water to flow out of the bathrooms and down the steps. A year in chemistry was not complete without killing Father Laurence's goldfish, so students dumped chemicals in the tank when he was not looking. Others reversed the gas jets in the lab, directing them to the cafeteria, a potentially dangerous stunt that was intended to stink up one of the school's common areas. Still others wrote the textbook publisher seeking the standardized final exam that Father Laurence always used. The scam backfired when the seniors were caught and barred from graduating.[45]

Students' shenanigans always livened up the routine of a school day, but so did unparalleled displays of students challenging authority. In the early 1960s, a series of protests straight out of the nonviolent playbook of the civil rights era empowered young men at St. Benedict's to confront the school's mandatory lunch program. During the 1960–61 school year, students began to complain about being billed for the school's new lunch program, especially when the quality of the food was poor. An editorial titled "A Fish Story" called the two-year-old, eighty-thousand-dollar lunch program to task, calling for more choice and fewer "substandard meals."[46] The following year, a more scathing review of the lunch program never appeared in the *Benedict News* because Headmaster Father Phillip Hoover decided that he could not allow it to be printed. Alumni, benefactors, and other schools received the newspaper, he said, and the "bad press" the school might receive troubled him. Father Boniface, dean of discipline and longtime moderator to the paper's editorial staff, literally cut the editorial from the newspaper and replaced it with other news before sending it to the printer.[47]

The furor that ensued led to demonstrations on behalf of members of the senior class. As part of the protest against the lunch fare and censorship of the *Benedict News*, "Senior A," a grouping of the brightest and highest achieving students, boycotted the lunch program and had pizza delivered to the school instead. The school administration suspended the entire section for two weeks as a result of their insubordination. One member of the newspaper staff recalled, "We had an entire issue printed and destroyed by the School Administration because of an editorial protesting low quality of food in our cafeteria. This was a great lesson on the importance of [being denied] free speech."[48] Throughout the 1960s, students challenged the status quo at the school, including the lunch program, dress code, and curriculum.[49] At the end of the decade, students and faculty joined together in a discussion of Vietnam, and a straw poll indicated that most were in favor of pulling out of the war. Students also initiated group discussions on race relations at the school as a growing number of African American and Latino students enrolled at St. Benedict's.[50]

In the late 1960s, the monks and staff at St. Benedict's Prep met to reevaluate the school's philosophy and objectives. A traditional approach to Catholic education was still advocated, but they could not ignore the sweeping changes in American society. "The contemporary world appears to be unstable, questioning, insecure, impersonal, mechanical, divided, in a state of flux," began the new mission statement. "Our students are of this age, this world, and at St. Benedict's Preparatory School we ask them to view the world as we see it, to consider our purposes, our values, our ends."[51] Of course, one of the means to their ends was discipline and punishment, and the 1971–72 faculty handbook even included an excerpt titled "The Good Teacher Is a Good Disciplinarian." A good teacher still had to be an effective disciplinarian, and good teaching, in turn, minimized discipline problems. Yet by the early 1970s, teachers and administrators began relying on recent studies in psychology and tossed around catchphrases like "all behavior is caused," "all behavior is learned," and "preventive discipline." The handbook now stated, "Do not reject the student. Determine the causes and help him learn"; it also counseled that "the best disciplinarian is the one who places the emphasis on avoiding disciplinary problems, rather than one who contrives and uses systems of punishment to control overt actions after they take place."[52]

It was a far cry from the days of Father Dunstan, who looked for incidents to set a fearful tone throughout the student body. Perhaps it was the turning of a new page in the history of discipline at the school. In their own way, the monks attempted to turn young boys into men, and in a real way, many graduates credited the monks' "endurance formula" of character education for helping them along the path to what one father called "manhood training." At times, that training could be brutal, especially if the Duke was involved. Yet, in stark contrast to many of the memoirs that condemned the repressive and authoritarian regime of various Catholic schools, "Benedict's men" believed the "dreaded disciplinary system" worked. Parents valued it too. But the violence, or threat of it, seemed out of place after the 1960s. Discipline was still important, perhaps even more so in a world loosed of its moral certainties, but the old ways of the Duke needed to ride off into the sunset.

6

Benedict's Hates a Quitter: Athletics at a Catholic Prep School

Jimmy "Jiggs" Donahue's last-minute hardwood heroics not only secured his school's first state prep basketball championship, it triggered a sequence of events that forever changed athletics at St. Benedict's Prep. In a "clash of speed and science vs. brawn and skill," the roving guard helped clinch a 33–29 victory over Blair Academy on March 15, 1919. "Snatching victory from the jaws of defeat in the last thirty seconds of play," Jiggs and the rest of his teammates finished the season unbeaten in dramatic fashion. Bernard M. Shanley Jr., a graduate of the class of 1883 and president of the St. Benedict's Prep Alumni Association, feted the team at an end-of-season banquet, and Paul Robeson, the third African American ever to enroll at Rutgers College, was among the speakers that night. The star athlete and future actor delivered an address on "Athletics and Life," and at one point described the Benedict's boys as "a team of brothers" whose "unselfish spirit prompted them to play always with the success of the team first in mind."[1]

Headmaster Father Cornelius Selhuber spoke last. He lauded basketball coach Frank Hill's own unstinting and unselfish efforts, especially since he continued to refuse a coaching stipend. Father Cornelius also acknowledged the "great prestige" gained through the recent victory, because "since then more than fifty applications from students have been made to enroll at St. Benedict's." The proud headmaster next lavished praise on Mr. Shanley for his financial support of the athletic program. Shanley, whose son Bernie played forward on the team, then made a surprise announcement, donating twenty-five thousand dollars to the school so it could build a state-of-the-art gymnasium in his late father's memory. Finally, Father Cornelius told the festive gathering that St. Benedict's planned on adding a year to its program, allowing young men to spend extra time "prepping" for college, academically and athletically. Reflecting on the succession of events, some predicted that Benedict's would go on to be an athletic powerhouse for years to come.

St. Benedict's Prep went on to win championships year after year, and school officials quickly saw the value of sport in advancing an institution. In many ways, sport put St. Benedict's "on the map," and helped make it an elite prep school. Athletic success brought free press and prestige as a handful of Newark-based newspapers provided extensive coverage of high school sports. In 1921, one newspaperman argued that such publicity elevated the school from "comparative obscurity" and "brought it forward to a position of the greatest prominence in the school world." Over a decade later, a report on the influence of athletics at the High Street school concluded, "The general public knows little about the scholastic reputation of a school. They judge a school by the excellence of its athletic teams and the company they keep, athletically speaking. Notre Dame without its football team would be just another Catholic college." Through the crucible of athletic competition, the world of a small Roman Catholic institution opened up, literally allowing it to keep company with both public and elite prep schools. St. Benedict's became so well-known for its sporting accomplishments that it earned a nickname: the Little Notre Dame of the East. In many ways, sport helped the school come of age.[2]

Sports helped the nation come of age too, as an American fascination with sport "provided the social glue for a nation of diverse classes, regions, ethnic and racial groups, and competing loyalties." According to the historian Steven W. Pope, sports helped produce a national popular culture, or "folk highway," during the first half of the twentieth century, and outsider groups, which still included Roman Catholics, eagerly pursued athletic opportunities. Importantly, St. Benedict's Prep used sport during this time to not only affirm its Catholic identity, but also to reconcile Catholicism with the mainstream Protestant culture. "Catholic victories brought pride, a measure of acceptance, and the reinforcement and celebration of an alternative culture, yet one that came to be more closely aligned with the other in its values, aspirations, and sense of American patriotism," argued the sports historian Gerald Gems. While sport and religion intersected in interesting ways at St. Benedict's Prep, so could sport and race, class, ethnicity, and gender. Notably, at all-male Catholic schools sport was seen as a character-building activity to be conducted by lay coaches of sterling morals and professional expertise. In short, contests on the gridiron, hardwood, or diamond often mirrored the competitive nature of society at large; as another historian of sport has put it, sports were often seen as a training ground for "learning how to win."[3]

To the monks, learning to win had to be consistent with the school's overall philosophy. Pushing the old adage "a healthy mind in a healthy body" a bit further, the monks went "old Seneca one better and [said] not only *mens*, but *anima sana in corpore sano*." For the Benedictines, "a healthy spirit in a healthy body" was paramount, and in conjunction with a strong academic program and strict disciplinary code, the athletic program helped make men. Father Cornelius believed athletics helped produce good citizens and men of character, saying in one speech, "I feel that they are the salvation of boys. With their minds and bodies engrossed in athletics, our boys will side-step other dangers. I would not attempt to conduct a school without athletics. First and foremost is education and then athletics." In addition, sports reinforced life lessons about working hard, being part of a team, and being held accountable. As one headmaster observed, "Well regulated athletic activities go a great ways in forming character, inculcating self-restraint, and training the young blood to discipline—more so than any other agency we know." And to no small degree, sports kept some students occupied and out of trouble. "If idleness is the devil's workshop," observed Father Cornelius in 1925, "what would we do without athletics?"[4]

"What Would We Do Without Athletics?"

Nary a ball was thrown, hit, kicked, or carried at the school until the mid-1890s. Initially, students could only join one of two groups that met after school, the Debating Society or the Library Association. In 1896, however, students formed the College Athletic Association, which focused on "the promotion of athletic sports for the general health and entertainment of the students." Students eagerly took care of the association's finances and scheduled games, most often against local high schools, athletic clubs, and colleges. By the early 1900s, the monks looked to control sports at the school and "regulate[d] and arrange[d] the games so that they [did] not interfere with the class work." In 1905, the school's catalog boasted that the athletic facilities, which included a playing field surrounded by a cinder track and a gymnasium, were "larger than those of any other institution in the City." Casino Hall, a wood building across the street from the school's main entrance, was used for gymnastics, basketball, shuffleboard, and bowling. The monks also enjoyed the new facilities, and on a sweltering June day in 1902 they accepted a challenge to play the first recorded student-faculty contest in Benedict's history. The "monastic nine" defeated their charges on the diamond, 4–0, as one monk hit a double and a home run, and another pitched a flawless game. When Father Bernard hit another home run, "the boys claimed it was too warm to continue, but the real cause was that [they] feared a severe defeat."[5]

American men suffered from their fair share of fears and defeats too. In particular, many middle-class men were in the throes of an identity crisis, dealing with the various anxieties and uncertainties caused by an expanding industrial economy, especially in cities like Newark. According to the historian Elliott Gorn, the nature of new work relationships often forced them to question their very manhood: "Where would a sense of maleness come from for the worker who sat at a desk all day? How could one be manly without independence? Where was virility to be found in increasingly faceless bureaucracies? How might clerks or salesmen feel masculine doing 'women's work'? What became of rugged individualism inside intensively rationalized corporations?" Orestes Brownson, a noted intellectual who converted to Catholicism and attended several graduation ceremonies at St. Benedict's, lamented the loss of "national virility" when he wrote, "The curse of our age is its femininity, its lack, not of barbarism, but of virility." Many students at St. Benedict's spent their days studying and

Late-nineteenth-century playing field across the street from the school, monastery, and church.

preparing for a lifetime of supposedly "feminine" white-collar work, so sport became a venue for them to show their mettle and prove their manliness.[6]

By the turn of the century an athletics craze swept through the country, preoccupying many young men in their quest to transform themselves from effeminate boys to manly men. President Theodore Roosevelt, one of the leading proponents of "Muscular Christianity," argued that certain sports would help prepare young men for adulthood: "In a perfectly peaceful and commercial civilization such as ours there is always a danger of laying too little stress upon the more virile virtues—upon the virtues which go to make up a race of statesmen and soldiers, of pioneers and explorers. . . . These are the very qualities which are fostered by vigorous manly out-of-door sports." According to Roosevelt, the sports craze had "beyond all question had an excellent effect in increased manliness," and he famously asked a new generation of American boys to "hit the line hard; don't foul and don't shirk, but hit the line hard!" Sport provided a proving ground for a young man, one where he could match his strength, courage, and skill against his peers. It also encouraged competition and stressed the importance of teamwork. Roman Catholic schools endorsed their own brand of "Muscular Catholicism," believing that sports complemented spiritual and intellectual endeavors.[7]

When Father Cornelius became headmaster, he upgraded the athletic facilities and encouraged student participation, finding that when games were properly controlled they stimulated rather than interfered with "the more important class work." Not unlike nineteenth-century headmasters at elite boarding schools, he indicated that due attention would be placed on "the health and strength and manly development of the students." Frank Hill became the school's first "physical culture instructor" in 1910, signaling a new era when only professionally trained laymen taught physical education and coached various team sports. For example, Hill was a leading light in metropolitan basketball circles—having played over three thousand professional games and coinventing the bounce pass and pivot turn—and he coached four teams simultaneously: Benedict's, Seton Hall Prep, Seton Hall College, and Rutgers College. Jim Cavanagh coached cross-country and track at his alma mater after graduating from Newark Normal School of Physical Education. Also an instructor in the city's playground movement, Cavanagh coached a Benedict's relay team to a national Catholic championship in 1917. A protégé of James Naismith, the inventor of basketball, joined the staff in 1925, and an acolyte of Knute Rockne, the famed football coach at Notre Dame in the 1920s, arrived five years later. St. Benedict's sought the best coaches and molders of men they could find.[8]

During wartime, physical instructors and coaches also looked to prepare young men for entry into the service. In 1917, amid the "preparedness crisis," a U.S. Army military instructor drilled students on the school's playing fields, and in ensuing years military drills and marching became routine components in the physical education curriculum. According to *Spalding's Official Foot Ball Guide*, during the 1918 football season some of the state's top players "shed their football togs" for khaki military uniforms, and "were busy tackling a bunch of fellows from Heidelberg and Leipzig, on the unchalked fields of France, with the Rhine River representing the goal line." After the war, Father Cornelius credited physical education classes and scholastic sports with playing a key role in American military success. "In the years gone by not enough importance was attached to athletics, but let me ask you where would we be in the World War without our athletes? We did not have a standing army of any size to speak of," he argued. "We depended on the men who received their training on the football field and on the baseball diamond and I most certainly believe that athletics played a most prominent part in America's success in the great conflict." But not all religious schools readily embraced physical education; for example, it was not compulsory in Boston until 1921, because of "opposition of Christian Scientists and Catholics who refuse to believe that we have bodies or that they are other than God's concern."[9]

Between German surrender in November 1918 and the signing of the Treaty of Versailles in June 1919, St. Benedict's Prep teams won everything in sight, including state championships in basketball and baseball, and another national crown for the track team. The only team to lose that year was the football squad. Perhaps Bernard M. Shanley Jr. would have donated a much-needed gymnasium to his alma mater without those championships, but the euphoria over sporting success did contribute to an increased commitment to the athletic program. During the 1918–19 school year the spirit in and around the school was palpable; in fact, school spirit—called by one newspaper the "Benedict spirit of indomitable grit"—became a staple as students rallied around one another and their teams. Some traveled far and wide to support their classmates, and one dedicated fan hitchhiked around the tristate area to follow the various teams. "The loyalty of the students was so magnetic. We were always the underdogs," boasted Ted Langan. "We were a young Catholic high school taught by priests and we were playing the best schools staffed by professional teachers and coaches." Athletic contests presented opportunities for the small Catholic prep school to compete with large public schools and prestigious prep schools, "carrying the Catholic flag" across the state.[10]

Bernie Shanley III, Owen T. Carroll, and other star athletes helped cement the school's reputation as a powerhouse. Just before graduation in June 1921, the *Newark Star-Eagle* announced that Bernie, Owen, Tom "Red" Nelson, and Frank Milbauer were all matriculating at Notre Dame in the fall. At the last minute Carroll opted for Holy Cross, but that did not stop Benedict's from becoming known as the "Little Notre Dame of the East." The trio joined other Benedict's alumni in South Bend, Indiana, including Gus Desch, a track star for the Fighting Irish who also won bronze medal at the 1920 Olympic Games in Antwerp, and Tommie Farrell, a star running back for Knute Rockne. Shanley left after his freshman year and enrolled at Columbia University, where he roomed with the future Yankee great Lou Gehrig, but Benedict's was clearly part of the network of Catholic schools with strong connections to Notre Dame. When Rockne's Fighting Irish came east to play Army in 1923, he stopped by the school and spoke to the entire student body. He invited students to attend the game at Ebbets Field, and afterwards he presented a signed game ball to the school's football captains.[11]

Although Benedict's sports fans took a keen interest in Notre Dame's affairs, especially since a dozen or so alumni studied and played there, the most followed Benedict's graduate of the era was Holy Cross's Owen Carroll, a Catholic Frank Merriwell of sorts. Carroll, called "our Ownie" by the Benedict's faithful, was "the most sought after college baseball player on earth," and his collegiate exploits were religiously reported in Newark newspapers. In May 1924, toward the end of his junior year, he met with the "law-and-order" commissioner of Major League Baseball Commissioner, Judge Kenesaw Mountain Landis. He verbally committed to play for Ty Cobb's Detroit Tigers, but only after heeding Landis's advice to finish college first. As they sat together at a New York City hotel, Landis told Carroll not to "give your books up and risk being a cop when the ball teams can't use you any more." Carroll went on to pitch for nine seasons in the big leagues before becoming the longtime baseball coach at Seton Hall University. Like Ownie, sport at Benedict's was increasingly becoming big business.[12]

Stung by the sporting bug, St. Benedict's adopted a new mascot amid a fund-raising campaign to build a new athletic facility. Originally called the "Saints," legend had it that one reporter started calling

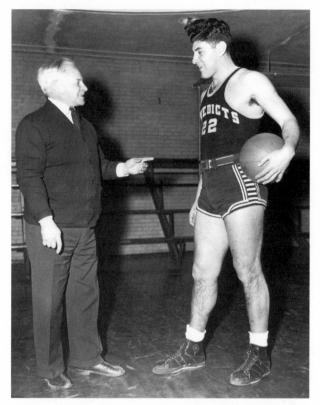

Ernest "Prof" Blood, the legendary basketball coach at both
Passaic High School (1914–24) and St. Benedict's Prep
(1925–50), provides a few pointers to one of his Benedict's
players.

the various teams the "Gray B's," as they sported a gray *B* on the front
of their uniforms. The nickname stuck, and Father Jerome Flanagan,
the athletic director, explained how appropriate it was, saying, "A bee,
with all its concentrated activity, just about symbolized the St. Benedict's spirit. We're a small school and we've adopted a bee. Maybe we
can do something to show that we're on the job, just as the bee does
on occasion." In designing the logo for the 1924 baseball uniform,
though, Father Jerome wanted a "he-bee," "a decidedly aggressive and
business-like bee." Like the new mascot, the aggressive and business-
like Father Cornelius eventually raised the necessary funds for the new

complex, even though a group of monks vehemently opposed the project because they viewed it as an unnecessary expenditure. Benedict Field opened in 1925, only blocks away from the recently constructed Newark Schools Stadium, and the complex included football and baseball fields, a cinder track, and a field house. It was a dream come true for the ambitious headmaster.[13]

A few months after Benedict Field was dedicated, Father Cornelius addressed his fellow Benedictine monks at the annual Benedictine Educational Association meeting, a summertime conference for monk-educators from the country's Benedictine colleges and high schools. The leading light on a variety of secondary education matters, the Benedict's headmaster began a talk on sport with the following: "I make the bold statement that next to the influences of religion, they are the salvation of our young generation. If it were not for the American love of competitive sport and games, what in the world would our young people be doing in these, our hectic times?" To be sure, sport was a character-building tool in that it kept them in top physical condition and forced them to live clean lives, control their tempers, and accept "hard knocks with equanimity." It also increased student enrollment, built school spirit, garnered free publicity in the local press, and attracted alumni support. Monks from around the country also saw the redeeming nature of sport, but they looked to keep its unseemly qualities in check, in particular an overemphasis on winning. They all endorsed the promotion of physical education and sports programs at their respective institutions, and some even indicated that it was a "sacred obligation."[14]

At one point in his talk Father Cornelius admitted, "Athletics may either be a great boon to an institution, or an unmitigated nuisance." It was an altogether fitting statement for the veteran educator to make, as sport helped bring his school to new heights but also led to his resignation. The rift between Selhuber and other monks over the practicability of the stadium project resulted in a group of monks questioning his ability to lead the Newark prep school. They said he was too powerful, and complained to Abbot Ernest about him. Dissension within the monastic teaching ranks forced Selhuber to offer his resignation in 1926. Benedict's lost another athletic booster a year earlier when Bernard M. Shanley Jr. died suddenly from a heart attack. Shanley's death and Selhuber's resignation could well have signaled the end of an era, as both men utilized athletics to build up the school's enrollment and reputation. In many ways, Cornelius Selhuber and Bernard Shanley epitomized the concentrated activity of the bee, the symbol of the school's very spirit. Fortunately, their losses did not upset the momentum gathered at the school during their tenures: Father Boniface Reger ably succeeded Father Cornelius as headmaster, and a handful of top-notch coaches, notably the trio of Jim Cavanagh, Ernest Blood, and Joe Kasberger, continued to field great teams and, more important, mold fine young men.[15]

The Gray-Thatched Wizard

Dressed in canvas high-top sneakers, gym shorts, and a sweatshirt, Ernest "Prof" Blood started every basketball practice with a lecture. With his team seated on the wooden bleachers, the soft-spoken Blood began one of his patented speeches with the simple phrase, "I want to show you something." He proceeded to throw a sixteen-pound shot put high in the air. As the metal sphere reached its apex and began its descent, he bent over, arched his back, and caught it in the nape of his neck. The seventy-year-old coach stood up, letting the shot put roll down his spine and into his right hand. He then looked at his squad and said, "Does anyone else want to try it?" "Monk" Meier, a tough and scrappy guy, bravely volunteered, but his failed attempt stunned him. Prof asked him, "Did it hurt?" and Monk, still gasping for breath, nodded his head up and down. Prof handed him the shot put and imparted the following lesson: "Do it again. Whatever you're afraid of in life, you've got to attack straight on. Whatever is bothering you, take it on first. Don't put it aside." Monk tried it two more times and then Prof started practice.[16]

When Father Cornelius hired Blood in 1925, he was already a national figure, as his "Wonder Teams" at Passaic High School won 159 basketball games in a row between 1919 and 1925. Like Selhuber, Blood believed athletics were the salvation of boys, and he spent over a decade as a YMCA physical director in New England before becoming a professor at Potsdam Normal School in upstate New York. Prof moved to the Garden State in 1915, and first visited St. Benedict's in March 1921 when his team played in Shanley Gymnasium. The already legendary coach was impressed by the spirit and enthusiasm of the Benedict's boys. In February 1924, while embroiled in a controversy with the Passaic Board of Education, Prof watched another Gray Bee game with Father Cornelius, Bernard Shanley Jr., and a handful of other monks. At some point, Selhuber likely broached the issue of Blood's bout with shortsighted city school officials who wanted to curtail Blood's influence, and offered him the opportunity to coach at Benedict's under a more cooperative and appreciative administration. Less than a year later, Blood resigned from his head coaching duties at Passaic, after which the fifty-two-year-old reappeared on the Shanley Gym floor, now tutoring the Benedict's basketball team.[17]

After only a month in charge, the "gray-thatched wizard" led the Gray Bees to victory in the city championship before seven thousand spectators at the Newark Armory, and when he returned the following fall as a full-time coach and physical instructor the high school basketball community took notice. At the outset of the 1925–26 campaign, the promoter George "Tex" Rickard invited Benedict's, instead of Passaic, to christen the hardwood of Madison Square Garden in the new venue's first basketball game. Ten thousand fans packed the Garden to watch Blood's team defeat New York City champion St. John's Prep of Brooklyn, 53–14. One Passaic newspaper reminded a bitter city of Blood's coaching prowess, reporting, "Blood Shows Madison Square Crowd Another Wonder Team."[18] The Gray Bees went on to have one of the best seasons in school history, losing but one contest and garnering both city and state crowns. "Bloodball" had come to the "Beehive."[19]

Blood and Selhuber liked to win, but they both saw athletics as a means to an end: saving boys and making men. The in-demand Blood was a popular after-dinner speaker and audiences often hung on his every word. "Victory Is Only Incidental," his topic one evening, encapsulated his thoughts on athletics; he felt that "the main goal of athletics was the inculcation of ideals, honor and the right spirit in the boys so that they could receive the best training for the game of life."[20] "The only kind of training I believe in is right living. Our lives are the reflection of what we think and feel. Think and feel on a high plane, with higher emotions, and you will live a higher life. We are what we make ourselves," declared Blood in another speech.[21] Blood's role in that process was as both guide and role model, much like the monastic staff at the school. His "right living" set the standard for his boys to emulate, and "Blood's Code" was a rather simple one: "I train boys for the game of life—not to win basketball games. If I succeed in that, I have accomplished something worthwhile."[22]

Sober and serious, proud and principled, Prof Blood was an impressive man who commanded respect. A stern disciplinarian who demanded perfection, Blood fit in perfectly with the way the Benedictines conducted their school in Newark. Even in his fifties, whether in his gym clothes or his trademark three-piece suits, Prof cut a muscular and powerful figure. "He wasn't more than five-five from the soles of his sneakers to the top of his curly head," observed one of the several newspapermen tracking Blood's every move. "But he was built like a top, with the neck, shoulders and chest of a heavyweight boxer and a waist as slender as a chorus girl's." His great strength and dexterity, honed and maintained through decades of gym work, complemented a sharp mind and a piercing set of blue eyes. His physical feats further enhanced his legend among his players and pupils.[23]

Most students came to know Prof through gym class, and it could become quite the spectacle as he often showed off for the boys. One of his classic tricks was to walk onto the gym floor with a forty-inch-long wand and ask a boy to throw a basketball up in the air. He then caught it, and after balancing the ball on the wand's tip, he swiveled and shot a hook shot into the basket. His gymnastic feats also dazzled generations of students, but perhaps the most bizarre stories come from his wrestling matches with the family pet. Prof maintained that one of the most effective parts of his physical regimen was a daily bout with Zep, the family's black bear cub. Zep even served as the basketball team's mascot, as Prof's son led him out on a leash each halftime and wrestled with him to the delight of disbelieving onlookers. Not surprisingly, Zep could even shoot a basketball, and his perfectly positioned paws suggested proper technical training from the famed coach himself.[24]

Prof's antics may well have amused students and spectators alike, but his well-drilled teams relied on intelligent play and unselfish team-work. Blood first played basketball at a Boston-area Y in the months after Dr. James Naismith first presented the new game at the nearby YMCA Training School in Springfield, Massachusetts, in 1891. By the time Blood became a YMCA physical director in 1897, he was con-vinced that passing the basketball was the key to team success. Drib-bling only led to individual play so Blood virtually outlawed its practice, maintaining that the ball always traveled faster when it was passed between players. "His theory of basketball was ahead of its time," stated one of his former players. "His basic theory was that no one could run as fast as the ball. So if you passed the ball and it never touched the ground, there was no way you could be defended against." Such play defined Prof's Wonder Teams at Passaic and then his cham-pionship-caliber quintets at Benedict's, and according to his biographer it also underlined his straightforward approach to life: "He trained his players to pass the ball and to sacrifice individual accolades for the good of the team. His reasoning was based on the belief that success in life required a cooperative effort with others." For Blood, teamwork "validated basketball as a teaching tool to prepare kids for life as adults."[25]

Some even called him the Knute Rockne of basketball because, "like all great coaches, Blood has a system that capitalizes on brains. The game 'from the shoulders up' played by Rockne on the field, is played by Blood on the court." Despite all the praise and press Prof Blood received, he remained a humble man. On the night he celebrated his one-thousandth career win, he simply said, "I couldn't see anything to get excited about. I'm just doing my job." Prof ably performed his job as a basketball coach and maker of men for fifty-five years, the final twenty-four at St. Benedict's Prep. Father Philip "Honey" Hoover, headmaster at Benedict's from 1949 to 1961, retired the coaching leg-end in 1949, noting with a twinge of remorse, "Prof wasn't a young man anymore and he'd doze off on the bench while a game was in progress." At seventy-seven, and with a tear in his eye, Ernest "Prof" Blood told Hoover, "I'll do whatever is best for St. Benedict's."[26]

"Much Harm to the Catholic Cause"

The two schools were both old, one founded in 1856 and the other twelve years later, in 1868. They first competed against each other in the 1890s, and since they were only four miles apart on South Orange Avenue, proximity bred contempt. The ancient rivalry between the Gray Bees of St. Benedict's Prep and the Pirates of Seton Hall Prep in nearby South Orange underscored the intense desire to vanquish a local foe. When Father Cornelius Selhuber spoke on the deleterious effects of rivalry in 1925, he may well have had the Benedict's–Seton Hall annual Thanksgiving football game in mind: "Dishonesty and poor sportsmanship in athletics have done much harm to the Catholic cause in many parts of the country." Ill will surrounding the annual football game worsened relations between the two schools and led to the cessation of the rivalry. Despite all the redeeming qualities of sport, a rivalry taken too far could undermine the stated goals of athletics and create a poor public image for two of the state's oldest and most well-respected Catholic schools.

The bad blood between the two schools reached a low point in 1932, when a "Celtic spat" erupted after a football game and the respective headmasters brought the series to a temporary halt. Restored two years later, the rivalry soon became characterized by tit-for-tat antics between the two sets of students. In 1937, for example, a handful of Gray Bee supporters snuck onto Seton Hall's campus two weeks prior to the Thanksgiving gridiron clash. Seton Hall students had begun collecting wood in anticipation of a traditional bonfire celebration, "but saw their efforts prematurely go up in smoke" as their stockpile was doused with gasoline and lit by the Benedictine interlopers. A group of Seton Hall students retaliated a week later, skulking onto Benedict Field in North Newark to paint the goalposts Pirate blue. They returned two nights later to cart the wooden goalposts away, and left behind an inflammatory note indicating that the posts would burn rather nicely in the victory bonfire.

Meanwhile, back on their South Orange campus, students busied themselves collecting more wood, but this time young men protected it by keeping a string of all-night vigils. On Monday night, in anticipation of another raid from their Newark rivals, strategically placed sentinels with trumpets sounded the alarm. Some eight hundred students sought "to repel the invaders that wanted to spoil their pep rally." Intent on defending their school's honor as well as the bonfire and goalposts, Setonians armed themselves with bats, clubs, and high-pressure water hoses. Two hundred Benedict's students crossed the Newark–South Orange border, and after a several-minute brawl a "riot call" brought both South Orange and Newark police to the campus. A few black eyes and sore heads later the ruckus quieted down, leaving one Seton Hall official quite pleased. A relieved Father James Carey, the school's athletic director, stated: "I'm glad it's all over. This business of climbing out of bed at an unreasonable hour to cater to the bulliency of youth is too much for an old man like me. But it's a fine thing for the school. I'm happy that I've boys around me that have spirit."[27]

The spirit of the boys was one thing, but the sensational press was certainly another. One headline in particular reflected poorly on the students of both institutions: "HUNDREDS OF STUDENTS RIOT ON CAMPUS AT SETON HALL!" A few days later, more than seven thousand spectators packed the bleachers and sidelines at Benedict Field to witness a Gray Bee victory in the closing minute. Quarterback George Conti's twenty-yard pass to Maurice "Horsey" Lonergan won the game for Joe K's squad, capping his second straight undefeated season. Both teams gathered for a "goodwill" dinner following the much-anticipated showdown, but some monks at St. Benedict's questioned whether the storied rivalry was worth playing anymore. The two athletic directors joked about it, though, when scheduling the annual "Turkey day game" for the 1938 season: "We had a verbal agreement [to play], and I suppose this year will be the same as last (without the riot of course)." In 1939, Benedict's threatened to cancel the football game following a controversy with Seton Hall at a track meet, but the archbishop requested that the game be played in order to avoid a public scandal. A year later, Newark patrolmen caught Seton Hall players smearing paint all over the goalposts and ticket booths at Benedict Field, retribution no doubt for the mysterious uprooting of the Pirate's posts a few nights previous.[28]

Relations deteriorated quickly after Seton Hall students vandalized Benedict Field once again in the wee hours of November 8, 1941, a month before the much more infamous "sneak attack" at Pearl Harbor. Headmaster Boniface Reger fired off an abrupt letter to Monsignor James Kelley, Seton Hall's president, stating that "this is but a repetition of yearly offenses which have caused great inconvenience and annoyance, and have resulted in much adverse publicity to Catholic schools." Further, Reger moved to cancel the annual game for a few years "in order that the unpleasantness attending the games will die a natural death." Kelley quickly replied, saying that "a few nit-witted, hair-brained students" should not be allowed to spoil relations. "I particularly fear that a breaking off of this game would cause the scandalous type of publicity that resulted when the game of two years ago was not scheduled," wrote Kelley to Reger, "and the newspapers played it up as an instance of how Catholics failed to get together even in sports." In a postscript, Kelley pointed out that St. Benedict's was not free of blame either; a night watchman caught several drunken St. Benedict's students tearing down Seton Hall's goalposts. He resolutely continued to push for the game, saying, "Since the few hoodlums on each side are not representative of our institutions, I hope they will not be permitted to spoil the pleasure of our fine Catholic young men."[29]

Father Boniface remained steadfast. He wrote Kelley, arguing, "If we now take a firm stand and show both students and alumni that we, as Catholic educators, cannot and will not countenance such behavior, even at a considerable financial loss, I believe their eyes will be opened and they will view their behavior in light of true Christian charity." Kelley pushed for a meeting between the two schools to resolve the matter, but before they could, the *Newark Evening News* reprinted a St. Benedict's press release stating that both schools agreed to drop the game by "mutual agreement." Father Boniface next received a matter-of-fact telegram from Seton Hall officials rejecting the "submitted release as untrue since cancellation was not by mutual agreement." The telegram also notified him of "severance of athletic relations in all sports," and it took another eighteen years for the schools to normalize relations. The rivalry illustrated the downside of intra-Catholic athletic competition. When accusations flew and tempers flared, students, teachers, and even the press attributed it to school spirit and the nature of local rivalry. But one teacher and coach witnessed the rivalry from inside both schools. Johnny Allen taught and coached at St. Benedict's and Seton Hall, and he recalled the ill feelings among the duo, saying, "You can't imagine the bitterness, lack of trust and hate between these schools. It was incredible," recalled Allen. "It didn't matter if they were priests or not; hate could exist. The schools absolutely despised one another."[30]

The Vailsburg Philosopher

When the Benedictines came for Joseph Michael Kasberger, they found the nineteen-year-old picking grapes on his family's Oregon farm. Two monks from Mt. Angel College approached him about studying and playing ball at their tiny Catholic college. Joe was eager to continue his studies, and his parents, both immigrants from Germany, agreed to send him to the Benedictine college situated atop one of the many peaks in the Willamette River valley. After spending two years starring in football, basketball, and baseball at Mt. Angel, Joe transferred to Oregon Agricultural College, where he remained a three-sport man. A six-month stint in the army briefly interrupted his studies, but Joe did earn a degree in agriculture there in 1922 before returning to Mt. Angel to teach and coach. A few years after a fire destroyed Mt. Angel, Kasberger decided to pursue a master's degree in physical education at Columbia Teachers College in New York City. A string of events landed "Oregon Joe" in Newark to coach the 1930 St. Benedict's Prep football team, and the move would continue an already promising and fruitful career.[31]

Frank Milbauer, a 1921 graduate of St. Benedict's and one of the "Seven Mules" for Knute Rockne's "Four Horseman," first met Kasberger in 1924 when Joe spent a season studying football at Notre Dame. After he returned to Oregon, Joe wrote Rockne to thank him for the opportunity, saying, "A season under a 'Wonder Coach' and at a school of 'He-Men,' with a perfect functioning football eleven, is an honor and favor not extended to every man." Milbauer and Kasberger struck an odd pair on the South Bend campus as the Newark native, a hulking 6′3″ and 285 pounds, towered over the 5′8″ and 180-pound budding coach from the rural Northwest. But their friendship proved critical to Joe staying in Newark, since Frank, now an insurance agent in the city, introduced Joe to the monks and other coaches at Benedict's. Impressed enough with the opportunity, Joe accepted a two-year contract worth $3,300 in annual salary to coach football and teach five sections of freshman English.[32]

With Joe's arrival, the athletic staff at St. Benedict's now had a trio of top-notch coaches, all men of sterling character. Jim Cavanagh, a 1913 graduate of Benedict's, was the first to join the staff and he

Joseph "Joe K" Kasberger, the longtime football and baseball coach at St. Benedict's Prep (1930–68), pictured with his assistant football coaches. He coined the phrase "Benedict's Hates a Quitter."

quickly demonstrated the merits of hiring full-time physical instructors and coaches. More and more students benefited from his rigorous gym classes, which included calisthenics, boxing, and games, and he assembled one championship team after another, whether in cross-country or indoor and outdoor track. Blood had already made a reputation for himself with the Passaic Wonder Teams. Joe Kasberger, though, brought unprecedented publicity and fame to the school as he coached numerous football and baseball teams to undefeated seasons. Perhaps more than anything else, his life example came to embody the fighting family spirit of the Gray Bees. He coined the phrase that encapsulated his philosophy—"Benedict's hates a quitter!"—and it has been central to the school's outlook ever since.

That simple mantra hung over the locker-room doorway as generations of Benedict's athletes walked out to train and compete each day: perseverance, as well as a host of other lessons, became ingrained in a young man for a lifetime. Kasberger demanded a certain ruggedness and toughness from his players, in particular because he pushed them toward perfection through long and tedious practices. Johnny Allen, a star quarterback for Joe K before returning to teach and coach at St. Benedict's, remembered practices as "those long ordeals," and Kasberger believed the longer he kept his charges the less likely they would fall victim to his three main dislikes: losing, smoking, and girls. For Joe, drinking and smoking were the "debilitation twins." Long and physically demanding sessions not only conditioned athletes and made them less susceptible to injury, he believed, they also sapped young men of their energies, making them less apt to keep late hours. In the fall, Joe K often kept his teams well after sunset and he produced white painted footballs so they could see the ball in the dark. Many of Joe's boys came from faraway places, and some of them observed they spent so much time at the school that they never saw the light of day in their own hometowns. Further, his teams practiced regardless of the weather; notably he still drilled his team in the middle of a hurricane.[33]

As a football and baseball coach, Kasberger had an almost religious dedication to teaching fundamentals. In the fall, he stressed hard-hitting, precision football, and in the spring he drilled smart, error-free baseball. After an undefeated football campaign, Kasberger revealed his secret to success: "We drill on fundamentals every day right up to the last game. Nothing can take the place of fundamentals." Joe's marathon football practices always emphasized repetitive blocking and tackling drills. "We wouldn't touch a football for days; we'd block and tackle for hours," recalled one former player. Joe's teams were so well drilled that they moved in perfect unison at some points, prompting a player to quip, "We were better than the Rockettes." Kasberger employed Knute Rockne's "Notre Dame Box," an offense that required complete and complex synchronization, and "its military-like precision demoralized a lot of teams." Some observers called it "Catholic football," and well into the 1930s his teams sought "to carry the Catholic flag" against some of the top prep and public schools in the region. Some prep schools even avoided competing against Joe K's gridiron juggernaut. During baseball season, he expertly wielded a bat to stage situational plays that his fielders had to solve over and over again. To him, mental errors were sins, so he sought to root out such "venial" offenses through practice and constant repetition.[34]

In addition to quitters, Joe K also hated injuries. If a player came to him injured, he took it as a personal affront, often ridiculing the young man: "You want out, guy? You're gutless. You're a gutless wonder." An extremely tough man himself, Kasberger had an outlook on life that included a "walk-it-off, play-in-pain" mentality. During an indoor baseball practice early one spring, Joe K caught an errant throw in the eye and when a fellow teacher came to check on him, he was washing his bloodied face in the sink. He muttered through the running water, "Gosh darnit, get out there and keep them throwing." On another occasion, he was struck in the groin with a line drive while pitching batting practice. He did not even flinch and kept tossing baseballs like nothing had happened. While mending a fence during one football season, Kasberger whacked his own shin with a sledgehammer but only asked for tape to close an open wound. One player confessed, "To be taken out by Joe was okay, but you never requested to be taken out. You never thought about taking yourself out. You'd sit for the rest of your life." Knowing full well his aversion to injuries, hurt players clammed up and routinely hid their aches and pains.[35]

For example, Adrian "Bud" Foley, a star quarterback, decorated World War II veteran, and highly successful New Jersey attorney, bragged about how he was "knocked out twice" during a football game but only managed to miss one play. The first hit took place a play before the first half ended and the second on the last play of the game. In another game, Foley hurt his leg, but his teammates picked him up off the ground, slung his arms over their shoulders, and walked him to the team huddle so he could continue playing. Kasberger loved him for it. In the late 1950s, Kasberger looked out the window of the coaches' room and noticed star lineman Tony Scotti dressed in civilian clothes. Joe turned to his assistant coach, John Allen, and asked him why Scotti had not suited up for practice yet. Allen reminded Kasberger that the young man had sustained a severe concussion during Saturday's game and even reported to the other team's huddle dazed and confused. Unimpressed, and perhaps unaware of the long-term implications of head injuries, Kasberger shot back, "Concussion, discussion, percussion. In my day they called it a knock to the head and sent you right back out there. Go tell Scotti to get dressed." Scotti changed, donned his helmet, and practiced per Kasberger's orders. Thankfully, several assistant coaches made sure Scotti was not involved in any contact. Ben Scotti, Tony's older brother, played for Joe before going on to star for both the University of Maryland and the Washington Redskins. He once said, "Joe never had to teach me technique but he taught me desire."[36]

More than most, Kasberger taught by example. He was tough and demanded that his players be too. He also believed in what Prof Blood called "right living," so he never smoked, consumed alcohol, or used profanity, and according to one monk, "a word from him about not drinking or smoking or swearing was worth five sermons from another."[37] In addition to his abstemious behavior, Joe's admirers always mentioned the fact that he walked the few miles back and forth from his home in Vailsburg to Benedict's each day in nothing more than a three-piece suit, regardless of the weather. While he could be loud and boisterous on the playing field, he could be quiet and soft-spoken off it. Harsh, demanding, and even unapproachable while coaching, Joe was warm, generous, and humble when he was not, especially when he called a student into his trophy-laden office to talk about school, sports, or life. Joe was a walking collection of aphorisms, and aside from the one about never giving up, others suggest a more humane side. Sayings that hung in his locker rooms or rolled off his tongue included: "Every man is guilty of all the good he didn't do," and "Kindness is a language that the deaf can hear and the blind can see." Joe could be sentimental and he often waxed poetic. One of his short poems, titled "What Is Success?" began, "It's doing your job the best you can, and being just to your fellow man," before ending, "It's serving, striving thru strain and stress, it's doing your noblest, that's success!" Some even referred to Kasberger as the "Vailsburg Philosopher."[38]

In an outline for a speech to parents, titled "Your Son Should Play Football," Kasberger listed a number of traits he sought out and tried to develop in his players. In particular, he wanted a young man who was "willing to go faithfully and daily through the drudgery that practice can sometimes be," knew "the meaning of obedience and does as he is told," and was "unselfish and thinks of the boys on the team." Joe K believed that "the football field is one place where democracy really works and a boy is judged by his ability and his effort, not by his color, his circumstances or his creed." Regardless of one's ethnicity, race, or religion, Kasberger rewarded the best players, and in addition to individual ability and skill he prized hustle, desire, and team play. A football team, Joe wrote, had to be "an eleven-man organization, and the different parts must work in unison to make up the finished whole. If a boy is to be a worthy member of this organization he must bow to the will of his coach; he must keep himself in top-notch condition; he must put the team's interest ahead of his own. In short, he must learn team play—and team play is the chief essential for success in any field of endeavor today."[39]

In another document, Kasberger reasoned, "The first glory of any school is a line of ideal graduates, gentlemen with character, personality, and apostolic zeal, who will be socially successful and be real citizens." For the faculty and staff at St. Benedict's, the foundation for a promising future was being laid on a daily basis in the classrooms as well as on its playing fields and courts. "School is your workshop for the time being, the place where you hang out your sign and go into business for yourself. You are not working for the teacher; you are working for yourself. Work, do not shirk." Effort, attitude, and a desire to excel dominated Kasberger's daily lectures to players. "Believe and have confidence in yourself and then play the game for all you're worth, every minute you're in it," he implored. "Have no fear but go out on every play and never quit HUSTLING! Whether you are studying, running a machine, or doing any one of the thousand and one jobs out in the world, have faith in your ability." Kasberger was a master motivator, urging his audience to offer the best that was in them, but above all he wanted them immersed in whatever they were doing at the moment. He often said, "We learn to swim by getting into the water. We build character by getting into the stream of Life."[40]

Above all, Kasberger saw himself as a teacher, whether it was in the classroom or on football or baseball fields. Over the course of his high school teaching career, Joe became convinced that teachers "should aim to prepare the boy to be a useful citizen and worthy of the ideals of our country." Moreover, he believed "the teacher should serve as a guide rather than a dictator," and that "teachers should keep constantly in mind that the real value of education is not the acquisition of facts but rather the establishment of character." In order to help form character in young men, though, teachers had to be "men of irreproachable character and becoming personality." While he could be dictatorial at times, especially as a coach, Joe was essentially a guide, a man of true character who led by his sterling example and tried to be "the one hundred point man" in everything he did. "As a man feels in his heart," Joe believed, "so will he teach."[41]

"Look the part. Act the part. Be the part" was one of Joe K's many mantras, and it summed up what St. Benedict's often asked and expected of its students and athletes. For some young men it took four years and for others it took even longer, but like many of his other sayings, "being the part" provided a young man with a masculine ideal. In detention one afternoon, a monk told an offending freshman, "I wish I could take a picture of you now and another in four years, after we're finished knocking the righteousness out of you. It'll be like night and day." A truism for generations of boys transformed into "Benedict's men" during their four-year journey on High Street, monks and laymen at the school served as guides along the way.[42]

The student body loved it when Joe K spoke at a pep rally or an awards ceremony. The "Voice" usually began by addressing those in the audience as "Bumbling, Buzzing 'Beehive' Workers!" He then gave advice to the young men about what it took to be a man, delivering staccato-like bursts of wisdom: "Be a man. Don't flinch. Don't look backward. Onward ever. Backward never!" A loyal "Beehive worker" for some forty years, Joe finally retired during the 1968–69 school year when doctors discovered that he had terminal cancer. Edwin Leahy, a young monk who was also a third-string quarterback for Benedict's in the early 1960s, spent many hours at Joe's bedside as a stream of visitors came to see the ailing legend. On October 1, 1969, students learned of Joe's passing when Headmaster Father Jerome Fitzpatrick announced: "God in His wisdom has seen fit to call from our company into His kingdom truly one of the great men of St. Benedict's Prep. He was to us what the redwood is the world of trees, he was giant among us, and we are saddened by his passing."[43]

Gene Schiller, the man who had taken over for Kasberger as football coach, delivered a moving eulogy at the memorial service. At one point, he focused on Joe's most recognizable phrase, "Benedict's hates a quitter":

This small quote plastered all over was for only one person. It was to be a constant reminder, a thorn—a yoke—for only Joe Kasberger. Joe had put it there for himself. It was there to remind him that he must never quit. He must never quit working with boys—turning them into men. He must never quit teaching the value of manliness and sportsmanship. He must never quit doing his part in the making of a great St. Benedict's.[44]

Athletics contributed to the success of St. Benedict's over the years and increased the school's profile and enrollment. The lessons of manliness, responsibility, and sportsmanship proved valuable and the monks, teachers, and coaches found that a strong athletic program complemented an intellectual, moral, and spiritual education well.

More than anyone else in the school's athletic past, Joe Kasberger, the man who Benedictine monks found picking grapes on an Oregon farm, proved to be an unflinching servant for generations of students and athletes. He was a giant. Shortly after he passed away, the monks planted a redwood tree in the middle of the monastic garden in Newark. Towering over all the red brick buildings, it served as a tribute to a legendary man and stood to remind others of what athletics can accomplish in an all-boys secondary school. Press clippings fade, trophies became chipped and tarnished, but the lessons learned in the crucible of athletic competition linger and become rooted in a man's being.

7

"He Was Afraid of the City": Abbot Patrick, the Monastic Family, and Postwar Newark, 1945–1967

In the months before the end of World War II, Abbot Patrick O'Brien appointed a committee to plan for the building of "a new and greater St. Benedict's, to be located in Newark, N.J." On four separate occasions in the 1940s, the monks agreed to build at Benedict's, but shovels never hit the ground as concerns repeatedly stalled their plans to expand. In particular, Abbot Patrick had major reservations. "He was afraid of the city. He saw no future in it," his successor revealed years later. After a decade of indecision, Abbot Patrick controversially switched the abbey's title from Newark to Morristown in 1956. Bitter about the decision, monks in Newark did not allow Abbot Patrick to move the school too. After "spurning strong overtures" to set up the ninety-year-old prep school in a suburban location, it was decided that St. Benedict's Prep would remain in Newark. Mayor Leo P. Carlin, a 1926 alumnus, chaired a fund-raising committee for a new school building on High Street. The campaign rallied behind the banner "Benedict's Builds with Newark."[1]

Ironically, as Abbot Patrick and his fellow monks debated their future in Newark in the late 1950s and early 1960s, St. Benedict's was a thriving, self-confident institution at the peak of its influence. More than seven hundred students jammed into the school's classrooms and an estimated five hundred qualified applicants were turned away each year for lack of space. Graduates went on to college in record numbers before distinguishing themselves in various professions, especially the church, business, law, and government. Joe Kasberger's football and baseball teams pieced together incredible winning streaks, garnering state and national recognition. With the school's reputation as an excellent academic institution and an athletic powerhouse that was also concerned with molding young Catholic men, St. Benedict's mirrored the generational tale of Philip Roth's "immigrant rocket": "As a family they flew the flight of the immigrant rocket, the upward, unbroken immigrant trajectory from the slave-driven great-grandfather to the self-driven grandfather to the self-confident, accomplished, independent father to the highest flier of them all, the fourth generation child for whom America was to be heaven itself." One monk-teacher of the era commented, "Everybody thought St. Benedict's would be the same for years and years to come. It felt secure in itself; it had its own niche and was set to go on that way forever."[2]

The sense of accomplishment and timelessness at St. Benedict's Prep, so characteristic of the Catholic Church at the time, was shattered by the dramatic changes wrought by events of the 1960s, including the civil rights movement and the Second Vatican Council. Additionally, suburbanization and deindustrialization continued at breakneck speed, and it did so at the expense of cities like Newark. In particular, the times influenced how individuals in the monastic family thought about the crucial issues of the day, and the interplay among religion, race, and community helped explain many of the individual and collective decisions made during such uncertain and unsettled times. It also sheds light on the debate over the futures of the monasteries and schools in both Newark and Morristown. Some monks no doubt empathized with Roth's character Lou Levov in *American Pastoral*; he looked back on the changes in his beloved Newark from the vantage point of the late twentieth century and said, "The changes are beyond conception. I sometimes think that more has changed since 1945 than in all the years of history there have been."[3]

Double-Cross Abbey

Most Newarkers believed the days and years following the conclusion of World War II held boundless opportunity. Beginning in 1946, the Port Authority of New York and New Jersey started to pour millions of dollars into the development of Newark Airport and Port Newark.

Newark's two largest insurance firms, Mutual Benefit Life and the Prudential, linked their futures to the city when both built new office complexes overlooking the historic Washington Park. Anheuser-Busch, the nation's largest brewer, planned construction of a twenty-nine-million-dollar plant near the airport. Rutgers and Seton Hall universities, along with Newark College of Engineering, all decided to expand and develop sprawling educational complexes in the downtown area. Newark's Central Planning Board prepared a master plan in 1947 that called for certain sections of the central city to be cleared and redeveloped. Equally important was the decision in 1953 to adopt a new city charter that created a mayor-council form of government, replacing what many felt was a corrupt and inefficient commission-style government. The first mayor under the new form was Carlin, and its second was another Benedict's alumnus, Hugh Addonizio.[4]

"The Committee for a Greater St. Benedict's" called for "a million dollar plan" to construct a new school building on High Street in the immediate postwar period. It was to include at least twenty-five classrooms and science labs, a combination gymnasium/auditorium to seat at least 1,500 people, offices, and even a swimming pool. But a fire at Delbarton in 1947 derailed the grandiose plans, and the monastic community voted to spend over one hundred thousand dollars to rebuild the destroyed buildings instead. It could be argued that the fire was the spark that set off more serious discussions about the future relationship between the city and country abbeys, as plans for development in Newark once again stalled in favor of helping Morristown. Abbot Patrick saw the aftermath of the fire as an opportunity to set forth a clear and coherent plan for future development, and another two committees were formed—one focusing on Newark and the other on Morristown—to examine the future, asking that they "determine the future for twenty years."[5]

The Newark committee recommended a round of meetings to begin in the fall, and on October 30, 1947, the minutes record that the monks discussed "separation" for the first time. One monk suggested that the Newark and Morristown houses might be growing apart because of "a legitimate difference in outlook and ideals." Father Ignatius "Iggy" Kohl, one of the students' favorite teachers, believed the Newark community "should be more interested in the children of the poor and in helping Catholic parents of low income give their children a Catholic education." Father Dunstan Smith spoke of his continuing frustration with the inadequacy of the facilities at St. Benedict's, implying what many deemed the crux of the matter: progress at Morristown continued to hinder growth in Newark. Although the community backed the expansion plans in Newark, eleven years passed before any monies were raised. In the interim, questions continued to surface about whether anything new or great would ever happen at the Newark school and monastery.[6]

In accordance with the bylaws of the American Cassinese Congregation of Benedictine Monasteries, each monastery in the country had to be visited by a panel of abbots at regular intervals. In 1955, a group of abbots visited both Newark and Morristown, observed life there, and decided that not much had changed since visits in 1949 and 1952. For some years the abbot visitors recommended a "complete union" of the two communities, stating in no uncertain terms after the 1955 visit, "Today we find little change in the conditions that existed years ago. The monastic family must be brought together, the whole family. . . . It is up to you as a Community to determine where that shall be, where that family shall live, and it is up to you as a Community to see that it is accomplished." At the height of World War II, Abbot Patrick told a local newspaper that the monastic community was "the ideal example of the family unit. It shows the world what family life consists of and can do." But in the postwar period, not unlike many other American families, the monks struggled to figure out where to live.[7]

Abbot Patrick had been contemplating the issue for some time and saw the need for a "definitive plan," one resulting in "all the constituent parts of a monastery under one roof—Abbot, priests, clerics, and brothers." He challenged the members of St. Mary's Abbey to find a suitable solution within the year. Upon hearing about new urban renewal plans for Newark, Father Philip Hoover met with Louis A. Danzig, longtime director of the Newark Housing Authority, and they discussed the redevelopment of a hundred-block slum area adjacent to the monastery's property. Danzig and Mayor Carlin both believed in

Abbot Patrick M. O'Brien, OSB, served as the spiritual leader of the Newark and Morristown abbeys from 1937 to 1967.

Newark's future, and Carlin even called together the CEOs of the city's eighteen largest corporations in an attempt to stop corporate Newark from leaving the city en masse. He also advised the monks to stay in the city. Eager to see the abbey and school commit themselves to renewal efforts, Danzig pledged "any help within the NHA's power."[8]

A few years earlier Father Philip conducted his own study and found that more than 70 percent of St. Benedict's students lived outside the city, a product of the first waves of "white flight" to the suburbs. He became convinced, however, that the school's central location still proved to be a major asset, concluding in 1951, "The fact obviates the possibility of any proposal for the change in the location of the school site. It lies in the center of a circle whose area embraces scores of communities and thousands of potential students. Transportation facilities make the school more readily accessible than if it were located in a suburban area." News of the redevelopment project further solidified his thinking that Benedict's should build with the city. Therefore, he wrapped up his report with the following conclusion: "The present site is adequate for any expansion of school or monastery, and that such a project would be justified in view of the city's redevelopment." Interestingly, *institutional* white flight lagged behind *residential* white flight. Families who left Newark apparently had no real problem sending their sons back into the city for a Benedict's education.[9]

Shortly after being presented with Father Philip's findings, Abbot Patrick appointed a second committee to undertake a more comprehensive study. Chaired by Father Matthew Hoehn, this committee sought more detailed information on the city's urban renewal plans as well as the community's mind-set on the issues of separation and union. Father Matthew walked downtown to the Newark Public Library to gather more information on the city's renewal plans and was most impressed by a recent survey conducted by Seton Hall University. It reported that more than 20 percent of the firms presently in Newark planned to leave in the near future because of "inadequate space and obsolete buildings." Meanwhile, Abbot Patrick visited Archbishop Boland to solicit his opinion. He wanted the Benedictines to stay in the archdiocese, but felt that High Street was not a suitable location for an abbey, specifically that it was impossible to train clerics there. Boland recommended that the monks look for property within the archdiocese (Morristown was in a different diocese) but outside Newark, and Father Matthew and others visited several possible locations, including sites in West Orange, Scotch Plains, and Livingston.[10]

At meetings in late 1955 and early 1956, Abbot Patrick encouraged people to voice opinions on the advantages and disadvantages of moving the abbey to a new site in the vicinity of Newark. Some monks argued that moving to a suburban location might be desirable because it provided an environment more conducive to a monastic lifestyle.

Another monk observed, "It might be said that the Newark of yester-day has moved out into the suburbs away from St. Benedict's Prep. Our moving therefore would not be running away from, but following of our former environment." Others clearly opposed leaving the city, arguing that the past ninety years of building the school and its scholastic reputation would be sacrificed by such a move. Although monks kept calling for unity, it was apparent that a wide range of opinions existed within the monastic family. The main question, though, was whether these differences were irreconcilable.[11]

With the Abbot's deadline for a solution fast approaching, there was no consensus on separation or unification. Separation might allow the men at Newark and Morristown to pursue their separate destinies, but it would surely put them under a great deal of psychological and financial strain. Some opponents of a split maintained that Newark stood to lose a great deal more than Morristown, especially when the unsettled situation in the country's urban areas was taken into account. The neighborhood had deteriorated in the last couple of decades, and all signs suggested that it would continue to do so. Indeed, there was no agreement on how to resolve the pressing issue, and one monk proposed that the abbot resolve the matter through a show of deter-mined leadership, as the chapter minutes indicated: "Many felt that they would rather Father Abbot make the decision and then call upon the Community to follow him."[12]

Abbot Patrick did so on May 24, 1956, when he asked his fellow monks to discuss two proposals: the first, to keep the abbey on High Street and develop the site in Newark while keeping Morristown as a dependency; and the second, to transfer the title of the abbey to Mor-ristown and establish Newark as a dependency. They once again re-hashed the pros and cons of each option, but "many chose to remain silent." Perhaps they were deferring to what they sensed were the ab-bot's wishes. Most had not agreed with the visitors that the "two com-munities abandon one or the other or both locations and assemble at one place." Instead, the monks preferred the status quo. Before calling for a community vote, the abbot indicated that he had been to see the archbishop, who agreed in principle that transferring the abbey to Morristown solved the problem.[13]

When the community reassembled for a vote on the proposal to transfer the abbey, Abbot Patrick began the meeting by reading from a prepared statement written in his flowery hand. Among other things, it highlighted the long debate over monasticism in the city versus the country, an issue dating back to Boniface Wimmer's ambivalence about founding a monastery in a major city. It even detailed how he spoke to at least ten abbots in the last year and "all were unanimous in the belief that a Benedictine Abbey could not function properly in a large city." Abbot Patrick also asserted that when Abbot Ernest Helmstetter purchased the Delbarton estate in 1925, he too planned on transferring the abbey one day. "It's incumbent on me to do what my predecessors intended to do," stated Abbot Patrick. "It is very evident to me that the situation calls for leadership and I feel impelled to assume that role. I'm convinced that the end we seek can be best achieved by relocating or transferring the Abbey to Morris County, Delbarton Estate."[14]

Following years of debate, the monks voted to transfer the title of St. Mary's Abbey to Morristown on June 13, 1956. After seventy-two years as an abbey, the monastery in Newark was now a priory, an unprecedented move in the history of the Benedictine Order in the United States. One monk compared it to changing the nameplates in the middle of the night. The vote crushed many in Newark who saw it as a loss of prestige and a denial of its long and generous history. The move also led to questions of the future stability of their now-dependent monastery. For years, monks loyal to Newark had made major sacrifices so that Manchester and Morristown could grow and expand. But now they worried whether their beloved monastery and school would be left to fend for itself amid a rapidly changing city. Was "a new and greater St. Benedict's" even possible? Such concerns clearly worried many monks, and some grew increasingly bitter toward Abbot Patrick. They quietly accused him of ignoring canon law in securing the vote to switch the titles, and of even influencing the votes of younger members. Such bitterness sparked a nickname for the new abbey in Morristown. A crucifix adorned each of the two entrances on either side of the long, multistoried monastery building set atop a hill on the four-hundred-acre Delbarton estate; they now called it "Double-Cross Abbey."[15]

"A Monastery on High Street?" Urban Anxiety
in an Age of Suburbanization

Abbot Patrick may well have been a reluctant "horse-trader," because in exchange for the title he promised that St. Benedict's would remain in Newark, "despite strong overtures to shift its educational facilities elsewhere." The day after the decision was made, the *Newark Star-Ledger* ran the following headline: "St. Benedict's Prep Won't Go." The ninety-year-old institution turned down proposals to move out of the city the article continued, and Abbot Patrick's decision had been "largely influenced by Newark's current redevelopment program." Headmaster Father Philip Hoover duly called for alumni and friends to raise $750,000 toward the construction costs of a brand-new building along High Street, and the fund drive's slogan, "Benedict's Builds with Newark," complemented the city's renewal plans. The three-story, yellow-brick building was dedicated in 1959, and it included an auditorium, cafeteria, offices, and classrooms. After waiting for nearly two decades, it was a dream come true for the monks and students: something new and great finally happened for St. Benedict's Prep.[16]

Newark had been in decline since the 1920s, when the impact of the Great Depression halted enthusiastic plans for various building projects in the city. The source of its so-called ghettoization, though, was to be found in decisions made in the 1930s and 1940s. During the 1920s, core industries started to vacate Newark as one-story plants could be built on cheap land in the suburbs, where taxes were considerably lower. Blue-collar jobs in the city began to dry up as a result.[17] Yet throughout the 1940s, African American migrants still flocked to cities like Newark in search of employment and educational opportunities. In Chicago, argued the historian Arnold Hirsch, a new ghetto appeared after World War II, distinguished by its racial segregation, poor quality housing, substandard schools, and continued lack of economic opportunity.[18] The rise of the "second ghetto" in cities like Newark has been of central importance for all urban schools, including Catholic schools.[19]

Leaving Newark has a long history, and the exodus to the suburbs has always been for those who could afford it. Commissioner Charles P. Gillen addressed the changing nature of Newark at a city hall meeting in 1932, saying:

The old American element that lived in Newark many years ago, the Yankee element, has moved out into the suburbs, up over the mountain and into Montclair. Into Newark had come a great immigration from many foreign countries, and today in Newark even the Germans who were so prevalent in Newark years ago, when Newark was known practically as the German city, when I was a boy, have moved out into Union and Irvington. A great many

After the monastic community decided to remain in Newark in 1957, school and city officials launched the "Benedict's Builds with Newark" campaign. The monastery and school planned to become part of the city's substantial urban-renewal program.

of my race, the Irish race, have moved out. In their places have come this great influx of Jewish population, of Italians, of Polish, Slavish, Spanish, Portuguese, Greeks, and today we have this great cosmopolitan population in the city of Newark.[20]

Conspicuous by its absence in Gillen's Newark mosaic was the African American community, yet they were the source of much of the anxiety that fed ensuing generations of white flight. That flight, beginning in the 1930s and accelerating in the postwar period, was subsidized by the federal government in the form of the GI Bill and Veterans Administration programs that enabled sixteen million veterans to purchase homes. To ease the severe postwar housing shortage, developers and builders transformed the suburban fringe; thirteen million new homes were built in the 1950s alone. Increased accessibility of the automobile and the construction of "superhighways" under the 1956 Federal Aid Highway Act sped up the mass departure, so that by 1960 as many Americans lived in suburbs as cities. The Federal Housing Authority and the VA enabled many Americans to buy new homes, mostly in the suburbs, with a long-term, low-down-payment, FHA-insured mortgage loan. In many cases it became cheaper to buy a house in the suburbs than rent one in the city, thus inaugurating a federally subsidized flight from urban areas.[21]

Postwar migrations transformed cities and suburbs, and in Newark's case it resulted in the city's population virtually turning color over the course of a few decades. Between 1940 and 1970, the African American population skyrocketed from 45,760 to 207,458 while the city's white population plummeted from 383,534 to 168,382. African Americans accounted for 10.7 percent of Newark's total population in 1940, but by 1960 that percentage more than tripled to 34.1. In 1960, whites still outnumbered blacks by a two-to-one margin, but by 1970 Newark's African American community became a majority. Population change was so swift and so pronounced that it led the historian Kenneth T. Jackson to proclaim in 1972, "It will soon become America's first virtually all-black city."[22]

One only had to look at FHA real estate appraisal methods to gain a notion that Newark was headed that way, as they undervalued old, dense, and diverse neighborhoods. Biased toward new, spacious, and racially segregated neighborhoods, underwriters favored new construction in the suburbs, effectively "redlining" whole areas and denying them access to loans. In 1939, for example, FHA appraisers using a scale of "A" for "First Grade" to "D" for "Fourth Grade" did not rate a single Newark neighborhood as "First Grade." The city's best neighborhoods, the largely Jewish sections of Weequahic and Clinton Hill and non-Jewish areas like Vailsburg and Forest Hill, characterized by single-family homes tightly packed together on tree-lined streets, only received a "B" rating. Average working-class neighborhoods garnered "C" classifications, while the crowded Ironbound section and every African American neighborhood were labeled "hazardous." Such ratings prevented the FHA from insuring new construction and renovation projects in the vast majority of Newark's neighborhoods.[23]

Overly concerned with the presence of "inharmonious racial or nationality groups," the FHA determined that "if a neighborhood [was] to retain stability, it [was] necessary that properties [should] continue to be occupied by the same social and racial classes." Panic selling, blockbusting, and violence all contributed to the preservation and expansion of all-black neighborhoods. Public housing and urban renewal plans directly affected their evolution too, because those programs "reshaped, enlarged, and transformed" African American ghettos. Between 1950 and 1960, seven of Newark's twelve neighborhoods displayed signs of considerable white entrenchment. Predominantly white neighborhoods like Forest Hill, Silver Lake, Roseville, Vailsburg, and Weequahic formed a ring around the core area of Newark's African American neighborhoods, and most of the nearly two hundred St. Benedict's students that still called the city home lived in that outer circle.[24]

While FHA housing policies favored white middle-class Americans by making suburban housing affordable, beginning in 1937 the federal government provided housing assistance to the urban poor. Local housing authorities received monies to purchase blighted land, tear down old buildings, construct new apartments, and rent them at subsidized rates to lower-income people. By 1966, the Newark Housing Authority operated seventeen public housing projects, a handful of which were within walking distance of the monastery and school, occupied by 10,531 families and 37,605 persons. Newark built more units of public housing per capita than any other city in the country, and one scholar criticized housing director Danzig's agency, concluding that "the program looms as a monument to the failure of impoverished ideas and uncritical politics backed by hundreds of millions of dollars from the federal government."[25] Put another way, Kenneth Jackson has argued that "the result, if not the intent, of the public housing program of the United States was to segregate the races, to concentrate the disadvantaged in inner cities, and to reinforce the image of suburbia as a place of refuge for the problems of race, crime, and poverty."[26]

The historian William B. Helmreich points to "America's love affair with the suburbs, with the idea of a backyard, a little green grass, and a private home they could call their own" in his attempt to explain the mass exodus out of Newark. He maintained that white Newarkers "were not running away from blacks," but simply lured to the towns ringing the city as jobs moved there and houses were built near them. Sure, city dwellers dreamed of leafy suburbs and backyard barbeques, but they also feared the changes occurring around them, including the racial transition and perceived decline of the city. Roman Catholics tended to remain longer in their urban neighborhoods than their Jewish and Protestant counterparts, in part because of their attachment to the "sacred space" of the old national parish. But they eventually left, for a combination of racial and financial reasons. Richard Lorenzo entered St. Benedict's Prep in 1959, which was also a momentous year in his North Ward neighborhood, as it was when a realtor sold a Park Avenue home to a black family. "It scared the crap out of white people," recalled Lorenzo. "The driving force behind the fear was that people thought their property values would go down."[27]

Abbot Patrick was among those who witnessed the rapid changes and struggled to make sense of them. His fear of cities influenced his decision to switch the titles in 1956, just as it factored into millions of other decisions made by white ethnic families to flee the city. While it is impossible to pinpoint when Abbot Patrick became afraid of the city, it was clear that he preferred not to spend time there, since he often visited St. Anselm Abbey in his hometown of Manchester, New

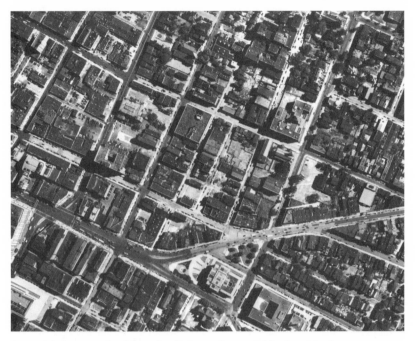

An aerial photograph of the school's immediate neighborhood in the 1950s.

Hampshire, and vacationed in Florida for long stretches of time. Some even intimated that he ran his monastery like Meyer Ellenstein, Newark's mayor between 1933 and 1941. Ellenstein was rarely seen at city hall, or even in Newark, and he later confessed, "I operate by remote control." When he was in Newark, Abbot Patrick warned his fellow monks against "the dangers of worldliness creeping into the monastery and into the individual lives of the monks," and advised monks to park cars in a different lot because the "Shipman St. location is hazardous, especially in the early morning and late evening hours. The area is ideally suited to hold-ups." Late one night Father Matthew Hoehn, the school librarian, was at his desk working on a book, *Catholic Authors*, and a bullet ripped through his window. A Newark policeman had fired it as he attempted to chase down a criminal. On another occasion, a Newark policeman chased after a man who stole a whiskey bottle out of his patrol car. He discharged his weapon and the stray bullet injured a St. Benedict's student looking to cross the street.[28]

The Third Ward was now called the Central Ward, and it still scared some monks. Their immediate neighborhood was perceived not as a sanctuary but as a liability. The blocks along High Street had transformed over time, from German to Jewish and now to African American. By 1959, Central Ward neighborhoods were 85 percent African American, up from over 60 percent nearly twenty years earlier, and in a very real sense Newark reflected the postwar urban experience in microcosm. The city "embod[ied] in intense form nearly everything that [was] happening in urban America. It might also be called the city that became a ghetto," argued the historian George Groh. In 1964, one monk wrote a paper to be read at a community meeting, titled "A Monastery on High Street?" It addressed issues of racism and civil rights, the changes wrought by Vatican II and urban renewal, and, fundamentally, whether a monastery belonged in Newark.[29]

Civil Rights, Vatican II, and the Catholic Encounter with Race

Although the monks really lived on the edge of one of the nation's most densely populated African American communities, most monks on High Street had little contact with their neighbors, at least through the mid-1960s. Father Benedict Bradley gave lectures on the liturgy at Queen of Angels, an African American Catholic parish on Belmont Avenue, as early as the 1930s. The abbey hosted a meeting of the Clergy Conference on Negro Welfare, and Catholic intellectuals, writers, and parish priests attended to discuss ways in which they could address Catholic prejudice. At that meeting the issue of admitting blacks to St. Benedict's was discussed, but Abbot Patrick squashed the idea as he worried about how his faculty might react, not to mention its potential impact on enrollment. The administration did not have a stated policy that barred African Americans from admission, and even though a few African Americans attended St. Benedict's beginning in the mid-1940s, the school remained virtually lily-white until 1970. Father Maurus McBarron, who served as pastor at St. Mary's, did engage the local community, beginning in the 1960s. His congregation and the parish school were open to African Americans, and he later took turns with other local clergy living in "the projects" during the 1970s.[30]

Since the majority of the school's clientele lived in the suburbs, it could be argued that St. Benedict's Prep was "*in* the city, but not *of* the city." Even though white ethnic Catholics saw their neighborhoods as "sacred" and resisted moving out of the city much longer than either Jews or Protestants, white flight effectively emptied out urban areas with relative quickness and ease after 1945. Racial attitudes of individual whites and "white" institutions facilitated the outcome: black inner cities and white suburbs. Interestingly, St. Benedict's remained a white institution in a black inner-city neighborhood, largely relying on graduates and friends to recommend the prestigious school to promising young Catholic students. Newark still boasted a transportation web that made the school's High Street location readily accessible. In addition, although there was some local competition in Seton Hall Prep and St. Peter's Prep, Benedict's stood near the top of the pecking order of the old guard of Catholic high schools. The burgeoning regional Catholic high school system, however, loomed on the horizon.[31]

In a letter to his old classmate Mayor Hugh Addonizio in 1962, Father Mark Confroy, Hoover's replacement as headmaster, pointed out, "As the only private school for boys that decided to remain in the city, we share in a common interest—that of the renewal of Greater Newark." But the decision to build in Newark was not particularly bold as Benedict's stayed the course, continuing to offer a traditional liberal arts curriculum to Catholic males from the suburbs in the confident hope that they turned out to be Catholic gentlemen. Even after the construction of the 1959 building, the faculty at St. Benedict's forged ahead with more elaborate building plans, mainly because of two factors: first, the drawing power from the vast Catholic population within a thirty or so mile radius, and, second, lingering animosity in the face of the switching of the title of the abbey to Morristown. A sibling rivalry with the monastery in Morristown, and indirectly Delbarton School, pushed the men in Newark to further develop the school and monastery. When the architect Victor Christ-Janer's firm produced a master plan in 1962, ironically called "St. Mary's: A Family," he soon found out that there was a great deal more at stake than just building a new monastic complex.[32]

He did not have to dig too deep to uncover a "particular problem." "General identification has been associated with the two schools that are being administered to by St. Mary's Abbey," Christ-Janer found out. Moreover, that identification stood as "an important factor both psychologically and spiritually" and was of great significance when planning for the future. Characterized by opaque language, the report suggested that the two monasteries could one day "evolve" into separate, independent houses. As for the "urban situation," the firm observed: "The Church has played an important and significant role in the integrated urban life throughout history. Is the role of the Church today passive or active? It may well be that the role of the Church in deteriorated areas might be reappraised." The firm submitted plans for an expansion of the monastery and school to Mayor Addonizio in 1962. The three-stage, three-million-dollar project was to be "an integral part of the contemporary rehabilitation and growth of the City of Newark . . . the 'City Reborn.'"[33]

Neighborhood decline and race were secondary matters for the time being, but soon the swirling changes in the Catholic Church and American society, not to mention within their own neighborhood, forced the monks to examine their vow of stability, especially after the summer of 1967. "There was not an explicit awareness of race at St. Benedict's Prep and St. Mary's Priory before 1967," recalled one monk. "Curiously, that only happened after they had the race riots here."[34] Individual monks did get swept up in the movements of the day, though, and the influence of these movements on the future direction of the school and monastery continued to grow.

Renewal and revitalization were the order of the day, not only in Newark but the country at large, and even within the Roman Catholic Church. When Pope John XXIII convened the Second Vatican Council in the fall of 1962, two years after Americans elected John F. Kennedy the first Catholic president in the country's history, he used the image of the Catholic Church opening windows that for centuries had been sealed shut. The pope said, "I want to throw open the windows of the Church so that we can see out and the people can see in." The council's main objective was aggiornamento, a modernization of the church that would enable it to read the "signs of the times" to better encounter the modern world. The first lines of *Gaudium et Spes*, one of a handful of the council's revolutionary documents, became a call to social action, especially among liberal Catholics throughout the 1960s: "The joys and the hopes, the griefs and the anxieties of the men of this age, especially those who are poor or in any way afflicted, these too are the joys and hopes, the griefs and anxieties of the followers of Christ." The church's pledge to serve "the whole human family" included a "preferential option" for the poor, and it also coincided with a renewed concern for issues of race and poverty in the United States.[35]

In April 1963, two months before he died, Pope John condemned racial discrimination in another document, *Pacem in Terris*, prodding Catholics the world over to reevaluate their views on race. That summer, confrontations between police and marchers in Birmingham, Alabama, shocked television audiences worldwide, and only a few months later more than two hundred thousand people gathered to demonstrate in Washington, D.C., in favor of civil rights legislation. Father Martin Burne was among the many clergy who traveled to the nation's capital to hear Dr. Martin Luther King Jr. speak at the March on Washington. King's oratory, in particular his dream about white and black children going to school together, left an indelible impression on the tall, lanky priest, who appeared amid the marchers on the cover of *Life* magazine. American bishops also met in Rome to call for equality within the church regardless of race, and the following fall the new pontiff, Pope Paul VI, met with civil rights leaders Martin Luther King and Ralph Abernathy to pledge his support for their cause.[36]

In Newark, the monks were involved in their own rights battle, one to declare independence from the Morristown abbey and an abbot toward whom many had grown bitter. In particular, Abbot Patrick had continued to push forward on the building of the new monastery in Morristown, and even suggested that St. Benedict's Prep alumni be approached for donations to help fund it. Benedict's alumni had just given freely in the "Benedict's Builds with Newark" campaign and some monks thought it was just too much to ask. To solicit alumni again, and this time for a project outside the city, would "meet with failure and will only breed ill-will," said one monk. Father Benedict Tyler detailed the situation in a letter on September 25, 1963, ten days after four girls died in a church firebombing in Alabama. "Morale here is not good. We have all experienced Abbot Patrick's kindness and I think that, to a man, we have loved and respected him as a father," he wrote. "But a feeling of bitterness is bound to develop among a group of men who are being treated as so many little boys who have misbehaved and must be made to toe the line." Nearly twenty monks maintained that the status quo could not be maintained, but only seventeen had the courage to sign a petition.[37]

Just seven years after Abbot Patrick had switched the titles, seventeen monks signed the petition that called for Newark's independence from St. Mary's Abbey in Morristown. The group argued that one abbot could not run two monasteries, saying, "The very geographical distance between the two communities at Morristown and in Newark precludes the effective rule of any one man." More important, though, was the insistence that "the two communities have begun to pull apart in the directions that their objectives and apostolates have taken. We feel that because of the special conditions of Newark regarding the Negro and Puerto Rican population, and the college and business area, this division will soon become even more pronounced." It was the first time that the monks referred to what other religious communities called the "racial apostolate."[38]

A significant portion, but by no means all, of the Newark group welcomed what they saw as the future, an apostolate in an urban setting serving largely African American and Latino populations. Others still questioned whether they should stay in the city at all. In a statement prepared for Abbot Patrick in 1964 titled "A Monastery on High Street?" Father Virgil Stallbaumer, a scholar of medieval literature, captured what some saw as a siege in progress:

Somehow Benedictines have gotten the notion that they should live on a mountain or in the woods. According to History, St. Benedict located on Monte Cassino to get away from the plundering and pillaging barbarians then on the move. . . . We could say that there is about the same reason today for moving from High Street. According to the present indications, this site will be surrounded on two, if not three sides by a prevailing Negro population. They in a sense are a threat in much the same way as the barbarians were in the sixth, seventh, and eighth centuries. It will take much time to bring them to accept our standards on private property, family life, and our social and religious ways.

In another telling passage, Father Virgil, who joined after leaving a rural, midwestern monastery, and who did not sign the petition, addressed some of the prevailing attitudes of the monks toward the local African American community:

During the past three years we have had samples of the problems that will confront us on High Street. Since bringing in Negro help to man the cleaning of the school, the cafeteria, and the kitchen, thieves have entered twice, something that never happened previously. Things have also been carried away in broad daylight. Lights have had to be installed in the parking lot as a means of safeguarding the cars. New locks have been put all through the monastery and school and a detective service has been put on duty at night, measures that have never been necessary before. We have also in late years seen something of what lies ahead in having Negroes as parishioners. Those who have come in contact with them in the church through work with the altar boys no doubt realize that as a race the Negro has a long ways to come.

Yet by the end of a statement filled with the racism and paternalism endemic to the time, Father Virgil declared, "To abandon High Street now would be going against the best tradition of Benedictinism. . . . Work has been put on our doorstep here and the best traditions of Benedictinism dictate that we make plans to do it." Father Benedict put it a different way: "I feel very definitely that my roots are here; I was born in Newark, I attended St. Benedict's Preparatory School and there I received my vocation, and it is at the High Street Community that my life as a monk, priest and educator has developed."[39]

Not surprisingly, the plans of the seventeen monks were at odds with Abbot Patrick's vision for the two monasteries. In a meeting following the petition seeking independence, Abbot Patrick delivered a statement that once again made his stance clear: the monastic family must not be broken up or separated. Even though he conceded that a monastic life could be led in the city despite "psychological hindrances from the proximity of the bustle and distracting activities of modern city life," he could not in good conscience bring himself "to believe the city either an ideal or suitable place" for the training of novices and clerics. He also maintained that plans for a larger monastery and school under the urban renewal program in the city were at a very premature stage, thus curtailing any attempt to grant independent status to the monastery in Newark. Abbot Patrick and Archbishop Boland both wrote letters that accompanied the petition seeking independence. In June 1964, the Vatican responded, declaring the time for Newark's independence as "inopportune."[40]

Race continued to mark many of the cultural changes sweeping through American Catholicism and American society, including those at the monastery in Newark. By the mid-1960s, maintained John McGreevy, "two distinctly Catholic visions of church, community, and authority clashed in the streets, parishes, and Catholic schools of northern cities." The battle lines for a similar clash began to form within the monastic family too: those who wanted to stay on High Street and work both in the school and community, and those who began to question their vow of stability to a place in a neighborhood under siege by the "prevailing Negro population."[41]

As the changes of the 1960s unfolded around the monastery and school, the Benedictines in Newark repeatedly sought outside advice on their present and future situation. An inward-looking group of prayerful men did not have ready answers for what was happening around them. A second study in 1966 hoped to develop recommendations to help the members of St. Mary's Abbey decide the future of the prep school in Newark. Among other things, the study explored whether St. Benedict's Prep ought to abandon its High Street location or remain in the city "under revised conditions with respect to size and other characteristics."

The New York consulting firm of Taylor, Lieberfeld and Heldman concluded that St. Benedict's "should continue in operation at its present location" since their research suggested that the school "could easily expand in enrollment to over 900 students by 1981–82 without compromising the quality of its student body or educational objectives." In the end, two reasons were put forth for why the school should remain in Newark: "First, the general population which the School services is concentrated in and around Newark. Second, the alumni of the School, who are particularly influential in affecting the decisions of either their children or friends in attending St. Benedict's, are similarly concentrated around Newark." Indeed, after exploring several other possible locations for the school elsewhere in the state, the consultants concurred that St. Benedict's should be "relatively optimistic about its enrollment potential." Newark was still the best possible location from which to draw the most students.[42]

Newark proved to be optimistic about its future too, especially in her tercentennial year of 1966. Three hundred years after Connecticut Puritans sailed down the Passaic River to set up a religious colony that hoped to be a "city upon a hill," the monks in Newark found promise and hope in the pages of the Taylor report. Looking back on the early days of the school, Father Luke Moosberger, who had immigrated to the United States from Germany in 1891, remembered when students "were seen prancing about the school in knee-high knickers and derbies." Born and raised in rural Germany, Father Luke was not prepared "to see the great wonders of a modern metropolis. Broad and Market Streets was a pandemonium of activity—crowds of people, horses, carriages, and street trolleys." Yet referring to the proposed urban renewal plans for the monastery and school, he proclaimed, "The school certainly has great plans. But, St. Benedict's will always be the same. Many great men have graduated from here in the past and many will graduate in the future. Yes, St. Benedict's will always be the same."[43] The urban renewal plans as well as the "expert" recommendations of various planners all proved to be overly optimistic. After July 1967, everything in the city changed.

8

"Camelot Is Dead": The Newark Riots and the Closing of St. Benedict's Prep, 1967–1972

On hot summer days in the city, the downtown monks loved to go to "Tin Beach." After climbing a dark, narrow staircase and ducking under a half door, the monks stepped onto the tin roof of the school building. There they often stretched out on chaise lounges in their bathing suits, reading, napping, chatting, or simply soaking in the sunshine. It was their quick summer getaway, an oasis four stories above Newark's busy, bustling streets. The spectacular panoramic views included the Manhattan skyline to the east, the leafy suburbs at the foot of the mountains to the west, and to the south, the noisy jets taking off at the airport. The bird's-eye view of the immediate neighborhood was a curious patchwork of churches, schools, businesses, wooden tenements, Victorian mansions, vacant lots, and massive public housing complexes. The neighborhood looked best at night, though, as the soft glow of downtown lights temporarily camouflaged the creeping signs of decay and decline.

The monks always gathered on Tin Beach on the Fourth of July to watch fireworks displays from a half dozen neighboring towns. In 1967, as they waited for the fireworks to begin, the monks were treated to a sideshow. For close to an hour, several neighborhood men tried to break in to the Masonic temple across the street. The determined men could not find a way in, much to the monks' amusement, and eventually one monk called the police, who then arrested the would-be thieves a few blocks away. Eight nights later, several monks again stood on the rooftop, this time for an altogether different kind of fireworks, the first of six nights of looting, rioting, and the subsequent "law-and-order" crackdown.

On July 12, 1967, Father Maynard Nagengast, a young monk who taught art at St. Benedict's Prep, looked down and watched the riots through his horn-rimmed glasses. African American teenagers looted nearby stores along Springfield Avenue, a major commercial thoroughfare. He heard smashing glass, frenzied shouting, wailing sirens, and intermittent gunfire, all sounds that became the neighborhood's temporary soundtrack. Hundreds of fires raged out of control. When the National Guard occupied the city early Friday morning, they did so in army jeeps and armored tanks. Helicopters circled overhead. The sights, sounds, and smells resembled a war zone. Later that day a National Guardsman rang the abbey's doorbell and said, "You can't go up on the roof anymore because there are snipers in the area." Father Laurence Grassman, the new headmaster, kept a diary that summer, and a mid-July entry simply read: "Riot Weekend. Wed.-Thurs.-Fri.-Sat.-Sun. Finished by Monday. Troops and State Police Withdrawn. Peace came by 3:00 P.M. Monday." Father Laurence left Tin Beach for Avon-by-the-Sea, a summer resort along the Jersey shore, for the long weekend, but other monks were quarantined inside the abbey on summer vacation. They followed the events outside their doors by watching television and reading the local newspapers. It was Newark's summer of discontent.[1]

Thirteen-year-old Bernie Greene witnessed the riots from street level. He wanted to see what was happening outside his first-floor apartment at the Stella Wright Homes, a public housing project, and convinced his mother to take a walk through their Central Ward neighborhood. They saw bands of looters strip stores in a matter of minutes, and members of one family lug a couch down the middle of the street. As Bernie, a strong, nearly six-foot-tall African American teenager, walked toward Springfield Avenue his heart jumped into his throat: a Newark policeman pointed a gun at his mother. Bernie, who would enter St. Benedict's Prep in two years' time as a tenth grader, instinctively shielded her from harm's way. The mother and son quickly made their way back home, where they slept on the floor of their apartment for fear of stray bullets. Bernie would sneak out several times during the next few nights.[2]

Father Martin Burne, a Newark native and St. Benedict's Prep graduate, was in Morristown when the riots hit his city. On July 13, 1967, when he drove the twenty-five miles to Newark in his Volkswagen Beetle to survey the situation, he had been abbot of St. Mary's Abbey for less than a year. After checking in with the monks, he decided to go for a mid-afternoon walk. A block or so away from the monastery and school he came upon three men leaning over the engine of a broken-down car. It was not far from the longtime Burne homestead on High Street, where generations of his family had made their way in the United States. One of the men looked up at the black-cassocked priest walking by and abruptly said, "Go home, white priest, go home." The abbot's initial reaction was to say, "I am home." But he uttered not a word. Instead, he put his head down and walked back to the abbey.[3]

The watershed event in Newark's recent history was six days of looting and rioting, death and destruction, some of it just outside St. Benedict's Prep's doors. At the time, a local attorney called the riots "a natural disaster." For others, including the monks looking down from Tin Beach, fire seemed to be a lasting image. Philip Roth lamented in his novel *American Pastoral* about post-riot Newark, "The fire this time—and next? After the fire? Nothing. Nothing in Newark ever again." "After the fires died, many say, the city did too, and as families fled Newark, they found good schools elsewhere to which to send their sons," observed a *New York Times* reporter. Yet Abbot Martin could not come to accept it. When he addressed students and faculty at a school-wide mass in St. Mary's Church, he asked each person present to lift their spirits. In a church that stood on the ashes of the one ransacked in the 1854 nativist riot, the former high school thespian implored his audience, "Play the part, be the man, be brave and steadfast. The Lord is by your side. Soon St. Benedict's will be one hundred years old. Are we to look back upon the hundred years while the school dies?"[4]

Abbot Martin Burne was an optimist, believing the very best about his city and the people who lived, worked, and went to school in it. But the recovery from the trauma of the Newark riots was too daunting, and St. Benedict's Prep closed for good in 1972. Sadly, one of the state's leading Catholic schools had shuttered its doors, an all-too-common tale for such institutions in the late 1960s and 1970s. In 1968, in the wake of the riots, Abbot Martin pushed the men in Newark to secure their independence for a second time. While Burne remained in Morristown, Newark Abbey elected Ambrose J. Clark as its first abbot, and he too believed in updating the mission of both the monastery and the school. But others did not, and the new abbey became mired in an internecine struggle for its very soul. Ultimately, in terms of St. Benedict's Prep, two sets of monks saw the times in diametrically opposed ways, bringing the conflict over whether a monastery-school could survive in the middle of a modern city to a divisive conclusion. In order to appreciate the most recent juncture in this century-long saga, one has to turn to six days in the middle of July 1967.

"A Pot on the Stove"

During Newark's summer of discontent, one hundred other cities across the nation also erupted in racial violence. Newark's turn came on July 12 when two Newark police officers pulled John Smith over for recklessly swerving around their parked cruiser. Smith, a cabbie for the Safety Cab Company, was driving while on the "revoked" list that fateful hot, humid night, but this did not warrant what was to happen next. A beating at the hands of two policemen sparked days of rioting that would take the city and its people decades to recover from, physically and economically as well as spiritually and psychologically. The wounds were deep and wide in what many called the worst city in the United States.

Like many American cities, Newark had suffered from decades of neglect and maltreatment. In particular, substandard housing, unsanitary living conditions, high unemployment, poor educational facilities, and insufficient social services made life in the city often overwhelmingly difficult. The United States, by virtue of the way its black and white populations lived, was a divided country, and as early as 1959 the U.S. Civil Rights Commission warned "against the division of society into Two Cities."[5] Two days after the rioting in Newark subsided,

Charles H. Percy appeared before a Senate committee and testified that city slums had become the "shame of our nation." The senator from Illinois went on to declare, "Urban America cannot survive half afflu-ent and half destitute. Metropolitan America cannot progress divided as ghetto black and suburb white."[6] In 1968, President Lyndon B. John-son's National Advisory Commission on Civil Disorders concluded that the house was in the process of dividing: "Our nation is moving toward two societies, one black, one white—separate and unequal."[7]

The glaring disparities between city and suburb were obvious for all to see, but perhaps what was even more telling was the contrast between Newark and other major American cities. By 1967, Newark was considered one of the worst places to live in the United States. Many residents, especially those living in the South and Central wards, had long complained about the lack of job opportunities, substandard housing, poor police-community relations, and failing schools. The lit-any of ills was staggering. Newarkers faced the highest percentage of inadequate housing, the highest crime rate, the most burdensome per capita tax rate, the most dramatic demographic shifts, and the highest rates of venereal disease, tuberculosis, and maternal mortality in the nation. Further, the city ranked second in population density, infant mortality, and birth rate. The absolute number of drug addicts residing in the city cracked the national top ten, and the unemployment rate ranked in the top five. Moreover, in 1967, 32 percent of families living in "ghetto" areas had incomes at or below the national poverty level of three thousand dollars, and fully half earned less than five thousand dollars annually.[8]

Paltry incomes resulted in substandard housing for most of New-ark's minority population. Three-quarters of the city's housing stock was in "old or rapidly aging frame structures," and more than 8 percent of the available housing was forty or more years old and "showing signs of substantial deterioration." Despite the prevalence of dilapi-dated housing throughout the city, Newark had been aggressively pur-suing public housing and urban renewal through government grants. Public housing afforded poor families a chance to move out of slum housing and into new housing projects at reasonable rents, and ini-tially many families were satisfied with their new surroundings. But by the mid-1960s residents observed that their apartments were the least likely to be properly maintained and policed. Charles Tuller, a caseworker for the Newark–Essex County Welfare Board, testified before a state civil rights commission that "city housing stinks." He added, "Whoever designed these forts must have had a prison in mind because they look like prisons. They were almost scientifically designed to make people feel like cattle."[9] "In the Central Ward, perhaps the worst ghetto in the East," observed reporter Fred Cook, "decent black families live as virtual prisoners in housing authority projects, afraid to let their children outside even to play."[10]

The city's schools were in no better shape. All of Newark's seventy-five public school buildings were more than fifty years old, and over half of them were built before 1900. Overcrowding, large student turnover, and high dropout rates were constant problems too. Test results indicated that Newark's minority schoolchildren were over a year behind their white counterparts in the city, not to mention middle-class children residing in the suburbs. Perhaps most troublesome was that many children came from "a home environment lacking in stability, in social, cultural and economic opportunities, frequently without a father at home and a mother away at work. These children carry complex and extensive needs into classrooms already overcrowded and inadequate." Like their neighborhoods, schools turned from white to black; for example, the formerly all-white high school in the predominantly Jewish Weequahic section went from 19 percent African American enrollment in 1961, to 70 percent in 1966, to more than 80 percent in 1968. It happened so quickly that the Board of Education could not update textbooks in time either. In a history class, a black youngster read the following from the class text: "The people of Africa are not white like we are."[11]

Politically, the African American community was still largely disenfranchised. By the time Mayor Hugh Addonizio, a 1949 St. Benedict's Prep graduate, took office in 1962, Newark had been desegregated for nearly two decades. According to a 1957 report on race relations in the city, "A quiet, bloodless revolution has altered the status of these minority groups. Newark's public record in establishing and protecting civil rights of all groups is exceptionally fine even among northern cities." As Addonizio proudly pointed to his city's civil rights record, southern rights activists mobilized around the strength of Martin Luther King's nonviolent leadership, and a ten-year battle for racial justice utilizing the tactics of the sit-ins, teach-ins, and freedom rides culminated in President Johnson signing the Civil Rights Act of 1964. Donald Malafronte, the mayor's administrative assistant, proclaimed that "Newark was not a red hot civil rights town," and while this might have been accurate for the early 1960s, it was not true for the years between 1965 and 1967, when the city's African American community became increasingly politicized. Dr. King sought to bring the battle for racial justice to northern cities, and after visiting in April 1967, he called Newark and several other cities "powder kegs." King predicted that the city could "explode in racial violence this summer."[12]

Monsignor Thomas Carey of Queen of Angels Church, an African American Catholic parish, testified before a civil rights commission in June 1966 that the variety of problems in the Central Ward could eventually "boil over." "We have a pot on the stove and it is cooking and we are all apprehensive about things that might happen," he said. Whatever the image—tinderbox, powder keg, or boiling pot—others predicted that Newark would not be spared violence either, especially after a series of events fostered a growing sense of both frustration and self-determination in the city's African American community. Police-community relations hit an all-time low in 1965, as black residents viewed the Newark Police Department as "the single continuously lawless element operating in the community." The following year Kenneth Gibson, an African American engineer, ran for mayor and lost, but not before he forced a runoff against Addonizio.[13]

The debate over the construction of a medical school in the city's Central Ward and the struggle over the appointment of an African American candidate to the Board of Education further radicalized the community in the months leading up to July 1967. The Addonizio administration enticed the University of Medicine and Dentistry to relocate from suburban Madison to Newark. Not only would the school bring new jobs, it would dramatically improve Newark's inadequate health care system. City hall met the medical school's demands of providing a large parcel of land, offering more than 150 acres of urban renewal land in the Central Ward, a good portion of which needed to be condemned and displaced citizens relocated. In order to speedily close the deal, city officials failed to consult the African American community; it was a classic case of "urban renewal" as "Negro removal."[14]

The second controversy came quickly on the heels of the medical school debacle. A more qualified African American candidate was looked over for a Board of Education appointment, in favor of a less qualified but politically connected white candidate. Fred Means, acting president of the Negro Educators of Newark, observed, "The Negro community is in turmoil over this injustice. If immediate steps are not taken, Newark might become another Watts." Harry Wheeler, a Newark teacher, emphatically stated that the decision was "going to be the catalyst for blood running in the streets of Newark like there has never been anywhere else in America." Unfortunately, Newark was ready to riot.[15]

It began with a routine traffic stop on Wednesday night, July 12, 1967. After arresting John Smith, the two arresting officers, Vito Pontrelli and Oscar De Simone, brought him to the Fourth Precinct. Once there, the Italian American policemen forcibly dragged Smith, an African American cab driver, out of the police car and up the steps of the building. Word spread quickly through the Hayes Homes, a high-rise housing project directly across the street from the precinct, and soon rumors of Smith's death circulated through the neighborhood. One resident called Robert Curvin of the Congress of Racial Equality (CORE) and within two hours community leaders demanded to see Smith to assess his condition. They also organized "a peaceful but angry demonstration" against police brutality. Smith had suffered head injuries as well as broken ribs. As the night wore on, tension mounted and some young men turned to hurling bricks and bottles. By midnight Molotov cocktails struck the Fourth Precinct's western wall, prompting Inspector Kenneth C. Melchoir to send out officers in riot gear. The crowd dispersed and though some looting took place, most of it targeted against price-gouging merchants, the scene had quieted down by early morning. As the new day dawned, Mayor Addonizio claimed that the previous night's incidents were "isolated instances."[16]

Thursday began with unwarranted optimism that the violence had come and gone. By late afternoon modest crowds gathered in front of camera crews sent from New York City's various newsrooms to capture a riot in progress. As if playing their part in a twisted tragedy, some African American residents in the Central Ward appeared on screen to be more jubilant than angry. Others had become quite destructive, smashing windows and looting stores. There had been no reports of gunfire, but as the riots entered their third day two notable shifts took place. First, "sporadic shooting" had been reported by city police; second, the riots had spread beyond the "contained area," south to Bergen Street and Clinton Avenue and west to Springfield Avenue, one of the city's main arteries, which originated right outside St. Benedict's Prep's front door.

Sensing that things had gotten out of control by early Friday, Mayor Addonizio called Governor Richard T. Hughes at 2:20 A.M. and requested the help of the State Police and the National Guard. The governor appeared on the scene at 5:00 A.M., and after touring various sections of the city he commented: "The thing that repels me is the holiday atmosphere I saw with my own eyes. It's like laughing at your own funeral." Upon arriving in Newark, Colonel David B. Kelly, superintendent of the New Jersey State Police, interviewed Mayor Addonizio to gather information in order to assess the situation in the city. According to Colonel Kelly, a despondent Addonizio simply replied, "It is all gone, the whole town is gone."[17]

In effect, the riots can be divided into two halves. The first half consisted of mainly young African American men vandalizing property and looting stores on Wednesday night and Thursday night, exactly what the monks witnessed from the school's roofline and Bernie Greene saw in his various forays into the neighborhood. The second half, from Friday through Sunday, was characterized by the indiscriminate gunfire of the police and the National Guard on the mostly unarmed African American community. "Trigger-happy guardsmen," who were overwhelmingly white, young, and inexperienced, expended more than ten thousand rounds of ammunition over the course of three days. The State Police unloaded nearly five thousand rounds. Twenty-six people died during the riots, all but two during the three days when the National Guard and the State Police occupied Newark. Assessing the role of law enforcement, one official report found that "the amount of ammunition expended by police forces was out of proportion to the mission assigned to them."[18]

The State Police and National Guard began leaving the city on Monday, officially signaling the end of the Newark riots. By Tuesday, most businesses opened again and the city was left to count its dead and assess the damage. Governor Hughes impaneled a committee to study the riots, headed by Alfred E. Driscoll, president of New Jersey Bell Telephone Company. Driscoll and his colleagues, including a young lawyer and graduate of St. Benedict's, John J. Gibbons, produced *Report for Action*, a no-nonsense, honest appraisal of the riots and their root causes. The report spared few from criticism.

During the course of the riots twenty-six people died, more than 1,500 were wounded, and at least 1,600 were arrested. More than one thousand stores and businesses were destroyed and there was over ten million dollars in reported losses. The report stated that "there is a clear and present danger to the very existence of our cities," and it placed the burden of responsibility on those in positions of leadership and power in the community. More specifically, it called for city educators to act swiftly to address the system's educational problems, and for suburban residents to understand that their future was "inextricably linked to the fate of the city."[19] It could be argued that the nadir of Newark's long history was July 17, 1967, the day it was left alone to ponder the future. "Newark had hit bottom," concluded the historian John Cunningham. "If it ever could rebuild, its new foundations would forever rest on the ashes of July 1967."[20]

During the riots St. Mary's Priory and St. Benedict's Prep lay mostly empty and quiet along the northeast border of the cordoned riot area. It was summer vacation, and aside from the renowned summer theater program, there were few students or visitors to the school in July. The monastery remained a contemplative community literally on the edge of open rebellion. National Guardsmen and local police authorities patrolled a checkpoint on the corner of William and High streets, and some Guardsmen sought respite in the abbey's vestibule and the school's gymnasium. Aside from a stray bullet that crashed through a window, the monastery, church, and school were untouched while other "white-owned" businesses in the city were destroyed. Father Theodore credited it to the school's increased involvement with the African American community, saying, "The black community said we were trying to do some of the things that needed to be done." Bernie Greene was a bit more practical, saying years later, "The rioters didn't steal anything because there wasn't anything to take." Yet he, as well as other African American males, would soon enter the school as students, looking for an education and a way out of the city.[21]

"The Challenge of a Lifetime": Abbot Martin's Vision for St. Benedict's Prep

On March 21, 1968, in front of more than nine hundred alumni and friends at the Robert Treat Hotel in downtown Newark, Abbot Martin Burne strode to the podium and delivered a speech that challenged most people's view of the mission of St. Benedict's Prep. Perhaps more so than anyone else in the banquet hall that night, Abbot Martin appreciated the complexity of the circumstances that situated St. Benedict's Prep in a post-riot city and a post–Vatican II church. He cited two reports on the previous summer's civil disorders, and remarked that "not a single monk-priest or lay teacher or student can emerge from the front door of St. Benedict's without looking up and seeing spelled out for him the very guts of these two reports. A teacher at St. Benedict's today, lay or clerical, has to be either cynical or blind if he believes himself to represent human society, while ignoring the situation that is at his very doorstep."

Abbot Martin did not ignore generations of good work, though, as he praised the Benedictines for giving one hundred years of teaching to the city. But he wanted that good work to continue and he had a clear vision on how to make that happen. At one point he asked the crowd, "Which way, St. Benedict's, you ask?" He replied, "Toward a deeper involvement in the society of which it is a part, toward an

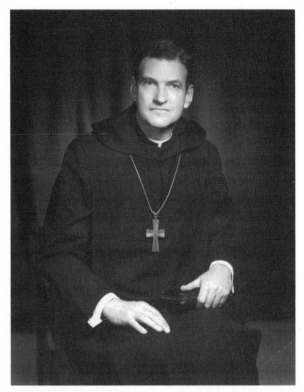

Abbot Martin J. Burne, OSB, a Newark native and St. Benedict's graduate, became abbot in 1966. He helped the Newark monastery achieve its independence for the second time in 1968.

increased endeavor to help parents in the education of their sons." The abbot went on to add:

Can we, the Faculty at St. Benedict's, begin to shape somewhat the situation at our doorsteps, by offering each year a college prep education to youngsters from the ghetto who need that type of education and who can well qualify for it? Or shall we turn our faces away from our front door, and pretend to the world around us that one really need not attend to his neighbor? The words of Christ are pure fiction!

I propose to the business Community of Newark, to the industry of Newark, to interested private citizens of Newark and its suburbs, the challenge
of a lifetime. I challenge a society that talks a great deal about helping the
underprivileged to let St. Benedict's do just that.[22]

Abbot Martin's speech was met with mixed emotions. Some praised
him for his own version of aggiornamento, his vision for updating St.
Benedict's Prep, while others, not unlike those who detested all the
new changes in the church, were resistant to change of any sort. One
alumnus's ambivalence became apparent when he approached the
abbot at the end of the evening and said, "That's okay, Abbot, but don't
forget about us."[23] Back in the monastery a monk was overheard saying, "He just doomed the school." While some monks believed in
Abbot Martin's vision for St. Benedict's, others came to blame him for
the troubles of the Newark monastery.[24]

Abbot Martin's vision for the future was completely out of touch
with the current reality of St. Benedict's. Only eight students walking
the halls that year were African American. Perhaps more alarming
than the minuscule number of African Americans students in the
school was the growing number of white students leaving St. Benedict's. Fifty-six young men transferred out of the school in the weeks
just after the riots.[25] Over the next two years, white students from the
suburbs often decided not to apply, or not to come when admitted.
The relatively new diocesan school system, often involving sprawling
suburban campuses, now posed a real threat to the tradition-laden center-city Catholic schools throughout the country. Benedict's suffered
more than most as a result of the riots, and the size of incoming freshman classes attest to this, as only 187 entered the school in the fall of
1967 compared to 214 in 1966. That number dropped to 148 in 1968,
109 in 1969, 123 in 1970, and 115 in 1971. All the while, the African
American and Latino population in the school grew incrementally.

When word spread of Martin Luther King's assassination in Mem-
phis on April 4, 1968, people in Newark feared another large-scale riot.
Several monks watched fires burn along Bergen Street from their perch
on Tin Beach, and others patrolled the halls of the school throughout
the night to insure that vandals did not start any fires. Isolated looting

and destruction of property turned to prayer and reflection as St. Mary's Church hosted a vigil for the fallen civil rights leader. The two youngest monks in the monastery, Philip Waters and Edwin Leahy, spent a few nights at Queen of Angel's Church with Monsignor Thomas Carey and Father Bill Linder. Together they planned a prayer service and a "March for Understanding," which "proceeded with dignity and camaraderie and elaborate courtesy." There was "pin-drop silence over the sea of human faces as the bells of St. Mary's on High Street slowly tolled 39 times to mark the years of Rev. Martin Luther King, Jr.'s life."[26]

In the wake of King's death, the monks in Newark waded into a long, tedious summer of discussion and reflection. Freewheeling talks proceeded, with topics ranging from how the school was perceived by whites and blacks, to discussions of an integrated society and the role of the monastic community in a rapidly changing church and city. One monk bluntly asked, "Do we have a right to stay here? Newark is going black. Will we be wanted by the black community?" Another responded, "Many of us feel we are not racist, yet we hear that much of white America is racist. Each of us must examine himself and discover whether or not the word applies to him. If we are racist, are we willing to try and overcome our racism?" Still another monk commented, "Our very presence in the black community is resented, but men in our position must be courageous, whatever the consequences. . . . We must listen, however, to the black man if we want to know what we must do. . . . We have something to offer others, and our remaining here gives us a chance to offer that."[27]

Most of the monks had little or no experience interacting with their neighbors. St. Mary's School had a large African American enrollment, but most of the monks had little to do with the grammar school. Even though a handful of extremely talented African American students more than "made the grade" at Benedict's, entrenched stereotypes of African American intellectual inferiority and criminality circulated in the monastery just as they did the rest of white society. Many monks actually felt under attack. "I don't think we knew just how deep things had gone in Newark until the riots," observed one monk. "And then when you saw the city go up in smoke and watched everything change, you realized that we were in a place under siege." Such a "fortress mentality" was not uncommon in the urban Catholic compounds of the era, but a paradigm shift was in order if the monastic community and its school stood any chance of relevancy. "We could no longer build this white enclave in the middle of the city and let a few bright black guys in," reflected Father Philip Waters.[28]

After much discussion the monks decided to adopt the following proposition: "The Benedictines of Newark believe that as one aspect of our continuing to establish a Christian Community here we must strive for the integration of society. This integration should be sought through well-planned, positive action in our prep school, parish, parish school and monastery." In addition, an invitation was sent to "Negro spokesmen" for a "suggested confrontation" in early August. It read:

We are a private school taught by a group of men who receive no outside funds—live on tuition. We are losing and have lost some of our students due to our location. As Christians we choose to stay, and we will stay. We want to extend ourselves toward the Negro Community with our brand of education. Education is our thing. Would you come in and help us by discussing our problem with us. Show us, if you can, how we can most effectively help. We feel that we do some things much better than other schools.

Another important factor was that Newark was many a monk's hometown. Someone in the monastic community once asked Father Theodore, "What do you want to stay in Newark for?" The Newark native, who grew up in the Clinton Hill section and attended Blessed Sacrament School before enrolling at Benedict's, responded, "Look, I was born in this city, and everybody can't leave it. Someone's got to stay. We started here and we can finish here." The end-of-year financial report, which did indicate that the monastery and school were still profitable, included the following statement to alumni and friends: "Others may talk of moving or closing their schools if they are afraid of the future. At Benedict's we propose to shape the future rather than be shaken by it."[29]

Monsignor Thomas Carey introduced the invited guests that Friday evening in August, and the first to address the monks was Bill Payne, a native Newarker and an assistant manager of public relations at Prudential. Payne began his opening remarks by divulging he had "snuck in" to the school the previous year to see a play because St. Benedict's had a "mysterious" quality about it. The same view of Benedict's was true for the African American community at large, as Payne explained: "They don't know what you have to offer, and it's kind of a mysterious thing. It always has had a good name scholastically and I think a lot of people just felt that you have to be, first of all, Catholic to get in, and, secondly, you had to be somebody really special and selected." Payne wanted to know if the school was targeting only middle-class African Americans. The monks assured him that they wanted to reach out to poor and deserving students from the neighborhoods just outside the school's front doors.

Barry Washington, a graduate of Queen of Angel's Grammar School and a current student at Catholic University, advised the monks to contact the guidance counselors in the grammar schools and explain that the school was actively seeking young men from the surrounding neighborhoods. Washington, a star football player while at Essex Catholic, a fierce rival of Benedict's, then revealed that Benedict's was spared "complete hostility from the community" because it played city schools in sports. Washington went on to add, "It may seem small, but the school is respected because they are not scared of Black people." But he then warned the monks that there was more to it than athletic competition because he could easily call St. Benedict's a "colonial establishment": "Your students come from outside the city the same way that business people come from outside the city; they come in to the city just like plantation owners who lived away from the fields, and they come into the fields to get their education."

Monsignor Carey concluded the meeting on an inspiring and encouraging note, telling the monks gathered around the table, "If you are going to do this with all the sincerity that is within you . . . I think you can really make a mark in Newark. And I don't think you ought to worry about the financial parts of it. I think all things will come to pass, and I think the main thing is to have the courage of your convictions. Then go, and the hell with the details. It will all work out. You'll do beautifully." In fact, the monsignor had managed to make wonderful things happen at Queen of Angel's and he thought that something fantastic could happen on High Street. Carey pointed out, "Who wants to be part of a funeral? But if something is alive and happening, you will have people coming across the world to get in on what you are doing. You are alive and vibrant and exciting because you've plunged in where no one else dares to walk."[30]

Seizing the moment, Abbot Martin sent word to Abbot Baldwin Dworschak, president of the American Cassinese Congregation, that a vote on Newark's status was imminent. In his letter to the abbot-president, Burne detailed the long, tortuous history of the two houses and Abbot Patrick's desire to advance Morristown at what many perceived to be Newark's expense. "From that time forward," wrote Abbot Martin, "men living in Newark suffered bitterly. Some wanted the place to shut down, others wanted Newark to move to a new location, others wanted some kind of action, but did not know what." Abbot Martin pushed the issue to a vote, declaring, "If we stay together, Newark is doomed. If anyone has got misgivings about Newark, for God's sake, come to Morristown!" He believed that "a well-knit, carefully organized Community approach [could] see Newark—as an independent Abbey —continue far into the decades ahead."[31]

The moment of decision came on October 14, 1968, and almost anticlimactically the community voted for Newark's long overdue independence. Abbot Martin petitioned the Vatican to allow the monastery to become an abbey for the second time in its history, and on December 14, 1968, the newly dubbed Newark Abbey elected Ambrose James Clark its first abbot.[32]

The Double Split: Newark Abbey, 1968 and 1972

The monks had every reason to celebrate the founding of Newark Abbey, the culmination of a long battle to reclaim its identity as an abbey. Deliberately choosing to put Newark in the new title, the monks saw it as "a reaffirmation on [their] part to stay with the city, to remain a part of it, to help lead it to a newness that will make its very name mean something again." Their decision to stay in Newark, and their willingness to readily identify with the city, ran counter to decisions made by many individuals, schools, and businesses after the riots. Many monks gathered in the monastery to celebrate "the separation" well into the night, toasting both the boldness and fortune of the new abbey. Father Bruno Ugliano recalled, "I had two cases of champagne in my room, and we had trouble getting to class the following morning." The euphoria did not last long, though, as Newark Abbey began to examine St. Benedict's Prep even more closely; after the election of Abbot Ambrose it became clear that the issue of the school, and just beneath that the issue of race, split the community in two. The divide was so wide, and disagreement so deep, that the monastic family became virtually "dysfunctional" by 1971. A year later St. Benedict's Prep closed.[33]

Separation made imminent sense in 1968, especially since one monastery was located in a troubled city and the other was situated in one of the richest per capita counties in the entire country. Their respective missions differed, and a monk chose either monastery according to his preference. Among the forty or so monks who identified with Newark, a range of motivations existed to stay in the city. Some wanted to remain in Newark because it was their home and they loved and believed in St. Benedict's. Others loved Benedict's and could not see themselves anywhere else, but they questioned the stability of the whole operation. Still others might have wanted to go to Morristown because it was a more secure situation, but they could not because they still harbored resentment over what they saw as Morristown's advancement at Newark's expense. Thus an assortment of monks made up the new monastery, confirming Alfred H. Deutsch's views on communal living: "One might think that a life patterned after a definite rule would produce one single kind of monk, one line of thought, one attitude toward life. Some disillusionment stems from the discovery that vows do not destroy personality and individuality."[34]

A good number of the forty men who identified with Newark Abbey agreed with Abbot Ambrose when he proudly stated after his election, "The community which chose me as abbot is a community dedicated to Newark. We have deliberately decided to stay in the ghetto area and provide the spiritual and educational leadership that our years of experience allow." The monks continued to seek advice from people outside the monastic community, and they found that no one suggested "any major upheaval." "Do not go all black, nor stay all white," they said. "Make St. Benedict's a center of understanding, a place where the dignity of the individual—not his color or creed—is what counts." The local press lauded the decision to commit to Newark too. One reporter admitted that it was not going to be an "easy job" because "cities are in turmoil; private schools are in great financial troubles; education is searching out new paths." But he predicted the following: "We can confidently expect great things of St. Benedict's Prep. We envision one of the most exciting prep schools in the East showing the way to all other schools around them."[35]

Behind the vision of what St. Benedict's could become were grim realities suggesting that the school had to fight for its very survival. First, the men of Newark Abbey had to become acclimated to one another and learn how to pray and work together. By the spring of 1969, though, one monk became concerned about a "polarization" between young and old monks, in particular over their ideas of how the school operated. Second, the number of applications to St. Benedict's Prep had decreased dramatically by 1969, resulting in a freshman class at the beginning of the 1969–70 school year of only 109, compared to entering classes of more than 200 before the riots. In light of the decreasing enrollment, Father Jerome Fitzpatrick, the new headmaster (Father Laurence served in the post for only a year), questioned whether the school should modify its admissions policies and accept students even if they could not handle the school's college prep curriculum. Third, at a meeting in late April, Abbot Ambrose reported for the first time that the school was in serious financial trouble in large part because of a declining neighborhood, rising tuition, a drop in enrollment, and a general move away from Catholic education.[36]

St. Benedict's Prep was not the only Catholic school facing such a predicament, and beginning in the late 1960s and early 1970s many inner-city Catholic grammar and high schools began to close at alarming rates. A newspaper article titled "The Plight of Jersey's Catholic Schools" detailed the story of one high school in Elizabeth that had to close because its largely Irish constituency had left the city. The principal coldly reported that the "reality for Catholic education at the parish level can be found through a simple equation. If the parishioners leave the neighborhood, and if the new residents are poor or are not Catholics, then there is little money available for the support of education." The network of Catholic schools throughout the country had been built on the backs of religious men and women, especially nuns, but after Vatican II they left religious life in record numbers. The main economic factor for St. Benedict's Prep was the declining student population, and for the first time in decades the monks ran the school at a loss. As Abbot Ambrose faced a modest twenty-thousand-dollar deficit for the 1969–70 fiscal year, and a projected deficit of thirty-two thousand dollars for the following year, he declared, "Gentleman, we are going out of business, if we continue this way!"[37]

The abbot continued to encourage his fellow monks throughout the spring of 1969, saying, "We're being put to a test. It's what we do now, in the next year, in the next three years that's going to count." Father Jerome became increasingly disillusioned and even charged some fellow monks with undermining the school administration, claiming in a written statement, "Unwarranted and irresponsible criticism, griping, questionable example, pot-shotting [sic] at the administration and faculty, encouraging students to defy rules or regulations; these things are going on and rest squarely on the shoulders of some of the members of our monastic community." He went on to condemn the "divisiveness and privatism which exists within our monastic faculty." Seven monks responded that evening in a prepared statement, suggesting that "a total restructuring of the administration of the school [was] needed in order to survive as a 1970s prep school." Father Jerome confessed that he had lost many of his friends since he became headmaster, and Father Boniface bluntly added, "It seems we crucify every man who has this job." A few months later, Abbot Ambrose read a melancholic statement lamenting his own lack of "inspirational leadership." "We seem to have run somewhat short of spirit, of élan," the abbot observed. "A good many of us seem tired, even discouraged."[38]

Interestingly, the school newspaper hailed the 1960s as "the most progressive years in the school's history," in large part because of the formation of a new abbey and the promise of urban renewal plans to be completed by 1975. In addition, the school had discarded "obsolete traditions," revised the old dress code, and dropped the mandatory Latin requirement. Further still, for the first time in its long history St. Benedict's formed a student council and hired female teachers. Some faculty members agreed with the students' assessment, as they too saw the 1960s as a decade of both progress and potential. When Paul Thornton returned to teach English at St. Benedict's after graduating from Harvard in 1967, he saw a school in the process of racial transition. Thornton recalled that he had "a very hopeful view of the way the school was going in the late 1960s in part because of the solid history of the school being where it [was] and having successfully absorbed successive generations from different ethnic groups."[39]

Some believed the school was making an honest effort at integration, as the administration supported an Inner City Scholarship Fund to pay for the education of talented minority students from Newark. In fact, the minority student population doubled every year from 1968 onward, and by 1972 eighty-five African Americans joined over four hundred white students at the school. A handful of Latino students enrolled too. For Father Benedict, the arrival of African American students at St. Benedict's made complete sense: "We had to provide an education for the people who were in Newark, and there were more and more black people here, and we knew that some of them were very much desirous of having this sort of education and eventually going on to college. Also, we wanted to get black kids to mix with white kids."[40]

Steven Walker, one of nine African Americans to enter St. Benedict's in 1968, always felt that race relations at the school were good. But he believed they improved over the course of his four years, especially as students bonded over shared experiences in classrooms, in locker rooms, and on athletic teams. Hank Cordeiro, a resident of the heavily Portuguese and Spanish enclave in Newark's Ironbound section, concurred: "Race was never an issue. The Class of 1972 was an equal opportunity class because we had brilliant guys who were white and black and we had idiots who were white and black. It didn't matter and there was never any tension." But in 1969 Father Albert spoke at a student assembly and said, "The same issues of racial relations that divide our nation, the same questions perhaps that disturb our neighborhoods, are now beginning to follow us to school." He posed serious questions to the students gathered, who then split into to smaller groups to discuss racial issues at the school.[41]

Some white students, for example, wondered why African American students often stuck together, in particular at several cafeteria tables during lunchtime. Steven Walker told some of them, "It's just a natural thing to sit and talk among ourselves because we have things in common. And until we have something in common with you, it's natural to sit by ourselves." Walker also revealed that African American students "didn't come to St. Benedict's on a mission to meet white students; we came here to go to school." Academically, almost all of Walker's African American classmates finished in the top half of the class, and most made notable contributions to student life. They went on to some of the best colleges in the country and later embarked on successful professional careers.[42]

For the most part, students from both races appeared to get along rather well in school, but local and national tensions did make for some interesting exchanges and result in some misunderstandings. For example, Amiri Baraka, a noted poet and black nationalist, established the headquarters of his bookstore/community center next door to St. Benedict's. Students commuting in from the suburbs had to walk by the front entrance of the Committee for Unified Newark, or CFUN, on a daily basis. "Members of Baraka's group were always outside," recalled a student. "There was always a couple 'brothers' just standing there looking intimidating. They never said anything to the students, but they were always there and it was a very tumultuous time in Newark in terms of race relations." Baraka often faced off against Anthony Imperiale, a race-baiting vigilante and politician from the North Ward, and in one particular episode Imperiale chained himself to a fence for days to block the construction of a low-income housing project sponsored by Baraka. It was theater for a polarized community, and one local leader observed, "Every day, [Imperiale] and Baraka would put on a show for the cameras."[43]

Racial tensions were at all-time highs in Newark after 1967, especially as African Americans and Italian Americans vied for power in a
post-riot city. The historian Clement A. Price has called the power contest between the two groups "Newark's fratricidal war." "The poison
of racial hatred really spewed from 1968 until 1972," observed one
resident of the North Ward. St. Benedict's alumnus Mayor Hugh Addonizio had been replaced by Newark's first black mayor, Ken Gibson,
and that power shift, argued journalist David K. Shipler, was "like step-
ping into a hall of mirrors where familiar images are inverted and
twisted into remarkable, confusing shapes that destroy any sense of
equilibrium. The familiar American patterns of racism and exploitation dissolve into a mad array of reversals and contradictions." Stephen
N. Adubato, a young leader in the Italian American stronghold, elaborated, saying at the time, "We're the niggers now, that's what happened. It's just who's on top. The group that's second's gonna catch
shit—they're gonna be niggers. This is what this country is really
about."[44] The effects of racial and ethnic transition, from the city's
neighborhoods to the corridors of city hall, also refracted on the St.
Benedict's situation, especially as more African Americans enrolled in
the school from the city's toughest neighborhoods.

In the summer after the riots, the two youngest monks, Philip Waters and Edwin Leahy, caught a handful of African Americans teens
breaking into Casino Hall, a decrepit old building across the street
from the school. They wanted to play basketball. Instead of shooing
them away, or even calling the police, Waters told them, "If you want
to play basketball, ring the doorbell and ask for me. I'll let you in."
Both monks formed an informal summer basketball league for boys in
the neighborhood, and as they got to know them they encouraged
them to apply to the school. When the Black Student Union sponsored
parties at the school, dubbed "Soulful Experiences," the young monks
found themselves there chaperoning. Affectionately called "Bro Ed" at
the time, Leahy recalled, "A lot of people were afraid of these kids.
Somehow Phil and I were 'in' with them."[45]

As the minority student population increased in the early 1970s,
there was a push to admit more than just a handful of academically
prepared African American students. In particular, Father Benedict
wanted disadvantaged students from nearby neighborhoods to attend

Abbot Ambrose Clark, the first abbot of the new Newark Abbey, pictured on "The Stoop" with members of the St. Benedict's Prep Black Student Union, 1968.

the school. As more students with poor academic backgrounds were admitted, a "standards debate" further divided members of the monastic community. No one except the blatantly racist took exception to the poor but high-achieving African American students. According to Father Albert Holtz, those types of students "bought what we were selling" and did not force faculty members to adjust much to accommodate them. "The problem for the faculty was much more the kids who didn't speak like us, didn't think like us, and sure didn't look like us. That's where some people got the shivers," he said. In the process, the strict and demanding entrance requirements were revised for some "so that the school wouldn't have to change its exit standards even if it changed its entrance standards."[46]

While some saw this as a more than reasonable approach at the time, others saw it as a blatant "watering down" of the school's curriculum. For these observers, it also proved the existence of two sets of standards: one for the white students and those minority students who could function in a prep school, and the other for educationally disadvantaged students who could not handle a college prep course of study. "We began taking people in who needed remediation," remembered Father Bruno, who was promoted to assistant headmaster in 1971, "and we didn't have a remedial program." St. Benedict's always educated "feisty kids with rough edges," but when students entered who had been "cheated on basic education, it's a different thing altogether. You could have two kids—black and white—and you would write your ordinary essay and get a B—; the other kid may write something substandard in Black English and get an A. Where's the justice? We had two standards."[47] Father Albert, then dean of studies, defended the use of a "different ruler": "If a way to keep St. Benedict's from taking black kids was to only take kids for whom we could predict A's, then that would've been a perfect way to keep the school white. So given that context, was it a disservice to bring a kid in and have a double standard?"[48]

Throughout the standards debate it became obvious that individual monks saw the same situation in diametrically opposed ways, and often differing racial attitudes among them contributed to another type of "fratricidal war." Philosophies differed, and where one man saw a "double standard," another saw a redress of past wrongs. Father Edwin Leahy quickly became attuned to the contrasting opinions of some of his fellow monks. From his point of view, talk of "standards" and "professionalism" reeked of discrimination and racism:

Overlaying the numbers problem was a tremendous concern for the changing face of the school. So the declining numbers are working on people's psyches in one way, and this increase of African American kids was working on it in another way. So as the numbers went down and "they" went up, the question came up of professionalism, which is camouflage in my judgment of what people don't want to say. None of those questions came up when the school went from being Irish to Italian, nobody was screaming about professionalism then. I remember hearing that word a million times, and saying to myself that that word is going to bury us. I have no idea what it meant, but I think I know what it meant, people couldn't say that they didn't want to deal with, or were afraid of, African American kids.[49]

Headmaster Father Jerome had found evidence that the school was "moving backward" in a lukewarm report submitted to the school administration by the Middle States Association in 1970. According to the report, the monastic teaching staff was at less than full strength and fewer students were being recognized through the National Merit Scholarship Program. Some colleges even reported back that the caliber of student coming out of St. Benedict's was not what it once was. The beleaguered Father Jerome resigned as headmaster in 1971, and he went out questioning whether St. Benedict's could even be considered a prep school anymore.[50]

At a February 17, 1971, meeting Abbot Ambrose discussed the financial crisis facing the new abbey. The school had not provided enough income for two consecutive years and the treasurer projected a loss of $87,800 for the current fiscal year. Most monks were stunned by the financial situation and astounded when they were asked to consider closing the school and moving it and the monastery out of the city. But Abbot Ambrose concluded the downbeat meeting with a question: "Should all of this go on if it is at all possible?" Father Bruno, who had become the mouthpiece for those who wanted to close the school, could not see the school continuing. The opinionated and outspoken monk had once proclaimed, "St. Benedict's will close over my dead body," but he now found himself admitting, "I must say in all honesty that I cannot see us doing anything in the present situation but closing. . . . We have been doing a good job, let's close with our heads high over that fact."[51]

Several monks countered the doomsayers. Fathers Boniface and Benedict, two staunch supporters of the school, disagreed with those who saw the financial problems as insurmountable. Father Boniface did not even recommend a tuition hike or substantial cuts; instead he asked that the school just economize, while Father Benedict argued that by choosing to close the school at this point the monastic community would place itself in a "bad predicament," since he did not see other viable options for supporting themselves. He told his fellow monks that he had an "intuition" that the school did have a "market value" and that "it will rebound in a year or two." After a few rounds of voting a few weeks later, Abbot Ambrose reported that "the split was a very honest one; two sets of people read the signs of the times differently on one thing: St. Benedict's Prep." He also maintained that a school was "a kind of work that requires a measure of unanimity," but in the next breath admitted, "There is simply too much pluralism among us to run St. Benedict's Prep."[52]

A most worrisome factor was the decline in total school enrollment below five hundred students for the first time since 1921. According to an admissions report, the number of students expressing interest in St. Benedict's on the archdiocesan entrance exam had plummeted too. Father Bruno visited the superintendent of schools to find out the number of interested students as of January 1972: it was only 491, down from 720 the previous year.[53] That low number raised serious doubts as to whether St. Benedict's could form a freshman class of 125, and it influenced the direction of discussions on the future of the school. To make matters worse, a handful of monks informed Abbot Ambrose that they could no longer work in the school that they considered to no longer be a top-caliber "prep" school, a reality that forced him to call another vote to close the institution.

Father Albert tried to make sense of the events in his personal diary. After hearing that other monks could no longer teach in the school, he compared the abbey to Father Timothy, an old monk he was caring for in the infirmary. He wrote, "Is he a symbol of the community, outlived its ability to rule its own destiny, disoriented, scattered, wondering when death will come?" Still larger questions loomed for Father Albert:

Will the school close in June [1972] despite a 2/3rd vote 3 weeks ago to keep it open? Will the "defection" of key people make it necessary to close? What will (would) life be like in Newark Abbey if St. Benedict's didn't exist? Does anything else hold us together? Maybe we've been preparing ourselves for this in stages: the agonizing weeks of March/April [1971] a year ago, where it became plain to all very really that the school might actually cease existing. We've had a year now to get used to the idea.[54]

When Father Albert decided to teach at St. Benedict's after being ordained in 1969, a monk from Morristown asked, "Why are you going there? That place will close in two years." Hours after Father Albert made the journal entry, Abbot Ambrose made the following announcement at a chapter meeting: "It has become very clear to me that St. Benedict's must close. Desperately low enrollment, the neighborhood and increased costs are the controlling factors. For these reasons I will ask Tuesday for a vote to close."[55]

Of the three "controlling factors," some monks contested the fact that enrollment was desperately low. In prior years the school administered its own entrance examination on High Street for which over five hundred students would sit, but now the school relied on an examination administered throughout the archdiocese. Prospective students took the exam closer to their homes, but they did indicate which schools were their top three choices. School officials closely examined and analyzed how many students showed interest in St. Benedict's, especially after the riots. In 1972, several monks accused Fathers Cornelius and Bruno of doctoring, or underrepresenting, the number of students interested in St. Benedict's Prep for the 1972–73 academic year. Years later, Father Benedict revealed that he had followed up with the archdiocese in the months after the school closed. "The one determining factor was the fact that the number of applications on the diocesan exam seemed to be less. I make that point—*seemed to be less*—because somebody gave an inaccurate figure," he said. "Actually they had gone up considerably the year we closed."[56]

On Tuesday night, February 15, 1972, the members of Newark Abbey voted on the following proposition: "That St. Benedict's Prep suspend operations indefinitely (this means close) as of June, 1972." The proposal fell one vote short of the necessary two-thirds majority, but Abbot Ambrose remained determined that the school close. Almost in anticipation of the inevitable, Father Albert wrote in his journal earlier that day, "Jean Dixon the prophetess predicted the world will end today at 4:10 P.M. EST. I just finished class for the day at the Hive, and am completely numb, as if I were drugged or drunk. Tomorrow morning may well be the end of the world, and in one sense it will be the end of the world that each of us involved has lived in."[57]

The following day, Ash Wednesday, Father Cornelius had the ignominious duty of informing both the faculty and student body that after
one hundred and four years in the city, St. Benedict's Preparatory
School would close in June 1972. Standing at the front of Conlin Auditorium, he delivered the news at what students thought was an im-
promptu assembly. "It was a total shock to the system. There was just
stunned silence for what seemed like an eternity," revealed Hank Cordeiro, a senior at the time. "Everybody walked around like zombies. A
lot of monks were extremely upset. I got the sense that it was a crush-
ing blow; they were teary-eyed and so, so sad."58 Some students just sat
and cried. Jack Dalton, a history teacher and basketball coach, simply
responded, "Camelot is dead."59

A stream of telegrams and letters came across the abbot's desk; the
overwhelming majority lamented the school's closure, and most asked
what alumni and friends could do to keep St. Benedict's open. One
telegram read: "EXTREMELY DEPRESSED ABOUT ST. BENEDICT'S PLIGHT.
KINDLY RECONSIDER YOUR VERDICT. WILL DO ANYTHING POSSIBLE TO ASSIST.
HOW CAN I HELP?" Another telegram simply stated, "BENEDICT'S HATES A
QUITTER." A suburban mother wrote Abbot Ambrose in her flowing
hand, "These boys today are the same as those in the past. They need
what you've got. The fear that has clouded your enrollments will pass
but because fear is the strongest of emotions, it will [last] a lot longer."
In her three-page note, she went on to add, "In my case, it's just the
reverse. When people asked me if I was afraid to send my son down
to St. Benedict's? I'd say, 'I'm afraid not to.' Boys need the strength of
St. Benedict's."60

In response to the closing of the school, a group of monks and
laypeople became interested in opening up a new school, one for "a
small group of students and [with] a more innovative approach to education." Shrouded in secrecy, the small "rump group" invited certain
guests to meet privately in order to discuss their ideas. When some of
the other monks learned of the secret meetings concerning the new
school venture, they became indignant because they had not been con-
sulted. They requested an immediate visitation to resolve the matter.
After spending a few days at the abbey, two visiting abbots concluded

that "at present there exists a deep and serious cleavage in the community, which has surfaced in recent weeks, because of a vote to keep St. Benedict's open, the reversal of this decision shortly after, and the interest of some in a new educational venture."[61]

The monastic family was in shambles. "There are some very embittered people walking around the monastery," noted Father Albert in his journal. "It's at the point where some of the men involved in the 'school venture' will not attend conventual mass when certain men are chief celebrant, and table talk can degenerate in a twinkling into catty, bitter, sterile remarks about 'them' at the other table." At community meetings there were confrontations. "It was not really hot, but you knew where someone stood," remembered Father Theodore. "I knew who was going to be on my side and who was not." "Those were very painful meetings because if you spoke your mind you knew you were hurting other people, and not hurting them because you wanted to but because their lives were so enmeshed in Benedict's," argued Father Bruno. "Then people weren't talking to each another and eating meals together was very difficult. A lot of people just shut down."[62]

Students had no sense of the depth of the rift in the monastery, as the monks did their best to present a "unified front." Hank Cordeiro, who spent most of his waking hours at the school and came to befriend a good number of the faculty, elaborated: "I was surprised to learn that there were sides because I thought they were like the Musketeers: 'All for one, and one for all.' In one sense, I was glad that we didn't know there was dissension in the monastery. If we did, students would've taken sides too. Maybe that was their pact: 'We can't let the kids know.'" The monks also left parents in the dark, as they learned of the school's closing from their distraught sons. When parents met with Abbot Ambrose and several school administrators, they pledged to help boost enrollment and even offered additional financial support. Abbot Ambrose declined, saying that the school could not be run on charity and that it had to be a viable business operation. "We didn't have the idea of going around asking other people to help us," said Father Albert. "So many monks felt the only solution was to close the school. We had never raised money before and the prospect of doing that was sort of unseemly."[63]

Parents could not understand Abbot Ambrose's refusal and some became suspicious that other reasons lay behind the decision to close. Reluctantly, the abbot admitted that there was a difference of opinion inside the monastery. Father Albert commented in his journal that outsiders would "find two main sets of ideas and attitudes operative—almost two distinct communities." One side thought that St. Benedict's was dying a slow death and ought to be closed as soon as possible, while the other side felt that the school should go on at all costs. Perhaps the most telling moment during the tense meeting was when one impassioned mother exclaimed, "You can't close our school!" A monk replied, "It's not your school, it's our school." For some in the monastery, it had ceased being about the students and their families; it was a bitter struggle for the soul of a monastery that was no longer a community.[64]

Events in early March signaled the end of any possible reconciliation between the two factions. In the process of electing advisers to the abbot's council, monks who favored closing the school rigged the vote. "It had all apparently been arranged beforehand," observed Father Albert. "The arrangement, however, was to grab all the marbles. . . . There will be no quarter given, no real dialogue allowed to those who want to talk about a commitment to the city, to the black people around us. Power is the order of the day." The group of men in favor of a Benedictine presence in the city feared that a vote to move out of the city altogether was in the offing. They met to plot a strategy and amidst a discussion for the need to respect the other side's opinions, Father Maurice Carlton, a large and imposing monk, interrupted. He blurted out, "Hey guys, hold it a minute, we're in a street fight here. We're in a street fight and you guys are talking about charity. We've got to take out chains and bats because this is a fight."[65]

Father Theodore contended that the monks had pledged a vow of stability of place and had a moral obligation to remain and work among the people in Newark: "We don't know the people of the city—they don't know us. Our present challenge is to learn how to work with the people we have always been living with. When we voted for separation we voted to stay here and implied in that we voted to be of service to those around us in the city of Newark." Father Jerome disagreed, saying, "I don't believe that this community is capable of or wishes to or wants to work among the 'poor' of the city of Newark. If this were the case there have been ample opportunities in the past in which this desire would have been activated and shown."[66] Father Laurence was a bit more blunt when he lamented, "I think God has been good to us, that no one has been seriously injured on the street here in this rat's nest."[67]

In anticipation of a pitched battle, Father Albert scoured the chapter minutes from the last nine years and provided one citation after another in favor of serving the city. He observed that such statements made in 1963 and 1968 went unchallenged at the time. If Albert and others expected a hostile showdown, though, it never materialized. The day after the monks in Morristown heard of the closing of St. Benedict's, Abbot Leonard Casell telephoned Abbot Ambrose and offered to accept elderly and infirmed monks in the case that Newark Abbey could not incur the expense of caring for them. Two monks moved to Morristown almost immediately, and another fourteen men joined in the weeks and months ahead. Individual Newark monks informed Abbot Ambrose that they wished to leave Newark Abbey and pledge their stability to St. Mary's Abbey in Morristown, and in the years ahead it came to be called "the exodus," or "the so-called exodus." Principally, men left for Morristown because they did not see a monastic future in the city; monks, many of them graduates of St. Benedict's, felt that they could observe the monastic life more authentically at a larger, more stable monastery. In June, a moving van with "Liberty" painted on the side of it pulled up in front of the Newark monastery. Nearly one-fourth of the community packed up their belongings and headed west for Morristown.[68] It was not an easy decision to make, especially since those monks had made the bold decision to remain in the city when Newark Abbey regained its independence in 1968. Now, four years later, those same men had to swallow their pride and admit they had made a mistake.

On the surface, St. Benedict's Prep's fate was the same as that of hundreds of other Catholic schools across the country. Citing financial woes as the cause of death, these schools all suffered from the same set of symptoms, including a declining neighborhood, a general move away from Catholic education, decreasing enrollment, and a lack of vocations to the religious life. In Newark, though, certain monks felt that the community had lost its way and that this factor, above all else, led to the closing of a revered institution. "There was fear, naked, justifiable fear. The racial and social questions of that time were overwhelming, and here we sat in the middle of it all with our nineteenth-century buildings and white student body," Abbot Melvin Valvano later observed. "We answered the explosion in the area with our own agonizing and confusion, and like any divided family, we split at the seams under the pressure." The monastic family no longer agreed about the "family" business—St. Benedict's Prep—and in the process overlooked the very Benedictine traits of stability and adaptability. Father Edwin Leahy saw it as a simple loss of vision. "Here is another revered institution in that city that 'those people' killed. It ran when it was Irish; it ran when it was Italian; it ran it was German," he recalled. "Soon as it got to be black people, they buried it. So that was the possible takeaway from people that were reading the papers, which wasn't true. People lost their vision, people were afraid to be courageous and make decisions."[69]

Bob Braun, a member of the class of 1963 along with Leahy, Philip Waters, and Paul Thornton, tried to make sense of the closing of his alma mater in a moving article in the *Newark Star-Ledger*. Braun's nostalgic look back on over a century of history proved to be a fitting tribute: "For thousands of men, young and old, scattered throughout New Jersey and the nation, St. Benedict's was the shortest distance between them and friends they will never see again, the straight line to memories of adolescent pranks, adolescent romances, to what was so simple because so much is so difficult now." Throughout its history, Braun maintained, St. Benedict's had been "the poor man's prep school," an opportunity for a top-notch education at an affordable price.[70] The monks of Newark Abbey had struggled for years over whether to keep St. Benedict's open, and just when it seemed possible that the school could realize Abbot Martin Burne's dream of a "new and greater St. Benedict's," it closed.

It all ended so abruptly too. Perhaps fittingly, the last day of school in the history of St. Benedict's Prep never happened. There had been a buzz that students would steal or destroy things around the school on the last day, so toward the end monks were seen scampering around the school taking down pictures, trophies, and other artifacts. To avoid any problems, the headmaster simply canceled the last day of school in the school's long and illustrious history. "So we had our last day of school and no one knew it was our last until it was already over," wrote Father Albert in his journal. "Better we shall go out with a whimper? No final masses. No final parties. No final adieux from teachers. No good-byes to classmates. It was just sort of called off." Graduation that year was a dark and dismal affair, more like a funeral as the school had already pushed out its last breath.[71]

9

"A Possible School": The Resurrection of St. Benedict's Prep, 1972–1977

"There were guys who said the ship was sinking, and they bailed out," recalled one monk.[1] Having just lost fourteen "brothers" to the abbey in Morristown, the monks in Newark walked around a half-empty monastery and a completely empty school. Dazed and disoriented, they did the one thing they could to survive: they jumped in a "lifeboat." For the first time in over a century the monks on High Street no longer had a common work, so individuals looked for "outside" work to keep the community afloat. Father Melvin Valvano became the chaplain at a nearby hospital. Father Albert Holtz taught French and religion at an all-girl's Catholic academy. Father Boniface Treanor and Father Theodore Howath taught at local grammar schools. The two youngest monks helped too. Philip Waters drove a delivery truck and Edwin Leahy counseled heroin addicts at a drug rehabilitation center. Other monks continued their studies or looked after duties at the monastery. Through the summer and fall of 1972, they met twice a week to figure out a course for the future. They did not know how, or if, the small community was going to hold together.[2]

During that uncertain summer, fifteen monks gathered around a massive oval table in the monastery. Father Albert likened it to the size and shape of a lifeboat, with its occupants clinging to the sides, setting out for murky and unchartered waters. In terms of common work, talk teetered from one side of the table to the other as the monks discussed opening a retreat house, a Newman center for local college students, a restaurant, or an adult school. By the end of September, though, the idea of running a high school resurfaced with someone proclaiming at one meeting, "Look, everybody knows we're gonna wind up saying, 'Let's run a school,' so let's cut the crap and start moving on it!" A week later, the soon-to-be ordained Edwin began the community meeting with a typically blunt statement: "We're running a school here next year."[3] Several monks laughed, but Edwin knew that a school was the right thing to try. It certainly made more sense than a retreat house in a riot-torn city.

On Thursday, October 12, 1972, the tide turned decidedly toward what came to be called the "new school venture" when the monks voted unanimously to plan for the opening of a school. As other men left the meeting buoyed by the decisive vote, Father Albert lingered in his seat, put his forehead down on the cold tabletop, and moaned. He did not possess the constitution of a risk taker; he was more likely to throw up over the side of the lifeboat than navigate it through stormy seas. He later confessed in his journal: "We must really be nuts. I ought to know better. But, Melvin just said to me we are forced into things by our values, and this is the essence of freedom." Albert could not be worry-free, though, and he continued to have reservations about opening up a school with limited manpower, zero students, and very little money. The turning point came after a late-night conversation with Father Edwin, who convinced him to put his faith in the new endeavor, and Father Albert later noted: "This may be the day I look back on and say, 'I believed beginning that night.'"[4] Others needed less convincing, but after the cataclysmic events of the last five years, it was that they all possess an unflinching faith for the voyage ahead.

In June 1972, 123 seniors, most of them white, walked across an auditorium stage to receive the last group of diplomas in the history of St. Benedict's Prep. Father Albert remembered that as he called out their names, he thought of a funeral. Yet in June 1977, twenty-nine young men, almost all of them African American, glided across the same stage, signaling the end of the pioneering years for the new St. Benedict's. Supporters pointed to that particular graduation ceremony as a major turning point, a clear sign that the school had completed its "unique reincarnation." The class of 1977 was the first class to spend four years at the new St. Benedict's Prep, and although it was officially the 103rd commencement exercises in the school's history, one monk appropriately called it "the end of the beginning."[5]

Father Albert suggested that the monks survived the tumultuous times after the school's closing by clinging to the sides of a lifeboat in search of safe harbor. Other monks compared the harrowing experience to that of the Israelites. After breaking away from bondage in Egypt, Moses and his followers wandered the desert in search of the Promised Land. With hindsight the comparison strengthened, and by 1976 a visiting abbot wrote the following about the experiences of the men of Newark Abbey:

[The desert experience] turned out to be a great gain for those who survived it: there is no Promised Land without the desert wandering, no resurrection without the passion. To continue the metaphor, it must be added with the prophets of old that the danger afterwards is to settle down comfortably in the Promised Land and forget the desert, to enjoy the gifts while ignoring the Giver. We should like to sound a warning against comfortably relaxing and thus losing what you have gained at the price of suffering.[6]

The "desert experience"—or, for that matter, the time spent in the lifeboat—was crucial to understanding the new St. Benedict's. Most Catholic high schools that close never have a chance to reopen; they simply shutter their doors and cease to exist. In that regard, St. Benedict's Prep was unique and special. The age-old vow of stability and the virtue of adaptability allowed for a group of Benedictine monks to remain in the middle of a modern city and keep doing what they had always done best: pray and teach. In the process, they continued to provide an educational safe harbor, or Promised Land, for future generations of young men.

Father Edwin's Election and a New School Vision

Part of the growing confidence in the "new school venture" no doubt stemmed from the fact that the depleted community had some distinct advantages. Most of the monks had training and experience as educators; the physical plant included classrooms, science labs, a well-stocked library, and a new auditorium; and there was a clear need for a quality school in the city. Perhaps another advantage was that over a dozen former monk-teachers had just left the school. While several monks lost their best friends to the "exodus" out of Newark, their departures proved critical to the success of the new operation. Key administrators, including three of the last four headmasters, all left for Morristown and the Delbarton School, leaving those in Newark to think and plan in new ways. It was an opportunity to create a new school, one that required "all crew and no passengers."[7]

A week after Richard M. Nixon was reelected to the presidency in a landslide victory, the monks of Newark Abbey voted for the first leader of the new school. The abbot had always appointed the headmaster, but at one meeting a monk jokingly suggested that anyone with an interest apply for the position. Two of the youngest men in the community, Albert and Edwin, presented their credentials, as did Fathers Declan Cuniff and Lucien Donnelly. Father Albert had been an administrator and teacher when St. Benedict's Prep closed and had recently earned a master's degree in educational philosophy at Columbia Teachers College. Edwin had just been ordained a priest and he had taught and coached at Benedict's prior to its closing. Of the four, Edwin was the least experienced, but he possessed the most enthusiasm for the possibilities of a monastic school in the middle of a down-and-out city. His novice master, Abbot Martin Burne, summed it up best, saying: "Edwin always had a great yen for Newark."[8]

When the monks gathered to vote on November 14, 1972, they agreed to drop the lowest vote getter on each ballot. Father Albert was the first to go, having suggested that he would better serve the effort in a supporting role. Father Declan went next, leaving Fathers Lucien and Edwin for the decisive third ballot. In the end, it came down to an eccentric candidate versus an eager but inexperienced one. When Father Lucien presented his credentials, he turned most monks off with his radical ideas on education and his vision for the future of St. Benedict's. The much younger Edwin could not recall much of what he said in support of his candidacy, except for the fact that he wanted to be able to fire a teacher if he so desired, even if that teacher happened to be a monk. But he did forward a more traditional program, one that his fellow monks could see themselves teaching in, and one that suggested the best of the "old" St. Benedict's would be preserved. Father Benedict Tyler, the man who helped integrate St. Benedict's in the late 1960s, voted for Father Edwin because he saw in him the vision, drive, and energy to lead the fledgling operation. But he also suggested that the twenty-six-year-old Leahy had won by default because "a lot of people feared what might have happened if Father Lucien was director."[9]

That night, Edwin, Albert, and Philip went to Paul's Tavern for a celebratory drink. Earlier, Father Edwin called his parents to share the good news, and when his mother learned of his election, she was

A young Father Edwin Leahy, OSB, was elected headmaster of the "new" St. Benedict's in 1972. His energetic and visionary leadership has been one of the driving forces behind the resurrected school's extraordinary success over the last four decades.

"dumbfounded." He was so young and she never saw him as a leader when he was growing up.[10] Others were flabbergasted too, especially some of the monks in Morristown, who privately maintained that the new school had little chance of making it because of the limited resources available and the less experienced and perhaps less qualified monks left behind. But Edwin had wanted the job all along and saw it as an opportunity to prove naysayers wrong. He knew there was a need for the school and he had friends to help him run it. He later reflected on the time just after his election:

At that time I was clearly a big mouth. I had no clue what I was doing, but I knew the kids in the city needed something from us and we were going to do it. I had no idea how I was going to take care of all the details and finer points, but I knew I lived in a community with people that knew how to get things done. I never felt like I was alone so I'd say outrageous things knowing that I had smart people with me that could get it all done.[11]

Father Edwin was the antithesis of a traditional Benedict's headmaster. Although he had taught for a handful of years, he held no advanced degrees and no administrative experience. But he did possess the pride, youthful energy, and sense of mission necessary to do the job.

Over the years some have called Father Edwin the heart of St. Benedict's Prep, and if that is true, then Father Albert has been its brain. The pair became an "odd couple," with Edwin generating a lot of the ideas for the school and Albert making them actually work. "A lot of Edwin's vision for education came from Albert," offered Father Philip. "Edwin was not a real academically interested guy. He was much more interested in the community, in relationships, and in sports."[12] The duo complemented each other well. Albert, the tall, lanky intellectual, had "serious doubts and cold feet" when monks first talked of opening a new school. He felt the project lacked "*Geist*, verve, élan, creativity— just the ingredients necessary to make a go of such a thing." But Edwin had just those qualities in abundance.[13] Albert needed Edwin to make a believer out of him, and like others involved in the new school, he fed off the headmaster's energy and enthusiasm. In return, Edwin relied heavily on Albert's organizational gifts as well as his knowledge of curriculum and educational trends.

But their partnership was not inevitable. Father Albert could have easily been elected director, but he was too scared of leading the new school and withdrew his name for consideration. He had attended St. Benedict's in the 1950s and, like Edwin, he had decided that he wanted to join the monastery in his sophomore year. A "timid soul" while in high school, Albert taught for three years at Benedict's before it closed, and his journal revealed how he agonized over whether to follow other monks to the abbey in Morristown. Just after deciding to stay, he encountered a hammer-wielding intruder looking to make off with a television set. The two wrestled briefly in a school hallway. Albert came away bloodied, requiring stitches in his head, but the incident did not change his mind. Newark was his home, and he felt that the monks "ought to look for ways to serve God where we are, on High Street."[14]

In the months before the school's opening, Father Albert was often unsure where he stood in his working relationship with Father Edwin, confiding in his journal at one point: "Should I be pressing the practical nitty-gritty with him, trying to get stuff organized ahead of time, or sit and wait? It doesn't seem like he wants to do things very much in advance." Edwin's fly-by-the-seat-of-his-pants style disturbed the detail-oriented monk. For example, when a parent asked at a meeting if they planned on teaching chemistry, Father Edwin replied, "Yes. We'll be teaching Chemistry." A stunned Father Albert almost fell out of his chair, and when he whispered in Edwin's ear that there was no one to teach the subject, the new director shot back, "Don't worry about it."[15] This became one of his staple responses. To Edwin, they were just details, but to Albert they resulted in sleepless nights and elevated stress levels. "Edwin taught me a lot about going with the flow," confessed Father Albert. "I had the choice of early coronary arrest or going with the flow." If Edwin captained the vessel referred to as the "new school venture," then Albert served as its ballast, counterbalancing his partner's "energetic, high-spirited improvisation" with some needed pragmatism and planning.[16]

In some respects, Albert marveled at his friend's nonchalance about the practicalities of opening a school. No doubt some called it naïveté. But at this point in the school's history, the need for a visionary leader, one not blinded by minutiae, was paramount. Father Albert had copied a passage from the philosopher Eric Hoffer's book *The True*

Father Albert Holtz, OSB, pictured here in the mid-1970s, was both a diarist and an organizational genius. His 1972 document, "A Possible School," became the blueprint for the new school venture.

Believer in his journal, and it seemed altogether appropriate given the task ahead of the Newark monks. In particular, it also served as a fitting description of the young director. "It is the true believer's ability to 'shut his eyes and stop his ears' to facts that do not deserve to be either seen or heard which is the source of his unequaled fortitude and constancy," wrote Hoffer. "He cannot be frightened by danger nor baffled by contradictions because he denies their existence. Strength of faith . . . manifests itself not in moving mountains, but in not seeing mountains to move."[17] More than anything else, Father Edwin believed in the need for St. Benedict's, the need for a Catholic secondary school for young men in Newark, and he did not allow any obstacles to get in the way. Father Albert once commented that the monks "never thought about not making it. We didn't have time to think about it."[18]

In the days following his appointment as director, Father Edwin outlined his initial thoughts on the school. He envisioned a small, racially diverse, and affordable school with a flexible approach to "some of the educational problems of our time." He did not want an exclusively "preparatory school" either. "The new school will, hopefully, prepare those students for college who want to continue their education," he told a *New York Times* reporter. "But if some decide to become carpenters or plumbers, we hope to provide them with a valuable four-year education. We're not going to shovel everyone into college education."[19] Father Edwin also saw school running eleven months out of the year, with unlimited possibilities for learning "outside the walls of the school proper." An additional hallmark of the new school was parental involvement; in particular, the monks had to count on parents to help maintain the school's buildings as well as "hustle" for money by participating in raffles and fund-raisers.

Benedictine values were still the bedrock of the school's existence, but a sense of adaptability had to accompany the monastery's commitment to place. "We must be willing to constantly evaluate the community we serve and ask how we might better serve them," urged Leahy.[20] This notion of service to those in the surrounding neighborhoods was at the core of the new mission for the school. As discussed in Chapter 8, when Abbot Ambrose and several other monks met with parents after the announcement to "suspend operations," one monk responded to a mother's plea to keep "our school" open with the curt reply, "It's not your school." For Edwin, that response "encapsulated the whole problem. The monks thought it was their own school, when it wasn't."[21]

Newark was in sorry shape. Fred J. Cook examined the state of the city in a July 1971 article in the *New York Times Magazine*, and he could have been talking about the very neighborhoods surrounding St. Benedict's Prep when he described "blackened, hollow shells of buildings, some boarded up, some closed off by iron grating, all in ruin."[22] Kenneth Gibson, Newark's first African American mayor, defeated incumbent Hugh Addonizio in a June 1970 runoff, but he inherited what many were calling the worst city in the United States. High employment, out-of-control crime, failing schools, unfinished "urban renewal" projects, and rampant political corruption all plagued a city in shambles. Racial tensions escalated too, especially during two teacher strikes in 1970 and 1971.[23] Amiri Baraka continued his long-running feud with Anthony Imperiale, a folk hero in the predominantly Italian North Ward. For his part, Addonizio, a Benedict's graduate, was sentenced to ten years in federal prison for extortion soon after his electoral defeat. An engineer by trade, Mayor Gibson literally had to rebuild a city still suffering from the terrible days and nights of July 1967.[24]

The city's troubles affected St. Benedict's Prep, which pledged to be a part of Newark's renewal in the riot's aftermath. The *Report for Action* maintained that renewal had to begin "at home, in the way we do business, on our streets, in our shops, our schools, our courts, government offices and wherever members of the black and white communities meet."[25] Mayor Gibson's mantra, "Wherever American cities are going, Newark will get there first," rolled off his tongue almost everywhere he went, including a congressional hearing in 1971. The short, stocky, mustachioed mayor went to Washington, D.C., to plead for government funding for what he called "the most decayed and financially crippled city in the nation." He also warned, "Do not misunderstand the implications of urban decay. We are not only talking of saving the 'Newarks' of America. We are talking about saving America itself."[26] The same could be argued of the fate of once-closed, but now reopened, urban Catholic schools: wherever they were headed, St. Benedict's Prep would most likely get there first.

Many Newarkers interested in salvaging their city were just plain angry; they could not understand how their once-proud city had fallen so swiftly and forcefully. Looking to apportion blame, some pointed a finger at the city's African American community. The same was true for St. Benedict's Prep. "This good thing was being strangled, killed, poisoned in a very unjust way because we just needed some people to go to school here," recalled one monk in the wake of the school's closing. "In my own thoughts, in a general way, I was blaming the African American community. If it wasn't for those people, then others might want to come."[27] Father Edwin "aired the monastery's 'dirty laundry' in public" on several occasions," namely talking about the motivations behind the "exodus" out of Newark to Morristown. He believed certain monks had abandoned their vows of stability of place and their commitments to the city and St. Benedict's Prep.[28]

After St. Benedict's Prep closed, some of the most heart-wrenching letters came from city's residents. Particularly disturbing was the fact that just at the moment when African American males had gained access to St. Benedict's, it closed, leaving many students and parents embittered and disillusioned. Upon hearing of the opening of another school, a mother wrote, "I am most happy that St. Benedict's has come back to our community. When I read of its closing last year it was heart breaking, especially when so many blacks were beginning to have an opportunity to attend the school."[29] Father Edwin's vision for the school was a return to what it had once been for the Germans and Irish in the late nineteenth century: a walking school in a working city. The school had belonged to the city once, to whatever immigrant groups were moving through it at the time. He believed it ought to return to that, and for him a clear sign was students from the neighborhoods walking to school each day sporting their school sweatshirts or jackets.[30]

"A Possible School"

Three days before Christmas in 1870, a handful of monks, including Archabbot Boniface Wimmer, the founding father of the Benedictine Order in the United States, sat around a wooden table in the monastery on High Street. On that occasion, they set down the bylaws for the Order in New Jersey that dedicated them to the provision of spiritual guidance and education of youth. Three days after Christmas, one hundred and two years later, thirteen Benedictine monks gathered in a hotel turned retreat house in Yulan, New York, to share their hopes and dreams and plans for a new school. St. Benedict's Prep had been dead for six months, not yet reborn or resurrected. Time was of the essence as only months remained before the anticipated opening of the "new school venture." Father Albert, ever the pragmatist and planner, had coauthored a twenty-eight-page workbook to provide the framework for the long and intense discussions during the three-day getaway. It was bitterly cold and over a foot of snow blanketed the ground outside, but inside the old hotel nestled in the Catskills, aptly named the "Inn of the Spirit," thirteen men searched for insight and inspiration on how to shape a new school.[31]

Rather surprisingly, it came from Brother Dennis Robertson, a sixty-three-year-old monk who was not an educator but the faithful operator of the abbey's mimeograph machine and the careful tender of its garden. Leading the discussion in the inn's front parlor room, Father Albert asked, "What is your theology of education?" Having recently completed a degree in the philosophy of education, Father Albert had his answer already prepared and he proceeded to give a "dazzling discourse on the dignity of the individual and the school's duty to call out the God-given gifts in each student." Brother Dennis spoke next. "My theology of education? Well, I guess you just love the kids," he sputtered out. "That's about it, I suppose. You just love the kids." A knowing silence accompanied several men nodding their heads in agreement. Five simple words had come to define everything that the group of monks would attempt to do in the new school: "You just love the kids."[32]

Philosophically, the sentiment that Brother Dennis proclaimed proved critical, but it alone could not run a school. The retreat was filled with "a spirit of openness, sharing, and camaraderie," the very opposite of the mood in the monastery leading up to the school's closing. By the time the carloads of monks made the two-hour drive back to Newark, Father Albert had a good sense of what the other monks wanted the new school to look like. In the next two weeks he took a "blank sheet of paper" and crafted a six-page school proposal. Modestly titled "A Possible School," it included a skeleton of the school calendar, a four-year curriculum, projections of student and faculty numbers, and a thumbnail budget. Six months earlier he had agonized along with everybody else about the fate of the monastery and school in Newark. In the process of coming to grips with his decision to remain in the city then, Albert quoted Friedrich Nietzsche: "We are prisoners of our own convictions." It was an exciting time for the Newark-born, Benedict's-educated monk. Fresh off reading and theorizing about education in graduate school, he now had the liberating task of creating a school.[33]

Holtz's ideas for the "possible school" met little resistance. The most controversial part of Albert's proposal was that it called for three distinct "phases" to the academic year: the Summer Phase (July 16–August 24, 1973); the Fall-Winter Phase (September 10, 1973–April 26, 1974); and the Spring Project Phase (May 6–June 7, 1974). The structure addressed some of the fundamental problems with the customary September-to-June schedule. Many students forgot what they had been taught during the summer months and spent much of September recouping those losses. At the other end, many educators believed that little work got done in May and June as the weather warmed and students eyed three months off. Additionally, at least in the city, the summer months had become increasingly more dangerous for young men. The Fall-Winter Phase satisfied traditionalists because it promised to deliver what the monk-educators did best: offer a traditional course of study geared toward college admission. Purposely designed to contrast the lecture-driven classroom experience, the Spring Project Phase in the springtime emphasized hands-on, experiential learning just when students, and faculty for that matter, started to tune out. The three-phase school sketched out by Father Albert during the first weeks of January 1973 remained an identifiable feature of the school for the next four decades.[34]

Another defining characteristic was its commitment to a diverse student body as both the monks and parents favored an integrated school. Fathers Albert, Edwin, and Philip studied together at St. Bernard's Abbey and College in Cullman, Alabama, in 1963 and 1964, a time of heightened civil rights activism that left an indelible mark on the young clerics. When the college made attempts to integrate, local Klansmen resisted. According to Father Albert, they told school officials, "If you allow 'niggers' in your school, we'll start out bombing the water tower and then bomb the other buildings one by one." When traveling throughout the Deep South, the trio saw "colored" water fountains, separate entrances to bus terminals, and the disparity between a newly constructed high school for white students and the one-room schoolhouse for blacks. During that year, four girls died in a church bombing in Birmingham and President Kennedy was assassinated. Locals celebrated with fireworks. The blatant racism and violence shocked the Newark monks, but the "horrid experience of looking at segregation" also helped inform their decision for a consciously integrated school a decade later.[35] In graduate school, Father Albert wrote a research paper titled "Creating an Educative Environment Suitable for Both Blacks and Whites: A Theological Critique."[36]

In the late 1960s and early 1970s, Edwin and Philip finished their studies for the priesthood at Woodstock Seminary in Manhattan, where they both encountered James Cone, a proponent of liberation theology. Even though in the presence of world-class theologians at Woodstock, Edwin often daydreamed about life back at Benedict's, in particular what was going to happen in football or wrestling practice that afternoon. Philip was an intellectual, but he was much more comfortable with poets and playwrights. He explained, "Ed and I were not great students of theology because it did not always resonate with us, but there was something challenging in what Cone was saying. It gave us a new model for understanding the inner city: we weren't dealing with a bunch of criminals that we were trying to insulate ourselves from, but we were in fact dealing with a community where God and the Spirit were at work." Abandoning "Benedictine insularity" represented a major shift in the monastery's thinking about St. Benedict's. It was to be a place both *in* and *of* the city.[37]

The monks began to engage the city and listen to people right outside their front doors. This approach guided the monks' first discussions with parents about the feasibility of opening a new school. Mr. Judge Walker, whose son graduated from St. Benedict's in 1972 and was now studying at Columbia University, responded enthusiastically, telling the monks that it was an important sign of life for Newark's African American community. Carl Quick, a white parent, said he believed so much in the monks that he planned on sending his son to the school. Others remained skeptical. How could the small school make enough money to stay open? One closing was enough, they said. Was it a college prep program? Would suburban students travel into the city to go to school?[38]

Both the tough questions and hopeful affirmations steeled the monks to press on, and the joint group hammered out important details over the next few weeks. Most notably they set tuition at six hundred dollars (double what the monks had originally talked about, because they believed the caliber of education offered warranted the higher price tag), targeted fund-raising possibilities, and zeroed in on the name for the new school. After two monks returned from a workshop on funding for private schools, they reported that they had to have "moxie" and "no longer be either afraid or ashamed to admit that we need help, and would be more than happy to help spend their money. We must be resourceful, imaginative and aggressive."[39] The approach was a decided shift from the old school, where it was unheard of and undignified to ask outsiders for help.

Most parents favored calling the school St. Benedict's though the monks had been split down the middle on whether to retain the name. One father said, "You can name it anything you want, but folks are gonna call it St. Benedict's anyway." Another asked, "If it was good enough when it was all-white to be called St. Benedict's Prep, how come it's not good enough when it's all-black to be called St. Benedict's Prep?" For the monks, there had been a clean break between the old and new schools so they suggested names like Phoenix School, after the mythical bird rising out of the ashes of a destructive fire, or simply High Street Learning Center. "It never occurred to us to call it St. Benedict's," remembered one monk. "St. Benedict's was dead and no one had the temerity to name it after a dead school. But the parents did."[40] By the July opening, the stationery proudly read, "St. Benedict's School," but boxes of it went unused as the name was officially changed to "St. Benedict's Preparatory School" in 1974. "A year and a half has shown that decision was foolish—most students and alumni ignored the change; many old friends were annoyed that 'Prep' had been dropped, much of our mail was delivered to St. Benedict's downneck, etc.," wrote Paul Thornton in an alumni newsletter. "We have happily resumed the full title. We hope it makes life here simpler and most of you happier."[41] In addition, Father Edwin's official title became headmaster.

What a difference a year made. In February 1972, Bob Braun had the ignominious task of reporting the closing of his alma mater, the news of which appeared on the front page of the *Newark Star-Ledger*. Just over a year later he wrote about the monks opening a smaller school, which only made the first page of the second section. Bad news always trumps good news in the newspaper business. Father Albert's journal entries also noted the shift in fortune; downcast, dispirited entries documenting the events leading to the school's closing had given way to joyful, hopeful ones. After one of the parents meetings, he wrote, "I am now more sure than ever before that we'll be all right next year. I'm starting to get enthusiastic now."[42] Father Edwin stopped working at the drug rehabilitation center in order to devote all his time to the new school. Other monks still worked their "day jobs" before returning to the monastery at the end of each day. They all looked forward to the coming school year and the "common work" ahead.

When former student Dennis Durkin, now a sophomore at Seton Hall Prep, read of the new St. Benedict's, he folded up his morning paper and walked to a bus stop on South Orange Avenue. Durkin's father and uncles all went to Benedict's and he reveled in the nearly four-mile ride back into the city. The freckle-faced lawyer's son bounded up the steps at 520 High Street as he had hundreds of times before, but this time he made a beeline for the new director's office. When he found Father Edwin, he asked, "So when do we get started?" Seated at his desk, the priest shot back, "What took you so long?" Dennis finished out the year at Seton Hall, but in June he joined other former students to form the backbone of the new St. Benedict's. Father Edwin reflected on the importance of former students returning, saying, "I wanted to get those kids back because I knew I could depend on them to build what I wanted to build."[43]

As Newark continued to decline during the 1960s and 1970s, the city's image suffered along with it; the butt of jokes nationwide, the old American city was no longer a destination, but rather a place to flee or avoid. Dennis Durkin, a resident of the exclusive Essex Fells community, wanted to return to Benedict's precisely because it was in the city, stating in a letter to be considered for readmission, "I want to know different people from different places. One of the reasons I went to Benedict's in the first place was to get away from all the green grass and country club nonsense." Durkin's mother agreed, writing, "We still want our children to know the city and its problems and not to become immersed in the ghetto that is suburban Essex [County]." When Father

Albert asked Mr. Durkin whether he had any questions about the new school's curriculum, the fiery lawyer retorted, "I graduated dead last in my class at law school. I graduated dead last in my college class. We Durkin's don't worry about that stuff; you're going to make a man out of my boy."[44]

The school provided an opportunity for the monks to "build bridges" between what the 1968 report commissioned by the federal government to investigate U.S. urban riots called "two societies, one black, one white—separate and unequal."[45] A mother living on nearby Prince Street, an African American neighborhood in the city's Central Ward, wrote, "With the school's racial grouping, I believe my son can learn to relate [to] and understand people of other racial and social backgrounds."[46] At Benedict's there existed the possibilities for cross-cultural exchange; a young man from the suburbs could study, play, and interact with someone from the grittiest section in the city. But perhaps more than anything else, parents, whether black or white, rich or poor, sent their sons to St. Benedict's for what Father Cornelius Selhuber had called "manhood training." Such training knew no age or race or class or religious distinction. "From past experience, Benedict's gave my son something money can't buy," noted a single mother who sent her son to the school before it closed. "Qualities like motivation, pride, dignity, empathy and kindness. I would like my youngest son to be given the best of chances to develop [into] manhood; a man that understands himself and can be an asset to his community."[47]

Other former students said they had missed the spirit of St. Benedict's and the close relationships between faculty and students.[48] New students often cited practical reasons for seeking admission: St. Benedict's was closer and cheaper than other private schools in Greater Newark. Also, it was not one of the city's large public high schools. Several former students who attended Newark public schools after St. Benedict's closed lamented the conditions they found there, including "overcrowded classrooms," "boring classes," and "racial tensions."[49] Parents also voiced their concerns with the public system, saying it was "all but lost" and that they had become "depressed and dissatisfied with the quality of public school education in Newark."[50] The school's close-knit community—where small classes meant individualized attention and where social interaction led to a better understanding among young men from different backgrounds—appealed to many parents and students. But the question remained whether Father Edwin and the admissions committee had enough time to enroll ninety students by September.

"Smoke and mirrors" and some good old-fashioned fibbing masked Father Edwin's attempts to fill the roster, as he later admitted: "I lied all the time because the monks would ask if we had students coming and I'd say, 'Yeah, no problem. There are lots of applications coming in.'"[51] Truth be told, the young headmaster waited until his fellow monks went to evening mass in order to sneak away and make recruiting calls in the secrecy of his office. He also visited local schools and attended high school information nights, but much of his effort came too late in the high school admissions process. The monks had announced the school's opening in late February and by mid-March most boys had already made their minds up on where to go to high school. Even though school officials fast-tracked the admissions process, they were unable to shape the type of school they had planned for, especially in terms of student diversity. Paul Thornton, a 1963 graduate who returned to teach after leaving a post at the prestigious Pingry School, observed, "Basically, we started with whoever showed up."[52]

It was an accident of history, then, that St. Benedict's was less integrated than it had planned for, as the overwhelming majority of those who "showed up" were African Americans living in Newark. While the junior class had a good number of white students reenroll (there was no senior class the first year), the freshman and sophomore classes lacked diversity. An open house for freshmen coincided with a demonstration outside the noted poet and activist Amiri Baraka's community headquarters, located next to the school. Chants of "Whites, go to hell!" probably did not help admissions that day. When Father Edwin assembled the freshman and sophomore classes for a mid-May orientation program the school was twenty students short of capacity, but that did not deter the dynamic priest from making a lasting first impression. He called his new charges pioneers and told them, "It's you guys who will make this thing work!" He also proclaimed, "From this date, May

19, 1973, you are to consider yourselves Benedict's Men and act accordingly. When people see you with a Benedict's jacket on, they'll know you're part of a one-hundred-year tradition. And they'll be watching you." People watched the monks too, most notably the men who left for Morristown after the school's closing, and that knowledge was "of no little motivational value" during the first months and years of the new St. Benedict's.[53]

Even though the Newark monks had insisted that the new school was not a reopening of the old one, Father Edwin blurred those lines by calling on over one hundred years of history and tradition. The split in the monastery in 1968 and the closing of St. Benedict's Prep in 1972 have to be considered crucial events in the school's modern history, allowing for a new vision to emerge on how to educate young men in a major city toward the end of the twentieth century. On the eve of the first day of school, several monks swept the floor in Conlin Auditorium, the venue where students first heard of the original school's closing. With broom in hand, Edwin turned to Albert and said, "It sure is a hell of a lot easier to close a school than to open one."[54]

The "New" St. Benedict's

"It is important that a school is opening in Newark," boomed Mayor Kenneth Gibson during the opening day festivities on July 2, 1973. "But that a school is re-opening, that is doubly important." Standing nearby, Father Albert, ever the worrywart, thought to himself, "It also means that the people involved in it are doubly crazy."[55] The impressive gathering of students, faculty, parents, alumni, city officials, Catholic clergy, and local educators underlined the significance of the event in post-riot Newark. After so much white flight and so many closures, something exciting and positive was happening in the city. Benedict's was rebuilding with Newark. Some could not help but think that "a new and greater St. Benedict's," the one alluded to by Abbot Martin Burne at the school's centenary, had finally arrived.

The public also got its first look at Father Edwin, and it soon became clear that the no-nonsense leader intended to run a student-centered school based on self-respect and responsibility. He also planned on creating a tight-knit family atmosphere where everyone knew one another and each individual played an integral part in shaping something meaningful. "We knew that those teachers and that staff wanted to be there and no place else. And if they wanted to be there and no place else, that was good enough for us," noted one of the returning students. "We knew we were going to build something great. They convinced us that we were doing a good, valuable, and important thing."[56] Operating on a shoestring budget, the monks relied on the founders' sweat equity to sidestep obstacles and avert crises, and one monk-teacher commented that the monks would look back on these early days fondly as "the good days of struggle and birth and new risks."[57] By the middle of the first school year, it became clear that the new school had not only survived but showed early signs of thriving. "We didn't stay in the lifeboat any longer than we had to," Father Albert admitted.[58]

Yet perhaps one of the last events that could have "rocked the boat" was the resignation of Ambrose Clark as abbot days after St. Benedict's reopened. It was the second time Clark planned on resigning, the first coming only months after the original school closed and the community was a shell of its former self. At that point, his confreres asked him to reconsider, knowing his departure would jeopardize the very survival of the urban abbey. Ambrose stayed on for another year, and his willingness to remain in office at a critical moment smoothed the passage to a new school and eventually a rejuvenated monastery. To his credit, Abbot Ambrose allowed the other monks to find their way as they "weathered the storm of the past year." The "upheavals and struggles" associated with the school's closing marked the monks of Newark Abbey as survivors; according to Father Albert, these experiences "helped shape us as a group, [gave] us an identity, clarif[ied] our goals, and prove[d] to others that we've got what it takes." Father Albert began his journal on February 10, 1972, when Newark Abbey was on the brink of crisis, but after the first day of the new school he reflected, "Now the chaos is over, the 'crisis' is past in the Greek sense of *Krisis* because the decision or judgment has now been made."[59]

The time spent in the lifeboat had been critical to the community's view of itself. They had stayed, survived, and now had a promising if somewhat precarious future in the city. But the monks needed a new spiritual leader, one with the vision and courage to duplicate what Father Edwin was doing for the school. On September 8, 1973, the monks elected Melvin Joseph Valvano the second abbot of Newark Abbey; at age thirty-four, he was the youngest abbot in the congregation's history. Valvano, a 1956 graduate of St. Benedict's, had once failed out of college and was not initially accepted into the monastery, trailed on two of the first three ballots. He capped his unlikely ascent by eventually winning on the sixth ballot. Over the course of the next decade, Abbot Melvin became known for his reforming spirit as he reacted to what he saw as a loose and lax monastic life prior to the split of the monastic family in 1968 and the school's closing in 1972. After his election, Abbot Melvin invited his brothers to return to the ideals of the Order's founder, emphasizing a prayerful existence consistent with the Benedictine vows of poverty and commitment to place.

With a recent history of family problems, financial woes, and unemployment, the monastic family shared some of the same experiences with the poor, disenfranchised, and broken families in its immediate neighborhood. By nature, monks did not live life "on the edge." But Father Albert warned against losing a "sense of being on the razor's edge," and becoming "complacent to the point of turning this monastery back into the self-centered anthill it once was, and thus provide fate with another chance to kick the anthill to bits and scatter us, dazed and lost, into a world that has again passed us by."[60] One kick was enough, and with the opening of the school and the election of Melvin Valvano as abbot, Newark Abbey began a new era, one that proved to be less serene and secure for sure, but also one full of excitement and exhilaration.

St. Benedict's buzzed with life from the outset and in many ways stood in stark contrast to the old school. It was much smaller, with ninety-three students as opposed to more than five hundred, and the staff included only two laypeople, a maintenance man, and a secretary. Students no longer had to wear collared shirts, ties, and blazers; jeans, T-shirts, and sneakers sufficed. There were very few rules and regulations in the new school, a significant departure from the rule-bound world of the old school's infamous disciplinarians. When a new rule made sense, students usually asked to add one. At first, the monks did not even grade students, only commenting on their performance and effort. But when they began to apply to college, letter grades reappeared. "We had freedom within a framework," noted one student. "They taught us life and told us not to get caught up in the details. They encouraged us to read, write, think, explore, and argue and said, 'You're going to grow, or you're going to leave.'"[61]

Community was built, or rather rebuilt, because the monks invited students back into their home and worked tirelessly at forging strong relationships. "We didn't leave in 1972 because this was our home," admitted Abbot Melvin. "We stayed because we were family."[62] That family atmosphere permeated everything the monks did. Close student-teacher relationships had been a defining characteristic of St. Benedict's for over a century, along with a real sense of unity among the students. Benedict's "sounded like one big family that cared for one another," wrote an applicant whose older brother attended the school before it closed.[63] In the new school the family proved to be smaller but even tighter. Father Edwin urged his fellow monk-teachers to spend time with the students both in and out of school, saying, "There is all sorts of stuff going on under our noses." In befriending students, some monks shot baskets or played handball, while others took students on field trips to New York City. Most spent time talking and listening to the young men about life, learning along the way on how to better serve them and the new school.[64]

Some of what the monks found out was quite shocking. Two transfer students, for example, revealed that Claude Brown's autobiography of his troubled inner-city youth, *Manchild in the Promised Land*, was the very first book they had been asked to read in high school. Other students shared details about the appalling state of the city's public schools, and the low level of expectations they had experienced there. But real breakthroughs came when young men began to trust the monks with their innermost feelings, including rejection by absentee fathers, fear of violence in their neighborhoods, and the tightening grip of drugs and alcohol on loved ones. The monks found out early that many young men had to navigate two worlds—school and street

—which affected how they dealt with the issue of language. They insisted on the use of "Standard English" in all written work, but also allowed for "Black English" in classroom discussions.[65] Father Edwin demonstrated a facility for language too, and an alumnus observed that he may well have been the only school head in the country to be "articulate in both ghetto street talk and Latin discourse."[66] Eventually, he became fluent in Spanish and possessed passable knowledge of Portuguese and several African dialects, always looking to converse with students and parents in their native tongues.

As much as Father Edwin loved to talk—he could rant and rave ad nauseam about a particular issue at an all-school meeting—he believed that listening was the key to the early shaping of the school. It also helped define his personal style as a highly effective school leader. "I learned a lot from kids and their parents," he admitted. "I think one of the things we learned early on was to keep our mouths shut as much as we could and keep our ears open." For example, "preparatory" was reinserted into the school's name because students and parents insisted on it. Moreover, parents kept telling the monks that they wanted a college prep curriculum because, as one monk put it, "they saw it as the next step up toward the American dream."[67] With many of the students coming from either all-white or all-black schools, parents favored a more diverse student body. Father Edwin explained, "We wanted to bring a lot of different kinds of people together—city, suburban, rich, poor, black people, white people—all bound by the common interest that concerned parents have for their children." The monks intended "to help bridge the gaps that exist[ed] in modern society by using the 1,500-year-old traditions of the Benedictine Order."[68]

Oddly, and perhaps schizophrenically, the monks did not teach religion during the first year of the new school. They were uneasy over imposing a "white value system" on the school community, but parents assured the monks that they desired an excellent education infused with Christian values and a healthy dose of discipline. "Religion is what got us this far; we've come this far by faith. You can't have a school without religion because that's what you're all about," interjected one African American parent.[69] The monks' values were the parents' values too. Religion was added to a curriculum that became all-encompassing according to Father Albert: "Our notion of curriculum became one in which the classroom was just one component. The curriculum was this whole collection of values, activities and attitudes from the time a kid came to us to the time he left us. It is everything that happens to him from the time he walks in that 520 door."[70]

Students also found out a lot about one another, and some of their friendships defied convention. "I used to watch the white kids get off the bus at the corner, coming from the suburbs and the Jersey shore, and I wanted to go to school there with them," recalled Virgil Griffin, a freshman the year the school closed. Although Virgil lived right across the street, he experienced a "culture shock" in his first months at St. Benedict's. He had never gone to a white-majority school, he had never been taught by Catholic monks, and he had never experienced such academic rigor. Virgil was in awe of the monks and intimidated by their high expectations (he usually felt ill before going to Father Boniface's algebra class), but older students eased Virgil's transition to the prestigious prep school a few minutes' walk from his front door.

But the school closed in his first year and he transferred to St. Peter's Prep in Jersey City. But he had a strange sense that it was not the end, saying, "I still had optimism that the school was going to open back up." After a year away, he was reunited with some of his former classmates, including Dennis Durkin, who all worked long and hard "to put the school back on the map." There were only ninety of them so they all had to become intimately involved in the school's success or failure. Virgil, for his part, played four sports and became a key student leader, saying of his important role, "It wasn't a big burden and I saw us leading the way back to the way it used to be. We had a lot of hope and faith in St. Benedict's. It still felt like Benedict's, with the same atmosphere and the presence of the monks."[71]

Tom Leahy, Father Edwin's younger brother, was one of four white students in the class of 1977, and recalled how everyone had to do his part. For example, almost everyone played sports because they needed to in order to field teams, plus no one thought of quitting because to do so meant letting down others. He also remembered the hilarious banter among his classmates sitting around the tables in the cafeteria or on the front stoop, in particular about racial stereotyping. Leahy recalled that he never heard a racist comment, perhaps because the school was too small to have cliques. "Did we mock each other and did race factor into that? Of course it did," he recalled. "I've been called 'cracker' more than once, but it was always in good fun. I never took offense to it."[72] At night, after practice, an older student escorted him down to Penn Station so he could take the train back home. It was far too dangerous for a white teenager to walk down Market Street alone after dark, his escort maintained.

The integrationists on staff reveled in the "cross-teaching about life-styles and outlooks." When Wallace Eng, the sole Chinese American student in the entire school, was dropped off at home following the dress rehearsal for the Christmas Program, he leaned back into the car to say goodbye to his friends, saying, "See you, niggers! See you, whit-eys!" That January, Eng served as a tutor in an after-school program, further amusing the monks when he was overheard telling his tutee, "No water until you finish your work!"[73] Over the next few years, the recruitment of white students was a constant concern, and African American parents even urged the monks to increase the number of suburban whites in the school. "We've become very much aware of the need to specifically recruit white kids," noted Father Albert at the beginning of the second year. When he left to attend a local high school fair, Father Edwin told him to be both "brief and brutally honest." The school was 75 percent African American and in the middle of the city, "but we've got a heck of an interesting program going, with the interaction of city kids and suburban. We're looking for students who are interested in taking advantage of this unique situation." Two years later, in 1976, Father Albert drew up a recruitment plan "to expand our apostolate of White/Black, city/suburb"; splashed across the top of white-lined paper was the plan's title: "Operation Whitewash '76."[74]

While many saw the reopening as great news for the city, many graduates of St. Benedict's still resented the fact that the school had closed at all. "Why didn't you move out to the suburbs? You could have saved the school," shouted one angry alumnus at a meeting shortly after the reopening. "I won't give you a dime because of what you did."[75] Some disgruntled graduates even hung up on former class-mates soliciting donations. But a group of loyal alumni did back the new school and put their faith in the monks to provide a quality education for young men in the city. Unsolicited, Bernard M. Shanley Jr. sent a personal check to Father Edwin shortly after the announcement of the school's opening. A small note accompanied the donation: "Father Ed, use this where it will do the most good."[76]

The Shanley name was huge not only in Benedict's history, but also in state and national legal and political circles. A partner in one of the Newark's largest firms, Shanley was also a stalwart in the Republican Party, having previously run (unsuccessfully) for the Senate and served on President Eisenhower's White House staff. Moreover, his great-great-great-aunt was Mother Elizabeth Ann Seton, the first native North American to be canonized by the Catholic Church. Another relative, James Roosevelt Bayley, was the first bishop of Newark and founder of Seton Hall University. Shanley's affinity for St. Benedict's was strong, so it was fitting that he gave Father Edwin the first check; after all, Shanley's father had donated the gymnasium in 1920, sparking an unprecedented surge in enrollment.[77]

Bernard Shanley Jr. was a "big Catholic layman," and as a staunch supporter of St. Benedict's, his prestige and reputation helped make it possible to reopen in 1973. While some alumni had turned their backs on the school for closing, others joined the effort, especially after they saw that Shanley backed the new venture. Paul Thornton, director of development, said at the time, "True, we lost some of the diehards among the alumni, but they have been replaced by the really dedicated." Graduates like Shanley, Foley, and John Magovern, the former president of Mutual Benefit Life Insurance Company, were the first "guardian angels" of the new school, observed Father Edwin, "even though they didn't give us huge sums of money, they gave us their names and that meant just as much." They all also served on the advisory board, lending expert advice to the monks on financial and legal matters.[78]

At one of the board's earliest meetings, an alumnus told the monks to be aggressive when seeking funds for the school, whether from alumni, foundations, or local businesses, imploring the monks to "camp on their doorstep. Don't let them go. Keep on them."[79] Soliciting

monies for the school's operating costs as well as for capital improve-
ments and endowment funds was relatively unheard of in the history
of the school. The last campaign, the Century II fund-raising drive in
the late 1960s, had failed miserably and the monks had no real experience in asking others for help. There had been no reason to, since the
tuition had always covered operating expenses. Now, they had to go
out and actively seek monies in order to make the plans of a visionary
headmaster materialize. They were able to make a compelling case at
the tail end of the civil rights era that St. Benedict's was quite
unique—a predominantly African American but integrated Catholic
school in the heart of a riot-torn city. Abbot Melvin and Paul Thornton
spearheaded what became one of the most intriguing and successful
development and fund-raising campaigns in the history of American
Catholic secondary education.

In the months before St. Benedict's reopened, many of the monks
and their advisers, regardless of whether they wanted to admit it, worried that the school and monastery were in dire straits financially.
Father Albert anticipated a funding predicament, only to later write in
his journal "that crisis never came, and, as it turns out, money is not
the ogre camped on our doorstep." It could well have been, if not for a
string of fortuitous events that started with the sale of the school's
athletic complex to the City of Newark just before Christmas 1973 for
the staggering sum of $525,000. Even though the Hayden Foundation
denied the school's first grant application, the Victoria Foundation of
Montclair was so impressed with the school's proposal they sent twice
the requested amount, an unbelievable $20,000. Visitors from various
foundations became commonplace, and students became so conscious
of these special guests that one young man approached a visiting reading specialist and mistakenly asked, "Pardon me, I don't like to be
nosey, but what foundation are you from?"[80]

The school and monastery were far from flush with money, even
with the annual interest from the sale of Benedict Field and the first
successes in securing foundation money. Abbot Melvin was told early
on in his abbacy, "Watch the money. We're not in that good of shape."[81]
The monks did employ a "sweat equity" strategy and utilized a "nickel-
and-dime" approach to keep costs down during those pioneering years.

For example, parents came for a series of "work parties" on weekends to clean and paint the interior of the school, and students cleaned up as part of their after-school routine. Father Edwin's father, Bill Leahy, helped purchase a used van to transport students, and another relative painted it the school's colors. As a member of the advisory board, Mr. Leahy took the term "working board" to heart. A union operating engineer, he often showed up in his work clothes to labor around the school before hastily showering in the bowels of Shanley Gym to make the start of a board meeting on time.[82]

Three central figures at those early board meetings were Carl Quick, a soft-spoken parent from South Orange who sent his son to the school in 1973, J. Franklin Cook, and his son Roger, a graduate of the school. At times, the threesome empowered the monks to push forward with their bold plans, and at other times they led the way for a group of priests that lacked financial savvy and risk-taking attributes. Mr. Quick never spoke above a hush but was a colossal figure, according to Father Albert: "We were feeling our way in the dark, talking about taking baby steps so that we didn't fall off a cliff. But Carl was the type that said, 'Let's just start walking.'" When discussions turned to acquiring urban renewal land, Quick rebuffed a monk who said, "I don't know how we can do it," by saying, "I don't know how we can't do it, Father."

The Cooks had been involved with Father Benedict in his efforts to integrate St. Benedict's in the late 1960s, paying tuition for a promising young African American man before the school closed. After the school's reopening, they insisted on two things when advising the monks: first, the monks had a "product" and that they had to "sell it"; and second, they needed to find a person to serve as a development director. When Abbot Melvin told the father and son that the abbey did not have the money for that, they threatened to no longer advise the school. Father Edwin observed, "We wound up following them. People thought we were driving it but [Quick and the Cooks] were really pushing us."[83] Paul Thornton returned to teach American studies in September 1973, and a year later he became the school's first director of development.

The sons of a 1939 graduate, Paul and his brothers really had no option but to follow in their father's footsteps. When the fourteen-year-old old Rahway resident entered Benedict's in the fall of 1959, he had already heard hundreds of "Benedict's stories" and was anxious to make his own. Four years later he not only graduated at the top of his class, but earned all-state honors as a pitcher for another of Joe K's stellar baseball teams. After graduation Paul headed north to Harvard, while classmates Leahy and Waters went south to study for the priesthood at St. Bernard's in Alabama. In Cambridge, Paul became immersed in the classic novels of noted African American authors—such as Ralph Ellison, Richard Wright, and James Baldwin—and he was also greatly influenced by the civil rights movement and all that was happening on the politically charged Harvard campus. Paul returned to New Jersey in 1967 to pursue a doctorate at Rutgers University. He began teaching at Benedict's in 1968, and when the school closed, he taught at the Pingry School in Elizabeth.

Thornton became the first layman to teach at the new St. Benedict's, and Father Albert noted that he "lent a real air of class to the place. He gave us a lot of academic legitimacy with his Harvard diploma and graduate work at Rutgers."[84] Over the years many have questioned why Thornton, with his Ivy League pedigree and intellectual acumen, returned to Benedict's, especially when it was a shadow of its former self. He once explained, "You have to remember, we are children of the 1960s. Either it meant something or it didn't. I think it did."[85] As a boy Thornton had wanted to become a medical missionary, but circumstances caused him to return to Newark. When he was thrust into an unfamiliar role as development director, though, Thornton responded with missionary zeal. As a man of letters he knew little of fund-raising and foundations, but he was willing to work hard at improving the school's financial future. Father Benedict presciently noted in a 1963 college recommendation letter that Thornton had "all the qualities of an able first lieutenant," including "willingness, intelligence and dependability."[86]

Over the years, Thornton used his facility with language to paint a "word picture" of what St. Benedict's was, what it could be, and why donors should support such a special place. His fund-raising partner was not so subtle, as Abbot Melvin made some alumni feel guilty and pressed them for donations. "He was brutal," observed a fellow monk, and alumni "cringed" when he called them on the phone or visited their offices. John Magovern, the former chairman of a Newark insurance company, told the monks that the school needed a "sugar daddy," a benefactor with deep pockets. Robert E. Brennan, a young and aggressive financier who graduated from St. Benedict's in 1962, soon pledged $10,000 to the school and in the ensuing weeks came with two checks to honor it. But Abbot Melvin was not satisfied. He asked Brennan for an even larger gift, saying, "For a gift to be a gift, it has to be sacrificial." He then pledged an additional $250,000 and over the next fifteen years he donated millions.[87] Newark businesses broke their own rules when Benedict's starting asking for corporate support. For example, Prudential rewrote their giving policy because they had previously refused to give money to either secondary schools or Catholic schools.

"The End of the Beginning"

With the early fund-raising successes the school was quickly "in the black," so the monks could focus their attention on students, a rewarding but often frustrating experience. Throughout 1975 and 1976, Father Albert's journals routinely made mention of students giving up and quitting when circumstances toughened, whether in the classroom or in athletics. "Many of our kids lack the drive to get up after being knocked down," he revealed. "Slap one of them down to provoke him and he'll just lie there and say, 'Yeah, guess you're right, I'm lousy.'" He also wondered, "How many guys will still be doing this when they're married and disappear some day, leaving the wife and the kids?" Such attitudes infuriated Father Edwin and he spent much of his time challenging students, imploring them to not give up, to work harder, and to stick up for themselves. While Edwin yelled and screamed, Albert sought other means of motivation. He raided a closet to produce class banners going back to the 1930s. The one that left a lasting impression was a giant maroon and gray banner that read, "Benedict's Hates a Quitter!" Father Albert's father, who had grown up in Newark, candidly told his son, "If you find the solution to that, you've found the solution to Newark's problem too."[88]

Weeks after the first group of seniors graduated in June 1975, Father Edwin spoke to students on the first day of the Summer Phase. Reflecting on the first two years of the new St. Benedict's, he delivered a cautionary speech about the prospects for the coming year:

Before this year we had no place to go but up. People didn't expect anything of us and said we'd never make it. Well, now we've gotten somewhere—state champs in track, reasonable showing in other sports, 500 people at a drama guild production—and all of a sudden we've got two directions we can go in. For the first time we can go either up or down. Let's be sure we put in the work it takes to go up. It gets harder the higher you go.[89]

Not surprisingly, in order to move onward and upward, Father Edwin tightened discipline around the school, in particular after he hired a former student to join the staff. When Bernard Greene returned to the school, he did not recognize it: there were no uniforms and fewer rules, and it was much smaller and had a relaxed atmosphere. In addition, almost all the students were like him, African American and from local neighborhoods. He knew them, knew the streets and the problems therein, but he also knew that his "grandmother's values" meshed well with Benedictine values of discipline, responsibility, and accountability. Greene had presence too. A large man, over 6'3" and muscular, he had a deep, booming voice and threatening demeanor that intimidated students. Like Father Dunstan Smith, Bernard Greene became a legend.[90]

In fact, St. Benedict's became more and more demanding on students during its first two and a half years. In particular, the monks and staff "came to the conviction that it [was] a great mistake to do for students things that they can do for themselves." A loose, free atmosphere gave way to a more rule-bound, traditional Catholic school environment. Disciplinary changes rolled back the clock as students now received detention for infractions like being late or for uncooperative behavior. Teachers and staff efficiently monitored academic progress, or lack thereof, and suspended students from activities if they did not perform well enough. One such student placed on probation received a letter at home outlining his status: "He will be dismissed if he cuts school twice; he will be dismissed if he fails any subject at the first marking period; and, he will be dismissed if he is not at home on any school night."[91] The monks monitored all aspects of a young man's life.

As the country planned to celebrate its bicentennial, the newly resurrected school prepped for the future as school officials formed a long-range planning committee and began a self-evaluation. "The excitement of 1976 was of a new kind," noted Father Albert. "Gone was the suspense, the cliff-hanging sort of exhilaration. [It] was a year of real forward movement, of harvesting some of the produce born of four years of work."[92] Paul Thornton produced a detailed account of the scholastic year's happenings in his second-annual president's report. Notably, the student body increased again, from 134 to 150, and by 1977–78, 168 students enrolled, with 56 freshmen selected out of 170 applications. A trial summer program for seventh and eighth graders resulted in an increased number of suburban students enrolling in the freshman class. Additionally, St. Benedict's joined the National Network of Complementary Schools, a nationwide exchange program with twenty elite private and public high schools. Sports teams began to win championships and Father Albert pieced together a gospel choir that performed throughout the tristate area and even recorded an album that sold through its first pressing. Fittingly, the group's signature song also became the school's unofficial alma mater, "We've Come This Far by Faith."[93]

The three-phase school dreamed up at the Inn of the Spirit proved to be both innovative and effective as it allowed students to learn and interact in dramatically different ways. Although students did not like going to school during the summer, they responded well to the eclectic offerings during the spring, when they became immersed in a particular subject or activity. Some took part in the law project at the Essex County Courthouse while others participated in bike hikes and canoeing. Some students could not be trusted in a group setting, so they were forced to take part in the "Backpacking Project."

Fathers Edwin and Philip conducted the first "penal hike" in May 1974 when they dropped students off at the Livingston Mall and told them to hike fifteen miles west to St. Mary's Abbey in Morristown. Strung out along Columbia Turnpike with pots and pans dangling from knapsacks, most students were experiencing the "outdoors" for the very first time. When one wide-eyed Newarker saw a handful of cows out at pasture, he commented, "Those are the biggest Dalmatians I have ever seen!" The next year a student spotted, killed, cooked, and then ate a rattlesnake.[94] Brother Mark Payne, a 1969 graduate of St. Benedict's and an experienced Boy Scout leader, took over the project in 1976, and it soon became the capstone experience of the freshman year. When a team successfully completed the five-week program, culminating with a week's hike on a portion of the Appalachian Trail, each member was congratulated on finally completing his first year at the school.

Brother Mark's organization of the Backpacking Project resulted in a new approach to grouping students at the beginning of Fall-Winter Phase in 1976. The "group system" divided the entire school into ten groups of fifteen students each. Modeled on the "house system" of British private schools, it also incorporated Boy Scout leadership principles. The cross-class groupings allowed for students in different grades to get to know one another and for older students to become effective leaders in a small-group setting. The groups competed against one another in academics, intramural athletics, and school service. Every group set up study halls, and by the end of the year faculty noted a school-wide "improvement in self-esteem, confidence and performance." Eventually, each group had been named after a prominent figure in the school's past, whether coaches like Joe Kasberger or Prof Blood, disciplinarians like Fathers William "The Eagle" Koellhoffer or Dunstan "The Duke" Smith, and headmasters like Fathers Cornelius Selhuber or Boniface Reger.[95]

June 5, 1977, marked the graduation of the first class to spend four years at the reopened Benedict's. Three-quarters of the graduates went on to college and others found work or joined the military. The 103rd commencement exercises were a joyous occasion for the monks, faculty, parents, and students, a sharp contrast to what was supposed to be the last graduation ever in the school's history back in June 1972.

Moreover, it was also "the end of the beginning." According to Father Albert:

We're different in many ways from what we were then. Especially striking is the difference in outlook and attitude: no longer flailing just to stay afloat, we are now concentrating on very specific directions we want to go in; no longer lying awake at night wondering where the money's gonna come from, we now can spend more time wondering about more exalted things. We can look back to the events of 1971–73 as history already.[96]

The trials of those troubling years were behind the group of monks that decided not to abandon ship on High Street. The embodiment of the adage "all crew and no passengers," the monks and their ever-growing team of helpers labored to resurrect a once-dead school. Reflecting on the early days of the new St. Benedict's, Father Edwin commented, "You don't laugh when there's a hole in the other guy's end of your lifeboat. You're in the same boat as he is, like it or not!"[97]

10 The Headmaster and the Street, 1977–1986

For the last three decades "the hand" has gone up at St. Benedict's Preparatory School. Like clockwork, at eight in the morning a young man strides to the center of Shanley Gymnasium and raises his right hand straight in the air. Other students follow suit and hundreds of hands instinctively shoot up. The gesture signals silence, and previously animated conversations are muted. Peace seems to blanket the gathering, and while sirens and horns may wail outside, inside the school community pauses to ready itself for the day ahead. Communal prayer is followed by school-related announcements, but the daily meeting—known as "Convocation"—does not end until Father Edwin Leahy has an opportunity to speak. For him, it is the most important thing the school does because each and every morning community is visible—it can be seen, heard, and experienced.

Above all else, Father Edwin, the son of an operating engineer and a homemaker turned banker, has been a master builder. Since the mid-1970s, he and his staff have been able to create a community for young men, many of whom come from broken families, fractured neighborhoods, and failing schools. It was built by honoring the Benedictine virtues of stability and adaptability and meshing them with core values of the African American experience, particularly faith and family. Many older alumni recognized the "old in the new," but as one graduate suggested, "Edwin has created a school that alumni return to not because of what the school was, but for what it has become."[1]

Sustained alumni giving and continued support from various foundations have enabled the school to embark on a new phase of "brick and mortar Benedictinism." In particular, a five-million-dollar gift from

Father Edwin Leahy, OSB, headmaster, in front of the school with students, 1977.

an alumnus in 1984 enabled the school to complete an aptly named development campaign, "A Bridge to the Future." Fittingly, a massive sky bridge spanned Dr. Martin Luther King Jr. Boulevard (formerly High Street) and connected the old school buildings, the first of which were constructed in the late nineteenth century, with a new complex that includes classrooms, a gymnasium, and an indoor swimming pool. The impressive facilities rivaled anything an urban Catholic prep school had ever built, and stood in stark contrast to the blighted plots of Newark's Central Ward. Of the new construction and what the school was able to accomplish in the decade after it reopened, the longtime benefactor and adviser Bernard Shanley Jr. said, "Now, the skeptics can go away."[2]

Benedict's had its doubters, and that fact certainly motivated Father Edwin and the other monks. When the school reopened, they wanted to prove to people that a Catholic prep school for mostly African American males from the city could not only survive, but could thrive. In 1980, the Schumann Foundation sent Gil Sewall, a former education editor at *Newsweek*, to study St. Benedict's Prep and find out why the school worked so well. Benedict's was able to overcome so many obstacles and produce extraordinary student outcomes, concluded Sewall, because it had a strong principal, high expectations, a rigorous but basic curriculum, dedicated teachers, tradition, discipline, devoted alumni, and parental trust. "St. Benedict's proves that school improvement in inner cities is possible, even in low-income and minority areas," wrote Sewall.[3]

By the mid-1980s a handful of other studies confirmed what Sewall had observed at St. Benedict's. Catholic secondary schools not only escaped many of the problems affecting public high schools, they proved especially effective when serving poor and disadvantaged minority students. Notably, Catholic high schools reduced racial and class achievement gaps whereas public high schools seemed to exacerbate them. Some researchers argued that the key to Catholic school success was the "common school effect," the fact that all students, regardless of background or prior scholastic standing, were taught in basically the same way. In Newark, a study confirmed the Catholic school academic advantage—"the quality of learning simply seems to be superior in the Catholic schools"—and provided evidence of "a profound respect for authority and order. . . . They reflect the quiet discipline and graciousness of another era." Another national survey highlighted the role of community, as Catholic school principals described their top goal as "building community among faculty, students, and parents."[4] This was Father Edwin's main priority too.

Father Edwin became so adept at building community and making at-risk young men feel a part of something special that people talked of "Father Ed's magic" or a "miracle on High Street."[5] Father Edwin always insisted that there was nothing magical or miraculous about what was happening at St. Benedict's. It was simply a case of "ordinary people doing the extra-ordinary."[6] After nearly a quarter century as headmaster, Father Edwin received a note from an aging Abbot Martin, his novice master and longtime confidant: "In 1966, who would have guessed what Edwin Leahy would be doing within the decade. Perhaps next time we meet we should talk of miracles, not of Lourdes or Fatima, but of Newark and St. Benedict's."[7] What follows is a portrait of the man who became the headmaster and performed that miracle on High Street.

"I Think the Boy Has a Vocation": The Making of a Headmaster

The longest-serving headmaster in the history of St. Benedict's Preparatory School did not get in to the school on his first try. Initially rejected for scoring poorly on the math section of the entrance exam, Dennis Leahy, a scrawny, freckle-faced boy, needed his pastor to intervene on his behalf. Monsignor Charles McCorristin of St. James Roman Catholic Church in Woodbridge, a working-class suburb in central New Jersey, asked that the school reconsider Dennis's case. In a short note, McCorristin wrote, "I think the boy has a vocation. I wonder if you could do something for [him] and thus help to foster another vocation?"[8] Dennis was one of 233 freshmen in the class of 1963, and after only a week at Benedict's he was taken by the place. He remembers that he stood in the hallway above Shanley Gym, looked out a window, and said to himself, "This is home. You're home." He later recalled, "It was the best thing my mom and dad ever did for me."[9]

In hindsight, it was also the best thing for St. Benedict's Prep, as Dennis Leahy became Father Edwin, the Benedictine monk who proved pivotal in saving his alma mater. Leahy has made St. Benedict's feel like "home" for thousands of other young men. His brilliant people skills allow him to feel equally comfortable with a teenager and an aging alumnus. According to one close friend, "Edwin has an almost unlimited capacity to make and to maintain close friendships."[10] Father Edwin also possesses a magnetism that draws talented people and resources to his school. His ability to understand, command, and hold the rapt attention of various audiences is impressive. So is his ability to read various situations, whether in the life of an individual or of an institution. A hands-on headmaster, he labors tirelessly and without rest. His mother, a spry octogenarian, says he is incapable of taking time off, and her own active life suggests from where he gets his drive and energy.[11]

In others, Father Edwin looks for what he sees in himself: toughness, endurance, and moral strength. Because of his uncompromising principles and straightforward, often confrontational approach, students have a love-hate relationship with him. But his influence has been undeniable and harks back to another prominent leader in the history of St. Benedict's. As mentioned in Chapter 3, of Father Cornelius Selhuber, the headmaster between 1910 and 1926, students said, "We all knew that all the students looked to him as their primary guide and counselor, and that all loved him. During our four years in his happy company, we had many opportunities to see that his interest, enthusiasm and generalship is the *secret motive power* of St. Benedict's."[12] If Father Edwin is the "secret motive power" behind St. Benedict's present-day success, then certain people and forces helped make him the headmaster he has become.

St. Benedict's felt like home for Leahy because it reminded him of his upbringing in Woodbridge, one dominated by the dual rhythms of the Catholic Church and the suburban sandlot. Born on December 2, 1945, Dennis spent much of his time playing sports in his neighborhood, and whenever the nuns at St. James needed an altar boy they called the Leahy household. Sometimes Dennis just slipped on his pants over his pajamas and ran down to the church. He had been playing priest since he was five or six, as he set up an altar at home and muttered away in indecipherable proto-Latin. When playing football or baseball, recalled his mother, "Denny was always the peacemaker so the game could go on." Glued together by church socials, backyard barbeques, and Little League games, neighborhoods in Woodbridge oozed community. They also had a very Catholic feel to them. Monsignor McCorristin strolled down Main Street each night and knew the intimate details of most residents' lives. He also signed and handed out every report card at the grammar school. The town fathers routinely came to the rectory to discuss local affairs.[13] Priests often visited the Leahy household, but it was Bill and Jean who provided the first spiritual examples for their children. "My mother was a saint and very active in the church, and my dad was tough as nails but I remember him hitting his knees every morning and every night," recalled their youngest son, Tom.[14]

Tough, hardworking, and intensely religious, Bill Leahy was a man of principle, believing that laws and rules, whether religious or secular, had to be obeyed. He was also his son Dennis's first hero. Spontaneous, funny, and a bit mischievous, Mr. Leahy was also a doer. For example, he arranged to borrow heavy machinery from a construction crew along the Garden State Parkway so he and friends could build Little League baseball fields in town. He also had a temper, especially when he sensed he had been wronged. A crane operator by trade, Bill became incensed at work one day, believing that the boss's son had shown him a lack of respect. He skillfully lowered a crane's bucket within a few inches of the son's head before warning, "Don't ever come out onto my dock again!"[15] As a young monk, Edwin spent time standing next to his father at work, listening to his stories and no doubt seeing some of the same traits in himself, especially his sense of humor, stubbornness, and ability to get things done.

Dennis's parents rarely saw their son after he enrolled at St. Benedict's in 1958, since he spent almost all his waking hours there. Nicknamed "Dee-Lay" by his classmates, the lively, athletic teen played all sorts of sports, including football, wrestling, and tennis, so he stayed for practice and always took the late train home. He improved in the classroom too, gradually moving up from the lowest academic grouping to the highest by his senior year. But he never really took his studies all that seriously. His calling to the priesthood remained in tact despite some attempts to hide it. "I just always knew," recalled Leahy. "I tried to forget it when I got to high school and met this girl, but it was always part of me. It was something that I always had in me."[16] In 1960, Father Benedict Tyler, his guidance counselor, noted in his student file that he was still considering not only a vocation to the priesthood, but one as a Benedictine monk.

At St. Benedict's, Dennis was immediately drawn to Joe Kasberger, an immense presence at the school, and quickly came to admire the legendary coach's ability to build a team. Kasberger set extremely high standards, always demanding excellence and insisting on a high degree of discipline, all things that could be readily observed in his own conduct. Although Leahy was a third-string quarterback and rarely saw playing time, he always had an eye on Kasberger, watching and studying how he worked. He told stories about "Joe K" to students and alumni over the years, always mimicking Kasberger's drawl and reciting his many aphorisms verbatim. The headmaster-to-be was also strongly influenced by a Kasberger protégé, Johnny Allen, saying many years later, "I was never a great athlete, but I spent a lot of my life in locker- rooms. I learned just being around great coaches—Joe K and Johnny Allen—and they taught me most of what I do in running a school." Over the last three decades, the master team-builder has used convocation to "huddle" his "players and staff" each and every morning in order to cajole, criticize, or motivate. "It's the most important thing we do. It's about building a team and it's critical to have them together at least once a day," he said.[17]

After graduating from St. Benedict's in June 1963, Dennis began his clerical studies at St. Bernard's College in Alabama along with his St. Benedict's classmate James Waters. On the crest of the last wave of large-scale vocations to the priesthood, the pair went on to study at St. John's University in Minnesota before returning to New Jersey to complete their undergraduate theology degrees at Seton Hall University. Both men entered the novitiate at the abbey in Morristown in 1965, and as new members of the Order of St. Benedict they changed their first names. Leahy took the name Edwin, after Edwin "The Hammer" Mullin, a much-admired but tough monk who taught mathematics, and Waters took the name Philip. A year later they professed simple vows and continued living and studying in Morristown, doing so until 1967. Both yearned for their weekly Wednesday visits to Newark, though, where they often scoured through old abbey and school scrapbooks. Abbot Martin Burne wanted them to become familiar with the Newark community and its history, probably because he saw in them the future of both the monastery and the school.

During their time as students at St. Benedict's, Edwin and Philip, both suburbanites, had developed a special attachment to the city and the monastery. Edwin had a "real yen for Newark," as Abbot Martin recalled, and often made that known to the other monks in Morris-town.[18] In particular, he harbored ill will over Abbot Patrick's switch-ing of the abbey title from Newark to Morristown in 1956, even though it occurred a full three years before he entered St. Benedict's Prep for the first time. He often joked with Philip about his dislike for what some Newark monks called "Double-Cross Abbey." He would ask his friend, "What's the best thing about Delbarton?" Philip dutifully re-plied, "Looking back at it in your rearview mirror!" The two young clerics returned to live in the monastic community in Newark and teach at their alma mater in 1967, but not before a monk in Morris-town handed Leahy a hardcover copy of *The Headmaster*, a "sketch" of the longtime Deerfield Academy headmaster Frank Boyden. Although Edwin never met him, the iconic schoolmaster instantly became one of his heroes.[19]

The author John McPhee called Boyden "the last man of his kind," one of a class of twentieth-century American school leaders who "cre-ated enduring schools through their own individual energies, main-tained them under their own absolute rule, and left them forever imprinted with their own personalities." Enamored by the larger-than-life portrait of the short, bespectacled headmaster, the young monk could not have known in the late 1960s how his life's work would come to mirror that of the revered New England educator. The Deerfield headmaster's philosophy was quite simple: "I believe in boys. I believe in keeping them busy, and in the highest standards of scholarship. . . . I try to do the simple things a well-organized home does for its boys." Essentially, he assumed responsibility for their lives, monitoring their academic, social, athletic, and even spiritual development. He was ubiquitous too, touring the school's buildings and grounds daily, and even coaching and playing on various athletic teams in the afternoons. He believed that the more students saw him, the more smoothly his school ran. It truly was Boyden's school, as McPhee's portrait aptly pointed out: "Those who stay in the Deerfield community for any length of time quickly become aware that they are living in a monarchy."[20]

Father Edwin has called St. Benedict's Prep a "benevolent dictator-ship," maintaining that "it has always been benevolent, at least in my mind, maybe not in other people's minds."[21] Like Boyden, he has been involved in students' lives, past and present, and he has always possessed an uncanny ability to recall their struggles, their achievements, and their family histories with remarkable detail and understanding. "You can only do that if you care about them and are totally passionate about making them succeed in life," recalled one faculty member.[22] Edwin, perhaps not unlike other great secondary school leaders, has remained a teenager at heart. According to Abbot Melvin, "He has a special empathy and sympathy for teenagers. A teen still lurks within him, even though he has become a great headmaster and priest. Teenagers never threatened Edwin; he's understood them always." Fred Smith, a talented African American student, entered St. Benedict's months after his own father died of a fatal heart attack and a year before the school closed in 1972. "I was very fortunate that right after I lost one role model, I found another," admitted Smith. "He's probably the blackest white man alive. He understands black kids better than some black people do."[23]

Abbot Martin Burne, a massive influence in Leahy's spiritual and professional life, told him as a twenty-four-year-old novice that he possessed "an instinct with kids and how to deal with them."[24] "Maybe it was the way I was raised, maybe it was my father's influence," offered Father Edwin. "His approach was always to surprise you so the reaction that you thought you were going to get was not the one you got. I don't know where this intuition came from when I was in my twenties, but I knew I loved Benedict's so much that nothing was going to get in my way."[25] Boyden also had a similar intuition. "His school evolved naturally, gradually, surprisingly. He had no plan and no theory, but he proved himself to be an educator by intuition," wrote McPhee.[26]

Perhaps Father Edwin was drawn to Frank Boyden because he too had no plan and thought little of educational theory. "I had no training and I absolutely had no plan. We set out on this thing not knowing what we were doing, not knowing where we were going or what was going to happen," confessed Edwin. "We just went forth with our faith."[27] Faith certainly helped the "new school venture," but in a strange way so did Edwin's inexperience and youthful exuberance. Father Albert, his trusted right-hand man, explained:

Edwin had no idea what he was doing in terms of being a professional educator. That was a huge help when we sat down with a blank piece of paper and said, "Let's make a school." That's why it's so student-centered. He didn't know how to make it structure-centered because he didn't know what the structure was supposed to be, or program-centered because he didn't know what the program was supposed to look like. But he knew kids and he knew parents. He knew what made kids tick and clearly he knows what motivates adults. It was all that stuff that he brought as his vision, and it was all very vague. But as luck would have it, he had some people around who could put some flesh and bones to that vision. It was always within the context of Edwin's vision, though: "It's got to be good for the kids." At this reinvigorated St. Benedict's, it was all about the kids.[28]

Put another way, for the man who failed the math portion of the entrance exam, the "new math" at St. Benedict's could be distilled down to a least common denominator. The right answer was always what was in the best interests of the kids.

The Headmaster, the Street, and a School

When Father Edwin found out about a student carrying a knife in school, he cornered him and then threatened, "If you ever show that knife in school, I'll use it to cut out your colon!" The student replied, "I'd rather be caught by you with a knife than by somebody on the street without it."[29] In the school's attempts to build and foster community, observed one reporter, "St. Benedict's relentless adversary [was] the street, where drugs and lethargy [were] ubiquitous, and where debased values compete[d] with the school's good works."[30] The school's emphasis on academics, its social and academic honor code, and its commitment to community stood in direct opposition to an anti-intellectual, dishonorable, and altogether individualistic street culture. "We were creating an alternative to the street," admitted Father Edwin, "especially since many kids coming here in the 1970s and 1980s did not have experiences of community. We were creating it for them."[31]

Father Albert reflected on what the monks and lay teachers sought to accomplish at St. Benedict's early on in the new school's reincarnation. "Contrary to our conviction that 'there's more,'" reasoned the monk in a Benedictine publication, "*the Street* was teaching our students that there's nothing more, and that the best they could do is to pursue grimly and recklessly those same worn out substitutes for meaning that have deluded people for ages: possessions, power and prestige." The monastic school stood against everything "the street" valued, and so it became an enemy in and of itself. Each year the school lost several students to the street's "allurements," but the school was up for a fight, ready and willing to grapple with students and their problems. Father Edwin told his mother once, "I hate to lose to the street." Growing up in Newark or one of the surrounding cities or towns was not easy, and the staff at Benedict's was aware of the inner struggle that went on within many students. "It's a struggle and it matters what kinds of adults are in their lives and it's why St. Benedict's is so important," admitted Edwin.[32] In surprising ways, then, St. Benedict's Prep has been able to a wage a successful battle with the street, combating and counteracting the negative forces that seek to influence many young men who grow up in the city.

An article in *Harper's Magazine* confirmed just how formidable an opponent the streets of Newark could be, even almost ten years after the riots. After analyzing twenty-four categories, including crime, health, housing, poverty, and education, the article dubbed Newark the worst city in the United States, concluding:

The city of Newark stands without serious challenge as the worst of all. It ranked among the worst five cities in no fewer than nineteen of the twenty-four categories, and it was dead last in nine of them. Adding one, two, or even three tables couldn't possibly jar Newark from last place, and there is every reason to suppose that more comparisons would simply bury it deeper. Newark is a city that desperately needs help.[33]

While Newarkers could not deny their city was in rough shape, some doubted if it was indeed the country's most terrible city. A spate of corporate and educational construction, largely in the city's downtown,

A morning convocation in Shanley Gymnasium in the mid-1980s.

prompted the Newark Chamber of Commerce to run a full-page advertisement in the *Newark Star-Ledger* that read, "A MESSAGE FOR THOSE
WHO THINK NEWARK DIED TEN YEARS AGO."[34] Even if the downtown had
been bouncing back from the blows delivered by the riots, the city's
ravaged neighborhoods were less resilient. And since St. Benedict's
Prep drew many students from twelve core schools in the heart of the
Central Ward, the problems of those neighborhoods were the problems
of St. Benedict's, whether it was crime, drug use, teenage pregnancy,
or high school dropout rates.

What often lurked outside the school's front door was altogether
disturbing and depressing. After visiting one student's neighborhood,
Father Edwin returned and told others how "shocked" he was by the
living conditions of one high-rise housing project and vowed to raise
money to build a dormitory in the future. Despite two decades of civil
rights gains and federal antipoverty programs, conditions in the predominantly African American neighborhoods in the Central Ward had
worsened, and a 1977 *Time* magazine article attributed much of the

decline in places like Newark to the emergence of an American "underclass." "Behind [the ghetto's] crumbling walls lives a large group of people who are intractable, more socially alien and more hostile than almost anyone had imagined," concluded the cover story. "They are the unreachables: the American underclass." Made up of "mostly impoverished urban blacks," members of the "underclass" produced "a highly disproportionate number of the nation's juvenile delinquents, school dropouts, drug addicts and welfare mothers, and much of the adult crime, family disruption, urban decay and demand for social expenditures."[35]

As policy makers and scholars debated the causes and effects of persistent urban poverty, Bill Moyers produced a compelling documentary titled *The Vanishing Family: Crisis in Black America*.[36] Focusing on field interviews in Newark in the mid-1980s, Moyers reexamined the impact of a disintegrating black family structure, which was first studied by Daniel P. Moynihan in 1965. Citing a "tangle of pathology" associated with the prevalence of out-of-wedlock births, welfare dependence, and female-headed households, Moynihan argued that "the Negro family in the urban ghettos is crumbling," and that as long as that persisted, "the cycle of poverty and disadvantage will continue to repeat itself."[37]

Twenty years on, the picture was even gloomier. Nearly 60 percent of black children born in the United States were born out of wedlock, many of them to teenage mothers. African American men took little or no responsibility for their offspring. Moyers interviewed a young Newark man who had fathered six children by four different women and supported none of them. "Well, the majority of the mothers are [on] welfare," he stated. "And welfare gives them the stipend for the month. So what I'm not doing, the Government does." Moyers commented at one point, "What happens to families when mothers are children, fathers don't care, and the street is the strongest school?"[38]

Moyers's documentary, as well as the *Time* magazine article, reached a national audience and left some viewers with the impression that places like Newark were all-ghetto and that each and every "underclass" family was on welfare. Of course, this was not true and it often led to simplistic and misleading stereotypes. The lack of jobs and the accompanying poverty in postindustrial Newark were root causes of many of the city's worst problems, and Father Edwin often spoke of the school's efforts in terms of missionary work. "You don't need to go to the Third World to do mission work," he would say. "What we're trying to do here is mission work; we're dealing with the Fourth World: the Third World in the middle of the First."[39] More than half the school's students came from single-parent households and more than one-third lived below the poverty line.

Father Edwin once received a letter from a struggling mother, enclosed along with twenty-seven dollars and a piece of cheap blue stationary. In neat print, the note read:

Father Ed,

I want to try and tithe my welfare check. I don't want my son to know. Your school has been good for both of us. Use this where it'll help.

Sincerely,

A mom.

The next month, after welfare checks were delivered, Edwin received another letter and payment:

Dear Father Ed,

I'm putting this in the envelope before I lose my nerve. Talking about tithing is easy, doing it sure is another matter. I get scared when all there is left is faith and no money. Thanks for all you've done for my son and for all the kids at St. Benedict's.

A mom.[40]

The note's emotional conundrum struck a nerve. It reminded the monks of the period of time after the school closed when they had no work and had to subsist on faith alone. It also validated the school's mission and sense of place in the larger Newark community.

Since the 1970s, the monks had been looking to shed the "fortress mentality" that long defined the relationship between the monastery-school and the local African American community. "We broke down that idea of a fortress," said Father Phillip, "and we try to pull the kids in, lock them up here, and provide them a safe place to learn and grow."[41] Of course, the college prep curriculum sought to prepare young men for the rigors of college, an avenue that many young men were the first to go down in the history of their families. But there also existed a not-so-hidden curriculum that helped to draw students into the Benedict's family. One old monk often told Father Edwin how to win over young men, saying, "Eddie, you attract more boys with honey."[42] Edwin and his staff did just that, as everything from the morning meeting to after-school sports brought students and adults together in the common endeavor to create community and provide a viable alternative to the street.

In large part, the effectiveness of the school was measured by the sheer amount of time students and adults spent at the school. The monks may well have lived there, but it seemed others did too. It was not uncommon for students and adults to arrive at seven in the morning and leave after eight in the evening. There was always something going on, including pickup games of all sorts like touch football, floor hockey, and whiffle ball. Young faculty members like Edwin, Hank Cordeiro (a 1972 graduate who returned to teach Spanish), and Mike DiPiano (the wrestling coach and athletic director) all played. They enlivened the games and blurred the lines between who was a kid and who was not. Students and faculty from the late 1970s and early 1980s recall an era that was "a laugh a minute." For example, some staff members caught a student cutting out of school on videotape. The next day at convocation, Cordeiro narrated the scene for the entire student body like Warner Wolf, a colorful New York sportscaster. In some respects, all the time spent together outside class was as important as what was happening inside it.

Instilling a sense of belonging to the Benedict's tradition was also a crucial element to Father Edwin's leadership style. Through storytelling, he included students in the school's glorious past and challenged them to create their own stories to place alongside those of the men who went before them. To that end, the headmaster told stories of legendary coaches like Joe Kasberger and Prof Blood and long-remembered teachers like Father Ignatius Kohl and Father Dunstan Smith. He usually told these stories at convocation, but he also did so in his office, where students often "hung out." He regaled them with the time he purposely left a tack on Father Iggy's chair in 1961. After sitting on it not once but twice, the monk uttered several obscenities before grabbing a detention slip and filling it out for the entire class. It read, "Junior C, jug the whole class! Tack on the chair, right up the old ass!" "I told stories to connect them to what had gone on here before them," admitted Father Edwin. "The African American community was here now. They owned it just as much as the Germans or Irish or Italians communities did before them."[43]

To make sure that the school's value system had a fighting chance, Father Edwin, Father Phillip, and Bernard Greene often visited students' neighborhoods on what they called "homework raids." An adaptive lot, many of the students found ways to live by two codes of conduct, the one expected of them at St. Benedict's and the one required by the street, ably switching between the two at a moment's notice.[44] Like "urban guerillas," the trio snuck into various neighborhoods at night to see if a student was where he was supposed to be and doing what he was supposed to be doing. "They didn't know where we were coming from next. The kids were afraid and thought we were crazy," confessed Father Edwin. At one house a single mother said, "Father, he's up in his bed. He should be studying. Go get him, but just don't hit him in the mouth because he just got braces." Edwin tore up the stairs and yanked the startled teen straight out of bed, yelling, "You should be studying! What are you doing up in the bed?" On other occasions, they found no one home and so questioned the student on his whereabouts the next day in school. Another time they caught a student riding his bicycle to McDonald's at nine o'clock at night, and they even discovered that one poor fellow had left his unopened book bag on the front porch for the entire evening.[45]

Father Albert attended one raiding party and made note of the experience in his journal: "I really think this was worthwhile, just to see where and how these kids live, while letting parents (often single mothers) know we're helping, and making the kid wonder a bit, too."[46] The "homework raids," as well as what was going on at the school, led to increased credibility and trust. The school was gaining an odd sort

of "street cred" among adults. As word traveled through the community, the message became clear: if you were having trouble raising your
son, or if you just wanted some help doing it, then send him to St.
Benedict's. Many mothers over the years arrived on the school's doorstep and said the same thing: "I'm afraid I'm losing my boy and they
told me to bring him to you, Father Ed." "Mothers just wanted any
help they could get," said Father Edwin, "They thought I was nuts, but
they appreciated the help."[47]

Students did too. Joe Scott lived in the Scudder Homes, a high-rise
project on Howard Street, but he spent most of his time only three
blocks away at St. Benedict's Prep. "If you come to my building, the
first thing that hits most folks is the smell—it changes—but usually
it's some variation on the burnt food–reefer–urine theme," remarked
Joe in 1981. "The rep of the place is pretty bad; in fact, for some
younger kids, it must be the epitome of hell to live there." For Joe,
Benedict's was heaven-sent. He finished atop his class, captained the
soccer team, and won the school's prestigious Presidential Award for
scholastic and athletic achievements. Scott went on to study at Trinity
College in Connecticut before embarking on a successful career as a
jazz musician. "Because of Benedict's," offered Joe, "I learned that there
is more to life than Howard Street, another world that I'd have to deal
with if I wanted to make it."[48]

Carl Blake was a directionless teenager from a tough city neighborhood, but oddly enough, a flashy maroon and gray gym bag changed
all that. Carl spotted a young man walking home early one night and
asked, "Hey, man, where'd you get the bag? I really like that bag." He
was told that it was from St. Benedict's Prep. Blake's curiosity led him
to visit the school. He liked what he saw and enrolled in the summer
of 1976. After a rocky start, he responded well to the hard work, discipline, and commitment asked of him by his teachers. By his senior
year, he earned admission to Bowdoin College, a prestigious liberal
arts college in Maine, from which he graduated four years later with a
degree in economics. His first job was in investment banking on Wall
Street. At twenty-two, he was already a Benedict's success story—a
poor but talented African American male who had raised himself up
against considerable odds by dint of his own industry and initiative.

But Carl knew that it did not have to be that way, saying in 1984, "I know I'd probably be in jail now if it were not for this place. That's where most of the kids I hung out with are now."[49]

On a basic level, the monks and staff at St. Benedict's Prep wanted to create opportunities for young men who had been deemed "unreachable" by some sectors of American society. Benedict's was able to reach many young men through building community, much as it had for over one hundred years. It was a "second home" where they could forge meaningful relationships with peers and adults. But not every St. Benedict's student turned his back on the street and went off to college and a career like Joe Scott and Carl Blake. Some never graduated, and others succumbed to the negative forces of the street. This always bothered Father Edwin, who had a messianic complex and hated to lose. It tormented him when someone left the school, and he recalled the time when he asked the following question at convocation: "Did we do everything we could do to give this guy a shot?"[50] Giving someone "a shot" was a start, but Edwin and the St. Benedict's he helped create always wanted to win.

The End Is in the Beginning: St. Benedict's Prep, 1977–1986

During the sixth game of the 1977 World Series, Reggie Jackson slugged three home runs to win another world championship for the New York Yankees. The brash, confident Jackson thrived under the pressure of the New York media and the club's megalomaniac owner, George Steinbrenner. Through the late 1970s to the mid-1980s, St. Benedict's was hitting home run after home run too. As the graduation of the first four-year class at the new school in June 1977 marked "the end of the beginning," it also signaled the start of a new era, one just as exciting and rewarding. This phase was one not of consolidation but of growth and opportunity. Significantly, many of the developments during the first decade of the *new* school mirrored those of the *old* school some sixty years previous, when Father Cornelius Selhuber made Benedict's a modern Catholic prep school by strengthening the curriculum, securing student discipline, improving the facilities, encouraging athletics, and increasing enrollment. Father Edwin, the headmaster-coach who spoke to his "team" each morning at convocation, was still motivated by what some had said, or thought, in 1972: a prep school for mostly minority males from the city could not exist on High Street.

Beginning in the summer of 1977, every freshman began his Benedict's career by going through an intense orientation program. The "Overnight," described by one monk as "part monastic novitiate and part Parris Island," began on the eve of Summer Phase and continued for an entire week. The newest students slept on the hardwood floors of Shanley Gym before rising together to face a rigorous mix of academic, physical, and psychological challenges, all aimed at indoctrinating them on how their new school and community worked. During Benedict's "boot camp," freshmen learned the school's history and traditions and memorized its fight songs and the alma mater. They also memorized each of their classmates' names and helped serve them at communal meals. By midweek, with the pressure mounting and homesickness widespread, many of the neophytes wanted to quit. "But that is what brings the class together, and makes the class a unit," observed one student. "It makes you realize you have to face things together. Like a family, like brothers." Another revealed, "We get to see right then whether a guy's got what it takes to be a 'Benedict's Man,' and just a man, period. There's no calling your momma."[51]

The orientation week marked a class, just as the Backpacking Project did at the end of the freshman year, as students long remembered who quit, who cried, who passed out in the summer's sweltering heat, or who rose to a particular challenge. Each night, Mike DiPiano, the athletic director, conducted a gym class where students sounded off, did calisthenics in perfect unison, and sang songs. He also asked them over and over again, "What does the sign say?" The entire class shouted back, "BENEDICT'S HATES A QUITTER!" Just when the class seemed ready to move on to much-anticipated dodgeball games, "Mr. D" would find something wrong with someone or something. More singing and more jumping jacks followed, but eventually out came the red rubber balls to commence a series of vicious dodgeball games. At week's end, each freshman had to pass a test on the school's history and when he did so, he received his first maroon and gray St. Benedict's gym uniform.

Many students had never been subjected to such a stringent routine in their lives, but once they made it through the "Overnight" and their first Summer Phase they looked back with a sense of accomplishment. They had done something hard together with what was fast becoming a group of "brothers." They had real-life experiences to go along with some of the school's mottos, in particular those about not giving up and "Whatever hurts my brother, hurts me." Discipline and respect permeated the school's atmosphere, especially in the honor system established in the late 1970s. In September 1978, after some students began stealing from others, the entire school received after-school detention for a whole week. The soccer team even forfeited a game because they could not be in two places at once. The following year, students agreed to remove locks on their lockers. It was more than a symbolic gesture for a school in the heart of a city with one of the highest theft rates in the country, and it quickly became the bedrock of the school's honor code. In 1983, Father Edwin closed school until students found out who was behind a rash of stealing and vandalism at the school. Students resolved the issues and committed themselves once again to the Honor Code, further proving to many what separated Benedict's from other schools.[52]

To be sure, running a school on such an expansive honor system was challenging at times, but many teachers and students felt it was entirely worthwhile. In terms of discipline, students often tried to get away with things, much as they had throughout the history of the school. But now there was no demerit system and no dean of discipline. Teachers took a team approach to dealing with student behavior, both negative and positive, but two men in particular, Father Edwin and Bernard Greene, dealt with discipline issues more than others. Father Edwin usually addressed student behavior at convocation, reminding students how they should treat one another and conduct themselves in public. Conduct was talked about all the time, but rules and regulations were never written down and codified. Benedict's also stuck with students longer than they had in the past, and since there was no longer a demerit system students were not "discontinued" for amassing too many, and the school often gave young men second, third, and even fourth chances. The school staff preferred to use a "modified program of 'JUG,'" as Father Edwin kept certain students after school as "an effective means of punishment." There were only two infractions that led to immediate expulsion: selling narcotics or carrying a weapon in school.[53]

Physical punishment did not have a place in the new school either, but there were isolated instances of it being used. Father Albert recalled striking a student the year the school reopened. It never seemed right, although it had been perfectly acceptable only two years previous in the old school. Father Albert elaborated:

We could be much more creative than that by using love rather than force and fear. All along in the new school we realized the difference between physical discipline and violence. The kids I went to school with at St. Benedict's, their parents would smack them around. It was understood; that was the context. That was what your father was supposed to do. But that wasn't working for kids in 1973. At times, they were coming from places where there was just plain old violence, a dysfunctional kind of violence.[54]

The disciplinarian Bernard Greene, a towering figure who "roughed guys up" during the 1970s and early 1980s, established a reputation resembling that of Father Dunstan Smith during the 1950s. Greene's legend carried him from year to year, and all he had to do to maintain order or discipline a student was to walk into a room, roll his eyes, clench his teeth, and shout in his deep baritone voice.[55]

Parents appreciated the school's efforts to build community, maintain order, and instill disciplined habits, but they also looked to St. Benedict's to provide a racially and ethnically diverse environment. In 1973, part of the school's mission was to bring together rich and poor, black and white, urban and suburban. But when the class of 1977 entered in the fall of 1973 it was not diverse at all. Nearly 90 percent of the students were African Americans and almost all of them lived in Newark. Six years later, when the admissions committee put together a "profile" for an ideal class, it consisted of forty African American students (60 percent), twenty white students (30 percent), and ten Latino students (10 percent). In addition, the school desired forty students from Newark and thirty from outside the city limits, and wanted at least twenty students who were academic "risks."[56]

In 1980, the newsman Bob Brown highlighted the school on *World News Tonight* and informed a national audience that the "reincarnated" St. Benedict's had become "a national model of an urban, integrated secondary school." By then, 20 percent of its student body was white, as more and more white students from the suburbs opted to come into Newark to attend the school. More sons of alumni started to make the trek into the city; some even enrolled in the new seventh and eighth grade program. It was the first time in fifty years that middle schoolers walked the halls of St. Benedict's.[57] Bob Brown concluded his brief story by saying, "And, whether they live in white suburbs or ghetto projects, both black and white students say that St. Benedict's revival has brought about greater racial understanding." One student then added: "It's sort of an island in the middle of the city, and it's really a symbol of what can be, if blacks, whites, Hispanics—if everybody pulls

A group of students, c. 1985.

together." For Father Edwin, Benedict's was a symbol indeed, one that was "helping heal the city's old wounds—and helping change certain pictures of Newark that people carry around with them."[58]

One event that helped change people's mind-sets, especially skeptical alumni, was Jack Dalton's return to teach and coach at the school. Dalton was legendary in Benedict's circles, having first played basketball for Prof Blood in the 1940s before playing college ball for two other Hall of Fame coaches, Joe Lapchik and Frank McGuire. Dalton began teaching and coaching at his alma mater in 1953, and during one stretch his Gray Bee teams captured six straight prep championships. Dalton had reacted to news of the school's closing with the lament, "Camelot is dead," but his return in 1977 was a significant sign to alumni and friends that a rebirth was underway. Like many things at the school over the years, it happened fairly serendipitously. Jack and his wife, Joan, brought their son Tim to an open house at the school, and Joan pulled Father Edwin aside and said, "Why don't you ask Jack to come back?" Edwin did and Dalton returned, saying to a local sportswriter, "I'm glad to be coming back. I've spent most of my adult life at St. Benedict's. They're going to be doing such great things."[59]

For Father Edwin's part, "great things" included restoring the school's reputation as an athletic powerhouse. He envisioned the day when dominating teams with outstanding coaches won championship after championship, much like Benedict's teams had done from the 1920s through the 1960s. "Our kids know of St. Benedict's great tradition in sports and are determined to live up to it," the headmaster informed alumni in a 1978 interview.[60] While certain teams and individuals fared well in the first few years, the basketball team suffered some heavy defeats. In the middle of one particular game, Edwin had to walk out of the gymnasium because a Benedict's team was getting beaten so badly; the lopsided score made him nauseous and he vowed to never let it happen again. Jack Dalton brought stability and success to the basketball program while Mike DiPiano began producing wrestling champions, notably Clarence Richardson, who won the New Jersey wrestling tournament in 1979. Father Philip rebuilt the track program, and soccer was once again played at the varsity level at the school, the first time since the 1940s.

Philosophically, Father Edwin's approach to athletics was similar to Father Cornelius Selhuber's stance on athletics. Selhuber once told a gathering of alumni, "I am a great believer in athletics. I feel that they are the salvation of boys. I would not attempt to conduct a school without athletics."[61] Edwin believed in athletics and what they could do for an individual too, especially since he felt that success in activities could translate into success in the classroom. He spoke on the role of athletics before a panel of congressmen in 1980:

Strange as it may sound coming from a headmaster of a well-regarded prep school, I believe athletics are as important as academics for our students. For some students at certain stages, athletics are even more important than class. That's not at all to say that schoolwork is neglected. Rather schoolwork can be tackled with greater confidence and success once a certain determination and toughness are present in a student. It's all too easy for a student to hide from a really tough challenge in the classroom.

But activities like sports help a kid face certain responsibilities head-on—in a clear way that neither he nor anyone else can ignore. . . . The demands are rapid, intense, clear, and the results are in right away. You have to meet the test, and pass or fail, almost instantly, and often alone.[62]

Not everyone agreed with the headmaster's view of the role of athletics. Some even suggested that the school should de-emphasize sports and concentrate more on academic and personal issues.

Fred Smith and a young Father Edwin used to roll around on the wrestling mats during practice in the early 1970s. When the school closed, Fred transferred to St. Peter's Prep in Jersey City and Edwin continued to coach him. While at Benedict's, though, Fred studied alongside the sons of lawyers and doctors, and later observed, "I think I borrowed some of their ambition—maybe I looted their incentive a little."[63] A superbright young man, Edwin and Paul Thornton persuaded him to attend Harvard University, where he studied economics, continued to wrestle, and worked as a night watchman to meet some of his college expenses. In 1977, he became only the seventh African

American, and the first black Newarker, to win a Rhodes Scholarship.[64] After studying at Oxford University in England, where he won a university-wide boxing contest and rowed crew, he returned to Harvard to pursue a law degree. Fred next practiced law and eventually became the first African American partner at McCarter & English, Newark's most prestigious law firm. When Fred returned to Benedict's over the years he often criticized his friend Father Edwin for overemphasizing athletics.

"He used to get mad at me, and, in fact, he stopped coming around for a few years," remembered Father Edwin. Smith even told him, "Father, I'm looking forward to the day when kids are sitting around the property and reading books, not playing sports." But after reflecting on his life and career, and what had helped him along the way, Fred changed his mind, saying, "I've learned that solving problems had little to do with how much of the law I knew; it had to do with how determined I was and how many times I was able to get up after getting knocked down. These were the things I learned wrestling, all the things I learned from you when you used to beat me up on the wrestling mat."[65] Hard work, effort, and attitude mattered, and people at Benedict's knew that when men looked back on their athletic experiences, they remembered those invaluable lessons. They had shaped them as men, and Leahy, along with Selhuber nearly six decades earlier, did not dream of running a prep school without them.

On a practical level, both headmasters realized the importance of a successful athletic program: it meant both prestige and publicity for St. Benedict's, but it also was of particular interest to alumni. In the 1920s, Selhuber's commitment to athletics included hiring top-notch coaches, building a new gymnasium, and instituting a postgraduate year. Not coincidentally, the comprehensive news coverage of the school's sporting exploits increased the school's profile and thus enrollment skyrocketed. Athletics at the new St. Benedict's helped put the school "back on the map" as various reports in the local newspapers served as "free press" for the financially strapped school. Like Selhuber, Father Edwin began assembling a staff of highly competent coaches, and in the late 1970s the school broke ground for a new recreational facility on urban renewal land, ultimately creating two playing fields, a cinder track, and two tennis courts.

A few years after a twelve-year-old boy came to the United States from Uruguay, he graced those new fields and inaugurated an era that witnessed St. Benedict's become a national soccer powerhouse. Tabaré Ramos first lived across the river from Newark in Harrison, but eventually moved to the soccer hotbed of nearby Kearny. In 1980, Tab's parents enrolled him at St. Benedict's because they preferred a Catholic school, and he soon became a soccer legend, ultimately setting a state record for goals scored in a career with 162. St. Benedict's also went on to win its first state championship since the school's reopening, and Tab eventually played professional soccer and represented the United States in three World Cups. After hiring Rick Jacobs in 1985, St. Benedict's has won countless state titles and five national championships. A modern-day Joe Kasberger or Prof Blood, Jacobs, a Jewish man raised in the affluent town of Millburn, has produced some of the greatest players and teams in the history of American high school soccer, including the former U.S. national team captain Claudio Reyna. His success has led to other programs striving for national prominence; Benedict's teams in basketball, wrestling, and track have all won national championships recently. Much as it was in the 1930s through the 1960s, St. Benedict's has once again become an athletic powerhouse.

While the athletic program has been able to recapture its former glory, the fairy-tale story of fundraising has been far more unexpected and compelling. When Paul Thornton became director of development in the mid-1970s, St. Benedict's had already experienced some success with receiving alumni donations and foundation grants. Initially, a proud Thornton photocopied five-thousand- or ten-thousand-dollar checks to commemorate someone's unbelievable generosity, but according to Father Albert, by the end of 1978 "donations and grants [were] coming in so fast [it was] hard to keep track of them."[66] The school benefited from sheer luck too. Abbot Melvin and Father Luke Edelen, a young monk, discovered Father George Bien's long-lost coin collection in the abbey library. In 1974 the monks learned it was worth sixty-five thousand dollars; when the price of silver started to climb a few years later, the monks voted to put it out to auction. An 1861 three-dollar gold coin fetched twenty-one thousand dollars and the entire collection, consisting of over 1,200 pieces, returned nearly nine hundred thousand dollars. Abbot Melvin reflected, "The price of silver went through the roof in 1980. It was at its highest peak in history at thirty-four dollars per ounce and it has never returned there."[67] The monks used some of the money to renovate the abbey church and monastery buildings.

The monks also discovered more than hidden coin collections, namely that many alumni were very interested in financially supporting the new school. Their enthusiasm for the new St. Benedict's led many alumni to make significant donations of time, energy, and money. Some gave because they recognized a similar school spirit from their own schooldays, while others gave because they believed wholeheartedly in the school's current mission. "I've had alumni tell me that they are more enthusiastic about supporting St. Benedict's as it is now than they would have been if we remained the same as when they were here," revealed Paul Thornton. He also added that over the years between a third to a half of the operating budget in a given year has been raised from tuition revenue, a staggeringly low number considering most private schools cover more than 90 percent of their operating costs with tuition. St. Benedict's Prep's reliance on gift support and its growing endowment funds mirrored that of two other iconic educational institutions in the United States: Harvard University and the Lawrenceville School.[68]

In the months after the school reopened, Father Albert dined with John Magovern, the former chief of Mutual Benefit Life. Magovern told Albert that the school needed a sugar daddy. Shortly thereafter Bob Brennan began his long and controversial relationship with St. Benedict's. One of nine children, Brennan grew up in a strict but poor Irish American family in postwar Newark. After attending a local Catholic grammar school, Bob Brennan followed in the footsteps of his father and four brothers by entering St. Benedict's in 1958. On the eve of his senior year, he faced imminent disaster for failing French not once, but twice. On the verge of being thrown out, Father Boniface Treanor intervened to salvage Brennan's future at Benedict's. With the help of a tutor, Bob eventually passed French and went on to study at nearby Seton Hall University. In 1974, he founded First Jersey Securities, a stock-brokerage firm, and soon thereafter began donating money to the resurrected school that had given him a second chance.

In the fall of 1984, Brennan invited Abbot Melvin, Father Edwin, and Paul Thornton to his estate near the Jersey shore to talk about the school's ambitious development campaign. Toward the end of the evening, Brennan handed the abbot a check for five million dollars. Amazed at the ungodly sum, a disbelieving Melvin covered his mouth with a handkerchief and passed it on to Edwin. They were all speechless. Early the next morning, the abbot showed the check to Father Theodore, the grouchy treasurer, and after looking at all the zeros, he said, "Where did he get this from?"[69] Maybe the monk was skeptical of its source, or the amount simply stunned him, but Brennan felt the monks deserved every penny of it, saying, "The monks of Newark Abbey demonstrated a commitment to the City of Newark, a commitment that came only with great personal sacrifice. . . . They never ran away from their commitment to the city and its people." Shortly after the school announced the gift, a grateful Father Edwin praised Brennan, saying that he "never forgot what it was like to be poor and growing up in the city."[70]

Bob Brennan met fellow alumnus Carl Blake at the luncheon held to celebrate the unprecedented gift to the once financially strapped school. Blake, a recent college graduate embarking on a career on Wall Street, was in awe of the spectacularly successful and wealthy Brennan. It was hard to believe that he had once struggled at Benedict's and needed the school's help to even graduate. In fact, both men were personal testimonies to how a Catholic secondary school helped city kids, and they vowed never to forget what the school did for them. Two decades on, Carl Blake, who as a young man said that Benedict's saved him from a likely stint in prison, is still an investment banker in New York City. But Brennan served a nine-year sentence for bankruptcy fraud in a federal penitentiary in New Jersey.

Without a doubt, Bob Brennan's gift was a major turning point in the fortunes of St. Benedict's Prep. The monks and their helpers had labored to bring the school back over the course of a decade, but the school's valiant mission had always rested on precarious financial footing. Brennan's donation had finally put the school on solid ground,

Alumnus and benefactor Robert E. Brennan receives the Medal of St. Benedict for his charitable contributions from Abbot Melvin Valvano, OSB (*center*), and Father Edwin D. Leahy, OSB.

and the St. Benedict's Prep community has always been grateful for his generosity. As one of the monastery-school's "guardian angels," his portrait hangs on a wall just inside the monastery enclosure. Abbot Melvin and Father Edwin visited him in prison on a routine basis.

One monk watched in anticipation as the Henry and Agnes Brennan Center slowly emerged "from the primordial ooze" across the street from the school's front door. Father Malachy McPadden, the author of *The Benedictines in Newark*, could not help but think back to his student days at St. Benedict's in the 1940s, especially since Newark was an altogether different place then. People did not live on both sides of William Street anymore and Springfield Avenue was no longer a major shopping artery. The Masonic Temple, an imposing bank, and Casino Hall had long been demolished. During World War II, the field in front of Casino Hall, the parish's activities center, had been littered with "walls, fences, barricades, tunnels and traps" from Joe Kasberger's and Prof Blood's wartime obstacle course. After the war it became a parking lot for the monastery and the school. So much had changed along High Street. Fittingly, the street's name had been changed too—it was now Dr. Martin Luther King Jr. Boulevard.

Change was inevitable, but Father Malachy insisted:

While faces and buildings and the shape of things change, the Benedict's Spirit remains. That's the genius of this school—a certain stability, a tradition that is handed down from one generation to the next. Though properties be traded back and forth, buildings be torn down and others be erected in their place, the spirit of St. Benedict's Prep lives on within its walls. I think that peculiar vow of Benedictines, Stability, with its resultant rooted-ness to one place, has a lot to do with it.

I am convinced that if any of those Benedict's men of years gone by . . . were to come back and climb those brownstone steps to 520 today, they'd feel that same old St. Benedict's spirit and know they were home. "They sons forever more are we!"[71]

When a Benedict's man of yesterday walks into Shanley Gym today at eight o'clock in the morning, he will see a hand go straight up in the air. Others will follow and silence will come over the gathering. He will see, hear, and experience community. It is what St. Benedict's Prep has always been about, and according to the monk who helped resurrect a dead school, "It is the most important thing we do."[72] It is the miracle on High Street.

Conclusion

The shadow from the cross high above St. Mary's starts early in the morning near where William Street and Springfield Avenue meet. Father Edwin Leahy once walked to that corner of the abbey's property in the mid-1980s and looked back toward the school buildings in front of the skyscrapers that dot Newark's skyline. He thought, "We have from here all the way down to the telephone company building on Arlington Street. How the hell did that all happen?"[1] Since then three buildings—a gymnasium with classrooms, a library, and a dormitory—have been built on the property that served as a ball field for the first students at St. Benedict's. "I look at what we've done, where we are now," added the headmaster, "and I wonder to myself—how the heck did we come so far? I guess I was just so naïve back then I didn't realize what we were trying to do could not possibly be done."[2]

When looking for explanation to what has happened at St. Benedict's Prep and Newark Abbey, the monks understandably turn to the divine. Abbot Melvin Valvano mentioned the "unexplainable hand of God" and "the utter mysteriousness of it all."[3] Ten years after starting his journal in 1972, Father Albert Holtz ruminated on doing the impossible:

The Lord has been awfully busy over the past ten years working with a group of men, a bunch of buildings and a wild variety of kids. The "God of Surprises" has stood by us: leading, chiding, guiding, and always, always surprising us. His goodness to us has been utterly amazing. All the forks in the road, and he'd point us the right way at each one; all the times of doubt and discouragement, and he'd cheer us with some new surprises each time. Just when we'd be encouraged by some great success, he'd top it with another even better. He's been lavish in His blessings: He's blessed us with trials and heartaches, with fears and apprehensions, with challenges and opportunities, with good friends and healthy bodies and strength and enthusiasm, with a holy abbot and a masterful headmaster, with fundraising success and a good reputation.

"Prosper the work of our hands, O Lord!" Didn't He ever! In His all-seeing foresight He knew that St. Benedict's and Newark Abbey would prosper over these ten years. As this has unfolded day by day in our lives He has been teaching us one lesson in so many ways: how much He loves us![4]

"You have to inject the mystery of God into it," offered Father Edwin. "It has been just ordinary folks doing extraordinary things through God's grace."[5] His mother, Jean Leahy, concurs, saying, "I'm convinced that the Holy Spirit was there, and still is, working through the men, women and children in Newark. There is something there that no one can explain, but everyone wants to know how it happened. It's the Holy Spirit directing it all and working through the people there."[6] Fred Smith, the Rhodes Scholar from Harvard University, called it a miracle.

While many see what has transpired on High Street over the last forty years as miraculous, it has been the monks' stability of place that has made the urban abbey and school remarkably resilient. St. Benedict's Prep's has evolved from a "day college" for the sons of white ethnic immigrants to an urban Catholic prep school for mostly minority males. Born as a result of one riot, the school nearly died in another. According to the historian Mike Davis, places like Newark have faced three phases of neighborhood destruction since the 1950s, when the twin forces of urban renewal and highway construction began to rip a hole right through old urban centers. Next came the events of the 1960s and the hundreds of urban riots that wreaked havoc on the commercial life of the inner city. Finally, in the 1970s and 1980s, a long period of "disinvestment" led by local banks and endorsed by federal policies created what another scholar has called the "urban prairie."[7] The monks survived all three cataclysms.

In particular, the monks survived the "desert experience" in the aftermath of the announcement to close St. Benedict's Prep in 1972. In fact, they thrived in those years immediately after the trauma of losing one-third of their monastic family and common work. Their vow of stability, as well as their ability to adapt to changing circumstances, allowed them to resurrect a school in a city where too many of its venerable institutions simply perished. Father Edwin's ability to build community over the years has allowed St. Benedict's to prosper while serving young men who are too often failed by our educational system. Each year it seems another Catholic school closes in the city, and Terry Golway wrote in *America* that it is usually announced in February, the same month that the headmaster at St. Benedict's announced back in 1972 that the school would "cease operations." Golway has called it "the cruelest month."[8]

Over the last thirty years the monks have provided a holistic education, with wondrous financial help from alumni and corporations, friends and foundations. "It's insane," stated Father Edwin in 2004. "We're a high school and we have to raise four million dollars each year."[9] Bob Brennan's generosity from the mid-1980s through the early 1990s came to a controversial halt when he was sentenced to nine years in prison in 2000. But Brennan's gifts over the years were soon overshadowed by the beneficence of another alumnus, Charles M. Cawley. A member of the class of 1958, Cawley's father died when he was a student at St. Benedict's and he never forgot how the monks took care of him. When Brennan encountered his legal and financial woes, Cawley, founder of MBNA America, a credit card company based in Newark, Delaware, surfaced to become the greatest benefactor in the school's history. Cawley and his company donated more than thirty million dollars to St. Benedict's Prep.

The miracle of miracles, though, will be vocations to the monastery. Historically, a handful of Benedict's graduates considered the monastic life each and every year, but that trend came to a grinding halt with Fathers Edwin and Philip. Since then, only a handful of men have joined Newark Abbey and the current community is both old and small. Many rightly observe that Father Edwin and his cohorts could be the last of the Benedictines in Newark. The monks continue to pray and hope for "fresh blood" to reinvigorate the monastery and provide needed monk-power for the school. Father Edwin, a youthful monk in his sixties, will go on serving as headmaster for the foreseeable future, but in a few decades' time the next school leader may very well be a layman. The faculty has comprised mostly laymen and -women for some time.

Frank Boyden served as Deerfield's headmaster for six decades, and Father Edwin is only a bit more than halfway to that staggering accomplishment, having celebrated his thirty-fifth anniversary as headmaster in 2008. Like Newark Abbey, he is both stable and adaptable, so there is every reason to believe that he will be able to match Boyden's long tenure. In fact, when Father Edwin dies and goes to heaven, he wants to first see his father and grandfather. The third person to seek out, though, will be Frank Boyden. He plans on asking him, "How did I do? Did I do a good job?"[10] One retired archbishop of Newark, Theodore Cardinal McCarrick, would have Father Edwin canonized one day, saying he is a "very special man. He would be the patron saint of high schools in inner cities."[11] But it would be much more appropriate to commemorate the actions and deeds of all the Benedictines in Newark. Many a monk in Newark has done well at providing for the guidance of souls and the educational training of youth. It has been their life's work.

Notes

Introduction: Downtown Monks and the Miracle on High Street

1. On Boniface Wimmer and the founding of the Benedictine Order in the United States, see Jerome Oetgen, *An American Abbot: Boniface Wimmer, O.S.B., 1809–1887,* rev. ed. (Washington, D.C.: Catholic University Press, 2004), 80, 108; and Joel Rippinger, *The Benedictine Order in the United States: An Interpretive History* (Collegeville, Minn.: Liturgical Press, 1990).

2. For a discussion of the "urban crisis" and Roman Catholics, see Thomas J. Sugrue, *The Origins of the Urban Crisis: Race and Inequality in Detroit* (Princeton: Princeton University Press, 1996); John T. McGreevy, *Parish Boundaries: The Catholic Encounter with Race in the Twentieth-Century Urban North* (Chicago: University of Chicago Press, 1996); and Gerald Gamm, *Urban Exodus: Why the Jews Left Boston and the Catholics Stayed* (Cambridge: Harvard University Press, 1999).

3. Frederick T. Smith, "Miracle on High Street," *New Jersey Monthly,* December 1981.

4. Augustine Curley, OSB, "The Attack on St. Mary's Church, Newark: A Prototypical Know Nothing Incident," paper presented at the Spring 2004 American Catholic Historical Association meeting at St. Thomas University, April 16–17, 2004 (forthcoming in *American Benedictine Review*).

5. *Newark Daily Journal,* September 1, 1874; *Annual Catalogue of St. Benedict's College,* 1873–74, 1–2, Newark Abbey Archives (NAA).

6. *Newark Star-Ledger,* February 20, 1972.

7. Interview of Reverend Benedict Tyler, OSB, January 13, 1998.

8. Smith, "Miracle on High Street," 92.

9. U.S. Bureau of the Census, *Sixteenth Census of the United States, 1940: Population* (Washington, D.C.: Government Printing Office, 1941), 2:901; *Seventeenth Census of the United States, 1950: Population* (Washington, D.C.:

GPO, 1951), vol. 2, part 30, p. 70; *Eighteenth Census of the United States, 1960: Population* (Washington, D.C.: GPO, 1961), part 32, p. 92; *Nineteenth Census of the United States, 1970: Population* (Washington, D.C.: GPO, 1971), part 32, p. 71.

10. Arthur M. Louis, "The Worst American City," *Harper's Weekly*, January 1975.

11. Abbot Martin J. Burne, OSB, "The Second Hundred Years," an address given at the Robert Treat Hotel, Newark, N.J., March 21, 1968, 6, NAA.

12. *New York Times*, August 7, 1977.

13. Reverend Albert Holtz, OSB, "Benedictine Conversion: In Dialogue with 'the Street' in Newark," *American Benedictine Academy*, August 1984, reprinted with the permission of the Benedictines of Mount St. Scholastica.

14. *Newark Star-Ledger*, October 21, 1988.

15. Reverend Mark Payne, OSB, "In the Shadow of the Cross," comments made in a speech to the Middle States Visiting Committee, 1990, NAA.

1. Newark's Forgotten Riot

1. Protestants and Catholics clashed routinely from the 1830s through the 1850s in places as distant and disparate as New York, Philadelphia, Boston, Louisville, St. Louis, Detroit, and Cincinnati. On nativism and anti-Catholic violence, see two classic studies: Ray A. Billington, *The Protestant Crusade, 1800–1860: A Study in the Origins of American Nativism* (New York: Rinehart, 1938); and John Higham, *Strangers in the Land: Patterns of American Nativism, 1860–1925* (New York: Macmillan, 1938). For a general history of rioting in the United States, see Paul A. Gilje, *Rioting in America* (Bloomington: Indiana University Press, 1996), 60–86. On the Know-Nothings, see Michael Holt, "The Politics of Impatience: The Origins of Know Nothingism," *Journal of American History* 60 (September 1973): 309–31; and Jay P. Dolan, *In Search of an American Catholicism: A History of Religion and Culture in Tension* (New York: Oxford University Press, 1992), 53–60.

2. *Newark Daily Eagle*, September 5–8, 1854; *New York Freeman's Journal*, September 16, 1854; *Newark Daily Mercury*, September 4, 1854; Raymond M. Ralph, "The City and the Church: Catholic Beginnings in Newark," *New Jersey History*, Autumn–Winter 1976, 116; John T. Cunningham, *Newark*, 2nd ed. (Newark: New Jersey Historical Society, 1988), 136–37; Joel Schwartz, "The Overturnings in the Earth: Firemen and Evangelization in Newark's Law and

Order Crisis of the 1850s," in *Cities of the Garden State: Essays in Urban and Suburban History of New Jersey*, ed. Joel Schwartz and Daniel Prosser (Dubuque, Iowa: Kendall/Hunt, 1977), 27–30; Reverend Hilary Stephan, OSB, "History of St. Mary's Abbey," unpublished manuscript, c. 1917, NAA, 29–52. On the 1854 Know-Nothing attack at St. Mary's, I am indebted to Augustine Curley, OSB, for his scholarship and supply of source material. See his unpublished paper "Attack on St. Mary's."

3. *New York Freeman's Journal*, September 16, 1854; Joseph M. Flynn, *The Catholic Church in New Jersey* (Morristown, N.J., 1904), 205–6; Edwin Vose Sullivan, "James Roosevelt Bayley," in *The Bishops of Newark, 1853–1978*, ed. New Jersey Catholic Historical Records Commission (South Orange: Seton Hall University Press, 1978), 18–21.

4. Stephan, "History of St. Mary's Abbey," 39; *New York Times*, September 21, 1854; *Newark Daily Mercury*, September 6, 1854.

5. Flynn, *Catholic Church in New Jersey*, 206–8; *Newark Daily Mercury*, September 6, 1854; *New York Times*, September 6, 1854, and September 16, 1854; *Newark Daily Advertiser*, September 6, 1854. For a description and analysis of the role of the press in the wake of the attack, see Curley, "Attack on St. Mary's," 9–15.

6. Timothy J. Crist, "Godly Government: Puritans and the Founding of Newark," lecture sponsored by the Newark History Society and the New Jersey Historical Society, November 9, 2009; Frank J. Urquhart, *History of the City of Newark, New Jersey: Embracing Nearly Two and a Half Centuries, 1666–1913* (New York: Lewis Historical Publishing, 1913), 49–50; Alexander MacWhorter, *A Century Sermon, Preached in Newark, New Jersey, January 1, 1801* (Newark: W. Tuttle, 1801); Stuart Galishoff, *Newark: The Nation's Unhealthiest City, 1832–1895* (New Brunswick: Rutgers University Press, 1975), 11–13; Brad R. Tuttle, *How Newark Became Newark: The Rise, Fall, and Rebirth of an American City* (New Brunswick, N.J.: Rivergate Books, 2009), 15–21.

7. Dermot Quinn, *The Irish in New Jersey: Four Centuries of American Life* (New Brunswick: Rutgers University Press, 2004), 62, 66–69, 81–82; Curley, "Attack on St. Mary's," 3; Galishoff, *Nation's Unhealthiest City*, 13–14.

8. Cunningham, *Newark*, 166–73; William B. Helmreich, *The Enduring Community: The Jews of Newark and Metrowest* (New Brunswick, N.J.: Transaction Publishers, 1999), 9–11; Ralph, "The City and the Church," 105–6; Urquhart, *History of Newark*, 1054–55; Galishoff, *Nation's Unhealthiest City*, 14–15.

9. On disease in Newark, see Galishoff, *Nation's Unhealthiest City*. For attitudes toward Irish Catholics, see Kerby A. Miller, *Emigrants and Exiles: Ireland and the Irish Exodus to North America* (New York: Oxford University Press, 1988); David R. Roediger, *The Wages of Whiteness: Race and the Making of the American Working Class* (New York: Verso, 1991), 107, 133–34. On attitudes toward German Catholic immigrants, see Colman J. Barry, OSB, *The Catholic Church and German Americans* (Washington, D.C.: Catholic University Press, 1953). For attitudes on Germans in Newark, see Cunningham, *Newark*, 100–103, 136–37; Urquhart, *History of Newark*, 1054–55; and Stephan, "History of St. Mary's Abbey," 31.

10. Timothy Walch, *Parish School: American Catholic Parochial Education from Colonial Times to the Present* (New York: Crossroad Publishing, 1996), 53–54; Sullivan, "James Roosevelt Bayley," 13–15; John T. McGreevy, *Catholicism and American Freedom: A History* (New York: Norton, 2003), 7–15; Barbara Petrick, *Church and School in the Immigrant City: A Social History of Public Education in Jersey City, 1804–1930* (New York: Upland Press, 2000).

11. Letter of Boniface Wimmer to Father Schwerzmann, Abbey of Einsiedeln, August 8, 1854, as cited in Rippinger, *Benedictine Order in the United States*, 109. On Balleis's resignation following the riot, see Felix Fellner, *Abbot Boniface and His Monks* (Latrobe, Pa.: Saint Vincent Archabbey, 1956), 20; St. Mary's Office, *Souvenir*, 1907, NAA.

12. Boniface Wimmer, "Concerning the Missions of America," in *Documents of American Catholic Heritage*, ed. John Tracy Ellis (Milwaukee: Bruce Publishing, 1953), 279–88. See also Felix Fellner, "Archabbot Boniface Wimmer as an Educator," *National Benedictine Educational Association Bulletin*, December 1942, 7.

13. Reverend Nicholas Ballies, OSB, to Reverend Boniface Wimmer, OSB, St. Vincent Abbey Archives, Latrobe, Pa. (SVAA), November 19, 1847; letter of Wimmer to Abbot Gregory Scherr, Archives of Metten Abbey, Metten, Germany (AMA), July 6, 1853, as quoted in Fellner, *Abbot Boniface and His Monks*, 45, 277. For Wimmer's 1854 letter to Bayley, as well as more on the Bayley-Wimmer correspondence, see Reverend Giles P. Hayes, OSB, *Unto Another Generation: St. Mary's Abbey/Delbarton, 1836–1990* (Newark: Newark Abbey Press, 2006), 4–5.

14. Letters of Wimmer to Bayley, September 12, 1854, and October 3, 1854; letters of Bayley to Wimmer, March 30, 1857, and April 13, 1857, NAA; Hayes, *Unto Another Generation*, 5–6.

15. For Wimmer's motto, see letter of Wimmer to Abbot Lang, May 15, 1860, SVAA. See also Oetgen, *American Abbot*, 169–73; and Francis X. Reuss, "Memoir of the Rt. Rev. James Zilliox, O.S.B., D.D.," in *Records of the American Catholic Historical Society of Philadelphia* (Philadelphia, 1900), 11:257–58.

16. *New York Freeman's Journal*, December 3, 1881; Stephan, "History of St. Mary's Abbey," 51–52.

2. "Necessary, Useful, and Beautiful": Founding Fathers and a Catholic Day College, 1868–1900

1. Urquhart, *History of Newark*, 1082–85; "Van Duyne and Sherman's Map of Newark, New Jersey, 1868," available at the Newark Public Library (NPL).

2. *St. Benedict's College Ledger Book*, July 13, 1870–July 15, 1875, NAA; Augustine Curley, OSB, "Monks and the City: A Unique New Experience," Archbishop Gerety Lecture at Seton Hall University, November 2006, 7.

3. Letter of Wimmer to Ludwig-Missionverein, November 7, 1851, Ludwig-Missionverein Archives, Munich, Germany (LMA), as cited in Oetgen, *American Abbot*, 80, 108. See also Fellner, "Archabbot Boniface Wimmer as an Educator."

4. *The Chronicle of St. Mary's Abbey*, 5, NAA; *Newark Daily Advertiser*, December 23, 1870.

5. Flynn, *Catholic Church in New Jersey*, 281, 298, 597.

6. Walch, *Parish School*, 53–54; Jay P. Dolan, *The American Catholic Experience: A History from Colonial Times to the Present* (Garden City, N.Y.: Doubleday, 1985), 266–75. On James McMaster, the editor of the *Catholic Register*, and his views on Catholic schools, see Thomas McAvoy, "Public Schools Versus Catholic Schools and James McMaster," *Review of Politics* 28 (1966): 19–46.

7. Letter of Chrysostom Foffa to Abbot Schmid, December 31, 1857, as cited in Albert Kleber, *A History of St. Meinrad Archabbey, 1854–1954* (St. Meinrad, Ind.: Archabbey Press, 1954), 122; letter of Adelhelm Odermatt to Abbot Villiger, August 15, 1881, Mt. Angel Abbey Archives, St. Benedict, Ore., as cited in Rippinger, *Benedictine Order in the United States*, 117.

8. Like all other Benedictine schools in the nineteenth-century United States, St. Benedict's was modeled after St. Vincent College, where four programs of study existed: seminary, college (classical and commercial departments), and preparatory. For the structure of the academic program at St.

Vincent, see Oetgen, *American Abbot*, 295–96; and Reverend Paul R. Taylor, OSB, "Boniface Wimmer and Saint Vincent College: The Beginnings of American Benedictine Education" (Ph.D. diss., St. Vincent College, 1997). For nineteenth-century Catholic colleges, see Dolan, *American Catholic Experience*, 292–93.

9. *Newark Daily Journal*, September 1, 1872; *New York Freeman's Journal*, July 10, 1872; *Catholic Institute Gazette*, July 15, 1872; *Newark Daily Journal*, September 1, 1874; *Annual Catalogue of St. Benedict's College*, 1873–74, 1–2, NAA; *St. Benedict's College Prospectus*, 1873–74, 6–7, NAA.

10. *Catholic Institute Gazette*, December 27, 1872, and February 5, 1874.

11. *Annual Catalogue of St. Benedict's College*, 1873–74, 3–4, NAA; *Catholic Citizen*, August 22, 1874; *Catholic Institute Gazette*, December 28, 1872.

12. *Chronicle of St. Mary's Abbey*, 5–6, NAA; *Newark Daily Advertiser*, December 28, 1870.

13. On the rapid industrialization of Newark, see Susan E. Hirsch, *Roots of the American Working Class: The Industrialization of Crafts in Newark, 1800–1860* (Philadelphia: University of Pennsylvania Press, 1978); Samuel H. Popper, "Newark, New Jersey, 1870–1910: Chapters in the Evolution of an American Metropolis" (Ph.D. diss., New York University, 1952), 14; Cunningham, *Newark*, chaps. 12, 13, 17, 18.

14. U.S. Bureau of the Census, *Twelfth Census of the United States, 1900: Population* (Washington, D.C.: Government Printing Office, 1901), 1:628.

15. The preceding profile is based on an examination of census data for over one hundred students and their families who entered St. Benedict's between 1870 and 1875. For quotations, see *Catholic Institute Gazette*, December 28, 1872.

16. *Annual Catalogues of St. Benedict's College*, 1870–80, NAA; *Prospectus of St. Benedict's College*, 1871–72, 1872–73, NAA; Martha Lamb, "Sketch of Newark," *Harper's New Monthly Magazine*, October 1876, 671, 675–76.

17. Lamb, "Sketch of Newark," 675–76; Urquhart, *History of Newark*, 1057–61, 1094–95, 1090–92; Cunningham, *Newark*, 198–99.

18. For a discussion of the national parish in the era of the immigrant church, see Dolan, *American Catholic Experience*, 162–63; Dolan, *In Search of an American Catholicism*, 60–61. For Newark, see Flynn, *Catholic Church in New Jersey*; Ralph, "The City and the Church," 105–6; and Anonymous, "History of St. Mary's," 7.

19. Letter of Boniface Wimmer to the Archbishop of Munich, March 1, 1847, as cited in Fellner, *Abbot Boniface and His Monks*, 92–93.

20. *Irish Citizen*, September 16, 1876. According to an early college catalog, "Christian Doctrine will be an obligatory branch of study for all students, with the exception of non-Catholics." *Annual Catalogue of St. Benedict's College*, 1870–71, 1, NAA.

21. The classifications are those used by Kenneth T. Jackson, *Crabgrass Frontier: The Suburbanization of the United States* (New York: Oxford University Press, 1985), 23–24. See also Sam Bass Warner, *The Private City: Philadelphia in Three Periods of Its Growth* (Philadelphia: University of Pennsylvania Press, 1968), 64–65.

22. Data from the 1860, 1870, and 1880 U.S. Census reports for the earliest families at St. Benedict's College. See author's files or http://www.ancestry.com/.

23. Ibid.

24. Letter of Boniface Wimmer to Archbishop of Munich, Archives of the Louis Missionary Society, Munich, August 9, 1852, as cited in Fellner, *Abbot Boniface and His Monks*, 36.

25. *St. Benedict's College Ledger Book*, 1870–74, 34, 39, 46, 48, 56, 61, 66–67, NAA; *Newark Daily Journal*, July 1, 1874.

26. *St. Benedict's College Ledger Book*, 1870–74, 41–42, NAA; 1870 and 1880 census reports for Carrolton family.

27. *Newark Daily Journal*, June 25, 1878; *New York Freeman's Journal*, February 10, 1872, and July 8, 1882; *New York Times*, February 20, 1890.

28. Cunningham, *Newark*, 211–14; Jean Anyon, *Ghetto Schooling: A Political Economy of Urban Educational Reform* (New York: Teachers College Press, 1997), 44–48; *Annual Catalogues of St. Benedict's College*, 1872–80, NAA; *St. Benedict's College Ledger Book*, 1870–72, NAA; Anonymous, "History of St. Mary's," 9.

29. *Catholic Institute Gazette*, December 28, 1872; *Newark Evening Courier*, August 6, 1872; *Newark Daily Journal*, August 18, 1874, and July 1, 1875.

30. Reuss, "Memoir of the Rt. Rev. James Zilliox," 257–80; "Abbot James Zilliox, October 14, 1849–December, 31 1890," *St. Mary's/Newark Abbey Necrology*, 1–3, NAA.

31. Western Union telegrams, March 23, 24, 30, 1881, in NAA; *Annual Catalogues of St. Benedict's College*, 1882–85, NAA; *Newark Morning Register*, June 19, 1885; *Newark Evening News*, June 19, 1886.

32. *St. Mary's Abbey Chapter Minutes*, August 10, 1885, September 3, 1885, February 25, 1886, St. Mary's Abbey Archives (SMAA); Hayes, *Unto Another Generation*, 9–12; Rippinger, *Benedictine Order in the United States*, 210.

33. Hayes, *Unto Another Generation*, 17–18; Curley, "Monks and the City," 8; Anonymous, "History of St. Mary's," 16.

34. Dolan, *American Catholic Experience*, 143; *Chronicle of St. Mary's Abbey*, 11–16; *Newark Evening News*, June 28, 1887; Dermot Quinn, "The Irish in Newark and New Jersey," exhibition catalog from the Newark Public Library, March 14–May, 11, 2007, 5–6.

35. *Newark Evening News*, January 4, 1910; "Abbot Ernest Helmstetter, October 7, 1859–July 9, 1937," *St. Mary's/Newark Abbey Necrology*, 1–4, NAA.

36. Dennis Clark, *The Irish in Philadelphia: Ten Generations of Urban Experience* (Philadelphia: Temple University Press, 1973), 56–57; Quinn, "The Irish in Newark and New Jersey," 5–6; William E. Sackett, ed., *Scannell's New Jersey's First Citizens*, vol. 1, *1917–1918* (Paterson: J. J. Scannell, 1917), 237–38.

37. *Newark Evening News*, June 19, 1891.

3. The Making of a Modern Catholic Prep School, 1900–1926

1. Howard Newhard, *Lifeletter* (Xulon Press, 2008), 44; *St. Benedict's College Catalogue*, 1910–11, 10–11, NAA; *Newark Evening News*, September 9, 1910; Newark Board of Trade, *Newark: The City of Industry* (Newark: Newark Board of Trade, 1912), 177.

2. *Proceedings of the Benedictine Educational Association, 1925*, 55, NAA. For a discussion of "conservative progressivism" in Catholic schools, see Francis Ryan, "Sparing the Child: Superintendent John Bonner's Philosophy of Classroom Discipline and Character Education in Philadelphia Catholic Schools, 1940–1945," *Vitae Scholasticae: The Bulletin of Educational Biography* 10, nos. 1–2 (1991): 209–33.

3. *St. Mary's Abbey Chapter Minutes*, August 27, 1909, SMAA; Anonymous, "History of St. Mary's Abbey," 28; Hayes, *Unto Another Generation*, 21–22; Curley, "Monks and the City," 8.

4. *The Trenton Monitor*, December 31, 1907; *Newark Evening News*, September 12, 1914; *Newark Ledger*, September 16, 1922.

5. *St. Benedict's College Catalogue*, 1874–75, 7; *St. Benedict's College Catalogue*, 1900–1901, 40; *St. Benedict's College Catalogue*, 1903–4, 12–19, NAA; *The Trenton Monitor*, May 8, 1909.

6. Reverend Anselm Kienle, OSB, "Method of Teaching," in *St. Benedict's College Faculty Minutes*, February 10, 1906 (presented again on October 29, 1910), NAA. Emphasis added.

7. *The Telolog*, 1920, 36; Burne, "Second Hundred Years," NAA. Emphasis added.

8. Paula S. Fass, *Outside In: Minorities and the Transformation of American Education* (New York: Oxford University Press, 1989), 3, 191; James McLachlan, "The Emergence of the Prep School," in *Education in American History: Readings on the Social Issues*, ed. Michael B. Katz (New York: Praeger, 1973), 198–219; *St. Benedict's College Faculty Minutes*, March 3, 1906, 41; December 10, 1910, 72; May 10, 1913, 127, NAA.

9. *St. Benedict's College Faculty Minutes*, December 9, 1911, 97–99; February 3, 1912, 102, NAA; *Newark Evening News*, December 5, 1912, and May 16, 1913; Reverend John Dillon, "Fourth Report of the Superintendent of Parish Schools, Diocese of Newark, Year Ending, June 30, 1914," 9–11, Seton Hall University Archives (SHUA). For estimated religious sect census in Newark, see Newark Board of Trade, *Newark: The City of Industry*, 40.

10. *St. Benedict's College Faculty Minutes*, April 8, 1911, 81; September 13, 1913, 130; September 27, 1913, 132; October 4, 1913, 132–33; October 18, 1913, 134; January 31, 1914, 137; September 12, 1914, 140; on private lessons, see September 25, 1910, 65, NAA.

11. *St. Benedict's College Faculty Minutes*, December 18, 1914, 145, NAA. For pre–World War I optimism and boosterism in Newark, see Cunningham, *Newark*, 232–49.

12. Richard F. Welch, "One Century Ago, Irish Immigrant John P. Holland Perfected the U.S. Navy's First Practical Submarine," *Military History* 16, no. 4 (1999): 16–20. See also Richard K. Morris, *John P. Holland, Eighteen Forty-One to Nineteen Fourteen* (New York: Ayer, 1980); *St. Benedict's College Faculty Minutes*, September 12, 1914, 140, NAA.

13. *Newark Evening News*, April 30, 1918; *The Telolog*, 1920, 26–29, NAA; Cunningham, *Newark*, 260–62; *Chronicle of St. Mary's Abbey*, 20, NAA.

14. *The Telolog*, 1921, 16, NAA; Cunningham, *Newark*, 262; *Newark Evening News*, November 11, 1918.

15. *St. Benedict's College Faculty Minutes*, June 1, 1918, 182; *The Telolog*, 1920, 21–23, NAA; 1922, 24; *New York Times*, October 6, 1917; Cunningham, *Newark*, 259–60.

16. *The Telolog*, 1922, 44.

17. Higham, *Strangers in the Land*, 266. For the urban origins of the Ku Klux Klan, Klan attitudes toward Catholics, and the role of the Klan in Newark and New Jersey, see Kenneth T. Jackson, *The Ku Klux Klan in the City, 1915–*

1930 (New York: Oxford University Press, 1967), 20–21, 178–79, 237–39; Marc Mappen, *Jerseyana: The Underside of New Jersey History* (New Brunswick: Rutgers University Press, 1992), 166–70; *Newark Evening News*, April 28, 1913; *The Newarker*, September 1912, 177–79.

18. *Newark Evening News*, December 21, 1922.

19. *New York Times* article reprinted in *The Kayrix*, January 16, 1924, 2; February 25, 1924, 1, NAA.

20. For census data on Catholics in the Archdiocese of Newark between 1900 and 1920, see *Official Catholic Directory* (New York: P. J. Kennedy and Sons, 1919); for 1930, see Joseph F. Mahoney, "John Joseph O'Connor," in New Jersey Catholic Historical Records Commission, *Bishops of Newark*, 74, 90–91.

21. John T. McGreevy, *Parish Boundaries: The Catholic Encounter with Race in the Twentieth-Century Urban North* (Chicago: University of Chicago Press, 1998), 10–20; Charles R. Morris, *American Catholic: The Saints and Sinners Who Built America's Most Powerful Church* (New York: Vintage Books, 1997), 158–64; Maloney, "John Joseph O'Connor," 74–75; *St. Benedict's College Faculty Minutes*, April 1, 1911, 80, NAA.

22. McGreevy, *Parish Boundaries*, 10.

23. David Steven Cohen, ed., *America, the Dream of My Life: Selections from the Federal Writers' Project's New Jersey Ethnic Survey* (New Brunswick: Rutgers University Press, 1990), 35–38; *The Telolog*, 1924, 39–40, NAA.

24. Dolan, *American Catholic Experience*, 356–57.

25. Interviews of John Kling '33, July 13, 2003; Paul Healy '33, July 13, 2003; Msgr. Carl Hinrichsen '39, July 18, 2003; Art Guarriello '29, July 22, 2003; Pat McAuley '40, July 23, 2003; and Fass, *Outside In*, 194–95.

26. James T. Farrell, *Studs Lonigan: A Trilogy Comprising Young Lonigan, the Young Manhood of Studs Lonigan, and Judgment Day* (Urbana: University of Illinois Press, 1993), 402.

27. These samples come from *The Telolog*, 1924. A perusal of other years results in similar findings, some more cutting than others.

28. On "whiteness" and "inbetween peoples," see David R. Roediger, *Working Toward Whiteness: How American's Immigrants Became White* (New York: Basic Books, 2005), 10–14; on the Italian American community in Newark, see Michael Immerso, *Newark's Little Italy: The Vanished First Ward* (New Brunswick: Rutgers University Press, 1997); Urquhart, *History of Newark*, 826; *The Telolog*, 1924, 16–17, 26, NAA.

29. *The Telolog*, 1924, 17, 19, 26; 1930, 66, NAA; interview of Reverend Boniface Treanor, OSB, June 10, 2003.

30. For the importance of the Great Migration and subsequent migrations northward, see August Meier and Elliott Rudwick, *From Plantation to Ghetto* (New York: Hill and Wang, 1976), 232. For an analysis of this time period in Newark, see Clement A. Price, "The Beleaguered City as Promised Land: Blacks in Newark, 1917–1947," in *Urban New Jersey Since 1870*, ed. William C. Wright (Trenton: New Jersey Historical Commission, 1975), 10–45; William Ashby, "Reflections on the Life of Negroes in Newark, 1910–1916," an address to the Frontier Club, February 16, 1972, 2–3, available at the Newark Public Library; Clement A. Price, "The Afro-American Community of Newark, 1917–1947: A Social History" (Ph.D. diss., Rutgers University, 1975), 2–3.

31. *The Telolog*, 1922, 20; 1925, 92; *The Kayrix*, March 25, 1924, 1; June 13, 1925, 3; *The Telolog*, 1934, 75; *Souvenir Program: First Annual Minstrel at St. Benedict's Preparatory School, at Proctor's Lyceum, January 22, 1930*, program booklet, 1–12, NAA; *Sixth Annual Minstrel and Dance of the Holy Name Society of St. Joseph's Church, Maplewood, N.J., April 28th, 29th, 1930*, program booklet, 1–6; Roediger, *Working Toward Whiteness*, 168–69. Seton Hall Prep sponsored a minstrel show as far back as 1867, and the proceeds went to the Southern Relief Fund "to aid in the rehabilitation after the Civil War." *The Pirate*, September 21, 1955, SHUA.

32. *Minutes of the Clergy Negro Welfare Conference*, dated May 24 but without a year, NAA. Most likely the meeting was hosted at St. Mary's Abbey in Newark in the early 1940s. See also Malachy McPadden, *Benedictines in Newark, 1842–1992* (Newark: Newark Abbey Press, 1992), 18–19; Burne, "Second Hundred Years," 2, NAA; interview of Msgr. Carl Hinrichsen '39, July 18, 2003.

33. *Newark Evening News*, February 1, 1924, and January 5, 1929; Paul Stellhorn, "Boom, Bust, and Boosterism: Attitudes, Residency, and the Newark Chamber of Commerce, 1920–1941," in Wright, *Urban New Jersey Since 1870*, 49–51; Tuttle, *How Newark Became Newark*, 103–4.

34. Stellhorn, "Boom, Bust, and Boosterism," 48; Martin V. Minner, "Metropolitan Aspirations: Politics and Memory in Progressive Era Newark" (Ph.D. dissertation, Indiana University, 2005), 5–6, 84; *Newark Ledger*, January 27, 1928; Porter E. Sargent, ed., *A Handbook of American Private Schools: An Annual Survey, 1922* (Cambridge, U.K.: Cosmos Press, 1922), 498–500.

35. *Proceedings of the BEA*, 1918, 6–7, 13; 1919, 19–22; 1920, 31–33; 1922, 12–13, 16–17; 1925, 19–24; 1927, 12, 77, NAA.

36. *Proceedings of the BEA*, 1918, 6–7; 1921, 11; 1924, 9–10, NAA.

37. *Newark Evening Star*, June 22, 1913; *The Telolog*, 1919, 6–7, NAA; interview of Ted Langan '23, *St. Benedict's Prep Oral History Project*, Spring 1980, NAA.

38. *The Telolog*, 1921, 56; 1941, 6–7, NAA; *Newark Evening News*, June 6, 1915; *The Kayrix*, June 6, 1924, 1, NAA.

39. *Newark Evening News*, October 6, 1924.

40. *The Kayrix*, May 16, 1924, 1; NAA; *Newark Evenings News*, October 6, 1924.

41. Letter of Reverend Cornelius Selhuber, OSB, to Abbot Ernest Helmstetter, OSB, July 30, 1926, in *Headmaster's Files*, NAA.

42. Burne, "Second Hundred Years," 1–2; *The Telolog*, 1920, 36, NAA.

4. St. Benedict's Prep from Depression to War, 1926–1945

1. Interview of John Kling '33, July 13, 2003; interview of Paul Healy '33, July 13, 2003.

2. Author unknown, "The Educational Activities of the Newark Benedictines," 1943, in *Headmaster's Files*, 6, NAA; David M. Kennedy, *Freedom from Fear: The American People in Depression and War, 1929–1945* (New York: Oxford University Press, 1999).

3. As quoted in Kennedy, *Freedom from Fear*, 10.

4. Interview of John Kling '33, July 13, 2003. For Alfred E. Smith's unsuccessful presidential campaign, see Oscar Handlin, *Al Smith and His America* (Boston: Northeastern University Press, 1987).

5. For the Great Depression with an emphasis on Newark, see Paul A. Stellhorn, "Depression and Decline, Newark, New Jersey, 1929–1941" (Ph.D. diss., Rutgers University, 1982); Warren Grover, *Nazis in Newark* (New Brunswick, N.J.: Transaction Books, 2003), 140–43; Tuttle, *How Newark Became Newark*, 104; William E. Leuchtenburg, *Franklin D. Roosevelt and the New Deal* (New York: Harper & Row, 1963), 3.

6. According to the historian David Kennedy, "Security was the leitmotif of virtually everything that the New Deal attempted . . . security for vulnerable individuals, to be sure . . . but security for capitalists and consumers, for workers and employers, for corporations and farms and homeowners and bankers as well." Kennedy, *Freedom from Fear*, 365, 377. On Newark during the 1930s, see Tuttle, *How Newark Became Newark*, 111–13; Stellhorn, "Depression and Decline," 27–28.

7. Interview of Reverend Boniface Treanor, OSB, June 10, 2003; Grover, *Nazis in Newark*, 141–43; Ira Katznelson, *When Affirmative Action Was White: An Untold History of Racial Inequality in Twentieth-Century America* (New York: Norton, 2005), x, xv, 17.

8. Price, "Beleaguered City," 451–53; *Newark Evening News*, April 20, 1938, and July 18, 1938; Cohen, *America, the Dream of My Life*, 217–23.

9. Price, "Beleaguered City," 442, 451; Barbara J. Kukla, *Swing City: Newark Nightlife, 1925–1950* (Philadelphia: Temple University Press, 1991), 2, 20, 109; Curtis Lucas, *Third Ward Newark* (New York: Ziff-Davis, 1946), 1, 67.

10. Letter of Margaret Ryan to Reverend Boniface Reger, OSB, August 12, 1935; letter of Reverend Boniface Reger, OSB, to Sister M. Emilita, Principal, St. Columba School, May 28, 1936, in *Headmaster's Files*, NAA.

11. Letter of Helen Monteith, Caseworker, State of New Jersey Emergency Relief Administration, to Reverend Boniface Reger, OSB, September 17, 1934; letter of Reverend Boniface Reger, OSB, to Helen Monteith, Caseworker, State of New Jersey Emergency Relief Administration, September 22, 1933; letter of Reverend Boniface Reger, OSB, to Millicent Laubenheimer, Caseworker, State of New Jersey Emergency Relief Administration, December 6, 1934, in *Headmaster's Files*, NAA.

12. Letter of Reverend Boniface Reger, OSB, to Ruth K. Jolly, Director, New Jersey Student Aid Survey, December 11, 1931, in *Headmaster's Files*, NAA.

13. Letter of Reverend Boniface Reger, OSB, to Harry Hopkins, Director, Federal Emergency Relief Administration, April 30, 1935; letter of L. R. Alderman, Director of Educational Division, Federal Emergency Relief Administration, to Reverend Boniface Reger, OSB, May 3, 1935; letter of Reverend John Doyle, OSB, to Reverend George Johnson, Director, National Catholic Welfare Conference, March 25, 1941, in *Headmaster's Files*, NAA.

14. Letters of Reverend Boniface Reger, OSB, to Dr. E. D. Grizzell, Chairman, Commission on Secondary Schools for Middle States Association, December 19, 1932, April 17, 1933; letter of Reverend Boniface Reger, OSB, to Dr. George W. McClelland, Commission on Secondary Schools for Middle States Association, December 11, 1934, in *Headmaster's Files*, NAA.

15. Letter of Reverend Boniface Reger, OSB, to Reverend William A. Stahl, OSFS, Rector of Northeast Catholic High School, May 6, 1935, in *Headmaster's Files*, NAA.

16. Letter of Reverend Boniface Reger, OSB, to Dr. Floyd E. Harshman, Principal, Nutley High School, February 10, 1941; "Headmaster's Messages," May 5, 1941, in *Headmaster's Files*, NAA.

17. Reverend Boniface Reger, "Philosophy of Education and Objectives of This School," undated, 1–2; addresses of Reverend Boniface Reger, January 13, 1941, and January 20, 1941, NAA.

18. Interview of John Dalton '44, May 15, 2002; *Newark Evening News*, December 8, 1941; interview of Reverend Maurus McBarron, *St. Benedict's Prep Oral History Project*, Spring 1980, NAA; *Newark Evening News*, May 3, 1942.

19. Reverend Lambert Dunne, OSB, "Activities of St. Mary's Abbey and St. Benedict's Prep During World War II," undated, in *Headmaster's Files*, 1–10, NAA.

20. Interview of Pat McAuley '40, July 23, 2003; interview of Msgr. Carl Hinrichsen '39, July 18, 2003.

21. Dunne, "Activities of St. Mary's Abbey and St. Benedict's Prep," 9, NAA.

22. *Newark Evening News*, December 4, 1943, and January 24, 1944; and *Newark Star-Ledger*, October 24, 1944, and January 7, 1945. For a short biography of Abbot Martin J. Burne, OSB, see Brother Eamon Drew, OSB, "Essay on the Life of Abbot J. Burne, OSB," in Hayes, *Unto Another Generation*, appendix 1.

23. Letter of David Liddell to Reverend Boniface Reger, OSB, September 1, 1945, in *Headmaster's Files*, NAA.

24. Reger, "The Educational Activities of the Newark Benedictines," 1943, in *Headmaster's Files*, 12, NAA.

25. Suzanne Geissler, *A Widening Sphere of Influence: Newark Academy, 1774–1993* (Livingston: Newark Academy Publishing Office, 1993), 182, 197.

26. *St. Mary's Abbey Chapter Minutes*, August 18, 1925, 73; April 23, 1932, 80; May 7, 1932, 80, SMAA; *Chronicle of St. Mary's Abbey*, 22; Reverend Giles P. Hayes, "A History of St. Mary's Abbey," unpublished manuscript, 1974, 19–28, SMAA; Hayes, *Unto Another Generation*, 35–37.

27. *Newark Advocate*, April 6, 1967; *St. Mary's Abbey Chapter Minutes*, August 10, 1937, 85–86, SMAA; McPadden, *Benedictines in Newark*, 30–31; Hayes, "History of Saint Mary's Abbey," 35, SMAA.

28. Kathleen Norris, *The Cloister Walk* (New York: Riverhead Books, 1996), 5; Timothy Fry, OSB, et al., *RB 1980: The Rule of St. Benedict in Latin and English with Notes* (Collegeville, Minn.: Liturgical Press, 1981), 165; *Newark Sunday Call*, February 4, 1945; Abbot Patrick O'Brien, "To the Reverend Fathers and Brothers of St. Mary's Abbey," October 2, 1943, in *St. Mary's Abbey Chapter Minutes*, 1–7, SMAA.

29. Abbot Patrick O'Brien, "To the Reverend Fathers and Brothers of St. Mary's Abbey," October 2, 1943, in *St. Mary's Abbey Chapter Minutes*, 1–5, SMAA; Norris, *Cloister Walk*, xix; St. Mary's Abbey Chapter Minutes, November 17, 1937, 88, SMAA; *Newark Star-Ledger*, December 17, 1937; *Newark Evening News*, March 7, 1938, and August 11, 1938. For the health and longevity of the Benedictines in the United States, see Marie Nordsieck and Oliver L. Kapsner, OSB, "Mortality Experience of the American Cassinese Congregation, 1952–56," *American Benedictine Review* 10, no. 3 (1959): 187–94.

30. Dom Wilfrid Upson, OSB, "From Hoboken to Hollywood," *American Benedictine Review* 1, no. 3 (1950): 357–59.

31. *St. Mary's Abbey Chapter Minutes*, May 12, 1938, 89–90, SMAA.

32. Ibid.; Hayes, "History of St. Mary's Abbey," 36–38; Curley, "Monks and the City," 1–10.

33. *St. Mary's Abbey Chapter Minutes*, February 3, 1941, 99; May 19, 1941, 100; July 12, 1943, SMAA. Abbot Patrick scaled down the five-thousand-dollar request for funds and took the matter to his Council of Seniors, a five-man advisory board representing the monastic corporation. By Benedictine statute he could have this body approve the measure, and he saw some of the members of the Senior Council privately before authorizing Father Vincent to continue the repair work at Delbarton. The abbot did not see two of the five members, though, and this no doubt angered members of the community. He later apologized for not following procedure. Hayes, *Unto Another Generation*, 51–56.

34. *St. Mary's Abbey Chapter Minutes*, November 10, 1943, 356, SMAA.

35. *St. Mary's Abbey Chapter Minutes*, December 13, 1944, 362, SMAA. For this quotation, see a statement read by Abbot Patrick in *St. Mary's Abbey Chapter Minutes*, June 13, 1956, 132A–132B, SMAA.

5. The Duke, Divine Comedy, and Discipline at St. Benedict's Prep

1. Interview of Reverend Boniface Treanor, OSB, June 10, 2003, and December 1, 2009; interview of Abbot Melvin J. Valvano, OSB, October 15, 2009.

2. This story has been recounted on a number of occasions. Interview of Reverend Boniface Treanor, OSB, June 10, 2003; interview of Reverend Edwin D. Leahy, OSB, March 21, 1997.

3. *Newark Star-Ledger*, July 18, 1971; *Proceedings of the BEA*, 1924, 14–15, 41; letter of William D. Quigley to Boniface Reger, OSB, December 17, 1932, in *Headmaster's Files*, NAA.

4. For a discussion of "conservative progressivism" in Catholic schools, see Ryan, "Sparing the Child," 209–33. For a depiction of Father Dunstan Smith's "modified violence," see interview of Abbot Melvin J. Valvano, OSB, December 2, 2009; *St. Benedict's Prep Faculty Minutes*, undated, 1949–50, NAA.

5. Willy Oldes, *Class of 1955 40th Anniversary Booklet*, 1995, 11, NAA. I am indebted to Reverend Gerard Lair, OSB, a graduate of St. Benedict's Prep, for the "divine comedy" metaphor. He first mentioned its appropriateness for describing life at St. Benedict's in the 1950s at an alumni function in 1997.

6. *St. Benedict's College Catalogue*, 1874–75, 3–5, NAA. For earliest records of student attendance and evidence of students paying for broken windows, see the back leaf of the *St. Benedict's College Ledger of Accounts*, 1870–75, NAA. For the entries from Seton Hall's punishment ledger, see "Punishment Ledger," 1867–68, SHUA, Record Group 50.3.

7. *Proceedings of the BEA*, 1924, 36–41, NAA.

8. Reverend Nicholas O'Rafferty, *Instructions on Christian Doctrine: The Commandments of God* (Milwaukee: Bruce Publishing, 1940), 3:192–93, 194.

9. Philip Greven, *Spare the Child: The Religious Roots of Corporal Punishment and the Psychological Impact of Physical Abuse* (New York: Vintage Books, 1990), 5–6, 47–48. On Protestant child-rearing practices, see Philip Greven, *The Protestant Temperament: Patterns of Child-Rearing, Religious Experience, and the Self in Early America* (Chicago: University of Chicago Press, 1977), 35–46.

10. Greven's Protestants participated in a far more literate society, one that centered its communication on letter writing and journal entries. Many Catholics were poor immigrants struggling for a foothold in American society, and so did not write letters or keep detailed journals. Jay P. Dolan contends that "the family lives of common folk remain hidden in the past. Such people did not leave behind diaries and voluminous correspondences, and if they did, it was most likely lost." Dolan, *American Catholic Experience*, 242–43.

11. Reverend Edgar Schmiedeler, OSB, and M. Rosa McDonough, *Parent and Child: An Introductory Study of Parent Education* (New York: Appleton Century Company, 1934), 158–59.

12. Reverend P. A. Halpin, *Christian Pedagogy, or, The Instruction and Moral Training of Youth* (New York: Joseph F. Wagner, 1909), 108–9.

13. *St. Benedict's College Catalogue*, 1874–75, 4, NAA. These statements on discipline remained consistent from the first catalogs in the 1870s through to 1900. See also *The Rule of Our Most Holy Father St. Benedict* (New York:

Catholic Publication Society, 1886), 97–99, 101; *Benedict News*, April 19, 1939; and *The Telolog*, 1947, 23, NAA.

14. Cornelius Selhuber, "On Punishment," in *St. Benedict's College Faculty Minutes*, March 31, 1906, 14, 20, 22–23, NAA; *New York Times*, March 20, 1894.

15. Selhuber, "On Punishment," 15, 20, 30; *St. Benedict's College Catalogue*, 1911–12, 16, NAA. Corporal punishment was forbidden in the following: *St. Benedict's College Faculty Minutes*, September 7, 1905, 2–3; September 29, 1906, 60; February 13, 1909, 44; October 8, 1910, 67; March 4, 1911, 79; September 16, 1911, 87; April 26, 1913, 127; September 13, 1913; 130; October 10, 1914, 142; January 22, 1916, 160; March 4, 1916, 162; November 8, 1919, 190, NAA. In 1906, the director warned against "calling boys names, as it may very easily be misunderstood and taken amiss by the parents of the boys." A year later the faculty was asked "not to use abusive terms in addressing students." *St. Benedict's College Faculty Minutes*, October 3, 1906, 62; October 19, 1907, 6 (for quotes above); October 8, 1910, 67; September 16, 1911, 87; January 11, 1940; September 16, 1941; *Proceedings of the Benedictine Educational Association*, 1922, 17, NAA.

16. Ryan, "Sparing the Child," 210–11. On Bonner and "conservative progressivism," see Francis Ryan, "Monsignor John Bonner and Progressive Education in the Archdiocese of Philadelphia, 1925–1945," *Records of the American Catholic Historical Association of Philadelphia* 102 (Spring 1991): 17–43.

17. *Proceedings of the BEA*, 1925, 55, NAA.

18. *Bulletin of Seton Hall High School*, June 1929, RG13.

19. Selhuber, "On Punishment," 15, 22–23, NAA; interview of Art Guarriello '29, July 22, 2003; "Father William Koellhoffer, March 18, 1879–August 11, 1938," *St. Mary's/Newark Abbey Necrology*, 2, NAA.

20. *St. Benedict's Prep Faculty Minutes*, March 3, 1922, 198–99, NAA; interview of Art Guarriello '29, July 22, 2003.

21. *Benedict News*, September 12, 1940, 1, NAA; interview of Reverend Maurus McBarron, OSB, May 21, 1980; interview of Ted Langan '23, *St. Benedict's Prep Oral History Project*, Spring 1980, NAA; *Proceedings of the BEA*, 1923, 28–29.

22. *Benedict News*, March 15, 1939, 2; interview of Msgr. Carl Hinrichsen '39, July 18, 2003; interview of Tom Gilligan '50, May 16, 2003; interview of John Kling '33, July 13, 2003; interview of Paul Healy '33, July 13, 2003; "Father Valerian Kanetski, April 20, 1888–March 8, 1939," *St. Mary's/Newark Abbey Necrology*, 1, NAA.

23. *Benedict News*, April 12, 1938; interview of John Kling '33, July 13, 2003; *Proceedings of the BEA*, 1927, 12.

24. Interview of Reverend Boniface Treanor, OSB, December 1, 2009.

25. James T. Fisher, *On the Irish Waterfront: The Crusader, the Movie, and the Soul of the Port of New York* (Ithaca: Cornell University Press, 2009), xi; interview of Reverend Boniface Treanor, OSB, December 1, 2009; interview of Abbot Melvin J. Valvano, OSB, October 15, 2009.

26. *Benedict News*, September 1939, and April 19, 1939, NAA; *Catholic News*, April 26, 1947.

27. Reverend John Doyle, OSB, untitled and undated document in *Athletic Director's Files*, NAA.

28. *Benedict News*, September 24, 1938, and September 12, 1939, NAA; *The Telolog*, 1947, 18, NAA; interview of Reverend Boniface Treanor, OSB, June 10, 2003; interview of Pat McAuley '40, July 23, 2003.

29. Interview of Reverend Boniface Treanor, OSB, June 10, 2003; letter of Reverend Gerald Flynn, OSB, to Mr. Andrew Eckert Sr., February 24, 1941, in *Headmaster's Files*, NAA.

30. On "word-of-mouth neighborhoods," see Alan Ehrenhalt, *The Lost City: The Forgotten Virtues of Community in America* (New York: Basic Books, 1995), 97; transcript of headmaster's broadcast, May 12, 1941; letter of Reverend Boniface Reger to Mr. Samuel Gruber, February 13, 1932, in *Headmaster's Files*, NAA.

31. Ehrenhalt, *Lost City*, 38–39; *Benedict News*, January 19, 1940, 2, NAA.

32. Interview of Pat McAuley '40, July 23, 2003; Richard J. Green, *Class of 1945 40th Anniversary Reunion Booklet*, 1995, NAA; G. Gordon Liddy, *Will: The Autobiography of G. Gordon Liddy* (New York: St. Martin's Press, 1980), 45–46.

33. Interview of Tom Gilligan '50, May 16, 2003; Charles A. Brady, *Class of 1953 45th Anniversary Reunion Booklet*, 1998, 2; Floyd J. Donahue, *Class of 1950 45th Anniversary Reunion Booklet*, 1995, 3; Robert J. Aikens, *Class of 1953 45th Anniversary Reunion Booklet*, 1998, 1, NAA; interview of Gene O'Hara '55, January 15, 2010.

34. Interview of Pat McAuley '40, July 23, 2003; "Father Paul Huber, August 15, 1896–November 29, 1981," in *St. Mary's/Newark Abbey Necrology*, 2, NAA; interview of Gene O'Hara '55, January 15, 2010.

35. *St. Mary's Abbey Minutes*, May 14, 1950, 65, SMAA.

36. "Father Dunstan Smith, February 17, 1914–November 7, 1965," *St. Mary's/Newark Abbey Necrology*, NAA; interview of Pat McAuley '40, July 23, 2003.

37. James F. Howe, *Class of 1958 40th Anniversary Booklet*, 1998, 14; Terrence McGovern, *Class of 1958 40th Anniversary Booklet*, 1998, 20–21; Ernie Iamundo, *Class of 1958 40th Anniversary Booklet*, 1998, 27, NAA. The Father Dunstan story of striking a freshman at an assembly has been retold many times, and the words are a paraphrase of what he said on that occasion. Interview of Reverend Albert Holtz, OSB, July 16, 2003.

38. *Benedict News*, October 21, 1941, 2; Michael Falivena, *Class of 1958 40th Anniversary Booklet*, 1998; Pete Prunkl, *Class of 1958 40th Anniversary Booklet*, 1998; *Benedict News*, October 6, 1961, NAA; interview of Reverend Boniface Treanor, OSB, June 10, 2003; interview of Reverend Albert Holtz, OSB, June 4, 2003.

39. Interview of Reverend Boniface Treanor, OSB, June 10, 2003; Mathias Hagovsky, *Class of 1962 35th Anniversary Booklet*, 1997, 11, NAA.

40. Interview of Reverend Albert Holtz, OSB, June 4, 2003; John A. Pisarra, *Class of 1958 40th Anniversary Reunion Booklet*, 1998, 27, NAA.

41. *New York Times*, May 31, 1943; April 17, 1946; March 31, 1951; December 11, 1955. See also Ryan, "Sparing the Child," 223–25.

42. Mark S. Massa, *Catholics and American Culture: Fulton Sheen, Dorothy Day, and the Notre Dame Football Team* (New York: Crossroad Publishing, 1999), 1–6.

43. *Benedict News*, October 18, 1965, NAA.

44. Interview of Reverend Boniface Treanor, OSB, June 10, 2003; interview of Abbot Melvin J. Valvano, OSB, October 15, 2009; Stanley E. Zeitz, *Class of 1962 35th Anniversary Booklet*, 1997, 22, NAA.

45. Interview of Reverend Boniface Treanor, OSB, June 10, 2003.

46. *Benedict News*, February 20, 1961, 2, NAA.

47. Interview of Reverend Boniface Treanor, OSB, June 10, 2003.

48. Interview of Reverend Boniface Treanor, OSB, June 10, 2003; Albert J. Ihde, *Class of 1962 35th Anniversary Booklet*, 1997, 14; John F. Hickey, *Class of 1962 35th Anniversary Booklet*, 1997, 13; Edward P. Kane, *Class of 1962 35th Anniversary Booklet*, 1997, 22, NAA.

49. For the shift to a more liberal dress code, see *Benedict News*, April 25, 1969, 1, NAA. A poll taken indicated that students no longer wanted to wear

uniform blazers, and the Student Council put forth a resolution that "dress is the individual responsibility of the student." A new schedule and the introduction of elective courses were among the changes for the opening of the 1969–70 school year. See *Benedict News*, October 8, 1968, NAA.

50. *Benedict News*, November 1969; June 1970, NAA.

51. *St. Benedict's Preparatory School Faculty Handbook*, 1971–72, 1, NAA.

52. Ibid., 1–2, 7–9, 59–64.

6. Benedict's Hates a Quitter: Athletics at a Catholic Prep School

1. *Newark Ledger*, March 16, 1919; *Newark Sunday Call*, March 16, 1919; *St. Benedict's Prep Athletic Scrapbooks*, 1920–21, NAA.

2. *Newark Evening News*, June 17, 1921. "St. Benedict's Athletic Board Memorandum on Athletic Policy," undated, 1–4, in *Headmaster's Files*, NAA. For the "Little Notre Dame of the East" reference, see letter of J. D. Gallagher Jr., Princeton University, to Father Cornelius Selhuber, November 16, 1923, in *St. Benedict's Prep Athletic Scrapbooks*, NAA; and *Newark Star-Eagle*, September 15, 1924.

3. Steven W. Pope, "Negotiating the 'Folk Highway' of the Nation: Sport, Public Culture, and American Identity, 1870–1940," *Journal of Social History* 27 (Winter 1993): 327–40; Gerald R. Gems, "The Prep Bowl: Football and Religious Acculturation in Chicago, 1927–1963," *Journal of Sport History* 23 (Fall 1996): 284–302; Pamela Grundy, *Learning to Win: Sports, Education, and Social Change in Twentieth-Century North Carolina* (Chapel Hill: University of North Carolina Press, 2001), 4–9.

4. For a copy of Father Cornelius's speech, see *St. Benedict's Prep Athletic Scrapbook*, 1920–21, NAA; see also his speech to fellow monks at the Benedictine Educational Association annual meeting, "Athletics: Uses and Abuses," *Proceedings of the BEA*, 1925, 32–35.

5. *St. Benedict's College Catalogue*, 1874–75, 13; *St. Benedict's College Catalogue*, 1896–97, 24–25; *St. Benedict's College Catalogue*, 1900–1901, 23–24; *St. Benedict's College Catalogue*, 1902–3, 36; *St. Benedict's College Prospectus*, 1905, 4, NAA. For the newspaper account of the baseball game from June 1902, see *St. Mary's Abbey Scrapbook*, 1899–1903.

6. Elliott J. Gorn, *The Manly Art: Bare-Knuckle Prize Fighting in America* (Ithaca: Cornell University Press, 1986), 117, 132–33, 192.

7. Theodore Roosevelt, *The Strenuous Life: Essays and Addresses* (New York: Century, 1900), 155–57. Numerous historians have explored white middle-class Protestant fears and anxieties brought on by industrialization, the growth of big business, continued non-Protestant immigration, and the women's rights movement. See Gail Bederman, *Manliness and Civilization: A Cultural History of Gender and Race in the United States, 1880–1917* (Chicago: University of Chicago Press, 1995), 18, 186; Mark Carnes, *Secret Ritual and Manhood in Victorian America* (New Haven: Yale University Press, 1989); Michael Kimmel, *Manhood in America: A Cultural History* (New York: Free Press, 1996); E. Anthony Rotundo, *American Manhood: Transformations in Masculinity from the Revolution to the Modern Era* (New York: Basic Books, 1993); Clifford Putney, *Muscular Christianity: Manhood and Sports in Protestant America, 1880–1920* (Cambridge: Harvard University Press, 2001), 2, 4–6, 69–71. Both Patrick Kelly and Christa Klein have used the term "Muscular Catholicism," but Klein challenged Kelly's premise that Catholics did not latch on to Muscular Christian ideals until the first part of the twentieth century. Klein detailed how two Jesuit Catholic all-male schools in New York established sports program by the 1890s. See Patrick Kelly, "The Sacramental Imagination, Culture, and Play" (Licentiate's thesis, Weston Jesuit School of Theology, 1999); and Christa Klein, "The Jesuits and Catholic Boyhood in Nineteenth-Century New York City: A Study of St. John's College and the College of St. Francis Xavier, 1846–1912" (Ph.D. diss., University of Pennsylvania, 1976), 318–22.

8. *St. Benedict's College Catalogue*, 1910–11, 39, NAA; *Newark Evening Star*, September 8, 1910; *The Trenton Monitor*, October 1, 1910. On Frank Hill, see Alan Delozier, *Seton Hall Pirates: A Basketball History* (Chicago: Arcadia Publishing, 2002), 16.

9. *St. Benedict's College Catalogue*, 1918–19, 40–41; *St. Benedict's Prep Athletic Scrapbook*, 1920–21, NAA; Walter Camp, ed., *Spalding's Official Foot Ball Guide, 1919* (New York: American Sports Publishing, 1919), 151–55. For a discussion of high schools and the "preparedness crisis," see Timothy P. O'Hanlon, "School Sports as Social Training: The Case of Athletics and the Crisis of World War I," *Journal of Sport History* 9, no. 1 (1982): 5–29. For Boston's reluctance to make PE compulsory, see Porter Sargent, ed., *Handbook of American Private School* (Boston: Porter Sargent, 1922), 17–18.

10. Interview of Ted Langan '23, *St. Benedict's Oral History Project*, May 1980, NAA; interview of Adrian "Bud" Foley '39, January 28, 2009.

11. Desch broke the world's 440-yard hurdle record at the Penn Relays in Philadelphia on April 29, 1921. See *Newark Evening News*, April 30, 1921. For the Gray Bee foursome headed to Notre Dame, see *Newark Star-Eagle*, June 14, 1921. For the 1923 Notre Dame–Army game and Rockne visit to St. Benedict's, see *Newark Ledger*, October 19, 1923; and interview of John Blewitt, *St. Benedict's Oral History Project*, May 15, 1990, NAA. For the Notre Dame network, see Raymond Schmidt, *Shaping College Football: The Transformation of an American Sport, 1919–1930* (Syracuse: Syracuse University Press, 2007), 108, 123–25.

12. *Newark Ledger*, May 8, 1924.

13. *Newark Ledger*, April 23, 1924.

14. *Proceedings of the BEA*, 1925, 24, 32–35.

15. Ibid.; *The Kayrix*, October 17, 1924, NAA; *Newark Ledger*, October 6, 1924.

16. Interview of Adrian "Bud" Foley '39, August 17, 2005; *Newark Sunday Ledger*, February 13, 1927; interview of Howard Newhard '45, October 14, 2003; Newhard, *Lifeletter*.

17. For a detailed biography of Prof Blood, see Dr. Charles "Chic" Hess, *Prof Blood and the Wonder Teams: The True Story of Basketball's First Great Coach* (Newark: Newark Abbey Press, 2003).

18. *Passaic Daily News*, December 7, 1925, as cited in Hess, *Prof Blood*, 345.

19. *The Telolog*, 1926, 47, NAA.

20. Hess, *Prof Blood*, 224.

21. *Passaic Daily Herald*, March 20, 1923, as cited in Hess, *Prof Blood*, 203.

22. *Passaic Daily News*, March 17, 1923, as cited in Hess, *Prof Blood*, 198.

23. *Passaic Herald News*, February 14, 1955.

24. Interview of Adrian "Bud" Foley '39, August 17, 2005; Hess, *Prof Blood*, 358–65.

25. Interview of Adrian "Bud" Foley '39, August 17, 2005. For the style of play preferred by Blood, see also Hess, *Prof Blood*, 28, 65.

26. *Newark Ledger*, October 20, 1925; *Jersey Journal*, January 31, 1940; *Newark Ledger*, February 2, 1940; *Newark Star-Ledger*, February 7, 1955.

27. *Newark Evening News*, November 23, 1937; *Newark Ledger*, November 23–24, 1937.

28. *Newark Evening News*, November 23, 1937; letter of Reverend James A. Carey to Reverend John Doyle, OSB, September 13, 1938, *Athletic Director's*

Files; "Special Meeting to Discuss Seton Hall Game," in *St. Benedict's Prep Faculty Minutes*, November 20, 1939, NAA; *Newark Evening News*, November 23, 1940.

29. Letter of Reverend Boniface Reger to Rt. Rev. Msgr. James Kelley, Ph.D., President of Seton Hall College, November 8, 1941; letter of Kelley to Reger, November 10, 1941, in *Headmaster's Files*, NAA.

30. Letter of Reger to Kelley, November 11, 1941; Western Union telegram from Reverend William N. Bradley, Headmaster of Seton Hall Prep to Reger, November 14, 1941; letter of Bradley to Reger, November 15, 1941, in *Headmaster's Files*, NAA; interview of John Allen '54, August 15, 2005.

31. *Newark Star-Ledger*, October 2, 1969. See also Dennis A. Joyce's extensive biography of Joe Kasberger, *Joe K: A Biography of Joe Kasberger* (Newark: Newark Abbey Press, 1998), 40–41.

32. Joyce, *Joe K*, 144, 191–95.

33. Interview of John Allen '54, August 15, 2005; interview of Adrian "Bud" Foley '39, August 17, 2005; *Newark Star-Ledger*, October 1, 1969; Newhard, *Lifeletter*, 89.

34. *Catholic Advocate*, December 11, 1954; Murray Sperber, *Shake Down the Thunder: The Creation of Notre Dame Football* (New York: Holt, 1993); interview of Adrian "Bud" Foley '39, January 28, 2010.

35. Interview of John Allen '54, August 15, 2005; interview of Adrian "Bud" Foley '39, August 17, 2005, and January 28, 2010; Joyce, *Joe K*, 221–22.

36. Interview of John Allen '54, August 15, 2005.

37. As cited in Joyce, *Joe K*, 170.

38. John Allen, who has collected nearly a thousand aphorisms during his long teaching and coaching career at area Catholic schools, commented on Joe's penchant for delivering well-timed pearls of wisdom: "Some were serious, some were humorous, most of them were wisdom in capsule form." Interview of John Allen '54, August 15, 2005. The poem "What Is Success?" appears, undated, in *Athletic Director's Files*, NAA.

39. Joe Kasberger, "Your Son Should Play Football," undated, in *Athletic Director's Files*, 1–2, NAA.

40. Joe Kasberger, "Advice to Baseball Players," undated, in *Athletic Director's Files*, NAA.

41. Joe Kasberger, "My Philosophy of Secondary Education," undated, in *Athletic Director's Files*, NAA.

42. Interview of Adrian "Bud" Foley '39, August 17, 2005.

43. Handwritten notes for St. Benedict's Prep Father's Club Father and Son Banquet at Military Park Hotel, May 25, 1966, in *Athletic Director's Files*, "Miscellaneous, 1966," NAA; Reverend Jerome Fitzpatrick, speech notes, October 1, 1969, in *Headmaster's Files*, NAA. See also Joyce, *Joe K*, 336–37.

44. For Schiller's eulogy, see *St. Benedict's Prep Alumni Newsletter*, Winter 1969, NAA.

7. "He Was Afraid of the City": Abbot Patrick, the Monastic Family, and Postwar Newark, 1945–1967

1. Interview of Abbot Martin Burne, OSB, June 26, 2001; *St. Mary's Chapter Minutes*, March 21, 1945, SMAA; *Newark Star-Ledger*, September 15, 1957; *Newark Evening News*, September 15, 17, 1957, and October 3, 1957.

2. Philip Roth, *American Pastoral* (New York: Houghton Mifflin, 1997), 122.

3. McGreevy, *Parish Boundaries*, 5; Roth, *American Pastoral*, 365.

4. For Newark's postwar development and promise, see Cunningham, *Newark*, 302–11; *Newark Evening News*, July 6, 1947.

5. *St. Mary's Abbey Chapter Minutes*, July 10, 1945; May 26, 1947, 17–18; June 20, 1947, 38, SMAA.

6. *St. Mary's Abbey Chapter Minutes*, October 30, 1947, 39–42; December 15, 1947, 44–47, SMAA.

7. *St. Mary's Abbey Chapter Minutes*, May 17, 1955, 105–6, SMAA; *Newark Evening News*, May 3, 1942, SMAA.

8. *St. Mary's Abbey Chapter Minutes*, May 17, 1955, 110–15; October 4, 1955, SMAA. On Louis Danzig's role in urban renewal, see Harold Kaplan, *Urban Renewal Politics: Slum Clearance in Newark* (New York: Columbia University Press, 1963).

9. Reverend Philip Hoover, OSB, "Headmaster's Report, 1949–1951," 6–7, NAA; "Report of the Abbot's Committee," *St. Mary's Abbey Chapter Minutes*, October 4, 1955, 110–15, SMAA.

10. *St. Mary's Abbey Chapter Minutes*, October 18, 1955; Hayes, "History of St. Mary's Abbey," 60–61, SMAA.

11. *St. Mary's Abbey Chapter Minutes*, October 18, 1955; December 19, 1955, 108–9; February 23, 1956, 124–26, SMAA.

12. *St. Mary's Abbey Chapter Minutes*, February 23, 1956, 124–26, SMAA.

13. Hayes, "History of St. Mary's Abbey," 62, SMAA.

14. "Prepared Statement, Abbot Patrick O'Brien," *St. Mary's Abbey Chapter Minutes*, June 13, 1956, 132A–132B; Hayes, "History of St. Mary's Abbey," 62–64, SMAA.

15. Interviews of Abbot Martin Burne, OSB, July 8, 1997, and June 26, 2001; interview of Reverend Boniface Treanor, OSB, July 12, 2001.

16. *Newark Evening News*, September 15, 1957; *Newark Star-Ledger*, September 15, 1957; *St. Mary's Abbey Chapter Minutes*, June 19, 1957, 136–40; July 20, 1957, 141–42, SMAA; various campaign announcements and letters in the *1957 Campaign Scrapbook*, NAA.

17. Stellhorn, "Depression and Decline," 11–12, chap. 2; Harland Bartholomew and Associates, *A Preliminary Report on the Background and Character of the City of Newark, New Jersey* (Kansas City, Mo.: Harland Bartholomew and Associates, 1944), 10. For the impact of the automobile on early suburbanization and Newark, as well as the departure of the city's elite for the suburbs beginning in the 1920s, see Jackson, *Crabgrass Frontier*, 174–89, 274–75.

18. Arnold Hirsch, *Making the Second Ghetto: Race and Housing in Chicago, 1940–1960* (Cambridge: Cambridge University Press, 1983). For subsequent scholarship on the development of the second ghetto, see Charles F. Casey-Leininger, "Making the Second Ghetto in Cincinnati: Avondale, 1925–70," in *Race and the City: Cincinnati, 1820–1970*, ed. Henry Louis Taylor Jr. (Urbana: University of Illinois Press, 1993), 232–57; Raymond A. Mohl, "Making the Second Ghetto in Metropolitan Miami, 1940–1960," in *The New African American Urban History*, ed. Kenneth W. Goings and Raymond A. Mohl (London: Sage Publications, 1996), 266–98; Thomas J. Sugrue, "The Structures of Urban Poverty: The Reorganization of Space and Work in Three Periods of American History," in *The "Underclass" Debate: Views from History*, ed. Michael B. Katz (Princeton: Princeton University Press, 1993), 87–117; Thomas J. Sugrue, "Crabgrass-Roots Politics: Race, Rights, and the Reaction Against Liberalism in the Urban North, 1940–1964," *Journal of American History* 82 (September 1995): 551–78; Hillel Levine and Lawrence Harmon, *The Death of an American Jewish Community* (New York: Free Press, 1992); Yutaka Sasaki, "'But Not Next Door': Housing Discrimination and the Emergence of the 'Second Ghetto' in Newark, N.J., After World War II," *Japanese Journal of American Studies* 5 (March 1994): 113–35.

19. Harvey Kantor and Barbara Brenzel, "Urban Education and the 'Truly Disadvantaged': The Historical Roots of the Contemporary Crisis, 1945–1990," in Katz, *The "Underclass" Debate*, 366–402; Anthony S. Bryk, Valerie E. Lee, and Peter B. Holland, *Catholic Schools and the Common Good* (Cambridge: Harvard

University Press, 1993), 33–35; Rippinger, *Benedictine Order in the United States*, 129. For the decline of public schools in Newark beginning in the 1920s, see Anyon, *Ghetto Schooling*, chaps. 4 and 5.

20. *City of Newark Board of Commissioners Meeting Minutes*, October 5, 1932, Newark Municipal Archives. I am indebted to Warren Grover for sharing this telling quote on ethnic succession in Newark.

21. Jackson, *Crabgrass Frontier*, esp. chap. 11, titled "Federal Subsidy and the Suburban Dream: How Washington Changed the American Housing Market." See also Kenneth T. Jackson, "Race, Ethnicity, and Real Estate Appraisal: The Home Owners Loan Corporation and the Federal Housing Administration," *Journal of Urban History* 6 (August 1980): 419–52; and John J. Harrigan, *Political Change in the Metropolis* (Boston: Scott, Foresman, 1989), 361.

22. See note 9 in the introduction of this volume; and Kenneth T. Jackson and Barbara B. Jackson, "The Black Experience in Newark: The Growth of the Ghetto, 1870–1970," *New Jersey Since 1860: New Findings and Interpretations*, ed. William C. Wright (Trenton: New Jersey Historical Commission, 1972), 37.

23. According to Jackson, "'Red lining' refers to the arbitrary decisions of government and private financial institutions not to lend to certain neighborhoods because of general characteristics of the neighborhood rather than of the particular property to be mortgaged." Jackson, *Crabgrass Frontier*, 196–98, 201–2, 362.

24. Ibid., 208; Hirsch, *Making the Second Ghetto*, xii, 10, 40–99, 215–16; Nathan Wright Jr., *Ready to Riot* (New York: Holt, Rinehart and Winston, 1968), 17–38; Lizabeth Cohen, *A Consumer's Republic: The Politics of Mass Consumption in Postwar America* (New York: Vintage Books, 2003), 212–13, 219. For the residence of St. Benedict's Prep students, see *Annual Catalogue of Students*, 1955–65, NAA.

25. Tuttle, *How Newark Became Newark*, 119–41; Kaplan, *Urban Renewal Politics*, 11, 156–57; David Levitus, "Planning, Slum Clearance, and the Road to Crisis in Newark," *Newark Metro*, September 2005, 1–7.

26. Harrigan, *Political Change in the Metropolis*, 31; *Newark Evening News*, January 27, 1957; New Jersey Advisory Committee to the U.S. Commission on Civil Rights, *Public Housing in Newark's Central Ward* (Newark: New Jersey Advisory Committee to the U.S. Commission on Civil Rights, 1968), 14; Jackson, *Crabgrass Frontier*, 219.

27. Helmreich, *Enduring Community*, 42–43; Dolan, *In Search of an American Catholicism*, 185. On the interplay of race and urban decline and the impact on Catholics in cities and suburbs, see McGreevy, *Parish Boundaries*,

79–110; Sugrue, *Origins of the Urban Crisis*, 231–58; Gamm, *Urban Exodus*, 222–60; Beryl Satter, *Family Properties: Race, Real Estate, and the Exploitation of Black Urban America* (New York: Metropolitan Books, 2009), 122–23; and interview of Richard Lorenzo, December 1, 2009.

28. *St. Mary's Abbey Chapter Minutes*, November 21, 1951, 86; May 7, 1954, 102, SMAA; *Newark Evening News*, October 6, 1951; *Catholic News*, August 2, 1947; interview of Reverend Boniface Treanor, OSB, June 10, 2003.

29. Kaplan, *Urban Renewal Politics*, 149; Anyon, *Ghetto Schooling*, 76; *St. Mary's Abbey Chapter Minutes*, May 24, 1956, 127–28, SMAA; George W. Groh, *The Black Migration: The Journey to Urban America* (New York: Weybright and Talley, 1972), 157; Reverend Virgil Stallbaumer, OSB, "A Monastery on High Street?" statement prepared for Abbot Patrick O'Brien, 1964, 1–6, SMAA.

30. McGreevy, *Parish Boundaries*. For the Catholic encounter with race in Chicago, see Eileen M. McMahon, *What Parish Are You From? A Chicago Irish Community and Race Relations* (Lexington: University Press of Kentucky, 1995). For a southern backdrop, see Gary Wray McDonogh, *Black and Catholic in Savannah, Georgia* (Knoxville: University of Tennessee Press, 1993); *Minutes of Clergy Conference on Negro Welfare*, meeting hosted at St. Mary's Abbey, undated, SMAA; Mary A. Ward, *A Mission for Justice: The History of the First African American Catholic Church in Newark* (Knoxville: University of Tennessee Press, 2002), 70–71.

31. Reverend Philip Hoover, OSB, "Headmaster's Report Covering the Period from September 1949 to January 1951," in *Headmaster's Files*, 1–11, NAA; interview of Reverend Bruno Ugliano, OSB, June 17, 2001.

32. Letter of Reverend Mark W. Confroy, OSB, to Honorable Hugh O. Addonizio, Mayor-Elect of Newark, May 17, 1962, in *1957 Campaign Scrapbook*, NAA.

33. Victor Christ-Janer and Associates, *St. Mary's: A Family: Master Plan Report* (New Canaan, Conn.: Victor Christ-Janer and Associates, 1962), 1, 15; Victor Christ-Janer and Associates, *St. Mary's Abbey/St. Benedict's Preparatory School Expansion* (New Canaan, Conn.: Victor Christ-Janer and Associates, 1962), 2–3, NAA.

34. Interview of Abbot Melvin J. Valvano, OSB, May 5, 2001.

35. Leonard Foley, OFM, "Vatican II: The Vision Lives On: Thirty Years After the Council," *Catholic Update*, nd, http://www.americancatholic.org/Newsletters/CU/ac0393.asp; Walter M. Abbott, SJ, ed., *The Documents of Vatican II* (New York: Guild Press, 1966), 197–203. Mark S. Massa has observed

that the language of Vatican II documents, especially the depiction of the church as the "People of God," was in complete "synergy" with social movements for racial and gender rights and helped shape a new Catholic identity. See Massa, *Catholics and American Culture*, 168–69. In the context of Vatican II's impact on Catholic schools, Bryk, Lee, and Holland discussed the transition from a "devotional" and "vertical" Catholicism toward a "horizontal" religion that emphasized Catholic responsibility for social justice in the modern world. See *Catholic Schools and the Common Good*, 33–34, 46–54.

36. On the rapid succession of events at the Second Vatican Council and in the American civil rights movement, see McGreevy, *Parish Boundaries*, 150–54; Morris, *American Catholic*, 322–30. See also interview of Abbot Martin J. Burne, June 21, 2001.

37. Letter of Reverend Benedict E. Tyler, OSB, to Right Reverend Bede Luibel, OSB, September 25, 1963, NAA.

38. "Statement of the Seventeen," *St. Mary's Abbey Chapter Minutes*, November 4, 1963, 1–3, SMAA. On the "racial apostolate" in Selma, Alabama, see Amy L. Koehlinger, *The New Nuns: Racial Justice and Religious Reform in the 1960s* (Cambridge: Harvard University Press, 2007), 1–19.

39. Stallbaumer, "Monastery on High Street?" 1–6, SMAA; letter of Reverend Benedict E. Tyler, OSB, to Abbot Patrick O'Brien, OSB, December 14, 1963, NAA.

40. "Prepared Statement Delivered by Abbot Patrick O'Brien," *St. Mary's Abbey Chapter Minutes*, November 15, 1963, 191–92; *St. Mary's Abbey Chapter Minutes*, December 10, 1963, 197–98; June 28, 1964, 201–3, SMAA.

41. McGreevy, *Parish Boundaries*, 3–5, 169, 205, 215.

42. Taylor, Lieberfeld and Heldman, *Report to the Order of St. Benedict of New Jersey: Development Prospects for St. Benedict's Preparatory School and St. Mary's Priory, 1966–67 to 1981–82* (New York: Taylor, Lieberfeld and Heldman, 1966), 3–5, 7, 25, NAA.

43. *Benedict News*, November 4, 1963, 2, NAA.

8. "Camelot Is Dead": The Newark Riots and the Closing of St. Benedict's Prep, 1967–1972

1. Interview of Reverend Boniface Treanor, OSB, August 2, 2002; interview of Reverend Maynard Nagengast, OSB, April 1, 2009; Father Laurence Grassman, OSB, "Headmaster's Diary, 1967–68 School Year," July 17, 1967, in

Headmaster's Files, NAA. Clement Alexander Price routinely calls the events of July 1967 "Newark's summer of discontent."

2. Interview of Bernard Greene, August 6, 2002, and April 2, 2009.

3. Interview of Abbot Martin Burne, OSB, June 26, 2002.

4. *Newark Evening News*, December 23, 1970; Roth, *American Pastoral*, 268–69; *New York Times*, December 27, 1992; *Benedict News*, December 29, 1967, NAA.

5. U.S. Commission on Civil Rights, *Report of the United States Commission on Civil Rights* (Washington, D.C.: Government Printing Office, 1959), 549.

6. *Newark Evening News*, July 19, 1967.

7. U.S. National Advisory Commission on Civil Disorders, *Report of the National Advisory Commission on Civil Disorders* (Washington, D.C.: Government Printing Office, 1968), 1.

8. New Jersey State Advisory Committee to the U.S. Commission on Civil Rights, *Public Housing in Newark*, 1–2; City of Newark, New Jersey: Newark Model Cities application, 1967, part 1 (A) 1–2, part 2 (B), table 1, part 2 (A), 24–28, 47–49, available at the Newark Public Library. Jean Anyon has used the data from the 1967 application to estimate that by 1970 one quarter of the city's 405,000 residents lived in the newly expanded ghetto areas, or "second ghetto" areas. See Anyon, *Ghetto Schooling*, 100.

9. New Jersey State Advisory Committee, *Public Housing in Newark*, 6–14.

10. Fred J. Cook, "Wherever the Central Cities Are Going, Newark Is Going to Get There First," *New York Times Magazine*, July 25, 1971.

11. Newark Model Cities application, 1967, part 2 (A), 17; Anyon, *Ghetto Schooling*, 110. For the impact of the dramatic demographic shifts in the Weequahic section of the city, see Sherry B. Ortner, *New Jersey Dreaming: Capital, Culture, and the Class of '58* (Durham: Duke University Press, 2003); *Newark Evening News*, December 22, 1967.

12. Clement A. Price, "The Struggle to Desegregate Newark: Black Middle-Class Militancy in New Jersey, 1932–1947," *New Jersey History*, Fall–Winter 1981. On race relations in Newark, see Chester Rapkin, Eunice Grier, and George Grier, *Group Relations in Newark, 1957: Problems, Prospects, and a Program for Research* (New York: Mayor's Commission on Group Relations, 1957); and Mayor's Commission on Group Relations, *Newark: A City in Transition* (New York: Mayor's Commission on Group Relations, 1959), 2:20–25; Donald Malafronte, *New Jersey Governor's Select Commission on Civil Disorder:*

Hearing Transcript, October 23, 1967, 16, Records of the Governor's Select Commission on Civil Disorder, box 5a, New Jersey State Archives; *Newark Evening News*, April 17, 1967.

13. New Jersey State Advisory Committee, *Public Housing in Newark*, 1; New Jersey Governor's Select Commission on Civil Disorders, *Report for Action* (Trenton: State of New Jersey, 1968), 32. Two incidents in 1965 clearly influenced the attitudes of African Americans toward the Newark Police Department. In the early morning hours of June 12, 1965, Lester Long Jr. was pulled over by Newark policemen for having a broken taillight and a noisy muffler. Long decided to flee from custody, and as he ran from the patrol car he was gunned down in the back by Officer Henry Martinez. The police immediately stated that Martinez's gun was fired by accident, but witnesses came forward to provide evidence to the contrary. See Ronald Porambo, *No Cause for Indictment: An Autopsy of Newark* (New York: Holt, Rinehart and Winston, 1971), 40–46. In August of the same year, Bernard Rich died in a Newark jail cell. Police reports stated that Rich had gone berserk and killed himself by banging his head against the wall. A pathologist's report revealed that although Rich suffered from head injuries, he had also sustained severe bruises on other parts of his body. See Nathan Wright Jr., *Ready to Riot* (New York: Holt, Rinehart and Winston, 1968), 5.

14. Cunningham, *Newark*, 315–16; Stanley B. Winters, *From Riot to Recovery: Newark Ten Years After* (Newark: Roman and Littlefield, 1979), 47; *Newark Evening News*, May 26, June 14 and 16, 1967.

15. *Newark Evening News*, May 29, July 19, 1967.

16. The best account of the Newark riots is New Jersey Governor's Select Commission on Civil Disorders, *Report for Action*, 104–44. See also Tom Hayden, *Rebellion in Newark: Official Violence and Ghetto Response* (New York: Vintage Books, 1967); and Porambo, *No Cause for Indictment*, 100–109, 113–53.

17. *New York Daily News*, July 15, 1967; New Jersey Governor's Select Commission on Civil Disorders, *Report for Action*, 104–16.

18. New Jersey Governor's Select Commission on Civil Disorders, *Report for Action*, x–xi, 125, 129–31, 133–43.

19. New Jersey Governor's Select Commission on Civil Disorders, *Report for Action*, x–xi, 125, 129–31, 138–41; Cunningham, *Newark*, 325–26.

20. Cunningham, *Newark*, 327.

21. Interview of Reverend Theodore Howath, OSB, January 15, 2003; interview of Bernard Greene, April 1, 2009.

22. Burne, "Second Hundred Years," 1–6, NAA.

23. Interview of Abbot Martin J. Burne, OSB, June 26, 2001.

24. Interview of Reverend Philip Waters, OSB, January 30, 2006.

25. "Transfers: Summer 1967," in *Students Files*, 1–2, NAA.

26. Interview of Reverend Philip Waters, OSB, August 6, 2002; Ward, *Mission for Justice*; *Newark Evening News*, April 10 and 13, 1968; *Newark Star-Ledger*, April 8, 1968; Tuttle, *How Newark Became Newark*, 178.

27. The preceding quotations are actually extracted from a rather detailed summary of a discussion among community members during a meeting in Newark on Saturday, July 20, 1968. They are not direct quotes of the proceedings, but they are taken word for word from the minutes of that meeting. *St. Mary's Abbey Chapter Minutes*, July 20, 1968, SMAA.

28. Interview of Reverend Bruno Ugliano, OSB, June 17, 2001; interview of Reverend Philip Waters, OSB, January 30, 2006.

29. *St. Mary's Abbey Chapter Minutes*, July 19, 20, 27, 1968, SMAA; interview of Reverend Theodore Howath, OSB, January 15, 2003.

30. "Minutes of Meeting, Friday August 9, 1968, Newark, N.J.," typed transcript, 1–22, SMAA.

31. "Letter from Abbot Martin Burne to Members of Abbot Baldwin's Council–President's Council of the American-Cassinese Congregation," August 29, 1968, in *St. Mary's Abbey Chapter Minutes*; and *St. Mary's Abbey Chapter Minutes*, September 30, 1968, 126–28, 132–33, SMAA.

32. *St. Mary's Abbey Chapter Minutes*, October 14, 1968, 141, SMAA; *Newark Abbey Chapter Minutes*, December 14, 1968, 1, NAA.

33. "Remarks of Abbot Ambrose J. Clark at Ceremony of Blessing, Sacred Heart Cathedral, February 22, 1969," NAA; interview of Reverend Bruno Ugliano, OSB, June 17, 2001. Father Matthew remembered cleaning up all the champagne bottles strewn on the floor the next morning. Interview of Reverend Matthew Wotelko, OSB, April 17, 2001.

34. Alfred H. Deutsch, OSB, *Bruised Reeds, and Other Stories* (Collegeville, Minn.: Saint John's University Press, 1971), 89.

35. *Newark Evening News*, December 15 and 16, 1968; *Catholic Advocate*, December 19, 1968, and January 2, 1969.

36. *Newark Abbey Chapter Minutes*, March 24, 1969, 29; April 28, 1969, 46; NAA. According to the chapter minutes, the monks decided to institute a summer school before the 1969–70 academic year for "blacks who needed help and for whites whom it will be required if they wish to enter St. Benedict's this fall." *Newark Abbey Chapter Minutes*, April 14, 1969, 33, NAA.

37. Research indicated that inner-city Catholic schools closed at a rate two to five times higher than did other Catholic schools during between 1967 and 1973. Thomas Vitulo-Martin, "How Federal Policies Discourage the Racial and Economic Integration of Private Schools," in *Private Schools and the Common Good*, ed. E. M. Gaffney (Notre Dame: University of Notre Dame Press, 1981), 25–43. See also Bryk, Lee, and Holland, *Catholic Schools and the Common Good*, 336–38; *Newark Star-Ledger*, April 7, 1968. The American Cassinese Congregation, of which Newark Abbey belonged, declined from 2,045 members in 1965 to 1,462 in 1985. "This erosion of what had up to the time of the Council been an uninterrupted growth in American Benedictine houses was due to the departure of many professed members and the abrupt termination of large novitiate classes." See Rippinger, *Benedictine Order in the United States*, 248.

38. *Newark Abbey Chapter Minutes*, April 28, 1969, 46–47; "Letter of Father Jerome Fitzpatrick, OSB, to Newark Abbey Community," *Newark Abbey Chapter Minutes*, October 1, 1969, 57A–57B; "Statement Signed by Fathers Eugene, Regis, Bruno, Sean, Matthew, Colman and Maurice," *Newark Abbey Chapter Minutes*, October 1, 1969, 57c–57d, 56–58; "Prepared Statement of Abbot Ambrose, Beginning the Community Meeting of Newark Abbey of December 1, 1969," *Newark Abbey Chapter Minutes*, December 1, 1969, 65A–65D, NAA.

39. *Benedict News*, December 1969, NAA; interview of Paul E. Thornton, July 23, 2001.

40. During the 1969–70 academic year, the scholarship fund provided for twenty-one students at a cost of $14,771. According to the 1970 Middle States report, the fund was "established and maintained through the begging of Abbot Ambrose for the education of the needy poor of the inner city." Interview of Reverend Benedict Tyler, OSB, January 13, 1998.

41. Interview of Henrique "Hank" Cordeiro '72, February 26, 2004; Reverend Albert Holtz, OSB, "Understanding Each Other," speech given at a student assembly, September 1969, 1–3, NAA.

42. Interview of Steven Walker '72, March 31, 2004.

43. Ibid. For Baraka's influence in Newark, see Komozi Woodard, *A Nation Within a Nation: Amiri Baraka (LeRoi Jones) and Black Power Politics* (Chapel Hill: University of North Carolina Press, 1999), 109, 123, 153, 242; *New York Times*, December 28, 1999.

44. Interview of Clement A. Price, May 15, 2009; interview of Rich Lorenzo '63, December 1, 2008; David K. Shipler, "The White Niggers of Newark," *Harper's Magazine*, August 1972, 77–83.

45. Interview of Reverend Philip Waters, OSB, January 30, 2006; interview of Reverend Edwin D. Leahy, OSB, January 26, 2001.

46. Interview of Reverend Albert Holtz, OSB, January 29, 2002.

47. Interview of Reverend Bruno Ugliano, OSB, June 17, 2001.

48. Interview of Reverend Albert Holtz, OSB, January 29, 2002.

49. Interview of Reverend Edwin D. Leahy, OSB, February 6, 1997.

50. "Evaluation of St. Benedict's Preparatory School by the Middle States Association of Colleges and Secondary Schools, November 11–13, 1970," 1–24; *Newark Abbey Chapter Minutes*, January 1, 1971, NAA.

51. *Newark Abbey Chapter Minutes*, February 17, 104–7; February 24, 1971, 117–22, NAA.

52. *Newark Abbey Chapter Minutes*, February 25, 1971, and March 15, 1971, NAA.

53. "January Report 1972 on the Status of St. Benedict's Prep School," *Newark Abbey Chapter Minutes*, January 12, 1972, 156A–156C, NAA.

54. Personal journal of Reverend Albert Holtz, OSB, February 10, 1972, 1:1–5, NAA. On his journal, Father Albert commented, "I was consciously writing it to keep a record. I could see that this institution that had been around for one hundred years was about to fall apart. I wanted to leave some tracks in the sand, and something told me it would be a valuable thing to do. I always did it in such a way that anybody could pick it up and read it. It was a chronicle of those times." Interview of Reverend Albert Holtz, OSB, February 27, 2002.

55. Interview of Reverend Albert Holtz, OSB, March 19, 2002; *Newark Abbey Chapter Minutes*, February 10, 1972, 176, NAA.

56. Interview of Reverend Benedict Tyler, OSB, January 13, 1998.

57. Personal journal of Reverend Albert Holtz, OSB, February 15, 1972, 1:11, NAA.

58. Interview of Henrique Cordeiro '72, February 26, 2004.

59. Interview of Jack Dalton, May 14, 2000.

60. Telegram of Mrs. Patrick Hanifen to Abbot Ambrose Clark, OSB, February 17, 1972; telegram of J. McCormick to Abbot Ambrose Clark, OSB, February 19, 1972; letter of Dolores Miller to Abbot Ambrose Clark, OSB, February 23, 1972, NAA.

61. *Newark Abbey Chapter Minutes*, February 15, 1972, 178–79; February 23, 1972, 180–90; "Visitation Report to the Community of Newark Abbey, March 5, 1972," 1–2, NAA.

62. Personal journal of Reverend Albert Holtz, OSB, March 9, 1972, 1:27, NAA; interview of Reverend Theodore Howath, OSB, January 15, 2003; interview of Reverend Bruno Ugliano, OSB, June 17, 2001.

63. Interview of Henrique Cordeiro '72, February 26, 2004; personal journal of Reverend Albert Holtz, OSB, March 1, 1972, 1:18, NAA; interview of Reverend Albert Holtz, OSB, February 27, 2002.

64. Personal journal of Reverend Albert Holtz, OSB, March 2, 1972, 1:21, NAA.

65. Personal journal of Reverend Albert Holtz, OSB, March 9, 1972, 1:27, NAA; interview of Reverend Edwin D. Leahy, OSB, February 6, 1997.

66. *Newark Abbey Chapter Minutes*, May 15, 1972, 212–17, NAA.

67. Personal journal of Reverend Albert Holtz, OSB, April 11, 1972, 1:37, NAA; interview of Reverend Philip Waters, OSB, January 30, 2006.

68. Personal journal of Reverend Albert Holtz, OSB, June 21, 1972, 1:59–60, NAA; Hayes, *Unto Another Generation*, 72–73; interview of Abbot Giles P. Hayes, OSB, August 20, 2009.

69. As quoted in Smith, "Miracle on High Street," 92; interview of Reverend Edwin D. Leahy, OSB, February 6, 1997; see also *Wall Street Journal*, December 24, 1984.

70. *Newark Star-Ledger*, February 20, 1972.

71. Personal journal of Reverend Albert Holtz, OSB, March 9, 1972, 1:47, NAA.

9. "A Possible School": The Resurrection of St. Benedict's Prep, 1972–1977

1. Robert J. Armbruster, "Bringing Back an Inner-City School," *America*, June 12, 1976.

2. Interviews of Reverend Edwin D. Leahy, OSB, February 6, 1997, and December 22, 2005; interview of Reverend Albert Holtz, OSB, December 22, 2005; *Newark Abbey Chapter Minutes*, September 28, 1972, 267A–267D, NAA.

3. Personal journal of Reverend Albert Holtz, OSB, September 29, 1972, 1:76; October 5, 1972, 1:79, NAA.

4. Personal journal of Reverend Albert Holtz, OSB, October 12, 1972, 1:80; October 26, 1972, 1:81, NAA.

5. Personal journal of Reverend Albert Holtz, OSB, June 5, 1977, 3:64, NAA.

6. "Recessus: Visitation of Newark Abbey, November 1–6, 1976," in *Newark Abbey Chapter Minutes,* NAA.

7. Interview of Reverend Albert Holtz, OSB, June 25, 2001; personal journal of Reverend Albert Holtz, OSB, May 25, 1972, 1:45; June 5, 1972, 1:57, NAA. See also *Newark Abbey Chapter Minutes,* June 5, 1972, 226–28, NAA; and interview of Reverend Theodore Howarth, OSB, January 15, 2003.

8. Interview of Abbot Martin J. Burne, OSB, June 26, 2001.

9. *Newark Abbey Chapter Minutes,* November 14, 1972, 264, NAA; interview of Father Benedict Tyler, OSB, January 13, 1998.

10. Interview of Jean Leahy, February 2, 2006.

11. Personal journal of Reverend Albert Holtz, OSB, November 14, 1972, 1:84, NAA; interview of Reverend Edwin D. Leahy, OSB, December 22, 2005.

12. Interview of Reverend Philip Waters, OSB, January 30, 2006.

13. Personal journal of Reverend Albert Holtz, OSB, February 15, 1972, 1:8–9, NAA.

14. Personal journal of Reverend Albert Holtz, OSB, May 15, 1972, 1:41, NAA.

15. Personal journal of Reverend Albert Holtz, OSB, May 14, 1973, 1:110; May 20, 1973, 114; September 8, 1973, 136, NAA.

16. See author's notes of Father Albert's remarks from a March 25, 2001, acceptance speech at the school's Annual Communion Breakfast.

17. Personal journal of Reverend Albert Holtz, OSB, June 4, 1972, 1:157, NAA. See also Eric Hoffer, *The True Believer: Thoughts on the Nature of Mass Movements* (New York: Harper & Row, 1951), 57.

18. Interview of Reverend Albert Holtz, OSB, June 4, 2003.

19. *New York Times,* April 1, 1973.

20. *Newark Abbey Chapter Minutes,* November 20, 1972, 268–69, NAA.

21. *New York Times,* August 7, 1977; interviews of Reverend Edwin D. Leahy, OSB, February 2, 2006, and February 17, 2006.

22. Fred J. Cook, "The Newark Teacher's Strike," *New York Times Magazine,* July 25, 1971.

23. For a detailed account of the strikes, see Steve Golin, *The Newark Teachers Strike: Hope on the Line* (New Brunswick: Rutgers University Press, 2002).

24. Cunningham, *Newark,* 329–37.

25. New Jersey Governor's Select Commission on Civil Disorders, *Report for Action*, 23.

26. As quoted in Cunningham, *Newark*, 339.

27. Interview of Reverend Matthew Wotelko, OSB, April 17, 2001.

28. Interview of Reverend Edwin D. Leahy, OSB, February 6, 1997.

29. Letter of Lillian Dreher to Reverend Edwin D. Leahy, OSB, March 13, 1973, in *Headmaster's Files*, NAA.

30. Interview of Reverend Edwin D. Leahy, OSB, February 6, 1997.

31. Reverend Albert Holtz, OSB, *Downtown Monks: Sketches of God in the City* (Notre Dame, Ind.: Ave Maria Press, 2000), 32–33. See also Father Albert's unpublished manuscript in author's files.

32. Holtz, *Downtown Monks*, 32–33; Holtz, unpublished manuscript, 29–30.

33. Personal journal of Reverend Albert Holtz, OSB, January 7, 1973, 1:85–87, NAA; Holtz, unpublished manuscript, 39–43; interview of Reverend Albert Holtz, OSB, April 16, 2002.

34. Reverend Albert Holtz, OSB, "A Possible School," 1–6, in *Newark Abbey Chapter Minutes*, January 12, 1973, 285A–285G, NAA.

35. Interviews of Reverend Albert Holtz, OSB, June 4, 2003; Reverend Edwin D. Leahy, OSB, June 6, 2003; Reverend Philip Waters, OSB, March 3, 2004.

36. Reverend Albert Holtz, OSB, "Creating an Educative Environment Suitable for Both Blacks and Whites: A Theological Critique," research paper, December 17, 1969, NAA.

37. Interview of Reverend Philip Waters, OSB, January 30, 2006. For an article on liberation theology and urban Catholic schools, see Edward St. John, "Integrating Liberation Theology into Restructuring: Toward a Model for Urban Catholic Schools," *Catholic Education: A Journal of Inquiry and Practice* 2, no. 3 (1999): 265–80.

38. *Minutes of Parents Meeting*, January 23, 1973, NAA.

39. *Newark Abbey Chapter Minutes*, February 1, 1973, 289–90, NAA.

40. For background on the naming of the new school, see *Minutes of Parents Meetings*, January 30, 1973, 1–2, and February 6, 1973, 1–7; *Newark Abbey Chapter Minutes*, January 16, 1973, 286–87, and February 1, 1973, 288–90, NAA. For Father Edwin's quote, see interview of Reverend Edwin D. Leahy, OSB, December 22, 2005.

41. *St. Benedict's Preparatory School Alumni Newsletter*, Winter 1974–75, 3, NAA.

42. Personal journal of Reverend Albert Holtz, OSB, February 5, 1973, 1:94, NAA.

43. Interviews of Dennis Durkin '75, March 3, 2004, and January 11, 2006; interview of Reverend Edwin D. Leahy, OSB, December 22, 2005.

44. Letter of Dennis Durkin to Reverend Edwin D. Leahy, OSB, March 29, 1973, in *Student Files, Class of 1975*; letter of Elizabeth M. Durkin to Reverend Edwin D. Leahy, OSB, March 27, 1973, in *Student Files, Class of 1975*, NAA; interview of Reverend Albert Holtz, OSB, February 27, 2002. See also an alumni publication on the Durkin family's legacy at St. Benedict's Prep titled "One Man's Family and St. Benedict's Prep," NAA.

45. U.S. National Advisory Commission on Civil Disorders, *Report of the National Advisory Commission on Civil Disorders*, 1.

46. Letter of Mrs. Mary Pearl Brown to Reverend Edwin D. Leahy, OSB, May 30, 1973, in *Student Files, Class of 1975*, NAA.

47. Letter of Lillie Riddick to Reverend Boniface Treanor, OSB, September 5, 1973, in *Student Files, Class of 1976*, NAA.

48. Letter of James Reed Jr. to Reverend Edwin D. Leahy, OSB, April 27, 1973, in *Student Files, Class of 1975*; letter of Kevin McNeil to Reverend Edwin D. Leahy, OSB, March 8, 1973, in *Student Files, Class of 1975*, NAA.

49. Letter of Kevin McNeil to Reverend Edwin D. Leahy, OSB, September 5, 1973, in *Student Files, Class of 1975*; letter of Edward Alston to Reverend Edwin D. Leahy, OSB, March 21, 1973, in *Student Files, Class of 1975*, NAA.

50. Letter of Mr. and Mrs. D. Mitchell to Reverend Edwin D. Leahy, OSB, May 16, 1973, in *Student Files, Class of 1975*; letter of Mr. Gene McCullough to Reverend Edwin D. Leahy, OSB, March 26, 1973, in *Student Files, Class of 1975*, NAA.

51. Interviews of Reverend Edwin D. Leahy, OSB, February 6, 1977, and December 28, 2005.

52. Interview of Paul E. Thornton, July 23, 2001.

53. Personal journal of Reverend Albert Holtz, OSB, May 20, 1973, 1:113; January 12, 1974, 2:23, NAA.

54. Personal journal of Reverend Albert Holtz, OSB, July 1, 1973, 1:119, NAA.

55. Personal journal of Reverend Albert Holtz, OSB, July 2, 1973, 1:118–19, NAA.

56. Interviews of Dennis Durkin '75, March 3, 2001, and January 11, 2006.

57. Personal journal of Reverend Albert Holtz, OSB, December 9, 1973, 2:13, NAA.

58. Interview of Reverend Albert Holtz, OSB, January 10, 2006.

59. Personal journal of Reverend Albert Holtz, OSB, September 6, 1973, 1:139–41, NAA.

60. Personal journal of Reverend Albert Holtz, OSB, September 6, 1973, 1:141, NAA; interview of Reverend Albert Holtz, OSB, January 10, 2005.

61. Interviews of Dennis Durkin '75, March 3, 2001, and January 11, 2006; interviews of Thomas Leahy '77, February 12, 2002, and March 1, 2002.

62. Interview of Abbot Melvin J. Valvano, OSB, January 30, 2006.

63. Letter of James Caruso to Reverend Edwin Leahy, OSB, undated, *Student Files, Class of 1977*, NAA.

64. Personal journal of Reverend Albert Holtz, OSB, February 12, 1974, 2:27, NAA.

65. Interview of Reverend Edwin D. Leahy, OSB, February 7, 2001; personal journal of Reverend Albert Holtz, OSB, September 26, 1973, 2:3; October 13, 1973, 5; December 9, 1973, 13, NAA.

66. Smith, "Miracle on High Street," 94.

67. Interview of Reverend Philip Waters, OSB, January 30, 2006.

68. "An Interview of Fr. Edwin Leahy, Headmaster of St. Benedict's Prep," undated pamphlet distributed by St. Benedict's Prep School Alumni Office, NAA.

69. Interview of Reverend Edwin D. Leahy, OSB, February 6, 1997.

70. Interview of Reverend Albert Holtz, OSB, April 16, 2002.

71. Interview of Virgil Griffin '75, February 2, 2006.

72. Interview of Thomas Leahy '77, February 12, 2002.

73. Personal journal of Reverend Albert Holtz, OSB, December 16, 1973, 2:17; January 17, 1974, 24, NAA.

74. Personal journal of Reverend Albert Holtz, OSB, October 26, 1974, 2:66, NAA; Father Albert Holtz, OSB, "Operation Whitewash '76," dated February 20, 1976, *Headmaster's Files*, NAA.

75. *New York Times*, July 13, 1975; *Newark Star-Ledger*, November 18, 1984.

76. Holtz, unpublished manuscript, 45, NAA.

77. *Newark Star-Ledger*, February 26, 1992.

78. *New York Times*, July 13, 1975; interview of Reverend Edwin D. Leahy, OSB, February 12, 2001; interview of Adrian Foley, August 17, 2005.

79. Personal journal of Reverend Albert Holtz, OSB, May 1, 1972, 1:108–9, NAA.

80. *Newark Abbey Chapter Minutes*, December 2, 1973, 249–51, NAA; personal journal of Reverend Albert Holtz, OSB, November 10, 1974, 2:66, NAA.

81. Personal journal of Reverend Albert Holtz, OSB, September 16, 1973, 1:146, NAA.

82. Interview of Reverend Edwin D. Leahy, OSB, February 12, 2001; interview of Thomas Leahy '77, March 1, 2002.

83. Interview of Reverend Edwin D. Leahy, OSB, February 12, 2001; interview of Reverend Albert Holtz, OSB, February 7, 2002.

84. Interview of Reverend Albert Holtz, OSB, February 7, 2002.

85. *Newark Star-Ledger*, November 18, 1984.

86. Letter of recommendation for Paul E. Thornton to Harvard University in *Student Files, Class of 1963*, NAA; interview of Paul E. Thornton, July 23, 2001.

87. Interview of Abbot Melvin Valvano, OSB, May 5, 2001.

88. Personal journal of Reverend Albert Holtz, OSB, January 12, 1975, 2:74–75; February 10, 1975, 78–79; December 14, 1975, 115, NAA.

89. Personal journal of Reverend Albert Holtz, OSB, January 12, 1975, 2:94–95, NAA.

90. Interview of Bernard Greene '73, January 11, 2006.

91. Interview of Reverend Edwin D. Leahy, OSB, February 12, 2001; letter of Reverend Edwin D. Leahy, OSB, to Mr. and Mrs. Alfred Tyson, July 30, 1976, in *Headmaster's Files*, NAA.

92. Personal journal of Reverend Albert Holtz, OSB, December 31, 1976, 2:31, NAA.

93. Paul E. Thornton, "Highlights of 1976–77," in *Newark Abbey Chapter Minutes*, September 8, 1977, 311f–311i, NAA; McPadden, *Benedictines in Newark*, 56.

94. Personal journal of Reverend Albert Holtz, OSB, May 2, 1976, 2:146–47, NAA; interview of Dennis Durkin '75, January 11, 2006.

95. *Newark Abbey Chapter Minutes*, September 8, 1977, 311f–311i, NAA; McPadden, *Benedictines in Newark*, 56–57.

96. Personal journal of Reverend Albert Holtz, OSB, September 8, 1975, 2:101, NAA.

97. As quoted in McPadden, *Benedictines in Newark*, 51.

10. The Headmaster and the Street, 1977–1986

1. Interview of Patrick Napoli '87, March 21, 2005.

2. Interview of Reverend Edwin D. Leahy, OSB, January 26, 2001.

3. Gil Sewall, "1980 Annual Report on Education in the City," in *Schumann Review* (Montclair, N.J.: Florence and John Schumann Foundation, 1980), 1–16.

4. Andrew M. Greeley, *Catholic High Schools and Minority Students* (New Brunswick, N.J.: Transaction Books, 1982); James S. Coleman, Thomas Hoffer, and Sally Kilgore, *High School Achievement: Public, Catholic, and Private Schools Compared* (New York: Basic Books, 1982). See also two National Catholic Educational Association's reports released in the mid-1980s: *The Catholic High School: A National Portrait* (Washington, D.C.: National Catholic Educational Association, 1985); and *Catholic High Schools: The Impact on Low Income Students* (Washington, D.C.: National Catholic Educational Association, 1986). For a comprehensive review of the literature and an explanation of the "common school effect," see Bryk, Lee, and Holland, *Catholic Schools and the Common Gold*, 58. On Newark, see Robert Mahon, ed., *Newark: Demographic Happening: Geographic Opportunity* (Short Hills, N.J.: Mahon's Financial Profiles, 1974), 13–15.

5. In 1979, Arthur Lenihan wrote an article for the *Newark Star-Ledger* titled "Father Ed's 'Magic,'" and two years later, alumnus Fred Smith wrote his well-received piece in *New Jersey Monthly* titled "Miracle on High Street."

6. Interview of Reverend Edwin D. Leahy, OSB, February 26, 2001.

7. Letter of Abbot Martin Burne, OSB, to Reverend Edwin D. Leahy, OSB, March 21, 1996, in *Headmaster's Files*, NAA.

8. Letter from Msgr. Charles McCorristin to Abbot Patrick O'Brien, March 15, 1958, in *Student Files, Class of 1963*, NAA.

9. Interviews of Reverend Edwin D. Leahy, OSB, February 26, 2001, and January 26, 2006.

10. *Newark Star-Ledger*, November 29, 1992.

11. Interviews of Abbot Melvin Valvano, OSB, January 30, 2006; Reverend Philip Waters, OSB, January 30, 2006; Reverend Albert Holtz, OSB, January 29, 2002; Jean Leahy, February 2, 2006; Keith Corpus, February 9, 2006; Richard S. Jacobs, February 7, 2006.

12. *The Telolog*, 1920, 36, NAA.

13. For this depiction of Woodbridge during the 1950s, see interview of Jean Leahy, February 2, 2006; and interview of Reverend Edwin D. Leahy, OSB, February 26, 2001.

14. Interview of Reverend Edwin D. Leahy, OSB, January 26, 2006.

15. Ibid.

16. Interview of Thomas Leahy '77, February 2, 2002.

17. Interview of Reverend Edwin D. Leahy, OSB, January 26, 2006.

18. For Edwin's attachment to Newark, see interview of Abbot Martin Burne, OSB, June 26, 2001. For conflicts between Edwin and other monks while he lived in Morristown, see interview of Reverend Bruno Ugliano, OSB, June 17, 2001.

19. Interview of Reverend Edwin D. Leahy, OSB, January 9, 2001.

20. John McPhee, *The Headmaster: Frank L. Boyden of Deerfield* (New York: Farrar, Straus and Giroux, 1966), 7, 10, 17, 22, 32–33.

21. Interview of Reverend Edwin D. Leahy, OSB, January 26, 2006.

22. Interview of Richard S. Jacobs, January 30, 2006.

23. Interview of Abbot Melvin J. Valvano, OSB, January 30, 2006; *Newark Advocate*, January 28, 1981.

24. Interview of Abbot Martin J. Burne, OSB, June 26, 2001.

25. Interview of Reverend Edwin D. Leahy, OSB, February 26, 2001.

26. McPhee, *Headmaster*, 7.

27. Interview of Reverend Edwin D. Leahy, OSB, January 26, 2006.

28. Interview of Reverend Albert Holtz, OSB, January 29, 2002.

29. Personal journal of Reverend Albert Holtz, OSB, December 9, 1973, 2:13, NAA.

30. Sewall, "Education in the City," 4.

31. Interview of Reverend Edwin D. Leahy, OSB, January 26, 2006.

32. Holtz, "Benedictine Conversion," 6–7; interview of Jean Leahy, February 2, 2006; interview of Reverend Edwin D. Leahy, OSB, February 26, 2001.

33. As cited in Cunningham, *Newark*, 342–46.

34. *Newark Star-Ledger*, July 19, 1977.

35. George Russell, "The American Underclass: A Minority Within a Minority," *Time*, August 29, 1977, 14–27.

36. For the "underclass" debate, see Michael Katz, "Introduction: The Urban 'Underclass' as a Metaphor of Social Transformation," in Katz, *The "Underclass" Debate*, 3–23.

37. The full text of the report "The Negro Family: The Case for National Action" can be found in Lee Rainwater and William L. Yancey, eds., *The Moynihan Report and the Politics of Controversy* (Cambridge: MIT Press, 1967), 39–125.

38. Bill Moyers, *The Vanishing Family: Crisis in Black America*, CBS, January 25, 1986. For the quotation, see the *New York Times*, January 25, 1986.

39. Interview of Reverend Edwin D. Leahy, OSB, February 26, 2001.

40. Both letters appear in Father Albert's first book; see Holtz, *Downtown Monks*, 72–73.

41. Interview of Reverend Phillip Waters, OSB, January 30, 2006.

42. Interview of Reverend Edwin D. Leahy, OSB, November 29, 2003.

43. Interviews of Reverend Edwin D. Leahy, OSB, January 26, 2006, and March 22, 2006.

44. On the practice of "code switching," see Elijah Anderson, *Code of the Street: Decency, Violence, and the Moral Life of the Inner City* (New York: Norton, 1999), chap. 1.

45. For details of "homework raids," see interview of Reverend Edwin D. Leahy, OSB, January 26, 2001; interview of Bernard Greene '73, January 11, 2006; personal journal of Reverend Albert Holtz, OSB, September 12, 1979, 4:36–37, NAA.

46. Personal journal of Reverend Albert Holtz, OSB, September 12, 1979, 4:36–37, NAA.

47. Interviews of Reverend Edwin D. Leahy, OSB, February 17, 2001, and January 26, 2006.

48. For Joe Scott's remarks, see Smith, "Miracle on High Street," 96.

49. *Newark Star-Ledger*, November 18, 1984.

50. Interview of Reverend Edwin D. Leahy, OSB, March 22, 2006.

51. *Newark Star-Ledger*, December 16, 1979.

52. Personal journal of Reverend Albert Holtz, OSB, September 26, 1978, 3:133; September 12, 1979, 4:32–33; March 13, 1983, 5:47, NAA.

53. Letter of Edwin D. Leahy, OSB, to William D. Smith, March 6, 1986, in *Headmaster's Files*; interview of Marc Onion '89, April 10, 2010.

54. Interview of Reverend Albert Holtz, OSB, June 4, 2003.

55. Interview of Bernard Greene, January 11, 2006.

56. Personal journal of Reverend Albert Holtz, OSB, January 21, 1979, 4:4–5, NAA.

57. *Catholic Advocate*, June 8, 1978.

58. "Transcript of Broadcast Excerpt on St. Benedict's," *World News Tonight*, ABC, June 8, 1980, NAA.

59. Interview of Reverend Edwin D. Leahy, OSB, February 17, 2006; *Newark Star-Ledger*, March 16, 1977.

60. "An Interview of Fr. Edwin Leahy, Headmaster of St. Benedict's Prep," 1978, NAA.

61. For a copy of Father Cornelius's speech, see *St. Benedict's Prep Athletic Scrapbook,* 1920–21, NAA.

62. Excerpt of testimony of Reverend Edwin D. Leahy, OSB, before congressional committee hearing on "Schools That Work," reprinted in the *Newark Star-Ledger,* February 17, 1980.

63. See profile on Fred Smith in Sewall, "Education in the City," 7.

64. *Newark Star-Ledger,* December 19, 1977.

65. Interview of Reverend Edwin D. Leahy, OSB, February 26, 2001.

66. Personal journal of Reverend Albert Holtz, OSB, November 26, 1978, 3:145–46, NAA.

67. Interview of Abbot Melvin Valvano, OSB, January 11, 2006. For details of the auction, see Harmer Rooke Numismatists, *The Coin Collection of the Benedictine Abbey of Newark, N.J.* (New York: Harmer Rooke Numismatists, 1980).

68. Interview of Paul Thornton, April 3, 2006.

69. Interview of Abbot Melvin Valvano, OSB, January 30, 2006.

70. *Newark Star-Ledger,* November 15, 1984.

71. See Father Malachy's editorial in *St. Benedict's Prep Alumni Newsletter,* September 1986, 2, NAA.

72. Interview of Reverend Edwin D. Leahy, OSB, March 21, 2006.

Conclusion

1. Interview with Reverend Edwin D. Leahy, OSB, January 26, 2006.

2. *Newark Star-Ledger,* November 29, 1992.

3. Interviews of Abbot Melvin J. Valvano, May 5, 2001, and January 30, 2006.

4. Personal journal of Reverend Albert Holtz, OSB, February 10, 1982, 5:9–10, NAA.

5. Interview of Reverend Edwin D. Leahy, OSB, December 22, 2005.

6. Interview of Jean Leahy, February 2, 2006.

7. Mike Davis, *Dead Cities and Other Tales* (New York: New Press, 2002), 388–89; Mindy Thompson Fullilove, *Root Shock: How Tearing Up City Neighborhoods Hurts America, and What We Can Do About It* (New York: Ballantine Books, 2005), 145–47.

8. Terry Golway, "The Cruelest Month," *America,* March 6, 2006.

9. Interview of Reverend Edwin D. Leahy, OSB, April 20, 2004.

10. Interview of Reverend Edwin D. Leahy, OSB, February 26, 2001.

11. Interview of Archbishop Theodore McCarrick, October 25, 2009.

Index

Abbett, Leon (New Jersey governor), 32

abbey transfer announcement, 141

abbots' visit, 137

academic advantage of Catholic schools, 226

academic year in new school, 202
effectiveness of phases, 221

accreditation, 56–57
Middle States Association of Colleges and Schools, 62, 69–70

adaptability, 1–2
as asset to monastic life, 13–14
establishment of college and, 20
overlooking because of fear, 188
reopening and, 256

admission standards, 22
post-separation, 174

African Americans, 53
admittance to St. Benedict's, 148
Black Student Union parties, 178
blackface minstrel shows, 54
Blake, Carl, 240–41
blamed for Newark's downfall, 199–200
Board of Education candidate, 162–63

Carey, Monsignor Thomas, boiling over of problems, 162

ghetto growth, 145

Great Depression, 65–66

integration of school, 170

mothers looking for help, 240

mysterious quality of St. Benedict's, 171

neighborhood preservation, 145

ownership of school, 239

parodies in school, 53–54

political disenfranchisement, 161–62

politicizing, 162

population rise, 144, 161

Queen of Angels parish, 148

respect for St. Benedict's, 171

Scott, Joe, 240

Scudder Homes, 240

Stallbaumer, Father Virgil on, 153

students
attitudes toward, 53–54
double standards, 180
high-achieving, 179
increasing numbers, 4
initial attendees, 54
professionalism and, 180–81

stereotypes, 169

textbook issues, 161

The Vanishing Family: Crisis in Black America (television documentary), 236

white flight to suburbs and, 144

Allen, Johnny, 125, 230

alumni, 25

Benedictine monks, 58

Brennan, Bob, 256

Cawley, Charles M., 256

college bound, 58

financial support, 224–25, 250

military service, 73

response to closing, 184

American dream, preparatory school as, 212

American Protestant Association, 7

American underclass, 235–36

anima sana in corpore sano, 110

anti-Catholic sentiments, 30

Smith, Alfred E. and, 63

anti-immigrant sentiments, 30

Appalachian Trail hike, 222

athletics, 56

anima sana in corpore sano, 110

athletic field, 59

Benedict Field, opening, 117

"Benedict's hates a quitter," 127

benefits of, 117

Blood, Ernest ("Prof"), 119–21

Carroll, Owen T., 114–15

Casino Hall, 111

Catholic football, 128

Catholic identity and, 109–10

Cavanagh, Jim, 113

championships, 109, 114

College Athletic Association, 111

Doyle, Father John, athletic director, 93–94

Gray Bees, 116

Kasberger, Joseph, 125–31

Little Notre Dame of the East, 109, 115

Madison Square Garden game, 119

making men, 110

monks' control of sports, 111

Muscular Christianity, 112

new school, 246–49

Selhuber, Father Cornelius, 113

Seton Hall College rivalry, 122–24

Shanley, Bernard M. Jr., support, 108

Shanley, Bernie III, 114–15

sports craze at turn of the twentieth century, 112

wartime, 113–14

authority

challenges, 105–6

hierarchy in church, school, and family, 85

Backpacking Project, 222

Balleis, Father Nicholas, 7–8

Baraka, Amiri, 177

Bayley, James Roosevelt (bishop of Newark), 10

church property growth, 13

education, 20–21

parochial schools *versus* public, 12

Protestant-dominated schools, 20

school establishment and, 20

Seton Hall College, 17

BEA (Benedictine Educational Association), 55–57

behavior

away from school, 95–96

psychology and, 106

Benedict Field, 59, 116–17

Benedictines. *See also* OSB (Order of
St. Benedict)
adaptability, 1–2
as asset to monastic life, 13
establishment of college and, 20
overlooking because of fear, 188
reopening and, 256
character formation, 85
graduates becoming, 58
prayer and, 78
riot of 1854 and, 10
The Rule of St. Benedict, 1
schools and, 21
sisters, 16–17
stability, 13
African American values meshing, 224
as asset to monastic life, 13
establishment of college and, 20
dedication to community and, 75
the exodus and, 187, 200
McPadden, Father Malachy on,
253
neighborhood decline and events
of 1967, 150
questioning vows under neighborhood changes, 154
reopening and, 192, 256
stability of place, 1
Benedictines and, 1
moral obligation to Newark,
186–87
relocation of school and, 75
school's resiliency and, 255
vows, 13
The Benedictines in Newark (McPadden), 252

"Benedict's hates a quitter," 127
Benedict's Men, 207–8
benevolent dictatorship, 231–32
bicentennial year, self-evaluation, 221
Bien, Father George, 38–39, 249–50
Black Student Union parties, 178
Black Tuesday, 63
blackface minstrel shows, 54
Blake, Carl, 240–41, 251
Blood, Ernest ("Prof"), 72, 118–21
bloodless revolution, 161–62
Bodee, Brother Robert, 54
Bonner, Monsignor John, 88
boosterism, 55, 59
boxing match with Father Paul, 98
Boyden, Frank, 231–32
boys targeting weaknesses, 51–52
Braun, Bob, tribute to St. Benedict's in
Newark Star-Ledger, 188
Breidenbach, Frederick (Newark
mayor), 48–49
Brennan, Bob, 250–52, 256
Henry and Agnes Brennan Center,
252
Brennan, William J. Jr., 62
Brown, Bob (*World News Tonight*),
245
building. *See* expansion plans
Burne, Abbot Martin, 28, 34
challenge of a lifetime, 4
on Edwin Leahy, 193
King, Dr. Martin Luther Jr. speech,
151
Leahy, Father Edwin, instinct with
kids, 232
note to Father Edwin, 227
riots, 158–59
support for St. Benedict's to Abbot
Baldwin, 172

vision regarding post-riot St. Benedict's, 166–68

Carey, Monsignor Thomas, 162, 171–72
Carlin, Leo P. (Newark mayor), 137–38
Carroll, Owen T., 114–15
Carrolton, William, 29
Casell, Abbot Leonard's care for elderly and infirm monks, 187
Casino Hall, 111
Catholic football, 128
Catholic gentlemen, 2–3
Catholic identity, sports and, 109–10
Catholic neighborhoods, 48–50
Catholic schools
    academic advantage, 226
    closings in 1960s and 1970s, 174–75
    public schools' impact on, 40–41
Catholics
    as danger to way of life, 12
    Ku Klux Klan and, 47–48
    New Deal and, 65
    population growth 1900 to 1930s, 48
    proving patriotism during World War I, 46
    violence against, 12
Cavanagh, Jim, 113
    athletic staff, 126–27
Cawley, Charles M., 256
Central Ward, 148
challenge of authority, 105–6
character education, 83
character formation, punishment and, 85

cheating, Koellhoffer, Father William and, 89
Christ-Janer, Victor, 149–50
Citizenship and Catholicism, 71
city upon a hill, Benedictine's plan, 10
civil rights activism, impact on new school plans, 202–3
civil rights uprising of 1963, 151
Clark, Abbot Ambrose James, 172
    closing announcement, 183
    morale loss, 175
    resignation, 209
closing
    announcement from Abbot Ambrose, 183
    Ash Wednesday, 4
    election of advisers, rigging of, 186
    fear of moving entirely, 186
    first suggestion, 181–82
    Holtz, Father Albert's "end of the world" journal entry, 183
    last day of school, 189
    Leahy, Father Edwin's loss of vision opinion, 188
    monastic family after announcement, 185
    new school talks, 184–85
    official news, 184
    parents' suspicions, 186
    public's response, 184
    soul of monastery and, 186
    vow of stability and, 186–87
coin collection of Father George, 39, 249–50
College Athletic Association, 111
college-bound graduates, 58
Committee for a Greater St. Benedict's, 136

comprehensive education, 23

Cone, James, impact on Fathers Edwin and Philip, 203

Congress of Racial Equality (CORE), 163

consolidation, Abbot Patrick O'Brien, 137–38

construction of new building, 23–24. *See also* expansion plans

Conti, George, 123

convenient location of school, 25

Convocation, 224, 253

Cook, Franklin, board meetings, 217

Cook, Roger, board meetings, 217

Cordeiro, Hank, on race relations at St. Benedict's, 176

CORE (Congress of Racial Equality), 163

corporal punishment, 92, 97

    Berger, Father Wibald, 97

    Doyle, Father John, yardstick of, 93

    Huber, Father Paul, 98

    increases nationally, 102–3

    Kohl, Father Ignatius "Iggy," 98

    new school, 244

    Protestant and Catholic, 85–86

    questioning, 87–88

    reasoning for, 86

    slaps rather than punches, 104

    Smith, Father Dunstan, 100–1

cultural changes, 154–55

Curvin, Robert, 163

Dalton, Jack, 71, 246

Dana, John Cotton, 47

day college, 2, 21

dean of discipline, 83, 87

    Doyle, Father John, 93

Dwyer, Father Timothy, 94

    Kanetski, Father Valerian, 90–91

    Koellhoffer, Father William, 89–90

    O'Brien, Abbot Patrick and, 92

    O'Connell, Father Francis, 104

    Smith, Father Dunstan, 99–100

    Treanor, Father Boniface, 104–5

declaration of war on Germany, 43

decline of Newark, 142–43

Delbarton

    financial issues, 80

    fire in 1947, 136

    O'Brien, Abbot Patrick and, 79

    purchase, 75–76

demerits

    Doyle, Father John, 95

    Dwyer, Father Timothy, 95

Depression class, 61–62

desert experience, 192, 255–56

detention, JUG (Justice Under God), 95, 244

diet and exercise for monks, 78

diocesan school system, 168

DiPiano, Mike, 242–43

    wrestling champions, 246

director of development (new school), 217

disadvantaged students, 178–79

disciplinarian. *See* dean of discipline

discipline. *See also* punishment

    behavior away from school, 95–96

    Catholic schools and, 83

    character education, 83

    deans of, 83, 87, 89

    demerits, 95

    detention, JUG (Justice Under God), 95

    disciplinary code memorization, 95

endurance formula, 83
family spirit, 91–92
garden metaphor, 85
Hasel, John, 84
JUG (Justice Under God), 95, 244
Leahy, Father Edwin, 220–21,
        243–44
manhood training, 83
parents' approval, 91
psychology of behavior, 106
punishment and, 83
Punishment Ledger, 84
The Rule of St. Benedict, 86
Selhuber, Father Cornelius, 87–88
severity, community consequences,
        88
spare the rod/spoil the child, 85
student numbers and, 92
systems of, 83
word-of-mouth neighborhoods,
        95–96
districts in city, 49
diversity in new school, 207–8,
        244–46
division of society, 159–60
donations, 224–25
    Brennan, Bob, 250–51, 256
    Cawley, Charles M., 256
    Shanley, Bernard M. Jr., 59
Double-Cross Abbey, 142
double standards for students, 180
Down Neck, 11
Doyle, Father John, 93–95
The Duke. *See* Smith, Father Dunstan
Durkin, Dennis, return to St. Bene-
        dict's, 205–6
Dworschak, Abbot Baldwin, Abbot
        Martin's letter to, 172
Dwyer, Father Timothy, 53, 94–95

The Eagle (Father William), 89
economic growth, 28
    anti-Catholic sentiments, 30
    anti-immigrant sentiments, 30
    new work relationships for men,
        111
Ehrenhalt, Alan, on guilt, 96
Ellenstein, Meyer (Newark mayor),
        65, 147
endurance formula, 83
enrollment
    high, 43
    lowest, 182
    post-riot, 168
entrance requirements changes,
        179–80
ethnic rivalries, 51
ethnicity, 50, 52
European monks' asylum during
        World War II, 74
expansion plans, 54–55
    abbots' visit, 137
    Committee for a Greater St. Bene-
        dict's, 136
    Confroy, Father Mark, 149
    Delbarton fire in 1947, 136
    discussions on moving, 139–40
    location arguments, 138–39
    new features, 136
    separation/unification talks,
        138–40
    sky bridge construction, 225
expulsion
    behavior away from school, 96
    infractions leading to, 244

family spirit, 91–92
"Father Ed's magic," 226

Feigenspan, Christian, 26
FHA (Federal Housing Authority)
  biased lending, 144–45
  grading system, 145
  projects during Great Depression,
    65
finances
  abbey development, 80
  coin collection sale, 249–50
  compared to Harvard's and Law-
    renceville School's, 250
  Delbarton, 80
  new school
    director of development, 217
    fundraising, 215–16
    nickel-and-dime approach,
      216–17
    work parties, 217
  1960s and 1970s, 175
  school closing consideration,
    181–82
  school closings and, 187–88
  school development, 80
Fisher, James T., 92–93
Fitzpatrick, Father Jerome, 174–75,
  181
Foley, Adrian ("Bud")
  football, 129
  new school and, 215
fundraising, 215–16
  Hayden Foundation, 216
  Thornton, Paul, 219, 249
  Valvano, Abbot Melvin, 219
  Victoria Foundation of Montclair,
    216

garden metaphor for discipline, 85
General Course creation, 70

German immigrants, 11, 25–26
  anti-German sentiment, 46
  distrust of, 52
  Krueger, Gottfried, 26
  Newark Turnverein, 26
  newspaper, 26
  number of, 27–28
  school children, 2
German language classes during
  World War I, 46
German monks, war and, 43
Germany, war with, 43–44
Geyerstanger, Father Charles, Blessed
  Sacrament retrieval, 8
Gibson, Kenneth (Newark mayor)
  election as mayor, 178
  opening day festivities, 208
gospel choir, 221
grades at new school, 211
grading system of FHA, 145
graduates. See alumni
graduation
  first four-year class of new school,
    222–23
  last, 191
Gray Bees, 36, 116
Great Depression, 61–63
  African American population,
    65–66
  Depression class, 61–62
  effects on Newark, 63–65
  Federal Housing Authority, 65
  National Relief Administration, aid
    for St. Benedict's, 69
  National Youth Administration, 69
  public schools' enrollment, 68–69
  Public Works Administration
    (PWA), 65

scholarships and, 67–68

stock market crash, 63

student body loss during, 66–68

Third Ward and, 66

tuition leniency from Father Boniface, 66–68, 74

  Liddell, David, repayment, 74

Works Progress Administration (WPA), 65

Great Migration, 53

Greene, Bernie

  discipline, 243–44

  homework raids, 239

  legend of, 244

  return to school, 220

  riots, 157

Griffin, Virgil, 213

group system, 222

growth of school

  early 1900s, 37

  Selhuber, Father Cornelius, 40

guilt, sin and, 96

Hauck, Peter Jr., 35

Haynes, Joseph (Newark mayor), attending graduation, 31–32

headmasters

  applications for new school, 193

  Bien, Father George, 38–39

  Confroy, Father Mark, 149

  Fitzpatrick, Father Jerome, 174

  Helmstetter, Abbot Ernest, 39

  Leahy, Father Edwin, 227

  Reger, Father Boniface, 62

  Selhuber, Father Cornelius, 40

  talks on sin, 96

  voting for new school, 193–94

Healy, Paul, 61–62

Hell, Father Roman, 19

Helmstetter, Abbot Ernest

  addition to school building, 38

  BEA (Benedictine Educational Association), 55

  Delbarton, 75–76

  headmaster years, 39

  methods of teaching, 39

  modernization of St. Benedict's, 36–37

Helmstetter, Joseph, 34

Henry and Agnes Brennan Center, 252

high school (Hochschul), 18

  St. Benedict's transition to, 41–42

High Street, 18

Higham, John, 47

Hill, Frank, 113

Hill District, 11, 18

Hoehn, Father Matthew, committee on moving, 139

Hoffer, Eric, Father Albert's quotes, 197

Holland, John P., 43

Holtz, Father Albert, 4–5

  closing and, 182–83

  feelings about new venture, 191

  journal entries

    accomplishments, 254–55

    "end of the world," 183

    homework raids, 239–40

    new school, 205

    students' quitting, 219

  Leahy, Father Edwin and, 195–97

  Magovern, John and, 250

  school proposal, 201

  the Street, 234

  on striking a student, 244

teaching style, 219–220

warnings, 210

home education at St. Benedict's, 2, 21

homeowners, suburban flight, 144

homework raids, 239–40

homework requirements, Father Cornelius, 42

honor code, 243

housing, minorities, 160

Huber, Father Paul, 98

immigrant rocket (Philip Roth), 135

immigrants

antagonisms, 49

generations, 135

German, 11, 25–26

growth of school in early 1900s, 37

Irish, 11, 26–27

St. Patrick's Day parade, 11

reactions to, 11

Imperiale, Anthony, 177

"inbetween peoples," 52

Indiana Klan, 48

influenza epidemic, 44

integration of St. Benedict's

new school, 202

praise for, 176

press about, 174

self-segregation, 177

sense of, 176

integration proposition, 170

interest shown by prospective students, 183

Irish Catholics

Fisher, James T. on, 92–93

newer immigrants and, 50

stereotypes, 52–53

Irish immigrants, 11, 26–27

distrust of, 52

number of, 27–28

St. Benedict's students, 27

St. Patrick's Day parade, 11

Italians as first students, 52

Japanese in Newark, treatment during World War II, 71

JUG (Justice Under God), 95, 244

Junior Red Cross chapter (World War II), 72

Kanetski, Father Valerian, 90–91

Kasberger, Joseph Michael

"Benedict's hates a quitter," 127

Catholic football, 128

contract, 126

debilitation twins (drinking and smoking), 127

demeanor, 129–30

as example, 131

fighting family spirit, 127

injuries, 128–29

Leahy, Dennis and, 229–30

letter to Knute Rockne, 125–26

move to St. Benedict's, 125

Notre Dame Box, 128

pep rallies, 132

right living, 129

as teacher, 131

teaching fundamentals, 127–28

walking to work, 129–30

writings, 130–31

Kienle, Father Anselm, 39–40

King, Dr. Martin Luther Jr.

assassination, 168–69

Burne, Abbot Martin, 151

Newark as powder keg, 162

Kling, John, 61–63

Know-Nothing Party, 7, 9, 10

Koellhoffer, Father William, 89–90
Kohl, Father Ignatius("Iggy"), 98,
    136–37
Kountze, Luther, 76
Krueger, Gottfried, 26
Ku Klux Klan
    Catholics and, 47–48
    Indiana, 48
    mayor's denouncement, 47
    Methodist service interruption, 47
    threats to state, 47

last day of school, 189
last graduation, 191
lay teachers, 22
Leahy, Bill, 229
Leahy, Dennis (later Father Edwin),
    227–30
Leahy, Father Edwin (Dennis Leahy)
    basketball with African American
        teens, 178
    Boyden, Frank, 231–32
    as builder, 224
    Burne, Abbot Martin and
        instinct with kids, 232
        note from, 227
    caring about students, 231–32
    closing of St. Benedict's as loss of
        vision, 188
    communication, 212
    comparison to Father Cornelius Sel-
        huber, 228
    connection with Newark, 230–31
    discipline, 243–44
        tightening, 220–21
    double standards and, 180–81
    "Father Ed's magic," 226
    headmaster

    election, 194–95
    longest serving, 227
    The Headmaster, 231
    Holtz, Father Albert and, 195–97
    homework raids, 239
    knife-wielding student, 233
    languages, 212
    "miracle on High Street," 226
    mission work locally, 236
    mystery of God, 255
    name change at Morristown, 231
    opening day, 208–9
    penal hike, 221–22
    people skills, 227
    plan, 232
    recruiting for new school, 207
    reopening, 5
    restoring athletic reputation,
        246–47
    role of athletics, 247
    secret motive power, 228
    sense of belonging, instilling,
        238–39
    smoke and mirrors, 207
    St. Benedict's as benevolent dicta-
        torship, 231–32
    storytelling, 238–39
    students' living conditions, 235
    teaching style, 219–20
    thirty-fifth anniversary as headmas-
        ter, 257
    traits in others, 228
    vision for new school, 198
    Woodstock Seminary, 203
Leahy, Tom, friendships, 213–14
Lemke, Father Peter Henry, 19
letters from residents, 200
Liddell, David, letter from, 74

Liddy, G. Gordon, Father Wilibald Berger, 97
lifeboat metaphor, 190, 192, 223
Lincoln, Abraham, statue, 42
Little Notre Dame of the East, 109, 115
Lonergan, Maurice "Horsey," 123
loyalty oaths from teachers during World War I, 46
L. S. Plaut & Co., 36
lunch program protests, 105–6

Madison Square Garden game, 119
Magovern, John, 215, 250
manhood training, 83
    athletics, 111
map of predominant nationalities, 49
McBarron, Father Maurus, permission to enlist as chaplain, 71
McCarrick, Theodore Cardinal, 257
McGurk brothers, John and William, 18–19
McPadden, Father Malachy, *The Benedictines in Newark,* 252
McQuaid, Father Bernard, preaching calm after 1854 riot, 10
Means, Fred, Newark as another Watts, 163
Middle States Association of Colleges and Schools accreditation, 62, 69–70
Milbauer, Frank, 125–26
military training at school, 44
    athletics, 113–14
"miracle on High Street," 2, 226
modernization of St. Benedict's, 36–39
monastery
    abbatial status, 31

Double-Cross Abbey, 142
rifts after closing announcement, 185
schism with school, 4
soul of in closing, 186
students' choosing, 256–57
transition to Newark Abbey, 172
urban location, 78–80
monks
    background, 92–93
    choosing between monastery and abbey, 173
    diet and exercise, 78
    enlisting in military, 71–72
    European, asylum during World War II, 74
    morale loss, 175
    Newark Abbey, 174–75
    outside work, 190
    permission to go out at night, 78
    racism question, 169
    recreational periods, 78
    sneaking in back door, 78
moral defects of children, 85
moral development, 22–23
morale loss, 175
Moran, Patrick, preaching calm after 1854 riot, 10
Morristown abbey (St. Mary's Abbey, Morristown)
    abbey transfer announcement, 141
    building project, 151–52
    Double-Cross Abbey, 142
    growing apart from Newark house, 136–37
    hindrance of Newark house, 136–37
    independence from, 151, 152

monks moving before close, 187
purchase, 75–76
residential high school plans, 76
separation/unification talks,
    138–140
mothers looking for help with sons,
    240
Moyers, Bill, *The Vanishing Family:
Crisis in Black America*, 236
Muscular Christianity, 112
mysterious quality of St. Benedict's,
    171

name change, 38
National Merit Scholarship Program,
    decline, 181
National Network of Complementary
    Schools, 221
National Relief Administration, aid
    for St. Benedict's, 69
National Youth Administration, 69
nationalism, Pearl Harbor attack, 71
nation's unhealthiest city, 12
native Newark monks post-riots, 170
neighborhood
    African American population rise,
        148
    Catholic, 48–49
    changes, 140–47
    in the city but not of the city, 149
    city districts, 49
    decline, 37
    demographic changes, 49–50
    ethnic rivalries, 51
    as liability, 148
    map of predominant nationalities,
        49
    monks' contact with, 148

    parish boundaries, 50
    word-of-mouth, discipline and,
        95–96
New Deal, Catholics and, 65
New Jersey Freie Zeitung, 26
new school talks, 184–85
new school venture, 191
    civil rights activism and, 202–3
    headmaster applications, 193
    integration, 202
    Leahy, Father Edwin's vision, 198
    letters from residents, 200
    naming issues, 204
    parents' opinions, 203
    phases to academic year, 202, 221
    planning, 203–4
    proposal, 201
    retreat planning meeting, 200–1
    as service to neighborhoods, 198
    voting for new headmaster, 193–94
    "You just love the kids," 201
Newark
    anniversary of founding, 19–20
    commission government, 43
    county park, 42
    death of after riots, 158
    decline, 142–43, 199–200
    demographics in last half of nine-
        teenth century, 24
    as destination, 42–43
    disparities with suburbs, 160
    Down Neck, 11
    Great Depression effects, 63–65
    growth of
        German immigration, 11
        post–World War II, 136
    Hill District, 11
    immigrants, reactions to, 11

industrialization, 10
influenza epidemic, 44
nation's unhealthiest city, 12
powder keg, 162
public housing, 145–46
redevelopment, 142
renewal of, 199
state of city 1971, 198–99
street names during World War I, 46
250th anniversary, 43, 55
worst city in U.S., 234
as worst place to live, 160
Newark Abbey
founding, 172
polarization of monks' concerns, 174
Newark Academy, 18
Farrand, Wilson, 75
relocation, 75
Newark Daily Mercury, riots of 1854, 10
Newark Industrial Exposition (1872), 19–20, 24
Newark Turnverein, 26
Notre Dame Box, 128
Notre Dame connections, 115

O'Brien, Abbot Patrick
abbey transfer announcement, 141
African American admittance to school, 148
bitterness toward after abbey transfer, 141
business as usual at school during World War II, 71–72
consolidation and, 137–38
dangers of worldliness, 147

dean of discipline type, 92
Delbarton estate, 79
diet and exercise, 78
discussions on moving, 139–40
election as abbot, 76–77
fear of city, 146–47
front door use, 78
future of St. Mary's Abbey, 80–81
list of reminders, 77–78
monastic family ties, 154
monks' treatment of students, 99
name appropriateness, 77
permission to go out at night for monks, 78
preference for country house, 79
recreational periods, 78
Rule of St. Benedict and, 77–78
St. Anselm Abbey, 146–47
O'Connell, Father Francis, 104
opening day of new school, 208–9
Operation Whitewash '76, 214
ora et labora (pray and work), 1
Order of St. Benedict of New Jersey, bylaws, 19
orientation week, 242–43
OSB (Order of St. Benedict), 13
"Our Alma Mater," 58
"Overnight," 242–43

Panic of 1873, 29–30
parents
monks' treatment and, 99
punishment cooperation, 94, 99
parish boundaries, 50
parochial school disease, 30
parochial schools *versus* public, 12
Payne, Bill, 170–71
Payne, Father Mark, 222

peaceful demonstration, 163

Pearl Harbor attack, nationalism following, 71

penal hike, 221–22

phases to academic year (new school), 202

Phraengle, Abbot Hilary, 37–38

physical punishment. *See* corporal punishment

Pope John XXIII
    call to social action, 151
    racial discrimination, condemning, 151
    Second Vatican Council, 150–51
    transformation of Church, 104

population
    Catholic growth 1900 to 1930s, 48
    explosion at school, 3

praise for new direction, 175–76

pranks, 105
    Seton Hall rivalry, 122–23
        administration involvement, 124

pray and work (*ora et labora*), 1

prayer, Benedictines and, 78

prejudices revival, 47

priests as teachers, 39–40, 56

priory, change to, 141

prison-like public housing, 161

professionalism, African American students and, 180–81

programs of study, 2, 21, 58

"Project Maker" (Boniface Wimmer), 13

protests, lunch program, 105–6

psychology of behavior, 106

public housing, 145–46, 160–61

public schools
    African American students, textbook issues, 161

Bayley, James Roosevelt on, 20

buildings, 161

Catholic newspaper attack, 20

enrollment surge during Great Depression, 68–69

home environment, 161

impact on Catholic schools, 40–41

overcrowding, 161

versus parochial schools, 12

preventing Catholic children from attending, 20

punishment, 83. *See also* discipline
    character formation and, 85
    corporal, 92, 97
        Berger, Father Wibald, 97
        Doyle, Father John's yardstick, 93
        Huber, Father Paul, 98
        increase nationally, 102–3
        Kohl, Father Ignatius "Iggy," 98
        Protestant and Catholic, 85–86
        questioning, 87–88
        reasoning for, 86
        The Rule of St. Benedict, 86
        slaps rather than punches, 104
        Smith, Father Dunstan, 100–1
        spare the rod/spoil the child, 85

Punishment Ledger, 84

PWA (Public Works Administration), 65

Queen of Angels parish, 148

Quick, Carl, board meetings, 217

Quinn, Dermot, 30

race relations
    Baraka, Amiri, 177
    city government power contest, 178
    Imperiale, Anthony, 177
    self-segregation, 177

racial discrimination, Pope John XXI-II's condemnation of, 151

racism question among monks, 169

Ramos, Taberé, 249

rebuilding of school, 23–24

recreational periods for monks, 78

recruiting white students to new school, 214

Reger, Father Boniface
accreditation ratings, 68
General Course creation, 70
headmastership, 62
leniency on tuition, 66–68, 74
Liddell, David's repayment of tuition, 74
move suggestion, 75
resignation, 74–75
sanatorium stay, 70

religion courses, 56
new school, 212–13

relocation of school, stability vow and, 75

remedial students, 180

reopening, 5–6

Report for Action, 165

residential high school at Morristown, plans, 76

Richardson, Clarence, 246

Rickard, George "Tex," Madison Square Garden, 119

riots, 4, 150
1854
American Protestant Association, 7
attempt to remove cross, 8
Balleis, Father Nicholas, 7–8
calls to burn church, 8
desecration of church, 8
Geyerstanger, Father Charles, 8

Know-Nothing Party, 7, 9
man who decapitated statue, fate of, 17

Newark Daily Mercury, 10
appearance of jubilance, 164
Burne, Father Martin, 158–59
closing of school and, 2
Greene, Bernie, 157
gunfire, 164–65
holiday atmosphere, 164
looting, 164
National Guard called in, 164
National Guard warning, 157
native Newark monks, 170
natural disaster, 158
origins, 159, 163
peaceful demonstration, 163
Report for Action, 165
sporadic shooting, 164
St. Benedict's Prep during, 165–66
St. Mary's during, 165–66
State Police called in, 164
"Tin Beach" view, 156
transfers out of St. Benedict's, 168
vandalism, 164

rivalry with Seton Hall, 122–25

Roaring Twenties, 47

Robertson, Brother Dennis, "You just love the kids," 201

Robeson, Paul, end-of-season athletic banquet 1919, 108

Rockne, Knute, 115

Roll of Honor, 73

Roosevelt, Theodore, Muscular Christianity, 112

Roth, Philip, 135, 158

The Rule of St. Benedict, 1
corporal punishment, 86
O'Brien, Abbot Patrick and, 77–78

scholarships, Great Depression and, 67–68

school reopening. *See* new school venture

schools, public *versus* parochial, 12

Schools at War program (World War II), 72

Schumann Foundation study, 226

Scott, Joe, 240

Scudder Homes, 240

Second Vatican Council, 150–51

segregation
  public housing and, 146
  self-segregation at school, 177

Selhuber, Father Cornelius
  athletic field, 59
  athletics, 56, 113
    benefits of, 117
    military success and, 114
  Benedict Field, 116–17
  classroom management goals, 89
  closing announcement, 184
  disciplinarian, 87–88
  end-of-season athletics banquet 1919, 108–9
  growth under, 40
  headmaster appointment, 40
  homework requirements, 42
  Klan and, 47–48
  modernization of St. Benedict's, 36–37
  praise at hundredth anniversary, 60
  recruiting from parishes, 49
  resignation, 59–60, 117–18
  secret motive force, 41
  students' praise, 40
  testing standards, 42

separation/unification talks, 138–40

Seton Hall College
  founding, 17
  sports rivalry, 122–25

Sewall, Gil, Schumann Foundation study, 226

Shanley, Bernard M. Jr., 35
  booster, 58–59
  death of, 59, 118
  donations, 59, 215
  end-of-season athletics banquet 1919, 108
  financial support of athletic program, 108
  Klan and, 47–48
  public life, 215

Shanley, Bernie III, 114–15

shooting by police, accidental, 147

sin, 96

Skid Row, 1

Smith, Alfred E. presidential campaign, 63

Smith, "Big Jim" Jim Jr., 35

Smith, Father Dunstan
  discipline, 82–83, 99–100
  the Duke, 100–1
  end-of-school chaos, 82–83
  as father figure, 102
  making examples of students, 101
  military service, 99
  new construction and, 136–37
  reign of terror, 101–2

Smith, Fred, 247–48

Smith, John. 163

soccer, 249

social classes attending St. Benedict's, 28

sports. *See* athletics

St. Anselm Abbey, 146–47

St. Benedict's College, 18–19
  academic year, 22
  admission standards, 22
  college graduates, 1881 to 1910, 38
  demographic makeup, 26
  founding, Newark events and,
    19–20
  growth, hindrances to, 29–30
  Home Education, 21
  lay teachers, 22
  name change, 38
  programs of study, 21
  school day, 22
  students
    attracting, 30
    typical, 24–25
  travel to, 24–25
  tuition, 19
    ability to pay, 29
  uniqueness of day college, 21
St. Benedict's College and Preparatory
  School, 38
St. Benedict's High School, 204
St. Benedict's Preparatory School
  advertisement as high school, 38
  changes since 1940s, 252–53
  in the city but not of the city, 149
  enrollment post-riot, 168
  as healthy four-year job, 58
  high school, transition to, 41–42
  name change, 38
  Notre Dame connections, 115
  transfers after riots, 168
St. Benedict's Preparatory School
  (new). *See also* new school
    venture
  activities, 238
  bicentennial year, 221–22

  building bridges between commu-
    nities, 206, 212
  contrasts with old school, 210–11
  director of development, 217
  discipline tightening, 220–21
  diversity, 207–8, 244–46
  family atmosphere, 211–12
  fortress mentality, breaking down,
    237–38
  grades, 211
  graduation of first four-year class,
    222–23
  group system, 222
  honor code, 243
  Leahy, Father Edwin, 208–9
  location's benefits, 206
  measuring effectiveness, 238
  mirroring of old school, 241–42
  opening day, 208–9
  Operation Whitewash '76, 214
  "Overnight," 242–43
  preparatory school as part of Amer-
    ican Dream, 212
  religion classes, 212–13
  resentments over opening, 214–15
  students
    befriending, 211–12
    friendships forged, 213
    recruiting white, 214
  students' reasons for attending,
    206–7
St. Mary's Abbey
  future of, O'Brien, Abbot Patrick
    and, 80–81
  Zilliox, Abbot James, 31
St. Mary's Benedictine Priory, 16–17
St. Mary's Church, 6
  demographic makeup, 26

St. Patrick's Day parade, 11
St. Vincent College, Irish students' admittance, 27
stability, 13
    African American values meshing, 224
    as asset to monastic life, 13
    establishment of college and, 20
    dedication to community and, 75
    the exodus and, 187, 200
    McPadden, Father Malachy on, 253
    neighborhood decline and events of 1967, 150
    questioning vows under neighborhood changes, 154
    reopening and, 192, 256
stability of place
    Benedictines and, 1
    closing and, 186–87
    moral obligation to Newark, 186–87
    relocation of school and, 75
    school's resiliency and, 255
Stallbaumer, Father Virgil, 152–53
standards debate, 179–81
state certification for teachers, 57
stock market crash, 63
The Street (underclass), 234–36
"Striver's Row," 1
student body, 2–3
    class, 50
    discipline among larger numbers, 92
    ethnicity, 50
    expatriate, 3
    loss during Great Depression, 66–68
    post-reopening, 5–6

remedial students, 180
suburban residents, 138–39
war effort support, 43–44
students
    academic background lowering, 179
    attracting to St. Benedict's, 30
    befriending at new school, 211–12
    choosing monastery, 256–57
    double standards, 180
    first Italians, 52
    friendships forged, 213
    interest shown by prospective, 183
    typical, 24–25
submarine inventor, John P. Holland, 43
suburban residents, 138–39, 143
    FHA biased lending, 144–45
    lured by jobs and houses, 146
    veterans, 144
suburban schools versus center-city, 168
suburbs, disparities with city, 160
Succisa Virescit, 85

teachers
    classroom management, 89
    lay teachers, 22
    priests as, 39–40, 56
    "school is what the teacher makes it," 39
    state certification, 57
testing standards, Father Cornelius, 42
Thanksgiving Day game with Seton Hall, 122–23
Third Ward, 37
    Great Depression and, 66

Thornton, Paul
  director of development election, 217
  education, 218
  fundraising, 216, 219, 249
  new school title, 204
  president's report, 221
  return to St. Benedict's, 176
    reasons for, 218
three-phase academic year (new school), 202, 221
"Tin Beach," 156–57
transfer announcement, detractors, 141–42
transition to high school, 41–42
Treanor, Father Boniface, 104–5
Tribal Twenties, 47
Truman, Harry S., World War II and, 75
Tyler, Father Benedict, 3, 178–79
typical student, 24–25

underclass, 235–36
University of Medicine and Dentistry relocation to Newark, 162–63
urban life, 11–12
  monastery location, 78–80
U.S. Civil Rights Commission, division of society, 159–60

Valvano, Abbot Melvin
  election, 210
  family atmosphere, 211–12
  fundraising techniques, 219
  and reopening, 5
  unexplainable hand of God, 254
vandalism, rash of, 243

The Vanishing Family: Crisis in Black America (television documentary), 236
Vatican
  call to social action, 151
  public school, preventing Catholic children from attending, 20
  Second Vatican Council, 150–51
veterans, suburb flight and, 144
violence
  against Catholics, 12
  and spiritual authority among Irish, 93

Walker, Steven on race relations at St. Benedict's, 176
Walter, Father William, 22
war bond drives during World War II, 72
wartime, athletics and, 113–14
Waters, Father Philip
  basketball with African American teens, 178
  homework raids, 239
  novitiate at Morristown, 230
  penal hike, 221–22
  Woodstock Seminary, 203
Waters, James (Father Philip), 230
wealth, amassing in neighborhood, 28
welfare mothers
  offer to tithe check, 237
  stereotype, 236
white flight to suburbs, 138–39, 144
Wimmer, Father Boniface, 13
  adaptability, 1
  on character, 96
  Jesus as a boy, 97
  on Know Nothings, 13

on manliness, 96–97
monastery construction, 13
move to Newark, 15–16
Pope Pius IX directive to grow,
    15–16
"Project Maker," 13
refinement, 97
reluctance to move to city, 14–15
on sin, 96
St. Mary's Benedictine Priory, 16
stability of Benedictines, 13
urban location, 75
Wolf, Warner, 238
word-of-mouth neighborhoods and
    discipline, 95–96
World War I
    Armistice Day celebrations, 44
    Catholics' proving patriotism, 46
    German language classes, 46
    German monks and, 43
    Germans, anti-German sentiment,
        46
    loyalty oaths from teachers, 46
    military training at school, 44
    start, 42
    street names in Newark, 46
    students' support of war effort,
        43–44

World War II
    alumni involvement, 73
    asylum for European monks, 74
    business as usual at school, 71–72
    declaration by Congress, 71
    Japanese in Newark, 71
    Junior Red Cross chapter, 72
    Liddell, David, 74
    monks and staff enlisting, 71–72,
        74
    navy "E" pennant, 72
    postwar years, attitudes, 135–36
    preparing students for military
        involvement, 72–73
    rifle team, 73
    Roll of Honor, 73
    school as air raid shelter, 74
    Schools at War program, 72
    Truman, Harry S., 75
    war bond drives, 72
WPA (Works Progress Administra-
    tion), 65

yearbook, patriotism during World
    War I, 46
"You just love the kids," 201

Zilliox, Abbot James, 31, 33